The Price of Scotland

Darien, Union and the Wealth of Nations

DOUGLAS WATT

First published 2007
Reprinted 2007

ISBN (10): 1-906307-09-1
ISBN (13): 978-1-906307-09-7

The paper used in this book is recyclable. It is made from
low-chlorine pulps produced in a low-energy, low-emission manner
from renewable forests.

Printed and bound by
Creative Print and Design, Wales

Typeset in 10.5 point Sabon

Quis talia fando temperet a lachrymis? (Who in speaking of such matters could refrain from tears?)

VIRGIL

The main hazard in an affair of this nature always has been, and ever will be, of a rash, raw, giddy, and headless direction.

WILLIAM PATERSON

To Julie, Jamie, Robbie and Katie

Acknowledgements

THIS BOOK WOULD NOT have been written without the support of the Stewart Ivory Foundation, who funded a research fellowship at Edinburgh University allowing me to conduct an exhaustive examination of the financial records of the Company of Scotland. I would like to thank the trustees of the Foundation and in particular Angus Tulloch, Janet Morgan and Russell Napier for generous advice and enthusiastic encouragement.

My research has been carried out in a number of archives. Thanks are due to the staff of the Bank of England Archive, British Library, Edinburgh City Archive, Glasgow University Library, Mitchell Library, National Library of Scotland and National Archives of Scotland. I would like to thank in particular Ruth Reed of the Royal Bank of Scotland Archive and Seonaid McDonald of the Bank of Scotland Archive for providing friendly access on many occasions to the records of Scotland's oldest financial institutions. The Duke of Buccleuch and the Earl of Annandale kindly allowed me to consult their private papers. Thanks to Sir Robert Clerk of Penicuik for permission to quote from *Leo Scotiae Irritatus*.

The Scottish History department of Edinburgh University has proved a very congenial environment for historical research. Thanks to colleagues there, especially Dr Alex Murdoch for guidance and support. My knowledge of the late 17th century has been greatly deepened by many informal conversations with 17th century Scottish historians Sharon Adams, Julian Goodare, Mark Jardine, Alasdair Raffe and Laura Stewart, and with students on my Darien honours course. Doug Jones very kindly provided a copy of his dissertation on Darien and popular politics and I am also indebted to Prof Femme Gaastra, Prof Charles Withers and Allan Hood for answering enquiries on a variety of topics.

Thanks to my parents for their love and support. My wife Julie has offered many helpful comments on the original manuscript. I would like to thank her and our children Jamie, Robbie and Katie for their encouragement, love and forbearance during my three year sojourn with the Company of Scotland.

Contents

List of Figures

List of Illustrations

Preface

THE ATTEMPT BY THE Company of Scotland to establish a colony at Darien in Central America is one of the best known episodes in late 17th century Scottish history. Most historians have naturally focused their attention on the dramatic events on the high seas and at the isthmus. The account set out here, which is the first major examination of the Company since John Prebble's *The Darien Disaster* published in 1968, takes a different perspective. It is primarily concerned with the Scottish context; the directors who ran the Company, the shareholders who provided the cash to fund the venture, the mania for joint-stock investment that delivered such a very large amount of capital, and the financial and political repercussions of the disaster. The events in Central America were important and are considered in detail. However, what made the Company particularly significant was not its colonial aspects, for there had been a number of attempts by Scots to establish colonies during the 17th century, but rather its position as an instrument of financial innovation, and as a central ingredient in the complex financial and political settlement that created the United Kingdom in 1707. In the tercentenary year of Union, the strange circumstances which gave rise to this long-lasting marriage of convenience, or inconvenience, are of particular relevance.

Conventions

All monetary amounts in the text are in pound sterling unless specified, as the Company of Scotland raised capital and produced accounts in sterling. A separate Scottish currency existed until 1707 with an official exchange rate of £12 Scots to £1 sterling. Personal names and place-names have been modernised. In quotations, abbreviations have been extended, but 17th century punctuation, spelling and capitalisation left unaltered.

Introduction

ON 5 AUGUST 1707 a dozen wagons carrying a large quantity of money arrived in Edinburgh guarded by 120 Scots dragoons. A mob was waiting to hurl abuse as they trundled up to the castle to deposit their load and, on the way back down, to pelt them with stones. This was how the infamous 'Equivalent' was welcomed to Scotland; the huge lump sum paid to the Scots by the English government as part of the Treaty of Union of 1707; a bribe, bonanza or bail-out depending on your point of view. The stoning of those who delivered the Equivalent reflected the acrimonious divisions within the Scottish body politic, and is perhaps symbolic of the way in which Scots have viewed the Union ever since; repelled by the surrender of their national sovereignty, but at the same time willing to take the cash and opportunities it offers.

A large proportion of this money (about 59 per cent) was earmarked for a group of investors, the shareholders of the Company of Scotland trading to Africa and the Indies, now better known as the Darien Company. This was a joint-stock company which had attempted to establish a Scottish colony at the isthmus of Central America, in present day Panama. The fifteenth article of the Treaty of Union ended the existence of the Company and provided a generous bail-out package for shareholders, who received all the money they had invested 11 years before, and an additional 43 per cent in interest payments. By 1706 most had expected to receive nothing as the Company had destroyed all its capital. Compensation by a foreign government came as a welcome but problematic surprise.

The United Kingdom of Great Britain was brought into being by the Treaty of Union of 1707. The history of the Company of Scotland was intimately connected with the creation of this new political entity. At the heart of the achievement of Union was not economic theory or political ideology but rather that 'root of all evil', money. Not the money paid in secret bribes to buy support of key politicians, although this was important, or the money to be made in the future by exploiting access to English colonial markets, but the money paid immediately as part of the transaction between the two parties; the political elites of Scotland and England.

In 1696 the Scots had experimented with financial capitalism to a degree that many would have thought was beyond the resources of a relatively poor northern European nation. They had invested capital in a joint-stock company which promised to develop colonies and boost the domestic economy. In large numbers they had handed over coins or bullion to the Company in return for a share of future wealth. This was a remarkable event and one that can only be fully understood, it will be argued, if viewed as an early example of a financial mania.

The Company failed and every penny of capital was lost. The Scots experienced the destructive force of the new financial world more acutely than any nation before them. A dose of realism followed which encouraged the political elite to trade sovereignty and independence for the more prosaic prospects of security, economic growth and cash in hand. What follows is a history of how this happened.

CHAPTER ONE

The Strange Dream of William Paterson

It will be manifest that trade is capable of increasing trade, and money of begetting money to the end of the world.

WILLIAM PATERSON, 1701[1]

ON 16 JUNE 1699, William Paterson was helped on board the *Unicorn*, a ship belonging to the Company of Scotland, anchored off the coast of Darien in Central America. Like many of his fellow Scots he had succumbed to one of the tropical diseases prevalent there, possibly yellow fever or malaria. It was the last time he was to see the isthmus of America; a place which had obsessed him for much of his life. Scotland's colony was being abandoned after only seven months and Paterson's vision of a trading entrepôt lay in tatters. Given his grim personal circumstances, and the disastrous attempt to establish a settlement, it might be expected that he would have sickened of the place, but on his return to Scotland he was to praise Darien in even more fulsome terms.

Paterson was a controversial figure in the 1690s. Within months of becoming a director of the Bank of England he had alienated the rest of the board and was forced to resign.[2] The London merchants Michael Kincaid and John Pitcairn regarded him as a 'downright blockhead' and Robert Douglas, a merchant experienced in the East Indies trade, described him as 'one who converses in Darkness and Loves not to bring his deeds to the Light that they may be made Manifest.'[3] Walter Herries, who sailed as a surgeon with the first

---

1   William Paterson, *A Proposal to Plant a colony in Darien; to protect the Indians against Spain; and to open the trade of South America to all nations* (London, 1701) in *The Writings of William Paterson, Founder of the Bank of England*, ed. S. Bannister, 3 vols (1968, New York), i, 158.

2   Bank of England Archive, Minute Book of the Directors, 27 July 1694 to 20 March 1694, 164, 166, 171.

3   Edinburgh City Archive [ECA], George Watson and George Watson's Hospital, Acc 789, Box 8 Bundle 1, National Library of Scotland [NLS], Darien Papers, Adv MS 83.7.4, f23.

expedition to Darien, and became one of the severest critics of the directors of the Company, called him a 'Pedlar, Tub-preacher, and at last Whimsical Projector'.[4]

Others were greatly impressed by this serious middle-aged financier. Poems were penned in Edinburgh in 1696 and 1697 to celebrate the 'judicious' and 'wise' Paterson. In one particular ballad, *Trade's Release: or, Courage to the Scotch-Indian-Company,* he was compared with the biblical Solomon:

> Come, rouse up your Heads, Come rouse up anon!
> Think of the Wisdom of old Solomon,
> And heartily joyn with our own Paterson,
> To fetch Home INDIAN Treasures.[5]

On 19 February 1696, Paterson and his business associates Daniel Lodge and James Smyth were made burgesses and 'gildbrethren' of the Scottish capital, and the Merchant Company of Edinburgh awarded the same triumvirate 'Diplomas in best form'.[6] These were impressive accolades and reflected the reverence in which Paterson was held at the time.

He was sought out in the coffee-houses of Edinburgh by lairds, nobles, doctors and lawyers eager to hear his ideas about trade, colonies and companies. 'Happy was he or she that had the Favour of a Quarter of an Hours Conversation with this blessed Man' commented Herries.[7] One historian has viewed him as a 'merchant statesman' and proselyte of free trade, and another as 'the Man who Saw the Future' – apparently he anticipated the global economy of the twenty-first century but not, unfortunately, the disaster that was to follow the attempt to establish a colony at Darien by the Scots of the late seventeenth.[8] In a more balanced account he has been portrayed

---

[4]   Walter Herries, *A Defence of the Scots Abdicating Darien: Including an Answer to the Defence of the Scots Settlement there* (1700), epistle dedicatory.

[5]   *Various Pieces of Fugitive Scottish Poetry; principally of the seventeenth century,* second series, 2 vols (Edinburgh, 1853).

[6]   *Extracts from the Records of the Burgh of Edinburgh 1689 to 1701,* ed. H. Armet (Edinburgh, 1962), 190, ECA, Minutes of the Merchant Company, i, 1696–1704, 4.

[7]   Herries, *Defence,* 5.

[8]   S. Bannister, *William Paterson, The Merchant Statesman and Founder of the Bank of England: his Life and Trials* (Edinburgh, 1858), A. Forrester, *The Man Who Saw the Future* (London, 2004).

as a 'financial revolutionary', a man intimately involved with, indeed one of the principal figures in the financial revolution of the 1690s.[9] This 'revolution' is not as famous as other ones beloved of historians, for it lacks a great central image, like the storming of the Bastille or the execution of a monarch, but in common with its more famous cousins it ushered in important aspects of the modern world. This sedentary revolution involved debate, disagreement, and the buying and selling of bonds and shares in the coffee-houses of London. It resulted in an explosion of capital markets that allowed the English government and companies to raise sums of money in larger amounts and more quickly than ever before. The 1690s witnessed the growth of a liquid government debt market and the first boom in the stock market. This was the era when stockbrokers, derivatives and a financial press make their debut in the field of British history and terms such as 'bull' and 'bear' were first used to describe those who were either optimistic or pessimistic about the direction of share prices.[10]

Paterson was described by contemporaries as a 'projector'. He was one of the characteristic figures of what Daniel Defoe called the 'Projecting Age'; one of the men who organised company capital raisings and persuaded investors to part with their money. Living by his wits, he was something like a mixture of a modern day investment banker and a stockbroker.

It is clear from his letters that he recognised an important feature of the new financial era; capital markets could be irrational in nature, reflecting the changing emotions of their human participants. In a letter to the Lord Provost of Edinburgh in 1695, he noted that 'if a thing goe not on with the first heat, the raising of a Fund seldom or never succeeds, the multitude being commonly ledd more by example than Reason'.[11] Paterson understood how the herd mentality, or the madness of crowds, as it was to be called, might be manipulated by those launching a company to raise huge sums of money in a short time, anticipating the speculative manias of the future, such as the South Sea and Internet bubbles.

Paterson's skills lay in communicating the new age and at heart he

---

9   D. Armitage, ' "The Projecting Age": William Paterson and the Bank of England,' *History Today*, 44, (1994), 5–10.

10   P.G.M. Dickson, *The Financial Revolution in England: A Study in the development of Public Credit 1688–1756* (Aldershot, 1993), 503.

11   *The Darien Papers*, ed. J.H. Burton (Bann. Club, 1849), 3.

was a gifted salesman. He sold shares in the Hampstead Water Works, a company established in London in 1692 to help supply the city with water. He sold shares in the Bank of England, founded in 1694 as a mechanism to supply cash for King William's war effort; and he sold shares in the Orphans' Fund, an investment vehicle recapitalised in 1694–5. He also, most remarkably, sold shares in the Company of Scotland to a relatively large number of Scottish investors at a time when Scotland was not at the forefront of financial powers. Finally, he sold his great idea of an emporium in Central America at Darien, which would act as a magnet for merchants and capital and control the trade to the East Indies, to the directors of the Company of Scotland. He even sold this idea to himself, although there is no evidence that he had ever been to Darien before. Paterson was able to achieve all this because of his gifts as a communicator. His writings mixed sober finance with flourishes of powerful poetry. The lyrical peaks that are glimpsed intermittently in his prose perhaps echoed the Covenanting preachers of his native Dumfriesshire, and proved a very persuasive tool for raising the mundane topics of cash, companies and credit onto a higher level, and making it more likely that potential investors would part with their money. Thus for Paterson a colony at Darien would be the 'keys of the Indies and the doors of the world' or the 'door of the seas and the key of the universe.' The two oceans linked by his vision, the Atlantic and Pacific, were 'the two vast oceans of the universe'. Trade and money would increase 'to the end of the world'.[12] And in his most quoted passage, in which he praised the potential of an emporium at Darien, he brought together all his favourite sound bites to provide a piece of powerful poetry, indeed a hymn to the mystery of trade and capital:

> Trade will increase trade, and money will beget money, and the trading world shall need no more to want work for their hands, but will rather want hands for their work. Thus this door of the seas, and the key of the universe, with anything of a sort of reasonable management, will of course enable its proprietors to give laws to both oceans, without being liable to the fatigues, expenses and dangers, or contracting the guilt and blood of Alexander and Caesar.[13]

---

[12] *Writings of William Paterson*, i, 147, 158–9.

[13] J. Prebble, *Darien: The Scottish Dream of Empire* (Edinburgh, 2000), 12.

It is easy to see why so many were influenced by him. Although these words were written in a pamphlet after his return from Darien, they surely echo the kind of language he used in 1696 when persuading Scottish nobles, lairds, merchants, lawyers, doctors, soldiers and widows to invest in the Company of Scotland.

Despite his visionary invocations, however, Paterson was selling an old idea. The Spanish reached Darien in the early 16th century, 197 years before the Scots. Rodrigo de Bastidas was the first European to land on the isthmus in 1501 and a colony was established at Darien by Vasco Núñez de Balboa in 1510. Three years later the local inhabitants, the Tule, led Balboa through the rainforest to reach the South Sea, or Pacific Ocean. In 1519 Pedro Arias de Avila founded Panama City on the Pacific coast, which became the seat of Spanish power when Darien was finally abandoned in 1524. The Spanish viewed the isthmus as a vital link between north and south, east and west, where the interests of the entire world would meet under their control.[14] There were even plans in the 16th and 17th centuries to link the two oceans by a canal.[15]

By the middle of the 16th century the isthmus was the fulcrum of the Spanish imperial economy. Each year convoys of merchantmen protected by armed ships sailed up the Pacific coast of South America, loaded with silver from vast mines such as Potosi (in modern day Bolivia). At Panama City, on the south side of the isthmus, the treasure was packed on mules across to Portobello on the north, and then transported by the Spanish 'galeones' fleet to Seville or Cadiz.

Gold and silver lay at the heart of Spanish imperialism, rather than trade. In the early years artefacts looted from the indigenous peoples provided the principal source, but after the great 'meltdown' of 1533 the mining industry was expanded.[16] There has been disagreement among historians about the quantities of silver transported across the Atlantic to Spain during the 17th century. It has been argued that by the end of the century the mines of America faced

---

14 D.R. Hidalgo, 'To Get Rich for Our Homeland: The Company of Scotland and the Colonization of the Isthmus of Darien,' *Colonial Latin American Historical Review*, 10 (2001), 312–13.

15 R.L. Woodward, Jr. *Central America: A Nation Divided* (Oxford, 1999), 120.

16 J.R. Fisher, *The Economic Aspects of Spanish Imperialism in America, 1492–1810* (Liverpool, 1997), 25, 27.

exhaustion and amounts declined.[17] But the use of unofficial sources indicates that in the late 17th century bullion shipments were in fact reaching new highs.[18] Paterson's colonial project was not therefore centred on a pleasant backwater, but on an area of huge financial and strategic importance. As a contemporary pamphlet put it: 'the Company has settled their Collony in the very Bosom and Centre of the three chief Cities of the Spanish-Indies, to wit, Carthagena, Portobello, and Panama, the first being about 45 Leagues, and the other two not above 30 distant from the Collony.'[19] Why the Scots believed they could maintain a settlement in the centre of the Spanish empire remains one of the great mysteries of the history of the Company of Scotland and is a question we shall return to later.

Paterson had been trying to sell his Darien 'project' for many years. In a pamphlet of 1701 he recalled the 'troubles, disappointments, and afflictions, in promoting the design during the course of the last seventeen years'.[20] Robert Douglas, a merchant with experience in the East India trade, who wrote a long criticism of Paterson's ideas in 1696, recalled that:

> The design he was carrying on in Holland at Amsterdam some years ago particularly in 1687 when I had occasion to reside in that City about six months together and was often tymes at the Coffee houses where Mr Paterson frequented and heard the Accompt of his design which was to Erect a Common Wealth and free port in the Emperour of Dariens Countrey (as he was pleased to call that poor Miserable prince) whose protection he pretended to be assured of for all who wold engage in that design.[21]

In 1688 Paterson travelled to the German state of Brandenburg with the merchants Heinrich Bulen, Wilhelm Pocock and James Schmitten, looking for a sponsor to back his plans for an American colony, presumably at Darien.[22] Although the Elector of Brandenburg decided

[17] *Ibid.*, 75, 100.
[18] H. Kamen, *Spain in the Later Seventeenth Century, 1665–1700* (London, 1980), 136.
[19] Herries, *Defence*, 164.
[20] *Writings of William Paterson*, 117.
[21] NLS, Adv MS 83.7.4, f23–4.
[22] F. Cundall, *The Darien Venture* (New York, 1926), 10.

not to support Paterson's project, the joint-stock Brandenburg Company seems to have been influenced by his arguments, for it attempted to secure a footing at Darien in the late 17th century, probably the 1690s, but was repulsed by the Spanish.[23] Brandenburg, like Scotland, was looking for a colonial base in the Caribbean and had sought to buy, lease or occupy a series of sites including St Croix, St Vincent, Tobago and Crab Island near St Thomas, but these attempts failed because of French, English or Dutch opposition.

The reason for Paterson's obsession with Darien remains as obscure as his own early years. He left Scotland at a young age and, according to Walter Herries, became a merchant in the Caribbean, which was then experiencing a period of explosive commercial growth. In 1655 the English seized Jamaica from Spain, and the island became a significant centre for contraband trade with the Spanish empire. This was the so-called 'Golden Age of Piracy' when buccaneers infested the Caribbean seas. Pirates were active in Darien itself, suggesting that despite its importance to Spain the area was difficult to control, especially the eastern part of the isthmus.[24] The Welsh buccaneer Henry Morgan captured Portobello in 1668 with 400 men, and in 1671 he crossed the isthmus to sack Panama City. It took 175 pack animals to carry the booty back to the Caribbean.[25] William Dampier, the 'pirate of exquisite mind,' traversed the Central American jungle in 1680 and, according to Herries, shared his experiences with Paterson.[26] Lionel Wafer, a buccaneer who crossed the isthmus with Dampier, was involved in negotiations with the Company at a later date.

It is clear that by the time of his return to Europe in the 1680s Paterson was convinced that Darien might be utilised in a new way, outside the Spanish monopoly system. Other states had picked off pieces of Spain's Caribbean cake over the previous century. The English had taken the island of St Kitts in 1624, Barbados in 1625, St

[23]   *Companies and Trade*, (eds.) L. Blussé and F. Gaastra (The Hague, 1981), 169.

[24]   I.J. Gallup-Diaz, *The Door of the Seas and Key to the Universe: Indian Politics and Imperial Rivalry in the Darién, 1640–1750* (New York, 2005), xviii–xix.

[25]   H. Kamen, *Spain's Road to Empire: The Making of a World Power, 1692–1763* (London, 2002), 428.

[26]   D. and M. Preston, *A Pirate of Exquisite Mind: The Life of William Dampier* (London, 2004), 53–61. He was called this by the poet Samuel Taylor Coleridge. Herries, *Defence*, 4–5.

Vincent in 1627, Barbuda and Nevis in 1628, Montserrat, Antigua and
Dominica in 1632 and most significantly Jamaica in 1655. The French
grabbed Guadaloupe and Martinique in 1635, Granada and St
Barthelmy in 1640 and St Lucia in 1660, and in 1697 obtained possession of St-Domingue (modern day Haiti). The Dutch had seized the
islands of Curaçao in 1634 and Tobago in 1678, and even the Danes
had staked a claim to the small island of St Thomas in 1672. Were the
Scots not entitled to a share?

In July 1696 Paterson presented his plans to a committee of the
directors of the Company of Scotland. By then he had been praising
the virtues of Darien for many years and his argument was surely well
polished. He backed up his words with maps and other documents:

> The said Committee upon viewing and peruseing of several
> manuscript-Books, Journals, Reckonings, exact illuminated
> Mapps and other Papers of Discovery in Africa and the East
> and West Indies produced by Mr Paterson, as also upon hear-
> ing and examining several designs and schemes of trade and
> Discovery by him proposed.[27]

The directors noted in their minutes that Paterson had discovered
'places of trade and settlement, which if duely prosecuted may prove
exceeding beneficial to this Company'. Particular 'discoveries' of great
significance were ordered to be committed to writing, sealed by
Paterson and only opened by special order. At this stage Paterson was
promoting a series of destinations, presumably including Darien, but
the directors believed his information was of substantial value to the
Company and resolved that 'A settlement or settlements be made with
all convenient speed upon some Island, River or place in Africa or the
Indies, or both for establishing and promoting the Trade and
Navigation of this Company'. The opaque language of the Company
minute book seems to indicate that at this early stage a number of
locations were being considered.

In early 1697 there was a change of emphasis. On 25 February a
committee of the directors was appointed to consider 'Mr Paterson's
Project', as it was now being called. They resolved that without the
help of significant amounts of foreign capital the Company 'is not at

27 The Royal Bank of Scotland [Group Archives] [RBS], Court of Directors
    Minute Book, D/1/1, 105.

Present in a condition or able to put Mr Paterson's said design in exe-cution'.[28] They had decided to pursue a policy of retrenchment which involved selling ships and postponing the attempt to establish a colony at Darien.

However, they soon made another volte-face, which was to have profound repercussions. On 7 October the director Mr Robert Blackwood, an Edinburgh merchant, expressed his view that it was crucial that an immediate decision be made about the place or places to which the Company's first expedition was to sail. He was probably reflecting the frustration of shareholders, many of whom were annoyed that little progress had been made in either trade or colonial development. A letter was sent to Mr William Dunlop, the principal of Glasgow University, who had been involved in the unsuccessful attempt to establish a Scottish colony in South Carolina in the 1680s, and who was viewed as an experienced hand in such matters, asking him to come to Edinburgh as quickly as possible to advise the direc-tors. In the afternoon a committee was appointed to re-examine the issue: three lairds, Sir Francis Scott of Thirlestane, John Haldane of Gleneagles and John Drummond of Newton, and two merchants, Mr Robert Blackwood and William Wooddrop, were chosen. It is not spelled out explicitly in the Company records but it seems the commit-tee recommended reverting to the original Paterson plan. This was then agreed by the full court of directors.

Like the Brandenburgers and the Scots, the English were also interested in the isthmus and were keeping a close watch on the Scottish Company. Indeed English interest in the area dated back to the days of the pirate Francis Drake, who raided Darien in the 1570s and died at Portobello in 1596.[29] In English government circles there was initially some confusion about where the Company intended to trade, but in April 1697 a letter from Mr Orth, the secretary of Sir Paul Rycaut, English Resident in Hamburg, noted that the Scots were not interested in the East Indies or Africa, as their Company name suggested, but rather America and in particular the Gulf of Mexico.[30]

---

[28]   *Ibid.*, 25 February 1697.

[29]   *Oxford Dictionary of National Biography* [ODNB], (eds.) H.C.G. Matthew and B. Harrison, 61 vols (Oxford, 2004), 16, 858–69.

[30]   *Papers Relating to the Ships and Voyages of the Company of Scotland trading to Africa and the Indies 1696–1707*, ed. G.P. Insh (SHS, 1924), 34–5.

By June the English government had precise intelligence about the Company's plans, although the Scots were in fact having second thoughts at this point. An English commission for 'promoting trade and inspecting and improving Plantations' called Dampier and Wafer to attend 'to enquire of them the state of the Country upon the Isthmus of Darien where signified Scotch East India Comp have a design to make a settlement'.[31] On 2 July Dampier and Wafer were questioned and on 10 September it was recommended that an expedition be sent from London or Jamaica to take possession of the area for England. Captain Richard Long, who had offered his services to salvage wrecks off the north coast of Darien, was provided with a commission and a ship, the *Rupert* prize, and set sail for the isthmus on 5 December 1697.[32] The English government therefore had a clear idea where the Scots were heading before the Company of Scotland had come to a definite conclusion about their destination. The efforts of the directors to maintain secrecy had been a waste of time. It was well known in merchant circles that Paterson had been peddling the plan for years. Don Francisco Antonio Navarro, the Spanish Resident in Hamburg, was informing the Spanish crown of Scottish designs on Darien from July 1697.[33] But while the English and Spanish knew where the Scottish expedition was sailing, some of the Scots who left on the first voyage in the summer of 1698 were not so clear about their destination. Ensign William Campbell of Tullich believed he was heading for Africa.[34]

Thus, under the influence of William Paterson, a Scottish joint-stock company decided to establish a colony in a vital area of the Spanish empire. This was an ambitious and, as it turned out, fool-hardy decision, but other small European nations were looking for colonial crumbs in the Caribbean at the same time. What gave the Darien project its particular importance was the large number of Scots who invested in the Company, not just merchants from Edinburgh and Glasgow, but many nobles, and a large number of lairds, doctors, lawyers, soldiers, craftsmen and ministers. There was also a signifi-cant number of female investors; nobles, widows and the daughters of

---

[31]   *Ibid.*, 48–9.

[32]   Gallup-Diaz, *Door of the Seas*, 87–9.

[33]   *Ibid.*, 82–3. One letter from Navarro reported that the Scots also had designs on Chile and an island in the Straits of Magellan.

[34]   National Archives of Scotland [NAS], Breadalbane Muniments, GD 112/64/14/21.

THE STRANGE DREAM OF WILLIAM PATERSON

lairds and merchants. Success or failure would impact a relatively large part of the Scottish political nation. The capital that was raised gave the directors of a Scottish company, for the first time, immense financial muscle. For a few months they were in a much stronger position than the Scottish government, which had significant problems raising revenue in the later 17th century. Briefly the Company became a 'state within a state'. What they did with their cash would therefore have considerable political as well as financial implications.

CHAPTER TWO

Imperial Bliss

Our Thistle yet I hope will grow Green.

LORD BASIL HAMILTON[1]

THE DIRECTORS OF THE Company of Scotland were summoned to an impromptu meeting by secretary Roderick MacKenzie on the afternoon of 25 March 1699. They met, as was usual, in the Company offices at Milne's Square on the High Street of Edinburgh, opposite the Tron Kirk. Mr Alexander Hamilton, a messenger from the other side of the Atlantic, was called into the chamber and 'very joyfully' received. He was the bearer of intoxicating news: the Company of Scotland had achieved its aim of establishing a colony at Darien on the isthmus of Central America. At last Scotland could think of itself as an imperial power.[2]

Rumours about this miraculous event had been circulating before the directors received official confirmation. George Home of Kimmerghame, a Borders laird and shareholder in the Company, had noted in his diary as far back as 18 January that the fleet of five ships had reached an unknown destination in America. The press also had wind of the story; a letter was published in the *Edinburgh Gazette* announcing the location of the colony and the paper had to apologise for pre-empting an official announcement by the directors. The scoop was, however, too good to ignore and on 23 March the *Gazette* ran the following advertisement: 'There is now in the Press a short Description of the Isthmus of Darien, Gold Island and River of Darien, chiefly in relation to these parts where the Scots African Company are said to be'. This was published in the next few days at a price of seven pence Scots.[3] The 'Scots African Company' was one of the many contemporary names applied to the Company of Scotland trading to Africa and the Indies.

As well as bearing sensational news, Hamilton delivered a large

---

[1]   NAS, Hamilton Muniments, GD 406/1/6487.

[2]   RBS, D/1/2, 25 March 1699.

[3]   *Edinburgh Gazette*, no.7, 20–23 March 1699.

sealed packet containing a journal of events on the voyage and at the isthmus, and a letter from the Council of the colony. He also carried more sobering information; a list of those who had died in the Company's service. Alexander Piery had been the first to succumb to fever on 23 July 1698, and Lieutenant John Hay's wife the first woman on 19 October. The printed news-sheet did not provide her Christian name. Mr Thomas James, one of the two ministers, died on 23 October and Thomas Fenner, William Paterson's clerk, on 1 November. Both were consumed by 'fever'. In total 44 had died on the ships and another 32 perished after reaching the isthmus, including Henry Grapes, a trumpeter, Hannah Kemp, William Paterson's wife, Mr Adam Scott, the other minister, the two boys William MacLellan and Andrew Brown, and Recompence Standburgh, a mate on the *St Andrew*, whose English name reminds us that there were some colonists from other nations. The death rate of 76 from a total of 1,200 (6.3 per cent) was not regarded as excessive and indicates the risks of long-distance travel in the 17th century. The list was immediately published by the Company and proudly proclaimed that:

> It may be some Satisfaction to the nearest friends of the deceased that their names shall stand upon Record as being amongst the first brave Adventurers that went upon the most Noble, most Honourable, and most Promising Undertaking that Scotland ever took in hand.[4]

The court of directors proceeded to make a number of resolutions; firstly that no time be lost in supplying the colony with provisions, secondly that a reward be given to Mr Hamilton for bearing such good news and finally that the ministers of Edinburgh and its suburbs be officially informed of the Company's success 'to the end that they in their discretion, return publick and hearty thanks to Almighty God'. The *Edinburgh Gazette* reported that on the next day, Sunday 26 March, after their sermons, the ministers carried out the request.[5] The sparse minute book of the directors provides no further details about this auspicious occasion, so we can only imagine the sense of

---

[4]   *An Exact LIST of all Men, Women, and Boys that Died on Board the Indian and African Company's Fleet, during their Voyage from Scotland to America, and since their Landing in Caledonia* (Edinburgh, 1699).

[5]   *Edinburgh Gazette*, no. 8, 23–27 March 1699.

achievement felt by those who ran the Company. A number had worked tirelessly over the three years since capital was raised in 1696. There must have been great satisfaction for the men at the heart of the management: the lairds Sir Francis Scott of Thirlestane and John Drummond of Newton, the soldier Lieutenant Colonel John Erskine, and the Edinburgh merchants James Balfour and James MacLurg.

At church in Edinburgh on Sunday, George Home of Kimmerghame heard confirmation of the news and wrote in his diary that the Scots had 'fortifyed themselves in a bay the place they have called Caledonia the old name of Scotland and the toune they designe they have called New Edinburgh'. The patriotic symbolism was completed by naming their defensive position Fort St Andrew. Despite the exotic location the Scots had not established their colony in an unknown corner of the world. Darien was a famous location in the late 17th century. Just as the colonists were clearing the tropical jungle, at home in the Borders George Home was reading *A New Voyage Round the World,* the best-selling travelogue by William Dampier, the buccaneer turned travel writer, which included a description of the Darien isthmus and was published in 1697.[6] Another best selling work, *A New Voyage and Description of the Isthmus of America* by Lionel Wafer, who had been in Darien with Dampier, was to be published in 1699. For many Scots therefore the word 'Darien' carried connotations of exoticism, adventure, buccaneers and wealth. As news of the establishment of the colony spread there must have been raised eyebrows in the coffee-houses of London, Amsterdam and other European cities. Scotland was a relatively poor northern European nation and such an attempt was audacious to say the least.

Mr Hamilton, the bearer of such glad tidings, was generously rewarded. The directors agreed to give him one hundred guineas; a very large sum for the late 1690s, equivalent to about £10,000 in today's money, and we might imagine that he would not have received such a handsome bonus if the news he had brought home had not been so hopeful.[7] It was also generous because the Company's cash reserves were under pressure, and it marked a significant personal

---

[6]   NAS, Diary of George Home of Kimmerghame, GD 1/891/2, 1 April 1699.

[7]   Hamilton was the brother of John Hamilton, bailie of Arran, NAS, GD 406/1/6488, Lawrence H. Officer, 'Comparing the Purchasing Power of Money in Great Britain from 1264 to 2005,' Economic History Services, 2005, http://www.eh.net/hmit/ppowerbp/.

achievement for the young Hamilton, who in March 1698 had been described as 'idle', and had only been appointed as chief accountant on the expedition through the efforts of his uncle.[6]

Other mouth-watering rumours were circulating. According to Mr Robert Blackwood, one of the directors, the indigenous people of Darien, the Tule, had assured the Scottish settlers that there was a gold mine within two days journey of the colony.[7] From the isthmus Samuel Veitch wrote to the Earl of Annandale that the settlement was situated in the very centre of the 'riches of America', within two or three days march of six gold mines. Three of these were mined by the Spaniards and three were not worked because of a lack of slaves. The Tule had promised to guide the Scots to the mines and assist in seizing them.[8]

The author of a contemporary pamphlet informed his readers that the Darien gold mines were so well endowed that each slave working them might produce a daily profit of thirty louis d'or (French gold coins) and provide in a week what an English sugar plantation would make in a year.[9] Another pamphlet stated that the precious metal reserves would outstrip those of Peru; indeed Peruvian gold and silver was 'like a Mouse to an elephant in comparison of the Mines of Darien'. The writer described other riches including silver horseshoes, jewel-encrusted bridles and household vessels of gold and silver. Perhaps realising that he might be stretching the credulity of his readers he concluded: 'I could Write much concerning vast Riches that are there in these places; but I know that my Countrey-men are generally Thomasses'.[10]

A small book published in 1699 called *The History of Caledonia* waxed lyrical on the same theme:

The Country tho it be Rich and Fruitful on the surface, is yet

───────────────

[6]   NAS, Letterbook of Robert Blackwood, GD 1/564/12, 12 March 1698.

[7]   NAS, GD 406/1/4393.

[8]   National Register of Archives of Scotland [NRAS], Earl of Annandale and Hartfell, 2171, Bundle 825.

[9]   *A Just and Modest Vindication of the Scots Design, For the having Established a Colony at Darien* (1699), 173.

[10]   *Description of the Province and Bay of Darian ... Being vastly rich with Gold and Silver, and various Commodities. By I. B. a Well-wisher to the Company who lived there Seventeen Years* (Edinburgh, 1699), 4.

far Richer in its Bowels, there being great Mines of Gold; for the Deputies were certainly informed that not above twelve Leagues from New Edenborough, was a great Mine of this pretious metal, on which were employed near a Thousand Blacks, and that in the River of Sancta Mena; which is not above Thirteen Leagues from this Colony, and which falls into the South Sea, the Spaniards every year get Gold dust to the value of a Million.[11]

Physical manifestation of the potential wealth of Darien was soon appearing in Edinburgh as small pieces of gold that had been sent home by the colonists circulated in the coffee-houses off the High Street.[12] Perthshire laird and director John Haldane of Gleneagles proudly exhibited a gold lip-piece.[13] The appearance of such items must have had an electrifying effect on shareholders of the Company; a clear indication that they had been right to invest. It was also a clever public relations exercise, making it more likely they would provide further cash for the Company as calls were made by the directors. Although the Darien project was officially conceived as an attempt to develop Scottish trade and boost the domestic economy, these extracts reveal that a strong motive was the magnet that had pulled thousands of adventurers across the Atlantic in the 16th and 17th centuries, the desire for gold and silver.

On 29 March the directors were back at business and resolved to send the *Rising Sun* and two smaller ships, with 500 colonists and 200 seamen. As a mark of long-term commitment they hoped that one hundred women might be encouraged to go. They also decided to raise more capital to fund relief ships at this 'extraordinary juncture' and a council general of the Company was convened to sanction this. Sixteen directors and 25 representatives of shareholders attended the

---

[11]   *The History of Caledonia: or, The Scots Colony in Darien in the West Indies. With an Account of the Manners of the Inhabitants, and Riches of the Countrey. By a Gentleman lately Arriv'd* (London, 1699), 18–19.

[12]   Coffee-house culture had come to the Scottish capital during the Restoration and by the late 17th and early 18th centuries there were a number of coffee-houses in the closes, vennels and wynds off the High Street, including the Flanders, the Exchange, the Caledonian and the East India. They were relaxed meeting places where coffee or chocolate might be drunk and news, gossip and politics discussed.

[13]   NAS, GD 1/891/2, 5 April 1699.

following day and authorised a 5 per cent call on the subscribed capital of the Company. This would involve each shareholder giving five per cent of the amount they had subscribed. They had already provided 25 per cent of their subscription in cash. Authority was also given for a further 2.5 per cent if required and it was agreed that letters giving an account of the establishment of the colony should be sent to the King and the two Scottish secretaries of state in London.[14]

Many were swept along in the frantic optimism of these months. Lord Basil Hamilton, who later became a director, praised Darien in a letter to his older brother, the Duke of Hamilton:

> A fine Countrey a good harbour and what not and very well received by the inhabitants ... if this affair goe on as it begins, I think it the greatest happiness, and advancement that could befall this poor Nation, and which may lift up our heads which wer joust a sinking ... its not to be told you how joyfullie it is received by all people, Our Thistle yet I hope will grow Green.[15]

Samuel Veitch wrote from Darien praising the location: 'for the conveniency of the harbour and being easily fortified can scarse be paralleled in all this vast Continent'. He added that a thousand ships might be protected from storms within the harbour and that the promontory was the 'pleasantest situation for a toun in the world'.[16] Descriptions also highlighted the burgeoning fertility of the land and the exotic array of commodities, such as indigo, cacao and Nicaragua wood, which would soon be in the hands of the Scots.

There was, however, one discordant note amongst all the celebrations and back-slapping, which was to return as a chord and then a symphony of criticism. Lord Basil Hamilton noted the arrival in Bristol of Walter Herries, a native of Dumbarton, who was employed as a surgeon on the first expedition, but had left the colony disillusioned and was, according to Lord Basil, making up stories about the mismanagement of the directors.[17] Herries spent the time after his return writing an account of his experiences, which was published in

---

[14]   RBS, The Acts, Orders and Resolutions of the Council General of the Company of Scotland, D/3, 30 March 1699.

[15]   NAS, GD 406/1/6487.

[16]   NRAS, 2171, Bundle 825.

[17]   NAS, GD 406/1/6484.

1700 as *A Defence of the Scots Abdicating Darien.* It was a vitriolic, abusive and powerfully written attack on the directors and has become the historical source most relied on by historians of the Company. Its pronouncements, however, must be treated with some care given its viciously partisan nature.

For a few blissful months in 1699 the Scots were a colonial power and the talk of Europe. Darien was not, however, the first Scottish colonial venture of the 17th century. An attempt was made by Sir William Alexander of Menstrie to establish a colony in Nova Scotia in the 1620s, until Charles I sold the land back to the French in 1632. In 1681 a memorial was prepared for the Scottish privy council, addressing the question of possible locations for a colony. The Caribbean islands of St Vincent and St Lucia were regarded as 'very fitt and proper.' Cape Florida and the Bahamas were also proposed, and it was suggested that the English might allow the Scots to colonise part of Jamaica.[18] Darien, it should be stressed, was not mentioned. Two unsuccessful attempts to establish settlements followed in the 1680s at East New Jersey and South Carolina, but both were relatively small in scale. East New Jersey ultimately merged with the English colony of New Jersey and the settlement in South Carolina was destroyed by a Spanish force in September 1686.

Although Scotland had failed to establish colonies, many Scots had crossed the Atlantic by the late 17th century, with the majority settling in the islands of the Caribbean. Some were prisoners from Cromwell's victories at the battles of Dunbar and Worcester, who were shipped out as indentured labour and had to endure seven years of back-breaking plantation work before receiving their freedom. Some were engaged in the logging trade in the Bay of Campeachy in present day Mexico. Others settled further north in New England, establishing the Scots Charitable Society in Boston in 1657.[19] However, Scotland was well behind other nations in the imperial race.[20] The Spanish and Portuguese established vast empires in the 16th century and the English and Dutch in the 17th. Now smaller nations like Denmark, Sweden and Brandenburg were seeking sites for colonisation. By the

---

[18] *Register of the Privy Council* [RPC], third series, vii, 664–5.

[19] D. and M. Preston, *Pirate of Exquisite Mind*, 42.

[20] Scottish colonialism may have been less developed because of Scottish emigration to Ireland during the 17th century. The northern counties of Ireland could be regarded as Scotland's first colony.

1690s the Scots believed they needed colonies as markets for Scottish goods in an era of economic nationalism, or mercantilism, which saw their merchants and ships excluded from English colonial markets by the Navigation Acts.[21] The establishment of Scottish colonies would boost the domestic economy and solve the perennial problem of unemployment of the poor.

The nascent media industry was not slow in taking advantage of the atmosphere of intense national excitement. Before the ships had sailed on the first expedition, poems, songs and ballads circulated celebrating the Company of Scotland and in particular the man at the centre of its early history, William Paterson. In early April 1699 George Home read a description of Darien written by a man called Isaac Blackwell, who claimed to have lived there for 17 years.[22] The Company itself employed James Young to engrave a map and print a description of the colony.[23] Sir John Foulis of Ravelston paid £6 Scots for one, and £5 Scots for a 'Darien song'.[24] Students at Edinburgh University were busy preparing theses on the legal rights of the Company to the isthmus and at their graduation ceremony Mr William Scott, professor of Philosophy, provided an 'Elegant Harangue' on the same theme.[25] In Holland, John Clerk of Penicuik was moved to celebrate the Company's success in a stirring cantata he composed, called *Leo Scotiae Irritatus* (The Scottish Lion Angered), with lyrics in Latin by his Dutch friend Dr Boerhaave. The words of a Dutchman caught the ecstatic mood of the Scots:

[21] By the English Navigation Act of 1660, all trade to and from the colonies was to be carried in English or colonial ships and the captain and at least three quarters of the crew were to be English or colonial men. N. Zahedieh, 'Economy' in *The British Atlantic World, 1500–1800*, (eds.) D. Armitage and M. J. Braddick (Basingstoke, 2002), 53.

[22] NAS, GD 1/189/2, 3 April 1699.

[23] RBS, D/3, 31 March 1699.

[24] *The Account Book of Sir John Foulis of Ravelston 1671–1707* (SHS, 1894), 252–3.

[25] C.P. Finlayson, 'Edinburgh University and the Darien Scheme,' SHR, 34, (1955), 97–8.

O cara Caledonia!
Deliciarum insula
O renovate Scotia!
Te querimus, te petimus.
Tu animas nostras trahis.
Daria suavis insula,
Sit Scotiae colonia.

Dear Caledonia!
Delightful country.
O Scotland renewed!
We ask you, we beseech you
To raise our spirits.
Darien, that sweet land,
Should be a Scottish colony.[26]

The majority of the nation was in a state of intense excitement but the news provided problems for the Scottish government. The chancellor Patrick Hume, Earl of Marchmont, wrote prophetically to Secretary of State James Ogilvie, Viscount Seafield, on 3 April:

There is ane unaccountable inclination among people here to goe thither and by what I can find that undertakeing is not likelie to want all the support this countrie is able to give it either of men or money ... but as you hint There is either a great advantage or a great prejudice acomeing God knowes which.[27]

Government ministers were in a difficult position. Marchmont was a shareholder but found himself caught between two masters – King William and the Company of Scotland – and it was not possible to serve both. The Glorious Revolution of 1688–9 had brought William and Mary to the throne and seen Mary's father, James VII of Scotland and II of England, forced into exile. William was already Stadholder

---

[26] NAS, Clerk of Penicuik Muniments, GD 18/4538/4/1–2. I would like to thank Sir Robert Clerk of Penicuik for permission to quote from *Leo Scotiae Irritatus*. A recording of the cantata with other music by Sir John is available from Hyperion Records Ltd, London.

[27] NAS, Hume of Marchmont, GD 158/965, 101.

of the United Provinces and now became King of England, Scotland and Ireland. His principal concern was opposing the expansionist policies of Louis XIV of France and most of his time was spent in London or on the Continent. He showed little interest in Scotland and never visited his northern kingdom despite many pleas for him to do so. Scots affairs were delegated to the Dutchman Willem Bentinck, Earl of Portland, who, like his master, never ventured north of the border. Under Portland in the administrative hierarchy was the King's favourite, William Carstares, a Presbyterian minister who had been in exile in the Netherlands, and below him two Scottish secretaries of state based in London. This distant and inefficient structure highlighted the inadequacies of absentee monarchy which Scotland had experienced since the Regal Union of 1603, when James VI also became James I of England. From the beginning King William viewed the Company's existence as an annoying distraction. The arrival of the Scots at Darien and the creation of a Scottish 'empire' in Central America would prove to be an even bigger diplomatic headache.

CHAPTER THREE

The Company of Scotland

Qua panditur orbis vis unita fortior.[1]

THE COAT OF ARMS of the Company of Scotland, illuminated by herald painter George Porteous, is a surprising image to find on the first page of a company minute book.[2] On a shield quartered by a saltire are a ship, an elephant and two other exotic foreign animals. At either side stands a native of a distant land and above is the rising sun of future wealth. A Latin motto proclaims the Company's vision: '*Qua panditur orbis / Vis unita fortior*' (Where the world stretches forth / Its joint strength is stronger).[3] The arms point to powerful strands in the Company's history: colonialism, dreams of wealth, exoticism, global vision and national symbolism.

At heart, however, the Company of Scotland was a more mundane financial entity; a joint-stock company, ancestor of the present day plc (public limited company). Joint-stocks had their origins in the medieval period but rose to prominence in the 17th century as instruments of colonialism and overseas trade. Characteristics included a permanent capital which was not reimbursed at the end of each venture, a separation of operating control from ownership, and a secondary market that allowed shareholders to buy and sell their holdings.[4] The Dutch East India Company (VOC) and the English East India Company (EIC) were the most successful joint-stock companies of the age and had provided investors with large dividends.[5] Their success as engines of capital accumulation was a prime influence on the foundation of the Company of Scotland.

---

[1]   RBS, D/1/1, frontispiece.

[2]   *Ibid.*, 96.

[3]   The two parts could constitute separate mottos. They are not classical proverbs or quotations from classical literature, although '*panditur*' is often used by authors (including Virgil) to indicate a great expanse of land, sea or sky. I would like to thank Allan Hood of the Classics Department at Edinburgh University for this information.

[4]   L. Neal, *The Rise of Financial Capitalism: International Capital Markets in the Age of Reason* (Cambridge, 1990), 8.

[5]   Verenigde Osstindische Compagnie (VOC).

The central position of the Company in late 17th century Scottish history has distracted attention from previous attempts by Scots to develop joint-stocks. A series of corporate experiments anticipated the Company of Scotland. In the first half of the 17th century two Scottish companies were created to compete in the African and the East Indian trade. In 1617 James VI granted a charter to a Scottish East India and Greenland Company, which had privileges similar to the existing English companies and was authorized to trade to the East Indies, Levant, Greenland and Russia. However, the company's rights were soon withdrawn on protests by the English East India and Muscovy Companies.[6] Another attempt was made in 1634, when a Scots Guinea Company was established with a 31 year monopoly on African trade. The four patentees named in the charter were Patrick Maule of Panmure, Thomas Maxwell of Innerwick, Sir Thomas Thomson of Duddingston and Henry Alexander, son of Sir William Alexander. Maule's grandson, James, fourth Earl of Panmure, was to become a director of the Company of Scotland. The company sent two ships to West Africa in 1636. The *Golden Lion* realised an impressive profit of over 50 per cent, indicating the potential offered by the African trade, but the fate of the *St Andrew* highlighted the significant risks of overseas ventures; her crew was seized by Portuguese authorities and massacred. The efforts of the company thereafter appear to have petered out.[7]

Other companies were established during the Restoration. The 'Royal Company for the Fishery in Scotland' received a patent in 1670 to exploit one of Scotland's principal natural resources, which at the time was dominated by the Dutch fishing fleet. This poorly documented company apparently raised capital of £25,000, but had squandered most of it by the time it was dissolved by act of parliament in 1690.[8] In 1681 the New Mills cloth manufactory in Haddingtonshire was established with capital of £5,000, promoted by Sir James Stanfield and Edinburgh merchant Robert Blackwood, who was to be a key

---

[6]   W.R. Scott, *The Constitution and Finance of English, Scottish and Irish Joint-Stock Companies to 1720*, 3 vols (Cambridge, 1910–12), ii, 55, 104, *Calendar of State Papers Colonial: East Indies 1617–1621*, 319, 323.

[7]   R. Law, 'The First Scottish Guinea Company, 1634–9,' *SHR*, 76, (1997), 185–202.

[8]   Scott, *Constitution and Finance*, ii, 376–7, *Acts of the Parliament of Scotland* [APS], ix, 224.

figure in obtaining the act of parliament establishing the Company of Scotland.[9] A significant amount of the capital was provided by a group of London Scottish merchants, and investors from Scotland included the Edinburgh merchant George Clark and advocate Hugh Dalrymple, who were later directors of the Company.[10]

The Carolina Company was formed in 1682 by a group of nobles, lairds and merchants predominantly drawn from Covenanting areas of the south west. In July 1684 Lord Cardross, William Dunlop, and others sailed to South Carolina and established the colony of Stuarts Town.[11] Again, a number of the investors in this venture later emerged as directors and shareholders of the Company of Scotland.[12] Walter Gibson, a Glasgow merchant, owned the ship that transported some of the colonists across the Atlantic. His brother, Captain James Gibson, commanded the *Rising Sun* on the second expedition to the isthmus.

The Quaker Robert Barclay of Ury led an attempt to establish a colony at East New Jersey that was to be free from religious persecution. A substantial number of the 50 or so investors in the venture were Scots and at least four ships sailed with Scottish emigrants between 1683 and 1685, establishing Perth Amboy, named after the Earl of Perth, who was one of the investors, as a free port on the trading route to and from New York. Unlike the later settlement at Darien, this colony benefited from a reasonable climate, rich farmland and a favourable location, but in the spring of 1688 the proprietors surrendered their authority and became part of New England.[13]

The pace of joint-stock creation increased substantially in the 1690s during the period of the financial revolution, with 47 companies established in Scotland during the boom years from 1690 to

---

9   *The Records of a Scottish Cloth Manufactory at New Mills, Haddingtonshire 1681–1703* (SHS, 1905).

10   G. Marshall, *Presbyteries and Profits: Calvinism and the Development of Capitalism in Scotland, 1560–1707* (Edinburgh, 1992), 153–5.

11   L.G. Fryer, 'Documents relating to the formation of the Carolina Company in Scotland, 1682,' *South Carolina Historical Magazine*, 99, (1998), 110–133.

12   William Dunlop, Archibald Muir, Sir John Shaw of Greenock, John Anderson of Dowhill, George Clark, Lord Cardross, John Corse and Sir Colin Campbell of Ardkinglass.

13   G.P. Insh, *Scottish Colonial Schemes 1620-1686* (Glasgow, 1922), 145, 162, 185, L.G. Fryer, 'Robert Barclay of Ury and East New Jersey,' *Northern Scotland*, 15, (1995), 7–8.

1695, including the White Paper Manufactory, the Scots Linen Manufactory and most famously the Bank of Scotland and the Company of Scotland.[14] The Bank was established by act of parliament on 17 July 1695 with a nominal capital of £1,200,000 Scots (£100,000 sterling) and a monopoly of joint-stock banking in Scotland for 21 years. There were 172 original subscribers, with 136 resident in Scotland and 36 in London.[15]

The Company of Scotland did not therefore spring from virgin soil. There were a number of attempts over the 17th century to establish companies, the idea of a joint-stock was firmly established in Scotland and many individuals concerned in earlier projects later became involved with the Company.

The urgency to use a joint-stock to develop Scottish overseas trade and fund colonial expansion quickened after the Glorious Revolution and was reflected in an 'Act for Encouraging of Forraigne Trade', passed by parliament in 1693, which stated:

> How much the Improvement of Trade concerns the Wealth and Wellfare of the Kingdom, and that nothing hath been found more effectuall for the Improving and Enlargeing thereof than the Erecting and Incourageing of Companies whereby the same may be carryed on by undertakeings to the remotest parts, which it is not possible for single persons to undergo.[16]

The act declared that merchants might establish societies and companies to trade with countries not at war with their Majesties and highlighted geographical areas for exploitation including Europe, the East and West Indies, the Mediterranean, Africa and 'Northerne parts'. If ships were attacked by pirates during the first seven years, recovery would be at the public expense but there would be no compensation for those taken by privateers who were authorised by other states.

The driving force behind this effort to expand Scottish overseas trade through joint-stock company creation was the Edinburgh merchant community. In 1693, 48 Edinburgh merchants subscribed a guinea each to fund an attempt to secure a patent from the King and Queen

---

[14]   Scott, *Constitution and Finance*, i, 356.

[15]   R. Saville, *Bank of Scotland: A History 1695–1995* (Edinburgh, 1996), 1–3.

[16]   *APS*, ix, 314–15.

for developing trade to Africa and the Indies.[17] Thirty-eight of them later became shareholders in the Company of Scotland. The lobbying effort was led by Mr Robert Blackwood and James Balfour.[18] On 22 June 1695, £33 5s Scots was spent by the merchants on dining with members of the parliamentary committee of trade. The menu consisted of lamb head, mutton, broth, herring, duck, chickens with gooseberries, fruit, cheese, wine, bread, ale, brandy and tobacco.[19]

Before an act of parliament was obtained, a group of investors based in England was brought on board to expand the amount of capital available and broaden the level of expertise, following the example of previous joint-stocks like the cloth manufactory and Bank of Scotland. Indeed all the London promoters of the Company of Scotland (James Foulis, David Nairne, Thomas Deans, James Chiesly, Thomas Coutts, Hugh Fraser and Walter Stewart), with the exception of Paterson and his associates James Smyth, Daniel Lodge and Joseph Cohen D'Azevedo, were investors in the cloth manufactory. All except Smyth, Lodge and D'Azevedo were of Scottish descent.[20] The Company was thus first envisaged as an Anglo-Scottish endeavour.

An 'Act for a Company Tradeing to Affrica and the Indies' was passed on 26 June 1695:

> His Majesty understanding that several persons as well Forreigners as Natives of this Kingdom, are willing to engage themselves with great Soumes of money, in an American, Affrican, and Indian Trade, to be exercised in and from this Kingdom, if enabled and encouraged thereunto, by the concessions powers and priviledges, needfull and usual in such cases.[21]

The King constituted the 20 promoters named in the act (see Appendix 1) and other investors who subscribed within 12 months of 1 August 1695 as 'one body incorporate, and a free incorporation, with

---

[17] G.P. Insh, 'The Founders of the Company of Scotland,' *SHR*, 25, (1928), 243.

[18] *Ibid.*, 241–54.

[19] *Ibid.*, 250. From this evidence, Insh showed that the prime movers behind the Company were the Edinburgh merchant community and not William Paterson.

[20] According to Herries, Lodge was born in Leith of Yorkshire parents.

[21] *APS*, ix, 377–81.

perpetual Succession, by the name of the Company of Scotland tradeing to Affrica and the Indies'.[22] The act specified that at least half the
capital should be held by 'Scottish men within this Kingdom' and the
shares of Scottish shareholders had to be sold to other Scots to maintain a 50 per cent level of ownership. The minimum and maximum
amounts that could be invested were set at £100 and £3,000 (£9,997
and £299,920 today) and the promoters and other subscribers were
authorised to make rules, ordinances and constitutions for the 'better
Government and improvement of their joint stock, or capital fond'.
The powers of the Company were specified:

> The said Company is hereby impowered to equip, fitt, sett out,
> fraught, and navigat their own, or hired ships … from any of
> the ports or places of this Kingdom, or from any other ports
> or places in Amity, or not in hostility with his Majesty, in war-
> like, or other manner to any Lands Islands, Countreyes, or places
> in Asia, Affrica, or America, and there to plant Collonies, build
> Cityes Touns or Forts, in or upon the places not inhabited, or
> in or upon any other place, by consent of the Natives or
> Inhabitants thereof and not possest by any European
> Soveraign, Potentate, Prince, or State.[23]

At the heart of the act were generous trading privileges, in particular
a monopoly on trade to Asia, Africa and America for 31 years, paying
only a nominal hogshead of tobacco to his Majesty as blench duty.[24]
The Company was thus given a global brief, very different from other
successful joint-stock companies, which specialised in trading with a
particular region such as the East Indies, West Indies or Africa. It is
unclear why the promoters wanted the Company to envelop so many
branches of foreign trade. This obviously provided significant power,
prestige and opportunities, but given their lack of experience in running a major company, perhaps a less ambitious model might have
been advisable from a business perspective.

The act contained another very generous provision: exemption
from customs, taxes, cesses, supplies and other duties for twenty-one

---

[22] *Ibid.*, 378.

[23] *Ibid.*, 379.

[24] Although there was an exception: areas of America where the Company
did not settle colonies.

years.[25] But this concession proved a double-edged sword, attracting the interest of potential investors but at the same time intensifying opposition from other companies, such as the EIC and Royal African Company, which feared competition.

Another clause specified the protection offered by the King:

> If contrar to the said rights, Liberties, priviledges, exemptions, grants or agreements, any of the Ships, goods, Merchandise, persons or other effects whatsoever, belonging to the said Company shall be stopt, detained, embazled or away taken, or in any sort prejudged, or damnifyed; His Majesty promises to interpose his Authority to have restitution, reparation and satisfaction made for the damnage done, and that upon the publik charge, which his Majesty shall cause depurse, and lay out for that effect.

This suggested that William would provide 'diplomatic' support, with compensation coming from the state.

A final sweetener was added; one which suggests the promoters were seeking to attract foreign shareholders. Those who invested would become 'free Denizons' of Scotland and those born in the Company's colonies, 'Natives of this Kingdom'.[26]

The act marked a significant achievement for the promoters. A company could be established with a very generous trade monopoly and highly attractive tax concessions. Those involved were entitled to a night of celebrations before the hard work began. But the parsimony of the festivities was in stark contrast to the largesse of the directors with the shareholders' cash. On 26 July a bash in an Edinburgh tavern to celebrate the passing of the act cost only £7 Scots.[27]

---

[25] With the exception of duties on tobacco and sugar that were not from the Company's plantations.

[26] *APS*, ix, 380.

[27] Insh, 'Founders of the Company,' 251. This was equivalent to about 12s sterling.

CHAPTER 4

London Scots

So our Act must be attacked in it's Swadling Cloaths, and persecuted in its Infancy.

LORD BELHAVEN[1]

THE RAPID EXPANSION OF London outpaced the growth of any other European urban centre in the 17th century and was driven by an international trade network of merchants, companies and colonies.[2] If Amsterdam was still the financial centre of the world, London was catching up fast and was soon to surpass the Dutch rival as a nexus for investors and capital.

A Scottish community witnessed this explosive growth at first hand. A small group of Scots, many religious dissidents, were resident in the English capital in the second half of the 16th century, but when James VI travelled south to become James I of England in 1603, he was followed by a train of nobles, courtiers and merchants who saw the opportunity for advancement. In the early 17th century the Scots established a mutual-aid society, or Scottish box club, which became the Scottish Hospital in 1665 when it received a royal letters patent from Charles II. The number of Scots in London grew as Scottish trade with England expanded. By the end of the 17th century, it has been estimated, 50 per cent of exports were heading across the border, with a significant amount destined for London.[3] By the 1690s the London Scots were a community of significant size and wealth, with over 300 members of the Royal Scottish Corporation signing an oath of loyalty to King William in 1696.[4]

[1]   Lord Belhaven, *A Speech in Parliament on the 10th day of January 1701, by the Lord Belhaven on the Affair of the Indian and African Company, and its Colony of Caledonia* (Edinburgh, 1701), 8.

[2]   *London 1500–1700: The Making of the Metropolis*, (eds.) A.L. Beier and R. Finlay (Harlow, 1986), 3, 37, J. Hoppit, *A Land of Liberty? England 1689–1727* (Oxford, 2000), 425–30.

[3]   T.C. Smout, *Scottish Trade on the Eve of Union 1660–1707* (Edinburgh, 1963), 238.

[4]   J. Taylor, *A Cup of Kindness: The History of the Royal Scottish Corporation, a London Charity, 1603–2003* (East Linton, 2003), 3–64.

William Paterson was one of these London Scots. In May 1695 he was told about the attempt being made by Scottish merchants to establish an overseas trading company and was encouraged to provide a 'scheme', based on his substantial experience in company creation, which was taken back to Scotland by fellow London Scots James Chiesly and Thomas Coutts. Although his model was not followed entirely in the act of parliament, Paterson emerged as one of the promoters of the Company in London and encouraged some of his business associates to become involved.[5] The London based promoters named in the act of June 1695 therefore included a contingent of Paterson's friends as well as a group of London Scots.[6]

Given Paterson's experience of the capital market it was natural that he should emerge as spokesman for those in London over the summer and early autumn of 1695, communicating with Edinburgh's Lord Provost Sir Robert Chiesly and other Scottish promoters by letter. Paterson and the contingent based in England were determined that the Company should first be established in London, where capital and colonial expertise were plentiful. Only when the Company was up and running might the management be transferred to Edinburgh. The promoters in Scotland, on the other hand, believed the Company should be established in Edinburgh, with those in London joining them for meetings north of the border.[7] Disagreement over strategy thus emerged at an early stage. In response to these disagreements, Paterson called for unity so that the Company 'may be reckon'd one intire body, and not of several interfering parts and interests'.[8]

In this early phase of the Company's history Paterson encouraged the Scottish promoters to remain vague about their exact intentions: 'as for Reasons we ought to give none, but that it is a Fund for the Affrican and Indian Company; For if we are not able to raise the Fund by our Reputation, we shall hardly do it by our Reasons'.[9] He also stressed that prejudice should not get in the way of the hard-headed process of raising cash:

---

[5] *Journals of the House of Commons* [JHC], xi, 400.

[6] See Appendix 1.

[7] G.P. Insh, *The Company of Scotland Trading to Africa and the Indies* (London, 1932), 46.

[8] *Darien Papers*, 2.

[9] *Ibid.*, 1–2.

> Above all, it's needfull for Us to make no distinction of Partys
> in this great and noble Undertaking, but that of whatever
> Nation or Religion a man be (if one of us) he ought to be
> looked upon to be of the same Interest and Inclination.[10]

It is unclear whether his tolerance extended to Catholics but it certainly
included Jews as the London Jewish merchant Joseph Cohen D'Azevedo,
an associate of Paterson, became a promoter of the Company.[11]

The English promoters wanted to arrange a formal meeting in
early November to formulate a constitution. Paterson thought their
efforts should remain private until three or four months before the
deadline of 1 August 1696 specified in the act, so that the upcoming
session of the English parliament did not turn its attention towards
the Company.

In a letter to Sir Robert Chiesly, Paterson began to articulate his
grandiose plans:

> We ought not to think that ever we can bring an Indian busi-
> ness to bear from Scotland by only apeing the English and
> Dutch. But we may be sure, should we only settle some little
> Colony or Plantation, and send some Ships, They would looke
> upon them as Interlopers, and all agree to discourage and
> crush us to pieces.

In other words the business models of the EIC and VOC should not be
followed; nor should those of unsuccessful states such as France,
Denmark and Brandenburg. The French king had wasted millions of
crowns promoting foreign trade; the King of Denmark more than
£500,000 and the Elector of Brandenburg up to £500,000 over 16 or
17 years.[12] Paterson, of course, was optimistic about Scottish
prospects:

> There are remarkable occurrences at this time, and many
> Disadvantages our Neighbours ly under, and a considerable

---

[10] *Ibid.*, 4.

[11] The size of the Jewish community in London might have been similar to
the Scottish one. The number of Jews in London and the English West
Indies in 1700 has been estimated to be 2,000. J.I. Israel, *European Jewry in
the Age of Mercantilism 1550–1750* (London, 1998), 140.

[12] *Darien Papers*, 3–4.

measure of the Genius of Trade and improvements seemes to
incline to Scotland, to give them a faculty and inclination to
gain some advantages for themselves and Posterity, all which
seem to be Harbingers of, and to portend glorious Success.[13]

By early August a note of urgency entered the correspondence. The
English promoters had heard nothing from the Scots since the end of
June. They wanted copies of the act of parliament sent south and
Scottish heralds consulted about a Company seal and coat of arms.
They also needed at least three of the Scots to come to London to
make up a majority of those named in the act so they could hold a
general meeting to rectify a couple of mistakes made in drawing it up.
James Smyth had been wrongly named as John Smith and Joseph
Cohen D'Azevedo appeared as two individuals, Joseph Cohaine and
Daves Ovedo, his exotic name baffling the Scottish clerk who penned
the act.[14]

On 29 August, Paterson and the London Scots James Foulis, David
Nairne, James Chiesly, Thomas Coutts, Hugh Fraser and Walter
Stewart attended the first meeting of the English promoters, for which
minutes survive. They each advanced £25 towards expenses and agreed
that all potential investors should inform Roderick MacKenzie, who
had been appointed secretary, of the amounts they intended to subscribe.[15]

By early September it was becoming evident that attempts to
maintain secrecy had failed. Paterson commented that their business
had taken 'more aire' than expected.[16] The English secretaries of state
and members of the House of Commons were inquisitive about the
new company and wanted copies of the Scottish act of parliament.[17]
Since the activity of the Company was now in the public domain it
was necessary to act quickly and requests for a majority to conduct
business in London intensified.

Despite this worrying sign, optimism prevailed among the London
promoters. Initially they had decided to raise capital of £360,000,
with half coming from Scotland. But on 22 October the target was

[13]   Ibid., 4.

[14]   JHC, xi, 402, APS, ix, 378.

[15]   JHC, xi, 400–1.

[16]   Darien Papers, 6.

[17]   NLS, Yester Papers, MS 7019, f36.

increased to a massive £600,000, with half to be provided by English investors, and a quarter paid at the time of subscription. The date for opening a subscription book was set at 6 November. This substantial increase reflected confidence that there would be significant demand for shares. Two days later it was decided the Company should be run by a court of directors consisting of those named in the act and 30 other proprietors who owned £1,000 or more of stock.[18]

The promoters in Scotland were finally persuaded that business should begin in London and Lord Belhaven, Mr Robert Blackwood and James Balfour travelled south in October. On Saturday 9 November, Belhaven presided over the first meeting attended by a majority of those named in the act, at the house of Nathaniel Carpenter in St Clement's Lane.[19] The names of Smyth and D'Azevedo were corrected and a debate ensued about the large size of the target of £600,000, which had unsettled the promoters in Scotland. Paterson was asked to justify the increase in writing to reassure them.[20]

At the same time he was offered very generous terms to organise the capital raising: 2 per cent of subscriptions and 3 per cent of the profits of the Company for 21 years, which could be redeemed at any time over the next five years for 2 per cent more of the stock. If the capital raising was successful Paterson would receive the vast sum of £24,000 (4 per cent of £600,000, or £2.4m today) and become an extremely wealthy man. This amount dwarfed payouts to other projectors at the time. In 1692 Paterson himself had received 35 'maiden shares' in the Hampstead Waterworks with a nominal value of £700; Nicholas Dupin was promised £500 of shares in the Irish Linen Company and John Asgill and Nicholas Barbon were to receive £3,000 and £2,000 respectively from floating a land bank.[21] In today's capital market an IPO (Initial Public Offering) will secure an investment bank between 1 per cent and 2 per cent of the capital raised.[22] Paterson's 4 per cent perhaps

---

[18]   *JHC*, xi, 402. They had to be deputed in writing by other proprietors who owned at least £20,000 of shares.

[19]   *The Case of Mr William Paterson In Relation to His Claim on the Equivalent; As the same is stated in A Petition given in by Himself and A Report made by Mr Roderick MacKenzie; To the Honourable Court of Exchequer in North-Britain* (Edinburgh, 1708), 3.

[20]   *JHC*, xi, 402.

[21]   Scott, *Constitution and Finance*, i, 342, iii, 5.

[22]   Information supplied by Angus Sprott of ABN Amro, London.

reflected the large amount of capital that was being targeted. His reputation and influence among networks of London investors would be
vital for success. The terms, however, were controversial and worried
some of those who were considering investment in the Company. The
London merchants Michael Kincaid and John Pitcairn cited them as a
principal reason for their scepticism, believing that £12,000 (2 per cent
of £600,000) was earmarked for ten of the men named in the act, with
Paterson as a front.[23]

The London book was opened on 6 November and within eight
to ten days the target of £300,000 was subscribed.[24] This was a major
achievement for the Company, reflecting Paterson's marketing skills
and the appetite of London investors for high risk paper. Indeed there
was demand for more shares and individual subscriptions had to be
scaled back.[25] There was also no difficulty securing the first quarter
from the subscribers, which was paid 'instantly' to James Foulis, who
acted as the Company's cash collector.[26] All the investors, of course,
were seeking a substantial financial return from the new company.
John Hay, a kinsman of the Marquis of Tweeddale, noted in a letter from
London that Paterson had encouraged him to invest the maximum
£3,000.[27] An English merchant, Mr Glover, subscribed because he
thought it preferable that 'an Englishman should have the Benefit of
it than a Foreigner'. Mr Lancashire was also an investor in the EIC and
was told the unlikely story that if he did not subscribe the Bank of
England would buy up the shares.[28] Many others were merchants
associated with the 'interloping interest' that had been attempting to
break the monopoly of the EIC over the previous decades.[29]

The English joint-stock companies and the majority of London
merchants did not welcome the new company. The EIC was particularly vociferous in its opposition. The directors were still reeling from
a parliamentary investigation into a bribery scandal during the spring
of 1695 and their sensitivity was intensified by efforts of the interloping

---

[23]   ECA, Acc 789, Box 8, Bundle 1.

[24]   *Case of Mr William Paterson*, 2.

[25]   *JHC*, xi, 402.

[26]   *Case of Mr William Paterson*, 4, 7.

[27]   NLS, MS 7019, f65.

[28]   *JHC*, xi, 401.

[29]   A. Anderson, *An Historical and Chronological Deduction of the Origin
       of Commerce*, 2 vols, (London, 1764), ii, 205.

interest to obtain a charter and break their company's monopoly.[30] In response to losses caused by French privateers and the activities of the Scots, the share price collapsed from 80 in May to 50 in October, a decline of 37.5 per cent.[31] On 30 October the directors of the EIC decided to raise more capital to improve their cash position and fund ventures to the East Indies in the following year, and called for a further 25 per cent from the shareholders which was to be paid on or before 15 December.[32] Competition for funds in the London capital market was unwelcome. On 11 November the Scottish Company was mentioned for the first time in the minute book of the directors. A question was raised whether any 'member', that is shareholder, had subscribed for shares and it was declared that any investors would be acting contrary to their oaths and against the interest of the English company.[33]

The Scots responded by publishing a pamphlet presenting their case to the London mercantile community. *A Letter from a Member of the Parliament of Scotland to his Friend at London* was written by secretary Roderick MacKenzie and published on 14 November 1695.[34] It described the Company as an 'honest and infant undertaking' and addressed the key concern of the 'unprecedented concessions and exemptions', arguing that Scotland was so far behind England in company and colonial development that such privileges were necessary for survival.[35] It attacked the 'self-monopolizing interest' and stressed that

---

[30] In 1693, £80,000 was disbursed by the EIC in secret payments and it was rumoured that the Earl of Portland, King William's favourite and the man responsible for overseeing his Scottish business, had accepted £50,000. The efforts of the interloping interest would ultimately result in the creation of a New English East India Company in 1698.

[31] Scott, *Constitution and Finance*, ii, 161.

[32] British Library [BL], India Office Records, Court of Directors Minute Book, B/41, 68–9.

[33] *Ibid.*, 74.

[34] Roderick MacKenzie, *A Letter from a Member of the Parliament of Scotland to his Friend at London concerning their late Act for establishing a Company of that Kingdom trading to Africa and the Indies* (London, 1695). A transcription of this pamphlet can be found in BL, India Office Home Miscellaneous Series, H/44, 263–317. MacKenzie admits he was the author in a later pamphlet. See Roderick MacKenzie, *A Full and Exact Account of the Proceedings of the Court of Directors and Council-General of the Company of Scotland Trading to Africa and the Indies, with relation to the Treaty of Union, now under parliament's Consideration* (1706), 39.

[35] *Letter from a Member*, 286–7.

English consumers would benefit from lower prices of East Indian goods resulting from Scottish participation in the trade.[36] The pamphlet referred to a 'new Scotch-English, or English-Scotch Indian Company' which would 'bury in oblivion, the distinguishing names of Scotch and English' and ended with a call for closer union between the two kingdoms:

> Nature seems to have intended us for one people, as having concentered us within the same liquid walls; we are the Subjects of one King; we speak the same language; differing only in dialect, as most Countries do we possess the same Religion, differing only in some forms, which may or may not be; our Laws point at the same end; to distribute justice, and defend liberty and property.[37]

Despite this attempt to deflate English concerns the issue quickly attracted the attention of English politicians. Charles Duke of Shrewsbury recommended that the Scottish chancellor Tweeddale should come to London immediately for discussions with the King.[38] The drafting of the Company's act in Scotland had been muddled. Tweeddale, as King's commissioner in the Scottish parliament, had touched the act with the sceptre, but it had been drafted by Lord Advocate Sir James Stewart on terms that were probably outside the intended limits of Tweeddale's instructions. Tweeddale himself had expressed some doubts about the very generous exemptions from customs, but support for them was unanimous in parliamentary committee.[39] His rivals in Scotland were now in close contact with Thomas Osborne, Duke of Leeds, and other English politicians who were vocal in attacking the act.[40] The Scottish politicians who framed it and the promoters behind it clearly underestimated the opposition of the English mercantile and political communities.

In response to a petition from the EIC about the collapse of their share price, William referred to the future of the East India trade for

---

36   *Ibid.*, 307.

37   *Ibid.*, 311–12.

38   NLS, MS 7019, f133. Charles Talbot, Duke of Shrewsbury (1660–1718).

39   P.W.J. Riley, *King William and the Scottish Politicians* (Edinburgh, 1979), 98.

40   *Ibid.*, 99.

the first time in his reign in his opening speech to the English parliament on 23 November: 'you will consider of such Laws as may be proper for the Advancement of Trade; and will have a particular Regard to that of the East Indies, lest it should be lost to the Nation'.[41]

In late November the management of the Scottish Company was broadened to include more London investors. Colonel Robert Lancashire, Mr James Bateman, Mr Robert Williamson, Mr Thomas Skinner, Mr Abraham Wilmer, Paul Domonique and Mr Robert Douglas took their places on the board as directors, having each produced a deputation in writing from proprietors who had subscribed £20,000 of stock. On 22 November the meeting was described for the first time as a 'court' and the following week an *oath de fideli* was approved and signed by the directors. A committee of treasury was appointed to oversee company finances, a committee of trade to investigate sending ships to the East Indies, and a proposal made 'for improving the capital fund', i.e. lending money raised from subscribers at interest.[42] The Company of Scotland was thus initially a London company with a centre of gravity in the English metropolis and was run by London Scots and English merchants. The influence from north of the border was negligible at this time.

Another storm was brewing. The generous financial terms offered to Paterson for raising capital had become a subject of controversy and on 29 November he was forced to relinquish them. In his statement, recorded in the minutes, he claimed that six years of his life had been spent promoting the interests of the Company, even though he had only been associated with it since May. This was a typically Patersonian manipulation of the truth. It was remarkable that his account was not challenged by other directors and must reflect Paterson's authority and unrivalled position amongst them.

On 4 December the directors resolved that one or more ships should be fitted out for the East Indies and sail from Scotland as soon as possible. Plans were also to be put in place for a Scottish capital raising.[43] On the same day the EIC appointed a committee to draw up for the House of Lords a list of reasons why the Scottish act of

[41]   *Journals of the House of Lords* [JHL], xv, 599, H. Horwitz, 'The East India Trade, the Politicians, and the Constitution: 1689–1702,' *Journal of British Studies*, 17, (1978), 7–8.

[42]   *JHC*, xi, 403–4.

[43]   *Ibid.*, 405.

parliament was detrimental to the trade of England.[44] Panic spread through the English company as rumours circulated that several of their own directors and shareholders had subscribed to the 'Scotch Act'. It was declared that those who invested would be excluded from the court and directors were forced to swear an oath that they had not done so.[45]

The cacophony of protest spread to the Houses of Parliament. In December the Lords decided that the EIC and those trading to the West Indies should be summoned to give an account of how the 'Scotch Act' would damage English trade.[46] During their investigations, Sir Robert Southwell compared the exemptions of the Scottish Company with the English trade 'clogged' with customs. The Royal African Company feared the Scots would establish outposts in Africa and take the African trade from them. Mr Doddington of the East India Company believed Scotland would become a 'free port for all East India commodities' and Scottish pedlars swamp England.[47] A paper by the commissioners of the customs highlighted the fatal effect the Scottish Company would have on the trade, navigation and revenues of England.[48] Other papers against the Scots were produced by the Hamburg Company, the Levant Company, and merchants from Jamaica and the Leeward Islands.[49] English sugar producers published a one page news-sheet highlighting how the Scottish Company would damage the trade of English sugar plantations; the Scots were already seeking to 'bribe and entice away our Master-Workmen'.[50] The entire might of mercantile London was hysterically ranged against the Company.

The Scottish promoters and the English directors were summoned to the Lords and questioned.[51] On 9 December the house investigated the reasons why English merchants had invested in the Scottish Company,

44   BL, B/41, 81.

45   Ibid., 81–2.

46   HMC, House of Lords Manuscripts, 1695–7, 3.

47   Ibid., 13–14.

48   Ibid., 17.

49   Ibid., 17–21.

50   Some Considerations concerning the Prejudice which the Scotch Act Establishing a Company to Trade to the East and West-Indies, (with large Priviledges and on easie Terms) may bring to the English Sugar Plantations, and the Manufactory of Refining Sugar in England (London, 1695).

51   JHL, xv, 607–8.

and was told by the merchants themselves it was because they had
experience of trading with Scotland: 'We were known in Scotland,
and so came in'.[52] Paterson was summoned from Denmark Street in
Soho and said that he had been solicited in May to give advice about
drawing up the act of parliament.[53] On 12 December, Blackwood and
Balfour were asked to produce the Company books but claimed they
had already been sent back to Scotland.

On the same day the committee of the House decided to address
the King to lay before him the 'great Prejudice, Inconveniencies, and
Mischief' caused by the Scottish act.[54] The address of the Lords sum-
marised the concerns of the London mercantile community:

> The Duties and Difficulties that lie upon that Trade in England,
> a great Part of the Stock and Shipping of this Nation will be
> carried thither, and by this Means Scotland be made a Free
> Port for all East India Commodities; and consequently those
> several Places in Europe which were supplied from England
> will be furnished from thence much cheaper ... Moreover the
> said Commodities will unavoidably be brought by the Scotch
> into England by Stealth, both by Sea and Land, to the vast
> Prejudice of the English Trade and Navigation, and to the
> great Detriment of Your Majesty in Your Customs. And when
> once that Nation shall have settled themselves in Plantations
> in America, our Commerce in Tobacco, Sugar, Cloth, Wool,
> Skins, Masts, &c. will be utterly lost.[55]

The act was discussed in the Painted Chamber in a joint conference
between Lords and Commons on 16 December and on the following
day the address was presented to the King at Kensington.[56] William's
answer was to echo down through the centuries and reflected his dissatisfaction with his Scottish ministers over the extensive powers given
to the Company by the act: 'I have been ill served in Scotland; but I
hope some Remedies may be found to prevent the Inconveniencies
which may arise from this Act'.[57]

[52] HMC, *House of Lords*, 5.

[53] Insh, *Company of Scotland*, 56.

[54] *JHL*, xv, 610.

[55] *Ibid.*, 611.

[56] *Ibid.*, 614, Insh, *Company of Scotland*, 57, *JHC*, xi, 364.

[57] *Ibid.*, 366.

The Lords continued their discussions and on 20 December recommended legislation to crush the efforts of the Company: bills discouraging inhabitants of England from investing or taking part in the management under severe penalties, prohibiting the assistance of English seamen and shipbuilders, and establishing the English East Indian and African companies with privileges to compete with the Scots.[58]

The political fallout for the Scottish government was painful. Annandale informed Tweeddale from London:

> There wes never annie thing taken soe warmlie by this nation as this is and I am affrayed itt may stopp and retard the Kings busness extremlie this session off Parliament and I doe take freedome to tell your Lordship that itt does vex and perplex the King more then can be Immagined and att our Conference he did nott appeare warme as to annie thing except this Act for he said itt wes granting such powers priviledges and Soveraignties as iff there had been no King off Scottland.[59]

Annandale noted that the issue had so exasperated the King that he could not bear to discuss Scottish business. Tweeddale's political enemies were hoping that he would be held responsible and dismissed.[60] From William's point of view the furore was an annoying distraction. There were more important issues to be concerned with, such as funding the war effort on the Continent, and dealing with an escalating financial crisis that was gripping England. The reaction to the Scottish Company highlighted the weakness of William's government in Scotland and his lack of interest in his northern kingdom. Somehow an act with significant repercussions for trade relations between the two kingdoms had been passed with terms going well beyond the King's expectations. If he had paid more attention to Scottish affairs, a different and less controversial act might have materialised.

In January another concern was voiced by the directors of the EIC; English shipping was being prepared for the Scottish Company: 'many private Ships, which are refitting in the River of Thames, on account of the Scotch East India Company'.[61] There is no evidence in the

---

58   Insh, *Company of Scotland*, 58.

59   NLS, MS 7019, f154.

60   *Ibid.*, f157–8.

61   BL, B/41, 3 January 1696.

Company of Scotland's records that any ships had been fitted out at this point, although unofficial approaches may have been made, and such fears probably reflected the paranoia of London merchants.

The Commons carried out its own investigations, appointing a committee on 17 December to examine how the act was obtained in Scotland, and to determine the identity of the subscribers, promoters and advisers.[62] They interviewed MacKenzie, Paterson, Bateman, Glover, Lancashire, Domonique and Wilmer. Lord Belhaven was summoned but had already left for Scotland. A copy of the subscription book was provided by MacKenzie.[63] On 21 January the report was placed before the Commons, who responded aggressively, unleashing what has been described as an 'orgy of impeachment.'[64] It was resolved that administering and taking an *oath de fideli* in England was a high crime and misdemeanour, as was styling themselves a 'company', acting as such and raising money in England. All the directors, Belhaven, Blackwood, Balfour, the London Scots and the English merchants, were to be impeached.[65] On 29 January it was reported that Roderick MacKenzie had tried to suppress evidence he had given against those who were to be impeached. He was ordered to be arrested by the sergeant at arms attending the House.[66]

For Belhaven, the behaviour of the English Houses of Parliament was a direct attack on Scottish sovereignty, striking at the 'Independency of the Nation, through the Bowels of the Company.' He later lamented the mixed reception in the English capital: 'So our Act must be attacked in it's Swadling Cloaths, and persecuted in its Infancy.'[67]

The court of directors of the Company of Scotland had already met for the last time in London, on 6 December. At the meeting they had decided to prepare a fair copy of a preamble for subscriptions in Scotland. The court was adjourned until Friday 13 December at 3pm but never met again in England.[68]

Perhaps surprisingly given the fury of English opposition, the

---

[62] *JHC*, xi, 365.

[63] *Ibid.*, 400.

[64] Insh, *Company of Scotland*, 59.

[65] *JHC*, xi, 407. The threat was sufficient to end the Company's attempt to raise capital and impeachment was not carried out.

[66] *Ibid.*, 420.

[67] Belhaven, *Speech in Parliament on the 10th day of January 1701*, 8.

[68] *JHC*, xi, 405.

Company did not relinquish all hopes of securing capital from London. Six months later, in June 1696, instructions were given to directors James Campbell and James Smyth to negotiate with those who had originally subscribed.[69] Smyth and Campbell organised a meeting in London on 22 July and sought to encourage clandestine payment by 10 August. But lack of an English subscription book proved a disadvantage as they had no list of original subscribers. Some protested their 'sincere Affection to the Undertaking' but believed it was not safe for anyone resident in England to be involved. Foulis declared that all the money he had received the previous November had been returned.[70]

The attempt to raise capital in London unleashed the full fury of English economic nationalism. Despite being an Anglo-Scottish joint venture, English vested interests opposed the Company implacably, reflecting intense sensitivity in the London merchant community during a decade of severe financial difficulties. The impact of the Nine Years War fought from 1688 to 1697 was traumatic on English joint-stocks and merchants. The Royal African Company had suffered 'many great Losses since the War.'[71] The London sugar merchants put their losses at £664,100 in the period 1694 to 1695, and the EIC at £1,500,000 for 1695 alone.[72] The financial crisis caused by problems of war finance exaggerated the hysterical atmosphere. As the Houses of Parliament considered the Scottish act they were also debating the state of the English coinage, which had collapsed in value.[73] This would ultimately precipitate one of the key events in English monetary history: the Great Recoinage of 1696 which re-minted silver coins back to full weight.[74] The reception of the Scottish Company in London demonstrated that England would vigorously oppose a Scottish

---

[69] *Case of Mr William Paterson*, 4.

[70] *Ibid.*, 8.

[71] *JHC*, xi, 375.

[72] D.W. Jones, 'London merchants and the crisis of the 1690s' in *Crisis and order in English towns 1500–1700*, (eds.) P. Clark and P. Slack (London, 1972), 320.

[73] S. Quinn, 'Gold, silver, and the Glorious Revolution: arbitrage between bills of exchange and bullion,' *EcHR*, 49, (1996), 473–89. By 1695, years of clipping and bullion outflows had lowered the average silver content of the English coinage to less than half original mint weight. The Recoinage of 1696 re-minted silver coins back to full weight.

[74] M-H Li, *The Great Recoinage of 1696 to 1699* (London, 1963).

attempt to compete in African, Asian or Caribbean trade. The intensity of this opposition should have been carefully noted by those who returned to Scotland to establish the Company on a Scottish footing.

CHAPTER FIVE

Raising Capital in a Cold Climate

They came in Shoals from all Corners of the Kingdom to Edinburgh, Rich, Poor, Blind and Lame, to lodge their Subscriptions in the Company's House, and to have a Glimpse of the Man Paterson.

WALTER HERRIES[1]

AT THE HEART OF the history of the Company of Scotland was a group of individuals who never travelled to Darien, who never felt the heat of the Central American jungle or smelled the stench of death in the huts of Caledonia, and as a result have not featured highly in the accounts of historians. These were the men and women who, in very large numbers for the period, became shareholders in the Company and provided the money to fund the venture. They spent the years from 1696 to 1707 on an emotional rollercoaster between ecstasy and despair, waiting expectantly for each crumb of news. An examination of who they were, and why they were willing in such numbers to invest in a joint-stock company in 1696, is of central importance not just to the history of the Company but also to explaining the passage of the Treaty of Union through the Scottish parliament in 1707.

The attempt to raise capital in London had failed because of opposition from English joint-stock companies and the intervention of the English parliament. The promoters of the Company were forced to concentrate their efforts on Scotland. At first sight this might have appeared a fairly grim prospect. Scotland was not in the premier league of financial powers in the late 17th century. There were certainly signs of economic improvement, but she had slipped far behind the Dutch and English in terms of trade, industry and financial muscle.[2] It was unclear whether a Scottish company would be able to raise the large sum of cash that was being talked about from the domestic capital market.

---

[1]   Herries, *Defence*, 8.

[2]   *The Transformation of Scotland: The Economy Since 1700*, (eds.) T.M. Devine, C.H. Lee and G.C. Peden (Edinburgh, 2005), 13–20.

William Paterson and his London cohorts Daniel Lodge and James Smyth, who arrived in Edinburgh in February 1696, were the driving force behind the Scottish capital raising. George Home noted in his diary on 13 February that 'ther are some English men come hither from London for carrying on the East India Trade'.[3] They spent their time in Edinburgh coffee-houses selling the merits of joint-stock investment to nobles, lairds, merchants, doctors and anyone else who might listen. Home himself met Paterson, 'the great projector for trade', on two occasions before the subscription books were opened, and his experience was no doubt typical of many who were contemplating investment in the Company.[4]

In order to get the fund raising off to a flying start, Paterson focused his marketing campaign on the top echelons of Scottish society. If some of the social heavyweights backed the venture with their money, many others further down the hierarchy might be persuaded to do the same. Particular attention was paid to the 'old lady' of the nation, the formidable 64 year old Anne, Duchess of Hamilton, who was head of Scotland's principal noble family, the Hamiltons. She had been born in London in 1632 and brought up in England before returning to Hamilton Palace at the age of ten. Her father James, first Duke of Hamilton, was executed in 1649 for supporting Charles I. She became duchess in her own right in 1656, at the age of nineteen, on the death of her uncle. Since then she had overseen the recovery of the Hamilton estates from debts accumulated during the Civil Wars and had begun an ambitious scheme to rebuild Hamilton Palace in the late 1680s with her husband William Douglas, younger son of the first Marquis of Douglas. The support of the Duchess and other members of her large family was vital for the success of the Company. One of her thirteen children, Lord Basil Hamilton, an enthusiastic supporter of the Company, wrote to his eldest brother, James Earl of Arran, on 25 February:

> Mr Paterson and some others have been with her and say it would be disheartning to the whole kingdome, and might occasion many people far below her Quality not to goe a greater length, she said she believed you, and many of her family would be considerably in it, so she thought it needless for her

3   NAS, GD 1/891/1, 13 February 1696.
4   Ibid., 14 February 1696.

to subscrive a greater soum in it designing thereby only to sho
her good will to it but they wer very earnest in it, and I
thought it reasonable and might of be of consequence to the
bussines for many of the world act by example, and they said
they would rather pay the proportions of the other two thousand pound than that Her Grace should not subscrive it.[5]

Under pressure from the promoters, Lord Basil and the 'earnest'
Paterson, the old Duchess relented. She wrote to two of her other
sons, Charles, Earl of Selkirk, and John Hamilton, urging them to join
her in an investment under her name and raising the subscription from
£1,000 to the maximum of £3,000. There were expectations that
Arran would announce the size of his investment in the next few days.

The promoters had appointed Sir John Swinton of that Ilk, a
Borders laird, and the Edinburgh merchant George Clark to prepare
an advertisement for the capital raising, which was published as a
large one page news-sheet.[6] An antecedent of the present day share
prospectus, it informed potential investors that the subscription book
would be opened on Wednesday 26 February 'at the House of Mrs
Purdie in the North side of the High-street over against the Cross'.
Subscriptions could be made every day of the week between ten and
twelve in the morning and two and four in the afternoon except, of
course, on the Sabbath. A quarter of the amount subscribed was to be
paid to the Company on or before 1 June; to encourage early payment
a discount was offered for providing money before this date.[7] Those
living at a distance from Edinburgh, who could not travel in person,
might appoint someone else to subscribe for them. The remaining
three quarters of the subscription was to be paid in equal instalments,
the Company only calling for a second quarter after a year, and the
remainder held as a 'fund of security' to be called upon 'some press-
ing occasion.'[8]

The promoters principally relied on word of mouth to sell shares
in the Company, which was already the main subject of gossip in the

---

[5] NAS, GD 406/1/6944.

[6] RBS, D/1/1, 1.

[7] At a rate of 12% per annum or 8d per day from the time of payment until
    1 June.

[8] *The Company of Scotland, Trading to Africa and the Indies, do hereby
    give Notice* in NLS, Yester Papers, MS 14493, f130–1.

coffee-houses of Edinburgh, indeed throughout the whole country, following the events in London. There was, however, some recourse to the written word to reinforce the investment case. A pamphlet published in January 1696 stated that the Company would contribute to Scotland's 'Security, Peace, and Greatness' and was an 'absolute Necessity to our Nation, to keep us from being destroyed'.[9] Paterson was singled out for particular praise:

> A person to whom, in a special manner we owe already the fair Foundation of this Design; and I hope shall owe many good and well grounded Advices to carry on the Trade; His great Experience, Universal Travelling, and Correspondence, Exact Observing and making it for many Years his Study and work to lay such a Design, as might benefite his Native Country, fitting him for the same: His laying the Design, and Projects first of the Royal Bank of England, and then that of the Orphans Fund, demonstrating both his Ability for such an Undertaking, and his kindness to our Neighbours; And his doing this to us, as it proclaims him a Worthy Country man, so it may encourage us all to venture part of our Fortunes, on a project of his frameing, who hath been so successful among our Neighbours.[10]

The author is unknown but it would come as no surprise to learn Paterson himself commissioned the pamphlet and his acolyte James Smyth composed it. There are certainly Patersonain flourishes in it: 'there is such a Mystery in Trade, that Trade createth Trade, and one Trade createth another, and encreaseth another.'[11] Smyth had already penned a pamphlet in London in 1695 defending Paterson's roles in the Bank of England and Orphans' Fund.[12]

---

9   *A Letter from a Gentleman in the Country to His Friend at Edinburgh: Wherein it is clearly proved, That the Scottish African, and Indian Company, is Exactly Calculated for the Interest of Scotland* (Edinburgh, 1696), 5.

10 *Ibid.*, 7.

11 *Ibid.*, 8, 11.

12 J[ames] S[myth], *Some Account of the Transactions of Mr William Paterson, In Relation to the Bank of England, and the Orphans Fund. In a Letter to a Friend* (London, 1695).

The capital raising began in Edinburgh on 26 February 1696. The throng of subscribers was described by Herries in an oft quoted passage: 'They came in Shoals from all Corners of the Kingdom to Edinburgh, Rich, Poor, Blind and Lame, to lodge their Subscriptions in the Company's House, and to have a Glimpse of the man Paterson'. A vast hoard of subscribers apparently descended on Edinburgh in a fervour of enthusiasm. However, Herries was probably not in Edinburgh at the time; he was engaged by Gleneagles in London in November 1696, and he was wrong in stating that subscriptions were made at the Company House, which was not bought until the summer. His description should be viewed as impressionistic, an exaggerated caricature; the 'poor, blind and lame' providing, in likelihood, only a tiny part, if any, of subscribers. On the first day sixty-nine Scots signed the book over the four hours available for subscription, an average of seventeen per hour.[13] Even allowing for servants, friends, relations, hangers-on and interested Edinburgh citizens, there was probably a crowd of a few hundred rather than the 'shoals' described by Herries. Nevertheless such a throng was impressive and unprecedented in Scottish joint-stock investment.

The first person to sign was Anne, Duchess of Hamilton, who pledged £3,000. The efforts of Paterson had paid off. She was followed by two other women: Margaret, Countess of Rothes, who subscribed £1,000 for herself and £1,000 for her fifteen year old son, Thomas, Earl of Haddington, and Lady Margaret Hope of Hopetoun, with £1,000 for herself and £2,000 for her son, Hopetoun. The Lord Provost of Edinburgh, Sir Robert Chiesly, was the first man to sign, with an investment of £2,000, followed by a series of lairds, merchants, lawyers and doctors. John Haliburton, younger of Moorehouselaw, was the first to subscribe the minimum amount of £100.[14]

As one might expect, some of the promoters named in the act of parliament subscribed on the first day: Chiesly himself, Adam Cockburn of Ormiston, the Lord Justice Clerk, the lairds Francis Montgomery of Giffen and Sir John Swinton of that Ilk, and the two Edinburgh merchants Mr Robert Blackwood and James Balfour, who had been instrumental in securing the passage of the act. There were also men who were to play an important role in the history of the

Company as directors: James Pringle of Torwoodlee, John Drummond of Newton, Lieutenant Colonel John Erskine, Lord Basil Hamilton, George Baillie of Jerviswood, Sir Francis Scott of Thirlestane, and Sir John Maxwell of Pollock.

George Home subscribed £500 on the following day. He recorded his subscription in his diary: 'I went to the Indian Company room wher many subscribers of all sorts come very fast in. Afternoon I returned thither and signed'.[13] Following another coffee-house encounter with the East Lothian laird Andrew Fletcher of Saltoun, James Smyth and Sir John Swinton of that Ilk, he felt even more positive and wrote encouraging his brother and tenants to subscribe.[14]

By the end of the first day an impressive £50,400 had been promised to the Company. On the next day a further £25,200 was subscribed, and then £10,100 and £5,300 on the following days. By the end of February, £91,000 had been pledged, almost a third of the target of £300,000, and subscriptions continued to pour in during March, when £216,865, or 54 per cent of the total finally raised, was promised. The busiest day of the entire capital raising was the last day of March, when 176 individuals subscribed £47,400. The crowds at Mrs Purdie's house were perhaps then approaching the 'shoals' described by Herries. This was an important cut-off point, for those who subscribed before 1 April were entitled to vote in elections for a committee that joined with the promoters to draw up a Company constitution.[15]

The enthusiasm of subscribers was not curtailed by disturbing external events. In late February there was news of a plot to assassinate King William and the government feared a French-backed Jacobite invasion of Scotland. Suspected Jacobites were arrested and held in Edinburgh Castle and the Tolbooth.[16] The atmosphere of insecurity was reflected in the launch of a witch hunt on 3 March, when the privy council established a commission to try the unfortunate Janet Wodrow from the parish of Kilmacolm in Renfrewshire.[17] Despite political uncertainty, the capital raising continued seemingly unaffected. Lord Basil referred in a letter to 'such strange news of assassinations and invasions that we are all agast here'. But the subscriptions continued

---

[13] NAS, GD 1/891/1, 27 February 1696.

[14] *Ibid.*, 2 and 4 March 1696.

[15] RBS, D/1/1, 5.

[16] NAS, Minute Book of the Privy Council, PC 1/50, 367, 393, 405.

[17] NAS, PC 1/50, 362.

'very fast' although the news had 'put it out of our heads a litle'.[18] The Scots were so positive about the prospects of the Company that nothing could dent their optimistic mood.

Another book was opened in Glasgow on 5 March to facilitate further subscription by tapping into the rising wealth of the western burgh and its neighbouring shires. The first to sign was Provost John Anderson, who pledged £3,000 for the burgh, followed by Dean of Guild, John Aird with £1,000 for the Merchants' House, and Principal of the university William Dunlop with £1,000 for himself and £1,000 for his kinsman John Dunlop of that Ilk. The devout Presbyterian William Dunlop was to become an important figure in the Company. He was experienced in colonial matters having sailed to South Carolina in 1684 to become chaplain at Stuarts Town and a major in the militia. His appointment as Principal of the university in 1690 was secured through the patronage of his brother-in-law William Carstares. Dunlop of that Ilk was to sail with the second expedition to the isthmus.

Other investors in Glasgow on the first day included the East Sugar Works, a business partnership, and the merchants John Spreul, William Wooddrop, and William Arbuckle. Spreul was another man of devout Presbyterian principles, who was better known as Bass John from his days of imprisonment on the Bass Rock in the 1680s for opposition to the Stuarts. By the end of the first day in Glasgow £13,100 had been subscribed, and over the following days many travelled from the nearby towns of Hamilton, Paisley, Irvine, Kilmarnock, Largs and Greenock. On 2 April the book was taken to the burgh of Ayr, where Provost Robert Moore subscribed £200 for the town and was followed by many of the burgh's merchants. Between 15 and 17 April a group of soldiers from Sir John Hill's regiment – five captains, a lieutenant and an ensign – subscribed the Glasgow book. The regiment was involved in the Massacre of Glencoe in 1692 and many of its soldiers were in Edinburgh in 1695 when parliament considered the report of a commission of enquiry into the slaughter. The act establishing the Company was passed at the same time and their interest in joint-stock investment may have been kindled then.[19]

In late March, Lord Basil Hamilton was still hoping for news from his elder brother, Arran: 'I must say this to you, it has bein much talked here of your forwardness in this affair, and your great promises to

---

[18] NAS, GD 406/1/7494.

[19] Prebble, *Darien*, 59, APS, ix, 377.

put in and encourage it, and they say they have wrett to you of it and given you accounts of their proceedings but have never heard of you'. Basil noted the Duke of Queensberry's £3,000 subscription, perhaps to spur his elder brother on.[20] Arran's reluctance was not caused by a lack of ready cash as he had money 'lying dead' in Scotland despite large debts. The earl's indecision was to infuriate many who looked to him for political leadership over the following years. His younger brother lamented: 'I should be sorry to see so great and good a worke to the kingdome and your name not in it'.[21]

The appetite of the Scots for joint-stock investment went beyond the expectations of the promoters. On 3 April a general meeting of subscribers confidently resolved to increase the target from £300,000 to £400,000 because there were still several noblemen, gentlemen and royal burghs 'who live at a distance from this place, not yet come in, occasioned partly for want of Timely Advertisement and through the badness of the Weather.'[22] Subscriptions continued over the following months, although at a lower rate (see Figure 1). On 1 August the books were closed at £400,000. Last minute subscribers included Alexander Stevenson, the Edinburgh merchant who had been sent to the Continent to oversee the building of ships in Hamburg, who authorised Daniel Lodge to subscribe for him; James Lord Drummond, who may have had problems securing capital because of imprisonment for suspected Jacobitism; the towns of Cupar and Queensferry; and the Convention of Royal Burghs. The capital raising had run out of steam and the final £8,000 was invested 'in trust' for the Company by directors John Drummond of Newton, James Balfour, Sir John Swinton of that Ilk, William Arbuckle and John Corse, dedicated Company supporter Mr William Dunlop, and the lairds Henry Rollo of Woodside and John Graham younger of Dougalston. The obligation to provide cash would remain with the Company. It was a cosmetic exercise to ensure that the target of £400,000 was reached and indicated that the capital raising had sucked in much of the liquid wealth of Scotland. It did not bode well for an aftermarket in the shares. There would be no stampede of investors to inflate the share price.

---

[20]   NAS, GD 406/1/7475.

[21]   NAS, GD 406/1/7496.

[22]   RBS, D1/1, 7.

Figure 1

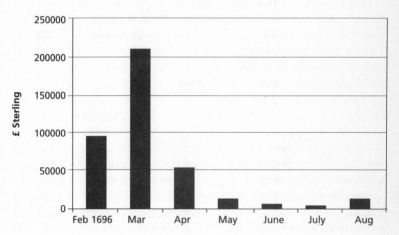

Monthly Subscriptions 1696

Source: *Darien Papers*, 371–417.

Investment in the Company of Scotland was not an anonymous affair like buying shares in today's stockmarket. The Company proudly published 'A perfect LIST Of the several Persons Residenters in SCOT-LAND, Who have Subscribed as ADVENTURERS in the JOYNT-STOCK of the Company of Scotland Trading to Africa and the Indies.' This provided an alphabetical list of subscribers with amounts pledged.[23] The level of financial commitment was therefore public knowledge.

As suggested by Herries, the subscribers hailed from many different parts of the country. Caithness was the only shire out of thirty-three not found in the subscription books.[24] Midlothian provided the most subscribers, with 425 pledging £111,650, but other shires, such as Angus, Ayrshire and Roxburghshire, were also well represented.[25] Those from the main urban centres subscribed large amounts of capital, Edinburgh accounting for 22.1 per cent and Glasgow 10.6 per

---

[23] NLS, Adv MS 83.1.8.

[24] W. Douglas Jones, '"The Bold Adventurers": A Quantitative Analysis of the Darien Subscription List (1696),' *Scottish Economic and Social History*, 21, (2001), 25.

[25] *Ibid.*, 26. Angus (77 entries, £15,625), Ayrshire (71 entries, £17,350), Roxburghshire (26 entries, £10,500).

cent. Captain John Blackadder, who was in Flanders, was the only subscriber based overseas.[26]

As we might expect given their active role in the establishment of the Company, merchants were significant investors, subscribing in total £96,195 or about a quarter of the capital. About 23 per cent of members of the Edinburgh merchant community were direct investors, 132 of them subscribing £49,750. 74 Glasgow merchants subscribed £24,775.[27]

The Scottish nobility pledged about 14 per cent of the capital.[28] The majority of the most powerful nobles promised money, including James, Duke of Queensberry, Archibald, Earl of Argyll and John, Marquis of Atholl. Arran himself did not subscribe in person but a proportion of the £3,000 pledged by Lord Basil Hamilton belonged to him, and other family members were significant investors.[29] Other noble subscribers included the Earls of Panmure, Leven, and Lothian, the Earl Marischal, Viscount Tarbat, Lord Belhaven and Lord Ruthven.

The Tweeddale family was especially enthusiastic in its commitment to the Company. The first Marquis of Tweeddale subscribed £1,000, his half-brother William Hay of Drummelzier £1,000, his sons John Lord Yester, Lord David Hay and Lord Alexander Hay £1,000, £500 and £400 respectively, his daughter, the Countess of Roxburgh £1,000, and his servitor John Hay £200.[30] This was a very substantial investment by a noble family and its size was commented on at the time. In his diary, George Home noted that the family and friends of Tweeddale intended to subscribe £20,000.[31] In fact the family's investment was just over £5,000 although Tweeddale's political 'interest', those who supported him in politics such as Sir Patrick Scott of Ancrum and Sir Francis Scott of Thirlestane, were major subscribers, providing him with a substantial voting block among the shareholders. Tweeddale and his eldest son were also investors in the White Paper Company and the Bank of Scotland, and items in the

---

[26] *Ibid.*, 25.

[27] Dingwall estimates that the size of the Edinburgh merchant community was about 585 in the 1690s, H.M. Dingwall, *Late Seventeenth-century Edinburgh: A demographic study* (Aldershot, 1994), 180.

[28] Smout, *Scottish Trade*, 150.

[29] NAS, GD 406/1/6440. Lord Basil noted in a letter of 31 October 1698 that 'your interest there is under my name.'

[30] *Darien Papers*, 371–417.

[31] NAS, GD 1/891/1, 21 February 1696.

Yester Papers indicate a healthy interest in finance and money making, perhaps stimulated by necessity; a way of freeing the family from significant debts, which were £24,000 in 1691.[32]

Surprisingly, the most significant group of investors was not merchants or nobles but lairds, small landowners beneath the nobility, who subscribed about 34 per cent of the capital. The wealth and influence of lairds had increased during the 17th century and was recognised at the Revolution when their representation in parliament was increased by 50 per cent.[33] This was very different from the English joint-stock companies, such as the Bank of England and EIC, where merchants dominated, and was to affect the complexion of the court of directors of the Company, where lairds formed a majority.

The professions of 17th century Scotland were also represented. The period from the late 16th century had seen the relentless rise of the legal profession in terms of wealth, power and influence, and a large expansion in numbers. Six out of 14 senators of the college of justice (judges) were subscribers, as were 21 advocates, 16 Writers to the Signet and 48 writers. Thus 58 per cent of the Faculty of Advocates, 33 per cent of Writers to the Signet and 27 per cent of Edinburgh writers subscribed.[34] The Faculty of Advocates itself made an investment of £1,000, so in theory all the advocates in Scotland had some financial commitment to the Company. The total pledged by the profession was £25,100.[35]

Many physicians, surgeons and apothecaries invested in the Company; 59 medical men subscribing £12,700 or 3.2 per cent of the capital. Some doctors made significant investments: John Baillie sub-

[32]   NLS, MS 1913, Scots White Paper Manufactory, f7. Bank of Scotland Archive [BS], Adventurer's Ledger, 1/92/1A, NLS, MS 14493, f114–15, 163–4: 'Memorial for Encouraging the Trade of the Kingdom of Scotland,' 'Proposals for a Guinea Trade' and 'A Short Discription of the Madagascare Trade And of the Commodities fitting for that place.' M. Lee, Jr., *The 'Inevitable' Union and other essays on Early Modern Scotland* (East Linton, 2003), 250.

[33]   Smout, *Scottish Trade*, 150, D.J. Patrick, 'People and Parliament in Scotland 1689–1702' (University of St Andrews PhD, 2002), 74.

[34]   21 advocates, 16 Writers to the Signet and 48 Edinburgh writers were subscribers. Poll tax records indicate that there were 36 advocates, 49 Writers to the Signet and 179 writers in Edinburgh in the 1690s. Dingwall, *Late Seventeenth-century Edinburgh*, 217.

[35]   *Darien Papers*, 371–417.

scribed £1,000, Thomas Dalrymple £700, Alexander Dundas, James Auchinleck and Sir Archibald Stevenson £600 each. Some were wealthy Edinburgh doctors, such as Robert Trotter, President of the Royal College of Physicians, and Sir Robert Sibbald, founder of the Royal Botanic Garden, but there were other less well known figures such as George Grieve, apothecary in Dundee, Hugh Hunter, apothecary in Kilmarnock, and Robert Rutherford, apothecary in Jedburgh.

Twenty ministers of the Kirk were shareholders, mostly investing smaller sums of £100 or £200, although John Hamilton, an Edinburgh minister, pledged £400 in two subscriptions of £200. There were about a thousand parishes in Scotland so only a very small proportion of ministers (about 2 per cent) subscribed.[36]

Shareholding in the Company was not the sole preserve of men. We have already noted the large subscriptions of the Duchess of Hamilton, Countess of Rothes and Lady Hope of Hopetoun. In total ninety-one women subscribed £21,000, or 5.3 per cent of the capital. Many were widows or heiresses who had control of estates or financial assets. They included Margaret Adamson, the eldest daughter of the late Patrick Adamson, merchant in Kelso; Agnes Campbell, relict of Andrew Anderson, his Majesty's printer; and Bessie Bogle, relict of Robert Bogle, merchant of Glasgow (see Appendix 7). There was no place, however, for women on the court of directors.

In the subscription books we also find the signatures of individuals from a variety of other trades: soldiers, sea captains, maltmen, baxters, vintners, fleshers, goldsmiths, weavers, tanners, hammermen, tailors and bookbinders. A selection of names taken randomly includes David Burton, glazier in Edinburgh; Andrew Brown, watchmaker; James Meikle, maltman in Leith; Robert Douglas junior, soap-boiler in Leith; William Brotherstone, harness-maker in the Canongate. There were a small number of teachers and professors including Thomas Darling, one of the doctors of the grammar school of Edinburgh; James Martin, late regent of St Andrews University; and Alexander Rule, Professor of Oriental Languages at Edinburgh University. There was also a lone medical student, James Gregory, who subscribed on two occasions. On 30 March, John Hay, Alexander Ramsay, and John Dickson, servants of the Marquis of Tweeddale, subscribed. There were also a few subscribers described as 'servitors,' such as William

---

[36] Following the ejection of Episcopalian clergy who did not support the Revolution there were a considerable number of vacant parishes.

Cleland, servitor of Lady Drylaw, and John Fraser, servitor of merchant Alexander Innes. These 'servitors' and 'servants' were elite members of the households of nobles and lairds, often administrative secretaries, or serving apprenticeships with merchants. They were paid reasonable wages and had access to some capital.

One further group of investors should be highlighted: the institutions of 17th century Scotland. There were no institutional investors in English and Dutch joint-stock companies in the 1690s and so the Company of Scotland might claim the distinction of marking the beginning of the institutional investment that now dominates the buying and selling of shares on global stockmarkets.[37] The role of institutions had been sanctioned, and indeed encouraged, by an act of the Scottish parliament of 1695: 'Act allowing the Administrators of the Common good of Burrowes to Adventure their Stocks or any part therof in the Company of Forraign Trade'. The act stated that it was legitimate for magistrates and administrators of the common goods of burghs, and deacons and masters of other corporate bodies, to invest in the Company, and indemnified them from personal liability if it should fail.[38]

Fifty-three institutions invested in the Company of Scotland (see Appendix 5). Almost all the principal corporate bodies in the kingdom were represented: the Good Town of Edinburgh, the Incorporation of Surgeons of Edinburgh, the Merchant Company of Edinburgh, the Faculty of Advocates, the burgh of Glasgow, the Merchant's House of Glasgow and the Convention of Royal Burghs. There was a series of smaller burghs; Dumfries, Linlithgow, Haddington, Perth, Brechin, Dunbar, Selkirk, Inverkeithing, Inverness, Queensferry, Cupar, Irvine, Ayr, Renfrew and Paisley, as well as merchant guilds and trade incorporations, such as the guildry of Stirling and the incorporation of the Maltmen of Glasgow. The institutions included one corporate investor, the East Sugar Works of Glasgow, whose partners decided to invest £3,000, and charitable institutions such as the Seamen's Box of Dundee and Cowan's Hospital of Stirling.[39] In total, institutions pledged £27,150 of the Company's capital, or 6.8 per cent.

---

[37] Dickson, *Financial Revolution*, 259–60. I would like to thank Prof Femme Gaastra of the University of Leiden for information about the VOC.

[38] APS, ix, 463.

[39] John, Robert and William Corse, James Peadie, John Luke, George and Robert Boyle.

The records of institutions provide some evidence about the decision to invest. The burgh council of Edinburgh was influenced by the act that indemnified administrators, referring to it in their discussion, and decided to invest £3,000, the maximum amount. The Lord Provost was empowered to sign the subscription book and the burgh treasurer to pay the first quarter in cash on subscription. A vote was taken with only one brave individual, Hugh Blair, dissenting.[40] A general meeting of another Edinburgh institution, the Merchant Company, met to discuss the 'virtuous and praise worthy designe of the Company of Scotland'. It was unanimously agreed to subscribe 'nemine contradicente' and another vote determined that £1,200 rather than £1,000 should be invested. It was also decided that half a per cent of the profits of individual subscribers should be paid to the treasurer for the use of the poor of the Merchant Company.[41]

The Convention of Royal Burghs made the decision to subscribe £3,000 on 8 July. Each burgh was asked to pay a proportion of the cash according to their position on the tax roll. But representatives of fourteen burghs protested they could not provide money because they had not been instructed to do so by their constituents. The investment by the Convention did not therefore represent all Scottish burgh communities.[42]

Small burghs were influenced by their larger cousins. The council of Lanark received a letter from the Lord Provost of Edinburgh in early March encouraging it to subscribe and on 23 April it decided to invest the minimum £100.[43] The guildry of Stirling noted that 'several burghs had given considerable sums of money' and unanimously voted an investment of £200, influenced by the herd mentality.[44] There was vigorous debate in some institutions. On 24 March the Faculty of Advocates decided to subscribe £1,000 'after much reasoning upon the said matter'.[45]

40 *Records of the Burgh of Edinburgh*, 190–1.

41 ECA, Minutes of the Merchant Company, Acc 264, i, 3.

42 *Extracts from the Records of the Convention of the Royal Burghs of Scotland, 1677–1711* (Edinburgh, 1880), 209–10.

43 *Extracts from the Records of the Royal Burgh of Lanark* (Glasgow, 1893), 259.

44 *Extracts from The Records of the Merchant Guild of Stirling AD 1592–1846*, (eds.) W.B. Cook and D.B. Morris (Stirling, 1916), 79.

45 *The Minute Book of the Faculty of Advocates*, i, 1661–1712, ed. J.M. Pinkerton (Stair Society, 1976), 167.

The act of parliament specified that the minimum investment was to be £100 and the maximum £3,000, equivalent to about £10,000 and £300,000 in today's money. Even the lower amount was a considerable sum and well beyond the vast majority of the population. In 1695 the average annual wage of a male servant in Renfrewshire was about £1 8s and a female servant £1 1s. Even if they saved every penny of their cash it would take a male servant over seventy years to save enough to invest £100 and a female servant a century. The daily wage of a master wright in Aberdeen in 1696 was 20s Scots and a building labourer 8s Scots.[46] The minimum investment represented one hundred days work for a master wright and about two hundred and fifty for a building labourer. Most of the subscribers therefore belonged to social groups who had access to capital: nobles, lairds, merchants, doctors, soldiers and skilled craftsmen. Investing in the Company was beyond the means of the majority of the Scottish population: small tenants, landless labourers, the urban workforce, the poor and the unemployed, who were very numerous in the 1690s.

Most of the shareholders subscribed either £100 or £200. Six individuals and four institutions subscribed the maximum £3,000; 35 invested above £1,000; and 92, £1,000 (see Appendix 4). Thus almost one in ten of the subscribers pledged at least £1,000 (£91,740 today), which was the amount required to be eligible to stand for election as a director.

Some subscribed the books on more than one occasion; a reflection of increasing confidence about the prospects of the Company, or ability to access more capital.[47] The director John Drummond of Newton made four separate subscriptions of £600, £400, £200 and £1,125. Lord Basil Hamilton made three subscriptions each of £1,000 and the Edinburgh merchant Mr Gilbert Campbell signed the book on five separate occasions: £400, £200, £100, £200 and £100.

During periods of excessive optimism it is often very difficult to stand apart from the crowd. In 1696 there were contrarians who did not invest in the Company. Significant numbers of the nobility did not subscribe, including the Earls of Carnwath, Crawford, Eglinton,

---

[46] A.J.S. Gibson and T.C. Smout, *Prices, Food and Wages in Scotland 1550–1780* (Cambridge, 1995), 310, 315, 334.

[47] As a result there has been some confusion about the total number of subscribers. If these multiple subscriptions are considered separately, a higher number is obtained.

Kintore, Mar, Morton, Glencairn, Loudon and Forfar, and the Lords Saltoun, Bargany, Blantyre, Forrester, Rollo, Rutherford and Bellenden. Indeed only 12 out of a sample of 44 earls (27 per cent) and 12 out of 41 lords (29 per cent) were investors. The reason for their absence is not known. It may reflect a shortage of cash, lack of interest in joint-stock investment, scepticism about the success of the Company, or simply old age or minority. James, second Earl of Airlie, who did not subscribe, was born about 1611 and was excused from parliament in 1693 on account of his old age. Many nobles who did not invest were Jacobites, or suspected Jacobites, such as the Duke of Gordon, Earl of Seaforth, Earl of Balcarres, Lord Dunkeld, Earl of Kinnoull, Earl of Perth, Earl of Melfort, Earl of Wigtown and Viscount Frendraught. The logistical and financial problems associated with imprisonment and exile may have made subscription impossible.

There were other reasons for ignoring the arguments of Paterson and his fellow promoters. In 1710 David, third Lord Falconer of Halkerton, was found to have been *non compos mentis* for the previous twenty years.[48] His insanity may have ensured that he did not participate in the investment mania of 1696.

One of the few institutions to stand against the tide of optimism was the Incorporation of Goldsmiths of Edinburgh. On 3 March the deacon asked the 'calling' if they would 'concern thair common box' in the venture. It was put to the vote but not carried. Perhaps they felt they were overextending themselves as an investment had already been made in the Bank of Scotland.[49] Ironically the incorporation did become a shareholder two years later in 1698 when they bailed-out Deacon Andrew Law, who had been imprisoned for debt. Law transferred his subscription of £200 to the incorporation after they provided his creditors with £300 Scots.[50]

Two important government figures were not subscribers: Sir James Ogilvy and Sir James Stewart. In December 1695 Ogilvy commented in a letter to Carstares that the Company 'will do little hurt to England, seeing we want a fleet'.[51] The lack of Scottish naval power

---

[48]   *Scots Peerage*, v, 249–50.

[49]   NAS, Minute Book of Incorporation of Goldsmiths of Edinburgh 1525–1725, GD 1/482/1, f217.

[50]   *Ibid.*, f225. This was at a 50 per cent discount to par value as a £200 subscription involved a quarter or £50 being paid to the Company, and £300 Scots was worth £25.

[51]   *State-Papers and Letters addressed to William Carstares*, ed. J. McCormick (Edinburgh, 1774), 270.

may have tempered his enthusiasm. Sir James Stewart had been a major opposition figure in the 1680s, spending time in exile in the Netherlands. He was appointed Lord Advocate in 1692 and helped to draft the Company's act of parliament.[52] John Clerk of Penicuik commented in 1702: 'I am no ane highflown East-India goose' but this was long after the subscription process and probably refers to his political position as a supporter of the Court rather than his reluctance to invest.[53] On the grand tour in the late 1690s, he was unable to subscribe because of his large debts, but he was an enthusiastic supporter of the Company and as we have seen, was moved to compose a cantata in its honour while in the Netherlands.

The effort to raise capital in a cold climate was a great success. The sum of £400,000 represented a vast financial commitment by the Scots and was at least four times the annual revenue of the government.[54] Investors were spread across the country and came from a variety of social groups and professions. The presence of many lairds and institutions was very unusual for the period. If it was not exactly 'popular capitalism', it did represent a very significant development in the history of capitalism.

---

[52] Ibid., 270, 331.

[53] Smout, Scottish Trade, 151.

[54] On the eve of union in 1706/7 annual public revenue was optimistically estimated to be £110,000. J. Goodare, State and Society in Early Modern Scotland (Oxford, 1999), 321.

CHAPTER SIX

Directors

They were fundamentally, at least, to understand arithmetic and accounts, with an inclination and genius for the knowledge and study of matters relating to trade and improvements, and unwearied in their application.

WILLIAM PATERSON[1]

THOSE WHO RAN THE Company of Scotland have also, like the share-holders, received little attention from historians. There are a number of reasons for the historical invisibility of the directors. Firstly William Paterson's dominant position in the Company in 1696 and his involvement in the dramatic events on the high seas and at Darien has overshadowed the role of the rest of the court. Secondly the directors did not belong to the powerful noble families that dominated Scottish society and politics at the time, and are thus less prominent in historical sources surviving from the period. And finally, their ambition to establish a Scottish empire failed and as a result none of them had any appetite for writing personal accounts of their experiences which might have ensured their historical fame.[2] Those who ran the show, the men who made the fateful decisions that resulted in a Scottish attempt to establish a colony at the isthmus of Central America, need to be restored to the centre of the Company of Scotland's history.

The act of parliament of 1695 outlined a constitutional framework and privileges but further details of the corporate structure, as it developed in Scotland, were not worked out until the following year. On 3 April 1696 a 'general meeting' of the subscribers elected a committee of 20 individuals to join the promoters listed in the act to formulate a constitution and rules for the Company.[3] We know more about the result of this election than about other elections to the court of directors, for a document in the Yester Papers provides the number of votes cast for each member of the committee, indicating their level

---

[1]   Bannister, *William Paterson*, 251.

[2]   They did, of course, produce collective pieces of propaganda.

[3]   RBS, D/1/1, 6-7.

of support among the subscribers. The man who received most votes was Sir Francis Scott of Thirlestane (2,272), followed by Lord Ruthven (1,900) and William Hay of Drummelzier (1,789). Those with the lowest number were Viscount Tarbat (841), the Earl of Panmure (930) and Sir John Shaw of Greenock (965).[4]

On 7 April, William Paterson presented proposals to the committee and promoters, and after extensive debate over individual articles a constitution was agreed by the middle of the month. The Company was to be managed by a court of directors and council general.[5] The court was responsible for executive decisions and might be compared to a present day board of directors. Each holder of £100 of stock was entitled to one vote in elections to the court, which was initially to number fifty.[6] A different president was appointed at each meeting ensuring no official hierarchy. This was unusual as most joint-stock companies possessed a designated leadership; for example the Bank of Scotland was headed by a governor and deputy-governor. The council general was a larger body, composed of the directors and other representatives of the subscribers; one for each £10,000 of stock. It was called to discuss and make decisions on issues of major importance such as raising capital, drafting petitions or addresses and the payment of dividends.[7] From 1696 to 1707 the court of directors met 578 times and the council general 84 times, indicating the huge amount of time and effort expended by the directors in running the Company.

The position of director was not open to all shareholders, for at

---

4   NLS, MS 14493, f112. The entire list in descending number of votes: Scott of Thirlestane (2,272), Lord Ruthven (1,900), Hay of Drummelzier (1,789), Lord Yester (1,672), Pringle of Torwoodlee (1,614), Mr Hugh Dalrymple (1,591), Lieutenant Colonel John Erskine (1,469), Lord Basil Hamilton (1,468), Mr William Dunlop (1,439), Robert Watson (1,410), Haldane of Gleneagles (1,366), Laird of Sornbeg (1,208), Baillie of Jerviswood (1,232), Sir Archibald Muir (1,043), Drummond of Newton (1,022), Fletcher of Saltoun (969), Shaw of Greenock (965), Earl of Panmure (930), Viscount Tarbat (841).

5   RBS, D/1/1, 9, 15, D/3, 1. In London in late 1695 there had only been a court of directors.

6   The very large size of the court may have been influenced by the VOC, which originally had 60 ordinary directors (62 by 1696) and a number of extraordinary ones (9 in 1696), J.R. Bruijn, F.S. Gaastra and I. Schöffer, *Dutch-Asiatic Shipping in the 17th and 18th Centuries* (The Hague, 1987), i, 13.

7   The directors were not allowed to take part in elections to the council.

least £1,000 of stock had to be owned. Thus 119 from a total of 1,320 subscribers were eligible to become directors.[8] The Lords of Session, the judges in Scotland's highest civil court, provided two boxes to allow a secret ballot at the 'High-Town Council House' for the first election and, on 12 May 1696, 25 directors were approved by a general meeting.[9] The election of the first court was a vitally important moment in Company history for under the constitution the court itself removed three directors each March, who were replaced by three nominated by the council general. Factions within the court could easily retain their positions and minorities or rogue directors could be removed.

The first court of directors included two nobles, eight merchants and fifteen lairds (see Appendix 2).[10] This was a highly unusual social composition for a joint-stock company of the time. The presence of merchants and a couple of nobles was to be expected but the very significant number of lairds was surprising and reflected the nature of the shareholders. As we have seen, the lairds were the largest social group among the subscribers, with 34.4 per cent of the shares, whereas merchants were dominant in the English joint-stock companies such as the EIC, Bank of England and Royal African Company.[11]

The two noble directors were not from the first rank of the nobility. Indeed the 39 year old John Hamilton, second Lord Belhaven, was not born a nobleman. In his early years he was known as John Hamilton of Biel, only inheriting his title in 1679 through his wife Margaret, the granddaughter of the first Lord Belhaven. The second Lord Belhaven was known for his temper and was famously described as a 'rough, fat, black, noisy Man, more like a Butcher than a Lord.'[12] He was a supporter of the Revolution and an active parliamentarian down to 1707. David, Lord Ruthven was a low ranking noble with a

---

8   1,267 individuals and 53 institutions.

9   RBS, D/I/I, 28–30. It should be noted that at this point the subscription books were still open and only those who had already subscribed were able to vote.

10 A broad definition of laird is employed here to include lawyers and merchants who made money and invested in land, and the younger sons of the nobility. Eight of these men were promoters named in the act of parliament of 1695. *APS*, ix, 377–81.

11 Smout, *Scottish Trade*, 150, K.G. Davies, *The Royal African Company* (London, 1957), 163.

12 *Memoirs of the Secret Services of John Macky* (London, 1733), 236.

penchant for business. A less colourful figure than Belhaven, he was a Presbyterian in politics, supporter of the Revolution and also a director of the Bank of Scotland.[13]

Seven of the lairds were close neighbours, giving the court a distinctive geographical flavour. Baillie of Jerviswood, Home of Blackadder, Hay of Drummelzier, Scott of Ancrum, Scott of Thirlestane, Pringle of Torwoodlee, and Swinton of that Ilk all owned estates in the Borders. Drummelzier was the half-brother of the first Marquis of Tweeddale, although 23 years his junior, and described as a 'Topping and leading man of the Company'.[14] Baillie of Jerviswood was the son of Robert Baillie, who had been hung, drawn and quartered in the Grassmarket of Edinburgh in 1684 on charges of high treason arising from the Rye House Plot. The 32 year old was the grandson of extreme Covenanter Sir Archibald Johnston of Wariston, the nephew of Secretary of State James Johnston, and in 1693 had been appointed receiver-general in Scotland. Pringle of Torwoodlee and Swinton of that Ilk were members of families who had been in exile in the 1680s, being staunch Presbyterians and supporters of William; Home of Blackadder was also a supporter of the Revolution and described as 'light in the forehead, full of notion, always talking and most uneasy to be in business with'.[15] Scott of Thirlestane and Scott of Ancrum, who had qualified as an advocate in 1676, were more moderate political figures who aligned themselves with the Tweeddale family.

The other lairds included the professional soldier Lieutenant Colonel John Erskine, the son of Lord Cardross, and John Haldane of Gleneagles, who owned lands in Perthshire. Hugh Dalrymple, the third son of the famous jurist Viscount Stair, was a gifted advocate who had built up a landed estate around North Berwick and was later to become President of the Court of Session in 1698. He was described as 'one of the compleatest lawyers in Scotland; a very eloquent Orator, smooth and slow in Expression, with a clear Understanding, but grave in his manner'.[16] Adam Cockburn of Ormiston, another supporter of the Presbyterian opposition to the Stuarts, was rewarded after the Revolution with membership of the privy council and was

---

[13]   BS, Minutes of Court of Directors, 1/5/3, 4.

[14]   Herries, *Defence*, 23.

[15]   Quoted in Riley, *King William*, 129.

[16]   *Memoirs of the Secret Services*, 211.

appointed Lord Justice Clerk in 1692. According to one commentator he was 'a Bigot to a Fault, and hardly in common Charity with any Man out of the Verge of Prebytery; but otherwise a very fine Gentleman in his Person and manners'.[17] Drummond of Newton and Muir of Thornton were merchants who had prospered and moved into the property market, and were now known by their territorial designations. Muir was elected Lord Provost of Edinburgh in 1691 and again in 1696; Drummond of Newton was 'reputed a man of substance'.[18] Only two lairds hailed from the west of the country: Sir John Maxwell of Pollock, another staunch Presbyterian who became a privy councillor after the Revolution and a Lord of Treasury in 1696, and Mr Francis Montgomery of Giffen, the second son of Hugh Earl of Eglinton.

The eight merchants on the court were divided into equal Edinburgh and Glasgow groupings. The Glasgow merchants William Arbuckle, William Wooddrop and Hugh Montgomery were active in the colonial trade to America and the Caribbean. Wooddrop had been a merchant in the Caribbean island of Nevis in the 1670s and he and Montgomery were partners in the Western Sugar Works of Glasgow.[19] The other Glasgow director, John Corse, was an investor in the Carolina Company. We have already met the Edinburgh merchants Robert Blackwood and James Balfour, who were instrumental in the foundation of the Company. Blackwood was also an investor in the South Carolina Company and the cloth manufactory at Haddington. He was described by Herries as a 'little busy-body'.[20] James MacLurg was a merchant and bill-broker whose niece ran the popular Edinburgh coffee-house of MacLurgs.[21] George Clark was also an investor in the Carolina scheme and the cloth manufactory.

Further important additions were made to the court by the directors themselves. On the afternoon of 12 May William Paterson was elected and two days later his cohorts James Smyth and Daniel Lodge

[17] *Ibid.*, 224–5.
[18] *The Lord Provosts of Edinburgh 1296 to 1932* (Edinburgh, 1932), 55–6, NAS, GD 158/966, 49.
[19] D. Dobson, *Scottish Emigration to Colonial America, 1607–1785* (Athens, 1994), 39, 77, NAS, Earls of Eglinton, GD 3/4/449.
[20] Herries, *Defence*, 46, Fryer, 'Carolina Company,' 124, NAS, GD 112/23/76/1.
[21] Smout, *Scottish Trade*, 88, 104.

were added to the court.[22] These 'Patersonians' aligned themselves with the merchants.[23] On 19 May Mr James Campbell, another London merchant, was elected as director of Company affairs outside Scotland and on 20 August Sir John Shaw of Greenock and the Edinburgh merchant Robert Watson were added.[24] The court now numbered 30 individuals; 20 short of the original target of 50 but still a considerable size.

Unfortunately only portraits of Lord Belhaven, Hugh Dalrymple, Baillie of Jerviswood and Adam Cockburn of Ormiston survive, and we have no pictures of the rest of the directors.[25] Perhaps paintings of the other lairds survive somewhere, but few merchants sat for portraits at this time in Scotland. The only representation we have of William Paterson is a crude black and white drawing.[26] From the portraits a few dominant characteristics emerge: the long periwig encasing a sober face; the white kerchief; the velvet jacket. As we shall see, the periwig was to have a central place in the history of the Company.

Some of the directors were more active in the management of the Company than others. Most of the key decisions taken by the court regarding the allocation of capital and the site of the colony were made in 1696 and 1697. In 1696 the court met 56 times. Those who attended more than two in three meetings were Sir Francis Scott of Thirlestane (55), James MacLurg (52), Daniel Lodge (51), John Drummond of Newton (49), William Paterson (48), Sir Archibald Muir of Thornton (46), Sir John Home of Blackadder (43), William Wooddrop (39), James Balfour (38), William Arbuckle (37) and

---

[22] It is unclear whether there was provision under the constitution for the court to do so. Paterson and his cohorts were not subscribers in Scotland and, lacking a dedicated support base, may have found it difficult to garner enough votes from shareholders. Direct election by the court was a way round this.

[23] NAS, GD 406/1/9078. Although at a later date, after his return from Darien, Paterson became a creature of the Queensberry interest.

[24] RBS, D/1/1, 48, 113.

[25] There are portraits of the Edinburgh merchant Hugh Cunningham, who was elected a director in March 1697, and the second Marquis of Tweeddale and fourth Earl of Panmure, elected in March 1698. Official position in government may have made commissioning a portrait more common. Belhaven was a privy councillor, Hugh Dalrymple later President of the Court of Session, Jerviswood Receiver-General and Ormiston Lord Justice Clerk.

[26] Forrester, Man who saw the Future, xv.

George Clark (37). In 1697 there were 89 meetings and only James MacLurg (71) and Sir Francis Scott (61) attended more than two out of three times (see Appendix 3).

During the most important years of the Company's history, from 1696 to 1701, there were 453 courts. Sir Francis Scott of Thirlestane, who attended 390, or 86 per cent, was the most active director by a large margin. Throughout the Company's history Sir Francis attended more courts than anyone else and his role might be compared with a modern chief executive. If the Company had established a Scottish empire in Central America his portrait would now adorn the walls of the Scottish National Portrait Gallery, but instead he is a forgotten figure and only the bare details of his life outside his work as a director are known. He was born in Dalkeith in 1645, the eldest son of Borders laird Patrick Scott of Thirlestane, and married Henrietta, daughter of William Ker, third Earl of Lothian. Only two of their ten children survived to adulthood.[27] If the family papers of the Scotts of Thirlestane had survived we might have a more detailed picture of this important man. What is clear from the evidence in the records of the Company is that he was a very hard working director over many years.

Other directors who were actively involved in the management from 1696 to 1701 were John Drummond of Newton, James MacLurg, Lieutenant Colonel John Erskine, the advocate Mr David Drummond, the Edinburgh merchant Hugh Cunningham, James Balfour, and John Haldane of Gleneagles.[28] With Scott of Thirlestane, these were the men who ran the Company of Scotland and allocated the capital. They are not well known names in Scottish history. William Paterson was active in 1696, but thereafter played a minor role in the management, attending only 35 meetings in the following years.[29]

A number of directors had poor attendance records and as a result were not closely involved in day-to-day management of Company affairs. In 1696 Cockburn of Ormiston, Montgomery of Giffen,

---

[27] For a brief account of his life see *Scots Peerage*, vi, 431.

[28] John Drummond of Newton (276, or 60.9 per cent), James MacLurg (266, or 58.7 per cent), Lieutenant Colonel John Erskine (252, or 55.6 per cent), Mr David Drummond (241, or 53.2 per cent), Hugh Cunningham (225, or 49.7 per cent), James Balfour (205, or 45.3 per cent) and John Haldane of Gleneagles (204, or 45.0 per cent). Mr David Drummond was elected as a director in March 1698.

[29] He was out of the country between July 1698 and December 1699 on the first voyage to the isthmus.

Dalrymple, Baillie of Jerviswood, Pringle of Torwoodlee, and Mr
Robert Blackwood attended less than 50 per cent of courts. Some of
these men held positions in the government and were busy with other
affairs. Over the longer period from 1696 to 1701, Lord Belhaven, Lord
Ruthven, Cockburn of Ormiston, Montgomery of Giffen, Hugh
Dalrymple, Maxwell of Pollock, Muir of Thornton, and Baillie of
Jerviswood were the least active directors. Lord Belhaven attended
twenty-nine out of fifty-six courts in 1696, but then lost interest, turning
up for only nine courts (2.3 per cent) in the five years from 1697 to 1701.

Director attendance proved to be a problem. In August 1696
Paterson commented that there were difficulties securing quorums,
and the Earl of Panmure later believed that poor attendance was the
'greatest mismanagement' suffered by the Company.[30] The position of
director of a powerful joint-stock company was a new role for most.
Paterson provided a description of the characteristics required of the
ideal director: 'They were fundamentally, at least, to understand arithmetic and accounts, with an inclination and genius for the knowledge
and study of matters relating to trade and improvements, and unwearied
in their application'.[31] It is unclear how many of them lived up to this.
The merchants were experienced men of business but some of the
lairds were not well versed in the world of trade and finance. The size
of the court was another obstacle to management efficiency. Paterson
admitted this after his return from Darien, recommending that twenty
was a more reasonable number: 'that the company's affairs may as little
as possible be liable to the raw and giddy influence of nominal and
honorary directors, whose time, temper, or business, may not, or cannot,
allow of their due and orderly attendance'.[32]

The English joint-stock companies had a politico-religious character.
Many investors were dissenters or from families with strong links to
nonconformity. For example, it has been estimated that 18 per cent of
the capital and 43 per cent of the directors of the Bank of England came
from the dissenting interest.[33] The task of determining the political and
religious views of the subscribers of the Company of Scotland is very

[30]   *The Annandale Book*, ed. Sir W. Fraser (Edinburgh, 1894), 124, NAS, GD
       406/1/4378.
[31]   Bannister, *William Paterson*, 251.
[32]   *Writings of William Paterson*, i, 81.
[33]   G.S. de Krey, *A Fractured Society: The Politics of London in the First Age
       of Party 1688–1715* (Oxford, 1985), 108–9.

difficult because little is known about many of the small shareholders, but the political complexion of directors can be established. In Scotland in the 1690s there was a complex array of political alignments. At one level the political nation was divided between those who held office or pensions from the government and those who did not. By 1698 this split had developed into a Court/Country party division. Other political groupings were dictated by the Revolution of 1688–9. Those who had supported the Revolution were given the contemporary name 'Revolutioner'.[34] Some of them had been in exile under James VII because of their opposition to his regime and others were actively supportive of William during the Revolution.[35] Jacobites opposed the Revolution and wanted the restoration of a Stuart king. Episcopalians represented the interest of Episcopalian clergymen who had lost their livings in the expulsions following the Revolution. Politics was complex, fluid and conspiratorial, with individuals often shifting their allegiance.

A number of members of the first court of directors can be identified as men who were strongly supportive of the Revolution: Lord Belhaven, Lord Ruthven, Cockburn of Ormiston, Montgomery of Giffen, Hugh Dalrymple, Lieutenant Colonel Erskine, Home of Blackadder, Scott of Thirlestane, Maxwell of Pollock, Swinton of that Ilk, Baillie of Jerviswood, Pringle of Torwoodlee and Scott of Ancrum.[36] The eight merchants of the court were also natural supporters of the Revolution, with strong Presbyterian connections. Before 1688 some were linked with exiles in the Netherlands. For example, James MacLurg, who was one of the most active directors in the Company's management, was a key man of business for a number of the exiled families, including Melville and his son Leven, the Dalrymples, and Gilbert Burnet.[37] James Balfour was associated with the Presbyterian opposition in 1684 and John Corse, George Clerk and Robert Blackwood were investors in the South Carolina Company, which was heavily dominated by Presbyterians from the west of Scotland.[38] Hugh

---

[34] Patrick, 'People and Parliament,' 62, footnote 175.

[35] Riley, *King William*, 141.

[36] G. Gardner, *The Scottish Exile Community in the Netherlands, 1660–1690: 'Shaken together in the bag of affliction'* (East Linton, 2004), Appendix 2, *Journal of the Hon. John Erskine of Carnock 1683–87* (SHS, 1893), 103, 188, 189, 192, Patrick, 'People and Parliament,' 176, H. & K. Kelsall, *Scottish Lifestyle 300 Years Ago* (Aberdeen, 1993), 88.

[37] Gardner, *Scottish Exile Community*, 69–70.

[38] *Journal of the Hon. John Erskine*, 76, Fryer, 'Carolina Company,' 132.

Montgomery was a staunch Presbyterian who was elected on several occasions as a ruling elder to the General Assembly of the Church of Scotland.[39]

There were some Jacobite shareholders in the Company, such as Lockhart of Carnwath, the Earl of Strathmore, Livingston of Kilsyth, and the Earl Marischal. On the council general James, Duke of Queensberry and Viscount Tarbat were associated with the Episcopalian interest, and James, Earl of Panmure and James, Lord Drummond were Jacobites. There is no evidence, however, of a Jacobite presence on the first court of 25 directors elected in May 1696. Haldane of Gleneagles may not have been a dedicated follower of William in the early 1690s, but he later emerged as a staunch supporter of Union and the house of Hanover. John Drummond of Newton may have been a Jacobite but the only evidence is his suggestive surname.

The political complexion of the first court of directors was therefore staunchly Revolutionary or Williamite and reflected the significant number of Presbyterian lairds and merchants who were shareholders in the Company, many of whom were members of families who had opposed the policies of Charles II and James VII and their investment was perhaps a statement of financial confidence following the Revolution, when fines and forfeitures imposed upon them by the Stuart Kings were rescinded.[40] A number had spent years of exile in the Netherlands, the centre of global capitalism in the late 17th century, and this may have been another powerful influence.[41]

There were important Company figures who were not directors. Roderick MacKenzie was employed as secretary in London in August 1695 and was to remain at the heart of the administration until 1707. On 22 May 1696 he was unanimously chosen as secretary in Scotland, on a salary of £150, and proved an indefatigable servant of the Company as an efficient and effective administrator.[42] He was described

---

[39]   *The House of Commons 1690–1715*, (eds.) E. Cruikshanks, S. Handley and D.W. Hayton (Cambridge, 2002), iv, 902–3.

[40]   *APS*, ix, 158, 164–70.

[41]   Lieutenant Colonel Erskine, Baillie of Jerviswood, Swinton of that Ilk and Pringle of Torwoodlee were exiles. For the primacy of the Netherlands in terms of economic growth and the sophistication of its capital markets see J. de Vries and Ad van der Woude, *The First Modern Economy: Success, Failure and Perseverance of the Dutch Economy, 1500–1815* (Cambridge, 1997).

[42]   RBS, D/1/1, 62, MacKenzie, *Full and Exact Account*, 39.

in one pamphlet as the Company's 'little Secretary and Oracle' and there is much evidence of his role as an energetic propagandist.[43] In 1695 he wrote a pamphlet to promote the Company's attempt to raise capital in London, oversaw the printing of five or six hundred copies of a petition to parliament for distribution to MPs in 1698, and was behind the publication of a collection of documents describing Company history from the directors' point of view.[44] MacKenzie's central role was highlighted by Paterson, who said he was 'better acquainted with the Threed and Train of their Affairs and proceedings, than any Body else'.[45]

The Company also employed an 'establishment' of accountants, cashiers, clerks, and other officers. On 20 May, James Dunlop became chief accountant and Gavin Plummer chief cashier, both on salaries of £120, and a series of other appointments followed (see Appendix 8). All those employed kept regular office hours from 8am to 12pm and 2pm to 6pm. The vast array of surviving accounts, journals, letters, minute books and ledgers, now in the National Library of Scotland and Royal Bank of Scotland Archive, is testament to their labour. The accountants were well versed in the techniques of double entry book-keeping and although at times the accounts slipped behind, the financial records of the Company, at least in the early years, were meticulously recorded.

On 21 May, three Company committees were established based on a blue-print provided by Paterson. The committee of improvements was responsible for securing supplies from domestic merchants and exploring business opportunities in Scotland; the committee of foreign

---

[43] Walter Herries, *An Enquiry into the Caledonian Project, with a Defence of England's Procedure (in point of Equity) in Relation thereunto. In a Friendly Letter from London, to a Member of the Scots African and Indian Company in Edinburgh, to guard against Passion* (London, 1701), 20.

[44] MacKenzie, *Full and Exact Account*, 39, RBS, D/3, 135–6, *A Full and Exact Collection of All the Considerable Addresses, Memorials, Petitions, Answers, Proclamations, Declarations, Letters and other Publick Papers, Relating to the Company of Scotland Trading to Africa and the Indies, since the passing of the Act of Parliament, by which the said Company was established in June 1695, till November 1700* (1700). In January 1700 he was overseeing the distribution of pamphlets and papers to members of the opposition, NAS, GD 406/1/4569. At a later date, in March 1702, he operated as an administrator of the Country Party and may have done so since 1698. NAS, GD 406/1/4982, 406/1/5002.

[45] *Case of Mr William Paterson*, 13.

trade oversaw shipbuilding and overseas business; and the committee of treasury managed the collection and safe keeping of the Company's cash.[46] All the directors were employed in one committee, except Paterson who, on 11 June, was the only director confirmed as a member of each, emphasising his exalted position in 1696.[47]

The Company also required a suitable residence. Robert Blackwood had provided a convenient room for a meeting of the promoters in February 1696 and a general meeting of subscribers was held in March at the 'Laigh Toun-Council-house of Edinburgh'.[48] On 13 May Paterson, Drummond of Newton, and MacLurg were empowered to look for a permanent residence.[49] But it was not until late July that two houses opposite the Tron Kirk on the High Street, in the 'great stone building called Miln's Square', were purchased for £396 and £451.[50] This investment of £847 in Edinburgh property was to prove the best capital allocation made by the directors. The rooms were filled with account books and ledgers, a copy of the printed acts of parliament since James I was ordered, and watchmaker Andrew Brown received £12 for making a standing clock for the directors' room.[51]

The Company of Scotland was a joint-stock established to raise a capital fund. As a financial entity, its life-blood was cash. A large chest and a series of smaller ones were procured to secure the Company's money and every night the chief cashier, or his assistant, balanced the cash before leaving the office. The elaborate lock mechanism on the

---

[46]   RBS, D/I/I, 56–7.

[47]   *Ibid.*, 74. During the Company's history a series of other committees were formed, including an executive committee of nine, a committee in constant waiting, a secret committee, and a committee for equipping ships.

[48]   RBS, D/I/I, 1, 3.

[49]   *Ibid.*, 38.

[50]   *Ibid.*, 94–5, 481. John Eidington sold one house and Sir Alexander MacKenzie of Broomhill and the widow of George MacKenzie of Pitcarro sold the other.

[51]   *Ibid.*, 133–4, 256. The other property asset of the Company was a Leith warehouse which was later constructed or purchased. On 30 July 1697 various members of the establishment were ordered to meet the directors there to inspect it. Sir Walter Scott refers to a tenement near Bristo Port which served as an office, but I have found no references to this property in the records of the Company. It may have been a house named after the Company rather than an asset belonging to it. Sir Walter Scott, *The Tales of a Grandfather* (London, 1933), 729.

main chest symbolised the security and financial probity expected of such a company.[52] Unfortunately for the directors, the shareholders, and the nation, the cash chest of the Company of Scotland was full for only a short time, and replenishing it proved very difficult.

---

[52] The main one is now on display in the Museum of Scotland in Edinburgh. RBS, D/1/1, 150–1.

The coat of arms of the Company of Scotland illuminated by herald painter
George Porteous

Reproduced by kind permission of The Royal Bank of Scotland Group © 2007

One of the Company of Scotland's cash chests; each night the chief cashier, or his assistant, balanced the cash before leaving the office.

The elaborate lock mechanism on the main chest symbolised financial
probity and security.

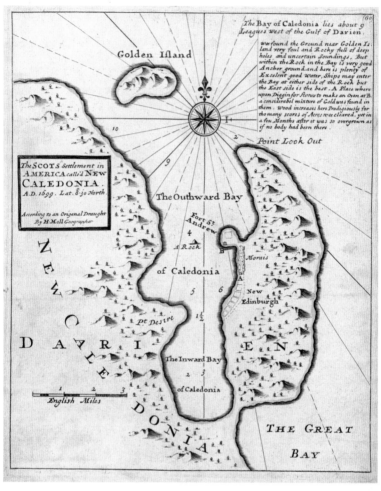

A Map of the West Indies by Moll, dedicated to William Paterson.

Sir

44

I send you here inclosed ye utmost proposalls I am able
to make you in order to my releate and that upon my
most solemn oath, if you can discouer any thing else
from my papers which were sealed in presence of Mr
Ja: Campbell and deliuerd to Mr Alexr Henderson when
you come to looke 'em ouer, I shall bee most willing
to allow itt, and if you suspect I haue more papers
im my other trunck itt shall bee opened in your presence
and exposed to your mercy, Itt is true I am unfortunate
in being the occasion of so great a disappointement to the
company, but I declare I neuer intended to cheate
them, if you daign to recouer what I owe, your
acaptinge of those termes now made and my speedy
releace is your interest, for if my imprisonement is
once known, att London itt will certainly incapacitate
me to perform this offers, but if you study reuenge
I shall uery soon fall a sacrifice to itt, I find my
self already indisposed under the sence of my present
misery and a little time longer shall putt an end
to my miserable life, and if youu do upon this termes
releace me and itt should afterward be disapproued
of by those concern'd with you or the company I
do solemnly promise you to deliuer my self up a
your prisoner when you shall require untill they
are satisfied your speedy resolution one way or
other will infinitely oblidge
                    Sir Your most humble
                    Sir Your unfortunate Servt.
                    James Smyth

The desperate letter by James Smyth from prison in Amsterdam in May 1697.

Sir John Clerk of Penicuik who composed *Leo Scotiae Irritatus*
(Artist unknown; after William Aikman).
Scottish National Portrait Gallery

Sir Mungo Murray who sailed on the second expedition and died at Darien.
(Artist: John Michael Wright)
Scottish National Portrait Gallery

CHAPTER SEVEN

Mania

He wont be looked upon as a true Scotchman that is against it.
LORD BASIL HAMILTON[1]

*No reasonable means or opportunity [be] omitted to make this
the most diffusive and National joynt-stock in the world.*
MINUTE BOOK OF THE COURT OF DIRECTORS[2]

THE QUESTION OF WHY SO many Scots invested in the Company of
Scotland in 1696 has troubled historians of the Darien debacle. In his
Tales of a Grandfather Sir Walter Scott believed it highlighted the
propensity of Scots to engage in manic behaviour when acting together:

> Human character, whether national or individual, presents
> often to our calm consideration the strangest inconsistencies;
> but there are few more striking than that which the Scots
> exhibit in their private conduct, contrasted with their views
> when united together for any general or national purpose. In
> his own personal affairs the Scotsman is remarked as cautious,
> frugal, and prudent, in an extreme degree, not generally aim-
> ing at enjoyment or relaxation till he has realised the means of
> indulgence, and studiously avoiding those temptations of
> pleasure to which men of other countries most readily give way.
> But when a number of the natives of Scotland associate for any
> speculative project, it would seem that their natural caution
> becomes thawed and dissolved by the union of their joint hopes,
> and that their imaginations are liable in a peculiar degree to be
> heated and influenced by any splendid prospect held out to
> them ... There is no greater instance of this tendency to dar-
> ing speculation, which rests at the bottom of the coldness and
> caution of the Scottish character, than the disastrous history of
> the Darien colony.[3]

---

[1] NAS, GD 406/1/7473.

[2] RBS, D/1/1, 92.

[3] Scott, *Tales of a Grandfather*, 725–6.

Sir John Dalrymple, writing in the 18th century, saw a religious intensity associated with investment in the Company: 'The frenzy of the
Scots nation to sign the Solemn League and Covenant, never exceed-
ed the rapidity with which they ran to subscribe to the Darien
Company'.[4] Thomas Babington Macaulay wrote in similar vein: 'of all
the ten thousand bubbles of which history has preserved the memory,
none was ever more skilfully puffed into existence; none ever soared
higher, or glittered more brilliantly; and none ever burst with a more
lamentable explosion'.[5] For one commentator the whole venture was
an 'amazing yet a natural product of that curious blend of cold, thrifty
common-sense and poetic idealism found in Scotsmen'.[6] Yet most
recent historians have not considered this aspect of the Company's
history in any detail.[7]

    There are a number of pieces of evidence, however, that confirm
the views of Scott and Macaulay. Investment in the Company of Scotland
was an early example of a financial mania. Firstly the Company had
a very significant number of shareholders: 1,320 subscribers comprising
1,267 individuals and 53 institutions.[8] This was a very large number
for the late 17th century as there were 1,267 shareholders in the Bank
of England, 1,188 in the EIC and about 800 in the VOC.[9] In absolute
terms the Company had more shareholders than contemporary
English and Dutch joint-stock companies. And subscriptions underes-
timate the actual number of investors as some investments were
pooled. For example, the shareholding of Anne, Duchess of Hamilton
was held jointly with her sons the Earl of Ruglen and the Earl of

4   Sir John Dalrymple, *Memoirs of Great Britain and Ireland from the Battle
     of La Hogue till the capture of the French and Spanish Fleets at Vigo*, 2
     vols (Edinburgh, 1788), ii, 96.

5   T.B. Macaulay, *The History of England from the accession of James the
     Second*, 8 vols (London, 1849–61), v, 204.

6   F.R. Hart, *The Disaster of Darien: The Story of the Scots Settlement and
     the Causes of its Failure 1699–1701* (London, 1930), 38.

7   Armitage has questioned whether the Company was a Scottish equivalent
     of the South See Bubble, D. Armitage, 'Making the Empire British:
     Scotland in the Atlantic World 1542–1717,' *Past and Present*, 155,
     (1997), 59.

8   *Darien Papers*, 371–417.

9   Scott, *Constitution and Finance*, iii, 477, BL, India Office Records, List of
     Adventurers, H/2, 97–144.

Selkirk.[10] Lord Basil Hamilton's subscription was shared with his brother the Duke of Hamilton, and the £1,000 subscribed by Maxwell of Pollock was a pooled investment with the lairds David Boyle of Kelburn and William Cunningham of Craigends.[11] We have no way of knowing exactly how many subscriptions represented collective investments by groups of nobles, lairds, merchants or lawyers, but the number of individuals with a financial stake in the Company was clearly considerably higher than is suggested by the signatures in the subscription books.

There were also institutional investments which represented large numbers of shareholders. The £700 invested by the burgh of Brechin included £100 from the common good, £50 from the guildry, £455 from 28 men and £95 from 13 women.[12] The £100 subscription by the Masons of Glasgow composed nine individual investments ranging from £5 to £25, and £10 from the institution.[13] Although pledges by most other institutions probably indicated adecision of the ruling elite, these investments did, in theory, reflect a commitment by the broader community.

A conservative estimate of the total number of shareholders, assuming 10 per cent of individual holdings were pooled and each institution represented ten shareholders, might be about 2,000; a very significant number for the late 17th century.[14] A more reasonable figure, using less conservative assumptions, for example 30 per cent pooling and 20 shareholders per institution, increases this to over 3,000. Prebble believed there were tens of thousands of investors, either influenced by the comments of Walter Herries, 'They came in Shoals from all Corners of the Kingdom', or based on the assumption that institutional investments gave every member of a community or corporation a financial stake in the Company. Although subscription was

---

[10] John Hamilton was created Earl of Ruglen in April 1697.

[11] NAS, GD 406/1/6440, NRA, Stirling-Maxwell of Pollock, 2312, T–PM 113/691. Boyle was a staunch supporter of the Revolution and an active member of the Court Party who was created Lord Boyle of Kelburn in 1699 and Earl of Glasgow in 1703.

[12] D.D. Black, *The History of Brechin* (Brechin, 1839), NRA, 2312, T–PM 113/691.

[13] Glasgow City Archive, Masons of Glasgow Minute Book 1681–1772, T–THI2 1/2.

[14] Prebble, *Darien*, 60, Herries, *Defence*, 8.

beyond the means of the poor there was certainly a contemporary view that the number involved was extremely large. The directors themselves drew attention to their democratic mandate in a pamphlet, referring to 'all Persons and Corporations directly or indirectly concerned in the African-Company participants thereof: Who (including such Incorporations) can by modest Computation be reckoned no less than 200000 persons.'[15] The view that 200,000 people, one fifth of the population, were directly or indirectly concerned, whether exaggeration or not, does reveal the exceptional level of psychological investment by Scots in a joint-stock Company, to a degree that was unprecedented in history. It is most likely that those with a direct financial stake numbered a few thousand, but this, it should be stressed, was a truly startling figure for a nation that until then was not in the vanguard of developments in financial capitalism.

Another indication of mania was the size of the capital raising relative to the liquid wealth of the kingdom. Exact figures for the Scottish coinage and money supply cannot be obtained because of a lack of monetary statistics and the complex mixture of foreign coins in circulation.[16] Estimates are based on sums found in contemporary pamphlets and extrapolations from the recoinage of 1707, and must be treated as indicative rather than authoritative. These sources provide amounts for the coinage of between £300,000 and £900,000, although the actual amount of money in the country was certainly greater due to an unknown quantity of hoarded coin and bullion.[17] Some shareholders, for example, paid for their subscriptions in bullion rather than coin, indicating that coin alone underestimates the liquid capacity of the nation.[18] Based on these estimates the subscribed capital of £400,000

---

[15] *Reasons For passing into an Act, an Overture in Parliament, for making Salt of a new Fashion* (Edinburgh, 1696). A recent historian has commented that the Company 'reflected the popular support of a democratic movement.' Hidalgo, 'To Get Rich for Our Homeland,' 326.

[16] Scotland was not atypical in this respect as by 1610 money changers in Amsterdam had to keep track of nearly one thousand different gold and silver coins. L. Neal, 'How it all began: the monetary and financial architecture of Europe during the first global capital markets, 1648–1815,' *Financial History Review*, 7, (2000), 120.

[17] *A Proposition for Remeding the Debasement of Coyne in Scotland (n.d.)*,7, *A Letter to a Member of Parliament concerning the Bank of Scotland and the Lowering of Interest of Money* (Edinburgh, 1696), 6 and Anderson, *Historical and Chronological Deduction*, ii, 245.

[18] For payments in bullion see RBS, D/1/1, 159, 165, 255, 301–2, 329–30.

was between 44 per cent and 133 per cent of the coinage, and the actual cash paid, of £153,448, between 17 per cent and 51 per cent. These were truly staggering proportions, even if we take the lower percentages as more likely. What seems clear is that the subscribed capital was a massive proportion of the coinage and the actual cash paid to the Company a very substantial proportion.

The ratio of shareholders to population, tax yield and money supply was significantly higher than for contemporary English joint-stock companies. Scotland had approximately 1/5 of the population of England, 1/36 of the tax yield and 1/40 of the money supply. Using an estimate of 3,000 for the total number of investors, the ratio of shareholders to population was about 13 times that of the EIC, shareholders to tax yield about 91 times and shareholders to money supply one hundred times[19] (see Table 1). The absolute numbers are not particularly important, but they do indicate the very large number of investors relative to the economic capacity of the country.

Table 1:

	Company of Scotland	Bank of England	English East India Company
No. of Shareholders	3000	1267	1188
Relative Population	1	5	5
Tax Ratio	1	36	36
Money Supply Ratio	1	40	40
Shareholders/Population	3000	253	238
Shareholders/Tax Ratio	3000	35	33
Shareholders/Money Supply	3000	32	30

Another piece of evidence was the broad social spread of the shareholders. The subscription process was extended to groups, such as ministers and widows, whose presence on share registers in significant numbers is often a key indicator of a mania or bubble in financial history. As we have seen there was also a very high ratio of lairds relative to merchants.[20]

---

19   Goodare, *State and Society*, 321, John Law, *Money and Trade Considered, with a Proposal for Supplying the Nation with Money* (Edinburgh, 1705), 74.

20   C.P. Kindleberger, *Manias, Panics, and Crashes: A History of Financial Crises* (New York, 2000), 28–9.

A liquidity injection of loose money is another common feature of a financial mania. Despite the problems of the agricultural economy from 1695 there was monetary expansion in Scotland in the first ten months of 1696, provided by the recently founded Bank of Scotland and the Company of Scotland itself. Lending by the Bank totalled £25,846 in four months to the end of July, and the Company lent £20,025 to its own shareholders between July and October.[21] Some of the money provided by the Bank was funding acquisition of shares in the Company and in May the Bank attempted to stop lending for this purpose.[22]

In 1696 poems and songs were composed in celebration of William Paterson and the Company. *The Golden Island or the Darian Song*, by a 'lady of honour', celebrated the spectacular returns shareholders were to expect:

> All Men that has put in some Stock,
> to us where we are gone;
> They may expect our Saviours words
> a Hundred reap for One.[23]

A Poem upon the Undertaking of the Royal Company of Scotland articulated the themes of freedom and the mystery of capital accumulation:

> Freedom draws such, and where there's many found,
> It is most certain, Riches will abound.
> One hundred such, ten thousand do imploy.
> Who find their *Wealth* increase, but know not *Why*,
> And as they Thrive, their numbers multiply,
> The want of money such joynt Stocks supply,
> When diverse gaine by few Mens industry.
>
> Thus as one Man the Nation has combin'd,
> And speedily a mighty Stock is joyn'd:
> A Stock so large, a Stock so very great,
> As must infallibly the Work compleat:
> That the Design is wise, I surely know,
> Tho' what it is, I justly may not show.[24]

---

[21] Saville, *Bank of Scotland*, 27, NLS, Adv MS 83.5.2.

[22] When Bank notes were then presented for conversion to cash, the Bank was placed under severe pressure and forced to suspend lending and raise further capital in the summer of 1696. Saville, *Bank of Scotland*, 34–5.

[23] *Various Pieces*, i, 4.

[24] *Ibid.*, ii, 11, 14–15.

The moral authority of the nation, the Presbyterian Church, or Kirk, of Scotland, also became actively engaged with the venture. Congregations prayed for the good fortune of the Company and ministers attacked its enemies. In February 1699 the General Assembly recommended that all ministers should 'pray for the success and prosperity of the trading Company of this Nation', and after the Company had met with 'severall cross providences' the Commission of the Kirk told ministers 'to be fervent in prayer to God for averting his wrath, and forgiving the sins of the Nation'.[25]

We have already seen that the legality of the Scottish settlement at Darien became a subject for Edinburgh University theses in the late 1690s, that at a graduation ceremony Mr William Scott, professor of philosophy, pronounced an 'Elegant Harangue' on the colony,[26] and that the Company even perforated into the world of refined music when it was celebrated by John Clerk of Penicuik, whose patriotic passions were inflamed by news of Darien while he was on the Continent as part of his grand tour.[27] This 'spill-over' of a financial event into the general culture is another classic sign of a financial mania. Poems about the stock market, for example, appeared in the United States in 1929 during the boom before the Great Crash.[28] Something similar could be said of the Company of Scotland in the period from 1696 to 1700. Everyone in the country knew about the Company, a large proportion of those with access to cash subscribed for shares, and much of the moral energy of the nation was invested in it.

For some there was a clear trigger that initiated the mania. Adam Cockburn of Ormiston, Lord Justice Clerk and a director, commented that 'twas the notice the parliament of England first took of it made the wholl nation throng in to have some share, and I am of opinion the resentments people are acted by are the greatest supplys [that] furnishes life to that affaire'.[29] Lord Basil Hamilton also believed that patriotism or nationalism was responsible for the extensive subscriptions:

[25] *Darien Papers*, 254–5.

[26] Finlayson, 'Edinburgh University and the Darien Scheme,' 97–102.

[27] NAS, GD 18/4538/4/1–2.

[28] R. Sobel, *The Great Bull Market: Wall Street in the 1920s* (New York, 1968), 126, 'By the summer of 1929 the market not only dominated the news. It dominated the culture,' J.K. Galbraith, *The Great Crash 1929* (London, 1975), 99.

[29] Fraser, *Annandale*, ii, xxvii.

> The bussines of our East india act make a great noise with you it makes no less here, where we are all very fond of it, and since its secured by an act of Parliament nothing but a Parliament can take it away, and he wont be looked upon as a true Scotchman that is against it.[30]

The writer of a contemporary pamphlet commented that 'the whole Kingdom of Scotland being more zealous for it, and unanimous in it than they have been in any other thing for 40 or 50 years'.[31] John Holland, an Englishman who had been an employee of the EIC, and became the first governor of the Bank of Scotland, wrote how it had become 'dangerous for a man to express his thoughts freely of this matter'.[32] It was difficult to voice opinions critical of the Company and those who questioned the bullish sentiment of the majority were viewed as unpatriotic. Nationalism or patriotism was therefore a key ingredient in triggering the mania.[33]

The directors themselves were aiming to achieve something unique in financial history. In July 1696 they noted that 'no reasonable means or opportunity [be] omitted to make this the most diffusive and National joynt-stock in the world'.[34] They were hoping to secure the widest social and geographical spread of shareholders in history. We may well ask where the motivation came from to achieve something so ambitious, given that the Scots were not among the first rank of financial powers in the late 17th century. The directors were hoping to jump from financial obscurity to stardom in one blazing performance.

Those who were organising the capital raising, the projectors of the Company led by William Paterson and aided by his London cohorts Daniel Lodge and James Smyth, manipulated the patriotic

---

[30] NAS, GD 406/1/7473.

[31] Herries, *Defence*, 24.

[32] John Holland, *A Short Discourse on the Present Temper of the Nation* (Edinburgh, 1696), quoted in B. McPhail, 'Through a Glass, Darkly: Scots and Indians Converge at Darien,' *Eighteenth-Century Life*, 18, (1994), 131.

[33] The capital raising has recently been described as a 'patriotic crusade.' T.M. Devine, *Scotland's Empire 1600-1815*, (London, 2003) 43.

[34] RBS, Court of Directors, D/1/1, 92. This was repeated in a news-sheet published by the Company at the time, *At Edinburgh, The 9th day of July, 1696* in NLS, Darien Pamphlets, RY.II.A.9, no. 5.

reaction to English opposition to encourage as much subscription as possible. Paterson was clear about his own role in the process: 'by his Reputation and Influence, the said Subscription was soon completed', he wrote about himself.[35] Paterson had already organised successful fund-raisings for the Hampstead Waterworks, Bank of England and Orphans' Fund, and his letters to Sir Robert Chiesly in the summer of 1695 reveal that he understood how a multitude of investors might be led irrationally into a joint-stock. The projectors skilfully wrapped the capital raising in the Saltire.

Sir John Dalrymple tells us that the famous Scottish financier and monetary theorist John Law, the son of an Edinburgh goldsmith who rose spectacularly to become Controller-General of France in 1720, and probably the richest private individual in the world, was influenced by the speculative nature of the capital raising:

> The famous Mr Law, then a youth, afterwards confessed, that the facility with which he saw the passion of speculation communicate itself from all to all, satisfied him of the possibility of producing the same effect from the same cause, but upon a larger scale, when the Duke of Orleans, in the year of the Missisippi, engaged him, against his will, to turn his bank into a bubble.[36]

Financial manias do not occur in a vacuum. This was the era of the financial revolution which witnessed the first bull market in British equities, beginning in London and spreading out to 'higher risk' destinations such as Scotland. There was a further vital ingredient: the Scots were financially confident in 1696. Some had returned from exile in 1688–9 and found their fortunes improved when estates were restored and forfeitures rescinded; others had accumulated capital over the previous generation, much of it no doubt put away for a rainy day. Now it came out to shine in the sun. Even the harvest failure of 1695 could not dent their optimism; after all, it was rare to have two failures in a row. In the course of 1696, however, confidence was transformed into overconfidence and then to 'irrational exuberance'.

The capital raising marked the peak of the British joint-stock bubble of the 1690s. In Scotland a significant number of joint-stock companies

---

[35] *Case of Mr William Paterson*, 2.

[36] Dalrymple, *Memoirs*, ii, 96.

had been established in the boom period from 1693 to 1695, but the vast majority of the capital was promised to one single financial entity: the Company of Scotland. The directors who controlled the capital were wielding vast power and influence over the financial future of the nation. Lord Basil Hamilton commented that the £100,000 raised from the first call was 'as considerable a soum if not greater as any kingdome in the world ever begun such a trade with'.[37]

The Company was thus the creation of economic confidence and the large number of Scots who subscribed such a vast proportion of the nation's liquid assets was testament to this. Investment reflected confidence about the future. It was a signal of a new world order breaking on the shores of Scotland, faith in the future being reflected in financial rather than religious terms, and has been described as a 'major shift in Scottish intellectual life'.[38] In other words the frenzy of Scottish investors in 1696 was a birth-pang of modernity.

Yet the mania did not develop into a full-blown asset bubble like the South Sea or Internet bubbles. Such a large proportion of the money supply was pledged to the Company that little liquidity remained in the financial system and monetary conditions were deteriorating significantly by the second half of 1696, with credit markets collapsing and interest rates rising. As a result there was little cash available for speculation and no inflation of the share price.[39] Very few references to transaction prices have been found in the historical sources until after the demise of the colony, when they were at very significant discounts to par (up to 90 per cent, i.e. the share price was 90 per cent below the amount originally subscribed), and for many years in the early 18th century there was no trading activity in the stock as it was viewed as worthless. Some small quantities did change hands, but this did not reflect the bubble mentality, rather its apotheosis, as when, for example, the Incorporation of Edinburgh Goldsmiths raffled twenty shilling divisions of their shareholding in 1700 in an attempt to get rid of it for some cash.[40] The Scots therefore only experienced the upside of the bubble as a psychological event. There was no opportunity for investors to sell out at miraculous profits, as there was in 1719 and 1720.

---

[37] NAS, GD 406/1/7779.

[38] Armitage, 'Making the Empire British,' 57.

[39] NLS, Adv MS 83.2.2.

[40] NAS, GD 1/482/1, f232–3. Because of a lack of data it is not possible to produce a share chart.

Sir Walter Scott believed the fervour of investment in the Company reflected the lemming-like behaviour of Scots when acting together. But other nations have been prone to over-optimistic phases. History is full of manias and bubbles, with speculation focused on everything from joint-stock companies to tulip bulbs, coffee, gold, bonds, and property; indeed anything that can be bought and sold.[41] The Dutch pushed the price of tulip bulbs to exotic heights in the 1630s and the stock market in Amsterdam experienced periods of speculative excess throughout the 17th century.[42] The Scots were no more or less subject to this than anyone else. Indeed, while the nation was enveloped in a frenzy for investment in the Company of Scotland, another Scottish joint-stock company was sowing the seeds of future greatness. In its office across the High Street, the Bank of Scotland weathered the financial storm of 1696–7, paid its first dividend in 1699, and thereafter its share price began to rise (see Figure 2).[43] The Bank was carefully managed on a lower cost base with much less capital, and was focused on lending money to Scottish nobles, lairds and merchants secured on land. It prospered and is still around today. Paradoxically, the Bank and Company of Scotland shared a number of directors and many Scots were shareholders in both institutions. The Bank's directors made a series of wise decisions and reaped the rewards; the directors of the Company of Scotland a series of very bad ones, with disastrous results for the shareholders and nation.

---

[41]   Kindleberger, *Manias*, 41–3.

[42]   *Extraordinary Popular Delusions and the Madness of Crowds and Confusión de Confusiones*, ed. M.S. Fridson (New York, 1996).

[43]   The graph suggests that monetary conditions were improving in Scotland before 1707 despite the liquidity crisis of 1704–5. As the prime financial institution in the country, the Bank was very sensitive to changes in the monetary environment.

Figure 2

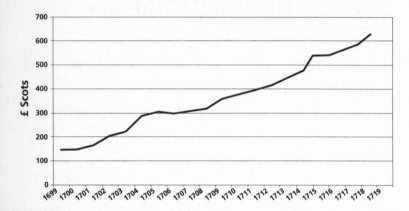

Bank of Scotland Total Return 1699–1719

*Source: Bank of Scotland Archive, Minute Book of the Court of Directors,
1/5/3.*

CHAPTER EIGHT

International Roadshow

*There has nothing fallen out of a long time that makes a
greater noise in the world than this does, and the Eyes of every
body is upon us.*

JOHN HALDANE OF GLENEAGLES[1]

FOLLOWING THE SUCCESS OF the domestic capital raising the directors
decided to persuade foreign investors of the attractive opportunity
offered by the Company of Scotland. Such an appeal is a common feature of the modern financial world as companies attempt to broaden
their shareholding base and secure more cash. In the late 17th century it
was an unusual exercise, although the Dutch had invested in joint-stock
companies of other nations.[2] The attempt to secure foreign shareholders
was not simply opportunistic, an effort to fill the coffers with as much
cash as possible, but had financial logic behind it. The Company was
spending large amounts of money on building ships in Amsterdam
and Hamburg, so if capital was raised there, the costs could be met
out of funds in these cities. The directors' confidence was buoyed up
by their success in Scotland and they strongly believed there was a
very good chance of convincing foreign merchants to invest in the
Company.

A high profile entourage was appointed for this important task. On
9 September 1696 the directors chose Lieutenant Colonel John Erskine
and John Haldane of Gleneagles to accompany William Paterson and
James Smyth on the overseas mission, or 'international roadshow' as it
might be called today.[3] William Paterson needs no introduction. His
business associate Smyth was a London merchant, who was an original
promoter of the Company in England and a director. Lieutenant
Colonel John Erskine was the son of committed Presbyterian David
Lord Cardross. He had joined Argyll's unsuccessful rebellion against
James VII in 1685 and thereafter lived in exile in the Netherlands.

---

[1]   NLS, Darien Company, MS 1914, f86.

[2]   *Companies and Trade*, 39–40.

[3]   RBS, D/1/1, 128.

After the Revolution he returned to Scotland, where he pursued a career as a professional soldier. In 1693 he was accused by the guildry of Stirling of illegal trafficking in 'all sorts of merchant wares', thus abusing his position as Governor of Stirling Castle, but revealing his entrepreneurial spirit.[4] John was 34 and described by Herries as the 'darling of the Kirk' because of his pious Presbyterian credentials.[5]

John Haldane of Gleneagles was a Perthshire laird of 36. Little is known about his early years except that he attended Aberdeen University, although recent research has suggested he displayed 'potential Jacobite behaviour' during the Revolution when he withdrew from the Convention of Estates.[6] However, he later emerged as a consistent supporter of the Union and the house of Hanover and in 1689 was made a captain in the staunchly Presbyterian Lord Ruthven's regiment.[7] His ambivalent position in 1688–9 may have been related to his association with the Marquis of Atholl, who had Jacobite sympathies, or he may have had some residual loyalty to James VII.[8]

Walter Herries was uncharacteristically charitable about Erskine and Gleneagles, describing them as 'Men of Honour and Worth', although he was unable to resist adding the gibe that they were 'altogether Strangers to Trade'.[9] Herries would certainly not have missed an opportunity to criticise or caricature, so it seems reasonable to take his description at face value. The inexperience of Gleneagles in financial matters is sustained by comments in his own letters to the committee of foreign trade. He and Erskine were both active directors of the Company, young men with energy and commitment, who were to serve it loyally over many years.

The court of directors set their sights high and authorised Paterson, Erskine, Gleneagles and Smyth to sell up to £200,000 of stock to foreign merchants and corporations and receive the first call of a quarter.[10] If they were successful the capital of the Company would be boosted by a mighty 50 per cent, and £25,000 made available on the Continent

---

4   *Records of the Merchant Guild of Stirling*, 78.

5   Herries, *Defence*, 12.

6   Patrick, 'People and Parliament,' 171.

7   General Sir J. Aylmer L. Haldane, *The Haldanes of Gleneagles* (London, 1929), 101, 103.

8   Patrick, 'People and Parliament,' 171, 247.

9   Herries, *Defence*, 12.

10   RBS, Instructions of the Court of Directors, D/2, f4.

to supplement expenditure on the fleet. A third of the shares would be in foreign hands, but the issue of representation of such a large body of new shareholders on the court of directors was not considered at this stage.

The fund raising effort was focused on two principal locations: Amsterdam and Hamburg. Amsterdam was the natural destination for a company looking to raise money as there was more wealth in the Dutch city than anywhere else in the world in the late 17th century. It was a trading entrepôt and financial Mecca; the site of the world's most sophisticated financial market, where a variety of commodities, bonds, shares and derivatives were traded, and the home of the most powerful chamber of the VOC.[11] Hamburg, on the northern bank of the River Elbe, about 80 miles from its mouth, had been a member of the medieval Hanseatic League, and remained an important trading, financial and shipbuilding centre, and home of Germany's oldest stock exchange, founded in 1558.[12]

The foreign contingent divided into two groups. Gleneagles travelled to the Continent by way of London to rendezvous with James Smyth and James Campbell, another director who was added to the mission. Campbell, who had been appointed director for Company affairs in England with Smyth, ran the merchant banking partnership of Stewart and Campbell with his fellow Scot Walter Stewart.[13] Paterson and Erskine travelled directly to the Netherlands by sea.

Gleneagles arrived in London by 3 November after a 'very uneasy and troublesome Journey' and spent time looking for potential employees for the Company and examining the accounts of Campbell and Smyth.[14] On the evening of 6 November he met a sea captain called Robert Pincarton, well regarded in the seafaring community and experienced in the West Indian trade. Proposals were made to him and he was later engaged to serve the Company, commanding the *Unicorn* on the first expedition to the isthmus.[15]

[11] de Vries and der Woude, *First Modern Economy*, J.I. Israel, 'The Amsterdam Stock Exchange and the English Revolution of 1688,' in J.I. Israel, *Conflicts of Empires: Spain, the Low Countries and the Struggle for World Supremacy 1585–1713* (London, 1997), 319–47.

[12] E. Simon, *Hamburg: A Gateway for the World, 1189–1989* (London, 1989), 54, 64.

[13] NLS, MS 1914, 79–80.

[14] *Ibid.*, 54–5.

[15] *Ibid.*, 58, 68.

Gleneagles also engaged three surgeons whom he met in Moncrieff's coffee-house: Mr MacKenzie, Mr Kier and Mr Herries, 'smart young men' with extensive experience of the sea. One of them had just returned from a voyage to China.[16] The employment of Walter Herries, a native of Dumbarton, was to prove unfortunate for the directors, as after he returned disillusioned from the first expedition to Darien, he turned his pen upon their incompetence. He proved the most gifted of those who wrote books or penned pamphlets about the Company's misfortunes and is often quoted by historians. At this stage Herries thought he was destined for a voyage to the East Indies.[17] Plans for an emporium on the isthmus of Central America were not being mentioned to new employees.[18]

Paterson and Erskine arrived at Veere in Holland in early November and proceeded to Amsterdam by way of Zealand and Rotterdam. During the following months they met many potential investors and faced many different responses, from genuine interest to hostility. The emotional ups and downs of the effort to raise capital – the shifts from optimism to bleak pessimism and back again – can be tracked in their correspondence with the committee of foreign trade in Edinburgh. On their arrival, perhaps influenced by the unpleasant voyage across the North Sea, they did not sound hopeful: 'we are affraid we are something too late in the Year and that we shall not gett in the Money to be raised here, time enough, to supply the Companys Occasions'.[19] Back in London, Gleneagles was more optimistic: 'I am told by several in this place that there is good appearances of our getting foreign Subscriptions'.[20]

Nevertheless, genuine interest in the Company did emerge and by the middle of December Paterson and Erskine were feeling more positive: 'a great many considerable persons well acquainted with the Trade and Navigation to the Indies present their selves to the Company, and some of them to be concerned in the Stock'.[21] However, they did raise a note of caution: 'we find the same Jealousy among the people here that we found in England'. Even Herries admits there was interest

[16]   Ibid., 67.
[17]   Herries, Defence, 13.
[18]   Darien Papers, 196.
[19]   NLS, MS 1914, 69.
[20]   Ibid., 77.
[21]   Ibid., 83–5.

among the Dutch, who were particularly attracted by the customs exemption specified in the act of parliament, which would allow the Company to undercut Dutch and English rivals by importing goods form the Far East into Scotland custom free.[22] The merchants of Amsterdam would thus be able to buy spices and exotic textiles at knock-down prices.

Gleneagles left London for Harwich on 3 December, accompanied by Smyth, Campbell and Herries. Fog and 'great Sholes of Ice' made the sea crossing difficult and the ship ran aground.[23] They eventually met up with Erskine and Paterson and reached Rotterdam by the middle of the month: 'there is a very good disposition in severals of this City to be concerned which we neglect not to improve and incourage'.[24] By the 1680s Rotterdam was the prime destination for Scottish shipping to the Netherlands, having eclipsed the medieval staple at Veere, and was a thriving trading centre with its own exchange bank, stock market and chamber of the VOC.[25] Perhaps the interest in the Company reflected the large community of expatriate Scots in the city.[26] Having tested the water, the directors decided to delay opening a subscription book there until a beginning had been made in Amsterdam.[27] They were still optimistic that a very substantial amount of cash could be raised on the Continent. When they wrote to Edinburgh asking for further funds to cover the cost of ship construction they informed the other directors that Scottish capital would only be required 'untill our Foreign Subscriptions put us in Condition not only to support the Companys undertakings here but also if need be in Scotland'.[28]

In January 1697 four 'good reputable' Dutch merchants, Jacob Larwood, Henry Wylenbrock, Isaac Cossart and Alexander Henderson, were appointed as factors for the Company in Amsterdam. They were to pay and receive money, buy and sell goods, promote subscriptions,

[22] Herries, *Defence*, 14.

[23] NLS, MS 1914, 86.

[24] *Ibid.*, 92.

[25] T.C. Smout, 'Scottish-Dutch Contact 1600–1800' in *Dutch Art and Scotland: A Reflection of Taste* (Edinburgh, 1992), 22, D. Catterall, *Community without Borders: Scots Migrants and the changing face of power in the Dutch Republic, c.1600–1700* (Leiden, 2002), 39.

[26] *Ibid.*, 92–3.

[27] NLS, MS 1914, 92.

[28] *Ibid.*, 97.

examine accounts, and oversee cargoes and provisions for the
Company ships. Henderson was Scottish, married to a wealthy Dutch
widow, and a major player in the Amsterdam and London bullion
trade.[29] At the time of their appointment they subscribed large sums
of stock: Larwood £1,000, Wylenbrock £1,000, Cossart £1,200, and
Henderson £3,000, putting them among the group of largest shareholders and presumably making them eligible at some point to be
elected as directors. Unfortunately the Company was never to see a
penny of the cash promised by these men.

The employment of such illustrious merchants was viewed as a
significant boost. Paterson, Gleneagles, and Erskine informed the
committee of foreign trade:

> We doubt not of doing materiall business here with the
> Assistance of Our new friends tho it may take a little time the
> Dutch being of an humor not to be courted too much into a
> Stock nor to sign great Sums but what they Sign is good when
> demanded not only in part but in whole the fixing of these
> four men in Our Interest conjunctly is lookt on here as a great
> matter and a certain presage of success.[30]

By early January the Company constitution and act of parliament had
been translated into Dutch and French, and copies distributed to provide information and assurances for potential investors. Yet there was
reluctance among the Amsterdam merchant community. In February
the Dutch factors were cautious: 'as yet few or none have been influenced by our Subscriptions what time may do we must with patience
expect'. Direct opposition to the efforts of the Scots had emerged from
the magistrates of Amsterdam and the directors of the VOC who were
doing all they could to discourage potential investors, in the same way
that the English joint-stock companies and the English parliament had
opposed the Company in London. Frustrated in Amsterdam, the directors
turned their attention to Rotterdam, where they had expectations of raising at least £20,000, sending James Campbell to open a subscription
book after an invitation in writing. But again their plans were foiled when
the magistrates of Rotterdam summoned those who were interested in
investing and threatened that they 'should not be very easy to any who
would Joyn'. This scared off potential subscribers.[31]

29   Quinn, 'Gold, silver, and the Glorious Revolution,' 485.
30   NLS, MS 1914, 112.
31   Ibid., f42–3, f45, f47, f63. This source only has page numbers up to 120.

By March the game was up in the Netherlands, as interest in the Company melted away. Gleneagles wrote from the Hague on 8 March: 'the expectations I have of Subsriptions in this Countrey is but very low'.

Factors had been appointed in Hamburg the previous August when the English merchants, Francis Stratford senior and junior, were proposed by director Robert Watson 'with assurance of their integrity and good inclinations to the Company'.[32] They proceeded to supply the directors with some honest and at times critical advice. It emerged at an early stage that the English government was committed to opposing the Company's efforts to raise capital in the German city. On 23 October 1696 the Stratfords had received private information that orders had been given to the English Envoy at the Court of Lunburg and Resident in Hamburg to obstruct the proceedings of the Company, but the tactics to be employed to achieve this were not clear.[33]

In Hamburg the Scots were faced with an experienced opponent, the indefatigable Sir Paul Rycaut, an English diplomat with a wealth of experience who was consul at Smyrna in Turkey from 1667 to 1678 and later chief secretary in Ireland, sitting on the Irish privy council. He was knighted in 1685 and after the Revolution became William and Mary's Resident at the Hanse towns of Hamburg, Lübeck and Bremen. Rycaut was the speaker of nine languages and pursued a successful literary career with works including *The Present State of the Ottoman Empire* and *The History of the Turkish Empire from the year 1623 to the year 1677*, which influenced among others Racine, Leibniz, Locke, Defoe, Montesquieu and Byron, and is still regarded as an essential source for the study of the Ottoman empire in the 17th century.[34] This remarkable man was keeping a close eye on the Company's shipbuilding activities in the city.[35] On 25 September he informed the English Secretary of State William Blathwayt of his determined opposition: 'nothing may be omitted to defeat the Scotch designes'.[36]

On 16 February, soon after their arrival, Erskine and Paterson met

---

[32]   RBS, D/1/1, 21 August 1696.

[33]   NLS, MS 1914, 52.

[34]   *ODNB*, 48, 439–42. He apparently felt the cold bitterly before discovering the joys of the duvet, which he is credited with introducing to England.

[35]   *Darien Shipping Papers*, 6.

[36]   Ibid., 8–9.

Rycaut and informed him that the Company had no ventures in mind that would undermine English trading interests in the city.[37] They clearly underestimated the experienced diplomat, as they wrote to Scotland that 'we find him an Old weak man And His nor the English Companys Interest is not very Considerable here'.[38] Rycaut told the other English secretary Sir William Trumbull: 'I can discover nothing farther but that their businesse reaches only to subscriptions, of which I believe they will find very few in this City, neither the Designe nor the people who manage it having any great reputation'.[39]

Initial indications were not particularly promising when the Stratfords, the Company's own agents in the city, began to distance themselves from subscription because of their large investments in London: 'it might draw some inconvenience upon us, to appear too publickly in your concerns'.[40] But again there was genuine interest in the Company from the investment community. Erskine and Paterson found some wealthy merchants 'inclinable to engage' and according to Herries 'the Hamburghers swallow'd the bait to a wish, for the more opposition the English and Dutch offer'd to the Project, confirm'd them the more that it was their Interest to embrace it'.[41] The merchants of Hamburg bought their East Indian luxuries from the English and Dutch Companies and then sold them to towns on the Elbe. The Scots might provide goods at a lower cost. The Company was again being marketed as a vehicle to compete in trade to the Far East and Darien was not mentioned.[42]

There was a large gulf, however, between serious attention and the actual act of subscription. Investors were willing to hear what the Scots had to say and may have appeared interested. What did they have to lose, after all, from listening? They might actually learn something. But handing over cash was a different matter.

Paterson was doing what he did best – promoting the opportunity for wealth creation offered by the Company of Scotland – but was being watched by Rycaut or his informants:

Mr Paterson, who is a diligent Projector, lyes hard at them, and

---

[37]   NLS, MS 1914, f51.

[38]   *Ibid.*, f57.

[39]   *Darien Shipping Papers*, 12–14.

[40]   NLS, MS 1914, f54–5.

[41]   *Ibid.*, f56–7, Herries, *Defence*, 17.

[42]   *Darien Shipping Papers*, 13.

representing nothing but riches and a golden age, and yesterday
gave a Treat at Altona to such of them as seem most inclinable
to this new designe, so that people beginne now to talk that the
Subscriptions may become in a short time very considerable.[43]

Paterson was attempting to butter up potential investors with free
meals and entertainment in the nearby town of Altona, in the same
way that investment bankers flex their company credit cards on
expensive restaurants or golf trips for investment managers today.

The Scots had a further trick up their sleeve: the ships they were
building in the city. In early March the *Caledonia* and the *Instauration*
(later named the *St Andrew*), were launched. Rycaut commented that
'they hope so to take the minds and hearts of the Dutch merchants of
Hamburg that none will be able to resist the temptation of being concerned in such fine ships, and then they think it may be the most proper
time to procure subscriptions'. The appearance of these impressive
vessels on the Elbe, and the anticipation of two more, did have an
effect on sentiment. Even Rycaut sounded less confident on 16 March:
'for as the world for the most Part is pleased with novelties so mens
harts are in a spetiall manner easily persuaded to new projects in
trade'. By this time he had heard rumours that the Company was not
to sail to the East Indies but to Africa and America and that they
intended to extend their capital raising by taking subscriptions at
Bremen, Leipzig, Dresden and Frankfurt: 'They also talk big that the
Dukes of Zell, Brunswig, and Wolfenbuttel will come in'. The Scots
were exaggerating the numbers who were interested to encourage subscriptions.[44]

Erskine and Paterson were not worried by the Resident's opposition: 'it but animates the people more and we find a great and General
Inclination here to be Concerned in the Company'. They ordered a
preamble for subscription to be translated into High Dutch and commented that 'the People here thinks it the most happy proposal ever
was made in Hamburgh'. There was also interest in the Company in
Danzig and Bremen and oozing confidence they believed that within
a month to six weeks cash would be provided by Hamburg investors:
'the hope of success in that matter Continues and increases'.[45]

---

[43] *Ibid,,* 16.

[44] *Ibid.,* 17–20.

[45] NLS, MS 1914, f67–8.

On 23 March they informed the committee of foreign trade in Edinburgh that they intended to proceed to subscriptions in a few days.[46] But on the same day the Stratfords confirmed they would not be involved because of their very large investment of £15,000 in English government bonds (tallies or short-dated Treasury paper). They did not share the confidence of the Scots: 'We know 2 or 3 that expect to lick themselves whole by the hopes of being made Directors may subscribe liberally but we scarce think that others will follow'. The factors continued by giving the directors some advice:

> Were the whole Concern our own, we should choose rather to Trade so much less, and only with our own Stock than to soare too high at first, the whole Stock of the Danish East India Company is but RD 180,000 specie, and they send out a Ship or Two every year and get one home and make every Year a Dividend besides the Advance of their Stock.[47]

It was dangerous for an inexperienced company to seek the 'keys of the universe'. Better to be more canny with their cash. The court of directors should have listened.

On 29 March a pamphlet was published called *A Letter from Amsterdam to a Friend at Hamburgh*. According to the Stratfords it gave many 'plausible reasons' against investment in the Company and was commissioned by Sir Paul Rycaut, who commented the following day that he would 'leave no stone unturned whereby I may disappoint their intentions'.[48]

On 6 April Rycaut reported to Secretary of State Trumbull that there was talk of the Company taking a public house and, with a licence from the senate, having written over the doors: 'This is the house of the Scotch Company'. But the Senate of Hamburg assured him such a request would be rejected. He was also informed by Paterson that Erskine, Smyth and Gleneagles had extended their marketing campaign to Glückstadt, Lübeck and Tormingen.[49]

---

[46]   *Ibid.*, f74.

[47]   *Ibid.*, f75. 'RD': rixdollars. 180,000 were worth about £38,000 based on an exchange rate of 4.69 rixdollars to £1 sterling. J.J. McCusker, *Money and Exchange in Europe and America, 1600–1775: A Handbook* (Williamsburg, 1978), 82.

[48]   NLS, MS 1914, f79, *Darien Shipping Papers*, 21–2.

[49]   *Ibid.*, 24–5.

But a diplomatic bombshell was about to explode; an official English government attack on the effort of the Scots.[50] The memorial to the senate of the city of Hamburg was modelled on letters Rycaut had already sent to Lübeck and Bremen and was composed in French.[51] In translation it read:

> We the Under-Subscribers, Ministers of His Majesty the King of Great Britain have, upon the arrival of Commissioners from an Indian Company in Scotland, represented at two several times to Your Magnificences and Lordships, from the King our Master, That His Majesty understanding that the said Commissioners endeavoured to open to themselves a Commerce and Trade in these Parts, by making some Convention or Treaty with the City, had commanded us most expressly to notifie to Your magnificences and Lordships, That if you enter into such Conventions with private Men, his subjects, who have neither Credential Letters, nor any otherwise authoriz'd by His Majesty, That his Majesty would regard such proceedings as an Affront to his Royal Authority, and that he would not fail to resent it.

It went on to emphasize English 'displeasure' that inhabitants of Hamburg 'forbear not to make Conventions and Treaties with the said Commissioners' and complained that the Scots had dared to erect a public office to receive subscriptions. The senate was requested to remedy the situation before good relations with England were damaged. This was an unambiguous diplomatic threat aiming to discourage the merchant community from having anything to do with the Scottish Company.

The directors in Hamburg and their colleagues back in Edinburgh, when they heard about the memorial, were furious. After all, the Company had been established by an act of parliament which had been passed by the King's commissioner. The claim in the memorial that they had 'neither Credential Letters, nor any otherwise authoriz'd by His Majesty' was untrue. Again the Company was faced with the grim reality that King William would side with his wealthier southern

---

[50] A translation is provided in Insh, *Company of Scotland*, 95. The original text is printed in *Darien Shipping Papers*, 28–9.

[51] Insh, *Company of Scotland*, 90.

kingdom rather than his poorer northern one. From William's point of view this no doubt made sound political sense, but for the directors, shareholders and most other Scots it seemed their King had forsaken them.

The memorial highlighted two key points. Firstly, the English government would do whatever it could to oppose and undermine a Scottish joint-stock company whether in England or abroad. This had been evident in London in the winter of 1695–6 and was emphasised by the events in Hamburg. Secondly, the constitutional relationship between the kingdoms was a hindrance to Scottish attempts to develop their economy. They were already excluded from legal trade with the English plantations through the Navigation Acts and now an effort to establish a colonial trade was being undermined by their own King. During the Revolution William had appeared as a saviour to Presbyterian Scotland, a deliverer from a Catholic tyrant. That he was now turning against them was a painful reality check. The memorial therefore symbolised the stranglehold placed on Scotland politically and economically by the Union of 1603 and became a key text in the political battles over the Company of Scotland and Darien in the following years.

The memorial produced the desired short-term effect. Subscription books were opened but the response was muted. Only £8,500 was subscribed on the first day and about £800 on the next.[52] Thereafter there was nothing. On 9 April Erskine and Gleneagles wrote to the committee of foreign trade: 'We are of opinion that our business in this place is over for most of the individuals have great effects in England'.[53] On 20 April Rycaut informed the English government of his success; the subscriptions were 'entirely quasht and the subscribers dishearted'.[54]

Back in Edinburgh a council general was called on 13 May 'to have their advice and concurrence in a matter of so great importance to the Company in particular and the Nation in General'.[55] Gleneagles wrote from Amsterdam that 'there has nothing fallen out of a long time that makes a greater noise in the world than this does, and the Eyes of every body is upon us'.[56] Erskine proceeded to the Hague to

---

[52]   *Darien Shipping Papers*, 30.

[53]   NLS, MS 1914, f79–80.

[54]   *Darien Shipping Papers*, 31.

[55]   RBS, D/1/1, 241.

[56]   NLS, MS 1914, f86.

voice the Company's grievances to William Carstares, the King's favourite.

The return journey was lengthened by bad weather and it was not until 16 June that Erskine and Gleneagles were back in Edinburgh, by way of London, having been delayed in the Netherlands for between eight and ten days. They gave the directors an account of events overseas and on 23 June their written report was presented to the council general.[57] The mission to raise capital on the Continent had been a complete failure. The massively expensive ships would have to be financed from cash provided in Scotland. This was a significant setback.

The directors had not expected such strong opposition to their plans in Amsterdam and Hamburg. Given their experience in London perhaps they should have. The court failed to assess the political risk associated with raising capital abroad. In Scotland subscriptions had flooded in and this success may have made the directors too confident. They ignored the intense competition between joint-stock companies in the difficult trading conditions of the 1690s.

What caused the directors particular gall was direct English interference sanctioned by their King. The chance of raising capital in Amsterdam and Hamburg might have been small – after all, they were selling shares in a new company with no experience of foreign trade – but English opposition provided a target to blame for the disappointment. The events in Hamburg thus marked an important point in the history of the Company; the beginning of a process that was to see the Company of Scotland transformed from a financial entity into a political one. Originally the aim of the directors was to invest capital and hopefully provide a return for shareholders. Now their aims broadened as men became involved in the management who had other objectives than trade and colonies.

English opposition was certainly important in scaring off investors in Hamburg. There was, however, another factor that contributed to the failure of the international roadshow that the directors were less keen to draw attention to.

---

[57] *Ibid.*, f91–2, RBS, D/3, 41.

CHAPTER NINE

The Talented Mr Smyth

The greatest vilan and most notorious lyar in Nature.
JOHN HALDANE OF GLENEAGLES[1]

NO COMPANY HISTORY WOULD be complete without a financial scandal and that of the Company of Scotland is no exception. Indeed, the emergence of swindles has been viewed as characteristic of speculative manias.[2] As with much else in the early history of the Company of Scotland, William Paterson was intimately involved. In 1696 he was riding high as champion of the Company, shareholders, and nation. His fellow directors entrusted him with £25,476 of the capital to transmit to London, which represented about 42 per cent of the Company's cash at this point, and was a huge vote of confidence in Paterson's trustworthiness. It proved to be a disastrous decision to risk so much of the Company's money on the reputation of one man.

Paterson recommended that some of the cash be transferred to London to take advantage of the weakness of sterling. In 1695 the English currency had collapsed, principally because of the vast quantities of money being sent overseas to fund King William's war effort on the Continent.[3] Bank of England notes were trading at large discounts to face value and Paterson argued that the Company could take advantage of this opportunity and earn some extra income on its capital if the directors purchased English notes and bills which then went up in value. It was also thought, quite reasonably, that having a fund in London would help business transactions, making payments in Hamburg and Amsterdam easier, as London was a larger and more developed financial centre than Edinburgh. If Paterson had transferred portions of the money to a number of the merchant banking partnerships that were then developing in London, all might have been well, and his reputation would have remained intact. But instead he transmitted £16,998, or about 66 per cent, to his close business associate,

---

[1]   NLS, Adv MS 83.7.4, f68.

[2]   Kindleberger, *Manias*, 73–90.

[3]   Quinn, 'Gold, silver, and the Glorious Revolution,' 477.

the London merchant James Smyth, who received £2,530 in cash and £14,468 in bank notes.[4] It was no doubt the largest amount of money that the young merchant had ever seen in his life, equivalent to about £1.7 million today.

Not a great deal is known about the man who was being entrusted with about 28 per cent of the Company of Scotland's capital. What we do know about Smyth suggests that he must have been an impressive communicator who was able to persuade many contemporaries that he was a merchant of sound financial probity. In the early 1690s he was active in the colonial trade between London and Charles Town in South Carolina and in 1693 and 1694 worked as a lobbyist for the Corporation of the City of London in their attempt to have an act establishing an Orphans' Fund pushed through parliament.[5] At some point he became a close associate, indeed acolyte, of William Paterson. Relations between the two men probably dated back to the late 1680s, when Paterson and three other European merchants, Heinrich Bulen, Wilhelm Pocock and James Schmitten unsuccessfully tried to raise capital in Amsterdam, Hamburg and Berlin for a venture to Darien.[6] It is highly likely that James Schmitten was the man who later emerged in London as James Smyth. Paterson was the kind of man who enjoyed the adoration of younger disciples. He was, after all, something of a radical in financial matters, a trailblazer of the financial revolution, and had influenced the financial elite of England to adopt his plans for state funding through the Bank of England. Smyth was no doubt attracted by the older man's visionary ideas, as well as the opportunity they might offer to feather his own nest. He became a loyal follower and was the author of a pamphlet in 1695 which defended Paterson's role in the Bank and Orphans' Fund. With Paterson and other merchants, Smyth became one of the promoters of the Company in London, although in the act of parliament of 1695 he wrongly appeared under the name of John Smith.[7]

Smyth arrived in Edinburgh with Paterson and Lodge in February 1696 to organise the Scottish capital raising. Bathing in the famous projector's reflected glory he was awarded diplomas from the Merchant Company of Edinburgh and the town council, and spent time in the Edinburgh coffee-houses selling the Company to potential

---

4   NLS, Adv MS 83.7.4, f52, 83.8.5, f200–1, 83.8.7, f153–4.
5   NLS, Adv MS 83.7.7, 1–7, Forrester, *Man who saw the Future*, 160.
6   *Ibid.*, 43–4.
7   RBS, D/1/1, 40, APS, ix, 378.

investors. He clearly made a big impression on the Scottish promoters for on 20 April he was one of five men appointed to receive cash paid by subscribers. The others were all Scots: Sir John Swinton of that Ilk, a Borders laird, who had worked as a merchant in exile in the Netherlands, and the Edinburgh merchants Mr Robert Blackwood, George Clark, and James Balfour.[8] Smyth was also ordered by the directors to provide lists and prices of goods from his mercantile contacts in London that might be suitable for trading ventures to Africa and the East and West Indies.[9] By 14 May he was back in London 'employ'd in the Particular Service of this Company' and *in absentia* was unanimously voted onto the court of directors. Paterson signified to the court that in Smyth's absence he would undertake that the young merchant adhered to his subscription in England of £3,000.[10] Smyth had made a rapid rise from relative obscurity to membership of a group of men who were destined, so the nation hoped, to create a Scottish empire. Further responsibility was placed in his capable hands on 18 June when he and James Campbell were appointed to oversee Company affairs in the English capital. This included attempting to persuade the London subscribers, who had been scared off by the opposition of the English parliament, to provide some cash for the Company.[11] He was clearly a dynamic young merchant who the directors had total faith in, and impressed them so much he was appointed to the high profile entourage, which included Paterson, Gleneagles and Lieutenant Colonel Erskine, sent on the important mission to raise capital on the Continent in late 1696.

Smyth was not English by birth but a Walloon, whose native name, according to Walter Herries, was Le Serrurier, and who was a master of most European languages, particularly English. Wallonia was an area in the Low Countries now in the southern part of Belgium. The name James Smyth was an English one he had adopted. Herries described him and Daniel Lodge, Paterson's other young sidekick, as 'subtle Youths, whose Office was to put Paterson's creud and indigested Notions into Form.'[12] Smyth was clearly a smooth operator with the gift of the gab.

---

[8]   RBS, D/1/1, 22.
[9]   *Darien Shipping Papers*, 1.
[10] RBS, D/1/1, 40–1.
[11] Ibid., 83, *Darien Shipping Papers*, 2.
[12] Herries, *Defence*, 5.

Beneath this trustworthy veneer, however, his personal and business finances were in a calamitous state. The first hint that all was not well with his financial dealings for the Company was on 17 September 1696. The directors ordered the factors in Hamburg, Francis Stratford senior and junior, and the Scottish merchants Alexander Stevenson and James Gibson, who had been sent abroad to build and buy ships, 'not to draw any more on Mr Smyth till further advice'. They also resolved that the transactions of Smyth and Campbell on behalf of the Company should be carefully examined.[13] As a result, in November Gleneagles was ordered to investigate Smyth's accounts in London on his way to the Continent, although at this point Smyth still enjoyed the confidence of the directors, receiving orders from them to convert money in London from bank notes to specie as soon as possible and remit these sums to Amsterdam to cover expenditure there.[14]

But in late November there were worrying developments. The Stratfords wrote to the committee of foreign trade in Edinburgh:

> We are very much Surpriz'd at the Receipt of a Protest from London for none payment of a Bill of £500 Sterling which we drew on Mr James Smyth the 11th of September by which we fear may expect Protests for all we drew since which reflects not only upon our Credit and reputation, but will cause a very considerable Charge to the Company.[15]

The bill of exchange was a common feature of international finance by the late 17th century and allowed funds to be transferred between countries without the cost and trouble of transporting coin or bullion.[16] A protested bill was similar to a bounced cheque, and indicated that inadequate funds were available to honour the promised payment. The effect of a protest was described by one contemporary merchant as a 'Thunderclap'.[17] By 27 November two more bills were protested.[18] For a new company attempting to establish its reputation the impact was devastating.

---

13   RBS, D/1/1, 139.

14   NLS, MS 1914, 57–8, 64–5.

15   Ibid., 72.

16   McCusker, Money and Exchange, 18–23.

17   John Spreul, An Accompt Current betwixt Scotland and England (Edinburgh, 1705), 14.

18   NLS, MS 1914, 80.

In January 1697 Gleneagles, Erskine and Paterson referred to 'Mr Smyth's Affair' in a letter to the Company.[19] The directors were faced with a full-blown financial scandal involving the Company's cash. The crisis had taken a few months to surface because of the confused state of the financial environment in Europe in 1696–7, when payment terms on financial instruments became extended as many merchants had increasing difficulties meeting their obligations because of a shortage of coin. By February the reality of Smyth's disastrous finances was becoming clearer. Gleneagles wrote from Amsterdam: 'the Disappointment we and the Company have mett with by Mr Smyth has made us resolve to be as slow as we can in taking on men and the like till we see what Train our Affairs take at Hamburgh'.[20]

By 14 March the news of the Smyth affair had leaked out to the broader financial community and was circulating in Hamburg. It was grist to the mill for inveterate opponent of the Company, Sir Paul Rycaut:

> One of the Scotch Company called Mr Smith was lately arrested at Amsterdam for default of payment of some bills or money which he had taken up belonging to the Scotch East India Company of which he could give no good account. It is said that he and Paterson are in contrivance to cheat the stock; which report, though there were nothing more in it than a report, yet it is sufficient to break the whole credit of the Company in these parts: as it hath already done, and some merchants here beginne to bless their good fortune that they have so well escaped the snare.[21]

Like all financial scandals, the details were quickly exaggerated and rumours of a worst case scenario, an alliance by Smyth and Paterson to swindle the entire capital of the Company, spread like wildfire. It must be emphasised that the emergence of a scandal during an effort to raise capital in foreign climes was a disaster of significant proportions, although most historians of the Company have followed the propaganda of the directors and accepted that the only reason for the failure to raise capital on the Continent in 1696–7 was English opposition.[22] In

---

[19] *Ibid.*, 111.

[20] *Ibid.*, f46–7.

[21] *Darien Shipping Papers*, 18.

[22] The one exception is Forrester, *Man who saw the Future*, which does stress its significance.

reality, the 'Smyth' affair and the dreadful financial backdrop were equally important.

With hindsight of course, Smyth was a rotten financial apple whose business or personal finances had become intimately linked with the cash he was supposedly safeguarding for the Company. Once the story of his embezzlement was in the public domain further tales of his financial ineptitude emerged. The Scottish merchant Alexander Stevenson had 'received an ill Character of him some time since' and had heard that he had failed in France some years before.[23] Investigation of his activity in London might have provided some warnings. In 1695 he was questioned by the House of Commons over allegations of the use of bribery to secure the passage of the Orphans' Fund, and in the same year was arrested with another man called Aubrey Price and held in jail for alleged involvement in an attempt to dump counterfeit Orphans' bonds on the Bank of England. They were not prosecuted as the Bank was fully reimbursed, but Smyth was not pardoned until 14 December 1695.[24] Paterson was therefore well aware that his young companion had a questionable history, but chose to overlook it, believing he would be useful for his efforts to raise capital in Scotland.

The Company now knew that a significant amount of their cash had disappeared. Smyth admitted his guilt when he decided to take flight, giving the directors the slip in Hamburg. Fortunately for the Company, he was seized in Amsterdam and held in a private prison. The directors threatened that if he didn't come to an accommodation with them in a few days he would be sent to the common jail; a much less agreeable prospect. Smyth told the directors they would have to take him back to England to gain access to his financial assets, and on 14 May wrote a desperate letter to Gleneagles from prison:

> Sir I send you here inclosed the utmost proposalls I am able to make you in order to my release and that upon my most solemn oath, if you can discover any thing else from my papers which were sealed in presence of Mr James Campbell and deliver'd to Mr Alexander Henderson when you come to looke them over, I shall bee most willing to allow itt, and if you suspect I have more papers in my other trunck, itt shall bee opened in your presence and exposed to your mercy, itt is

[23] NLS, MS 1914, 72, 104–5.

[24] Forrester, *Man who saw the Future*, 74, 77, 161.

true I am unfortunat in being the occasion of so great a disa-
pointement to the compagny, but I declare I never intended to
cheate them, if you design to recover what I owe, your accepting of these terms now made and my speedy release is your
intrest, for if my imprisonement is once known, att London itt
will certainly incapacitate me to perform this offers, but if you
study revenge I shall very soon fall a sacrifice to itt, I finde my
self already indisposed under the sence of my present misery
and a little time longer shall putt an end to my miserable life.[25]

He was offering to pay the Company £5,000 in four instalments of
£1,250, payable in three, nine, fifteen and eighteen months. The first
payment was to be met out of an ongoing trading venture, and the rest
from his other assets in London, which included 'some interest in the
waterworks' and 'something due by the government'. He would also
provide his own bills to cover the rest. Following this declaration Smyth
was released, provided the directors with his papers, and assured them
he would deliver all his assets when they were back in England.[26]

Gleneagles tried to placate rumours that were circulating in
Scotland about the nature of the scandal, informing the committee of
foreign trade that 'there is no great mysteries in this matter as people
imagine he is a proflagat person and had debt' and lamenting that he
'never had a ticklisher point to manadge than this'.[27]

The 'Smyth affair' was to be a long drawn out distraction for the
Company and it proved extremely difficult to recover any of the cash
that had disappeared in the morass of Smyth's liabilities. In early June
1697 Gleneagles and Erskine were still in London attempting to
recover some of the lost funds: 'we are likewise doing whats possible
for us to clear with Mr Smyth'.[28] They drew up a list of his assets,
which included goods on a trading venture to Charles Town in
Carolina, a shareholding of £300 in the ship *Good Success*, £700 of
goods in the hands of Charles Town merchant Henry Noble, a shareholding in the Hampstead Waterworks of £600, investments in
English government bonds of £400, and £1,000 owed him by fellow
Company of Scotland director Daniel Lodge.[29]

[25]   NLS, Adv MS 83.7.4, f48.
[26]   NLS, MS 1914, f92.
[27]   *Ibid.*, f85–6.
[28]   *Ibid.*, f94.
[29]   NLS, Adv MS 83.7.8, f213.

After the return of Gleneagles and Erskine to Scotland, others became involved in the debt recovery process. In June 1697 William Wooddrop, a Glasgow merchant and director who was going to London on private business, was authorised to settle and adjust in 'the affair of Mr Smyth', and in March 1698 Dr John Munro, a Company employee, was prosecuting Smyth in London. The only success came when London Scot, Hugh Fraser, who had taken over as debt collector, managed to retrieve £200 in August 1698.[30] This was a very small part of the sum that had been lost. Smyth's assets proved as elusive as his own identity.

Smyth was clearly a merchant who operated on the razor's edge and was juggling too many liabilities. It is unclear whether he deliberately planned to swindle the Company or whether he was simply a casualty of too much debt. He was able to sustain his position in the boom conditions of the early 1690s when credit was plentiful, but the monetary crisis that reached its peak in 1696–7 put severe strains on those who were overextended, and Smyth and the Company of Scotland were among the casualties. He operated in a world in which there was no clear division between a man's personal assets and the assets of the company he was working for. This issue has continued to haunt the financial world, down to the Maxwell pension scandal and beyond.

The European financial crisis of 1696–7 was a disaster for men like Smyth who had borrowed too much. In England prices of shares and bonds collapsed and the monetary situation was so severe that the government took the drastic step of calling in all the 'clipped' silver coinage and minting it afresh, intensifying the deflationary environment as the money supply contracted severely and interest rates rose.[31] Bank notes traded at large discounts (in other words they were worth less than the amount appearing on them) and the credit markets came to a standstill. There was a run on the Bank of England in May 1696, and suspension of payment. Scotland was not immune from these events. The agricultural economy fell into crisis with a bad harvest in 1695, pushing up the price of grain and requiring imports. The most prevalent symptom of this economic malaise was an intense scarcity of money in Scotland, England, and throughout Europe. Interest rates rose substantially, with the Scottish government being offered rates as

---

[30]   RBS, D/1/2, f11.

[31]   Scott, *Constitution and Finance*, i, 350.

high as 25 per cent in 1696–7.[32] The scarcity of money in England and
the high rates there were a problem for Scots who sourced credit in
the London market.

This monetary catastrophe was partly the result of the strains of
financing the Nine Years War, which was fought at massive cost, and
partly the downside of the boom of the early 1690s. The Scottish context was greatly worsened by the collapse of the agricultural economy
and the drain of cash from the country to buy ships, provisions and
goods for the Company of Scotland.[33]

The exalted reputation of William Paterson was another casualty
of the Smyth affair. Paterson had been the darling of the Company
and nation, but was responsible for Smyth's involvement, choosing him
as the recipient of the cash he had been entrusted with. The directors
were obviously exasperated by what had happened and the council
general ordered an investigation into Paterson's role in the scandal,
led by the highly respected Mr William Dunlop, Principal of Glasgow
University, and the director Mr Robert Blackwood.[34] The report they
produced was something of a whitewash: 'after serious and long reasoning, We cannot find the least ground to think that Mr Paterson had
any design to cheat or defraud the Company'. A series of arguments
were provided for Paterson's innocence, including the claim that if he
had intended to cheat the Company he could have absconded with the
full £25,000, or taken an opportunity to escape while on the
Continent. There was also the testament of Gleneagles and Erskine
that he was very 'surpriz'd and afflicted when he heard of the disappointment and how earnest and careful he was to get ditto Smyth
to make a discovery of his effects, to the end the Company might be
secured therein'.

The report did accuse Paterson of an 'easy credulity and folly' and of
being 'the instrument of conveying that trust upon Smyth who mis-used
the same to the Company's and said Paterson's manifest prejudice'.[35]
The same criticism should have been made of the court of directors.
The investigation did not consider the key question of why so much

[32] NAS, GD 158/964, 96, 303.

[33] Some historians have seen the whole period from 1680 to 1720 as one of
      severe monetary difficulties. See K.N. Chaudhuri, *The Trading World of
      Asia and the English East India Company 1660–1760* (Cambridge, 1978),
      455.

[34] NLS, Adv MS 83.8.7, f148–9.

[35] *Ibid.*, f148.

of the capital was entrusted to one individual. The report sanctioned Paterson's participation in the first expedition to the isthmus, because of his knowledge of overseas colonies and his considerable reputation in 'several places of America'. Paterson agreed to travel to Darien as a way of restoring his tarnished reputation.

Official exclusion of Smyth from the court of directors did not come until later. A representation was made to the court on 8 March 1698:

> James Smyth merchant in London had been formerly chosen a Director of this Company, but it being now made manifest that he had fraudulently embezel'd and misapplied a considerable sum of the Company's money, it was fitt he should not only be prosecuted to the outmost for the same; but also turn'd out of the number of Directors with as great a mark of disgrace as can be.

The motion was agreed as 'highly reasonable' and the directors resolved to continue to prosecute Smyth for recovery of debt and for his 'villanous violation of the trust reposed in him.' He was not only expelled from the court, but also declared forever incapable of being in any way employed directly or indirectly in the Company's service.[36] Paterson himself remained a director until 1703, when he was finally voted off the court, but he attended only a handful of meetings after his return to Edinburgh from the Continent in 1697, and his hands-on role in the management came to an end, although paradoxically the directors decided to pursue his visionary plan for a colony in Darien.[37] His relationship with Smyth was a personal disaster.

In October 1698 Gleneagles referred to Smyth as 'the greatest vilan and most notorious lyer in Nature'.[38] The history of Smyth's involvement with the Company ended in dramatic fashion. Business opportunities were now limited for him in London so, perhaps planning another change of identity, he attempted to flee to the Continent with his wife and children, but he was arrested at Dover and taken back to prison in London.[39] In December 1698 he escaped from the

---

[36]   RBS, D/1/1, 406–7.

[37]   RBS, D/1/3, 4 May 1703. Prebble wrongly states that Paterson was excluded from the court after the investigation. Prebble, *Darien*, 90.

[38]   NLS, Adv MS 83.7.4, f68.

[39]   Forrester, *Man who saw the Future*, 178–9.

King's Bench prison and fled the country.[40] According to Herries his destination was Carolina.[41] At this point the talented Mr Smyth disappeared from the history of the Company of Scotland, but he later re-emerged to play a role in other historical events.

What was the total financial loss to the Company? There are a number of accounts dealing with the losses from the Smyth affair in the vast array of ledgers in the National Library of Scotland. In the *Balance of the General Trading Ledger* the total loss is recorded as £9,268. Other accounts provide figures of £8,169, £9,268 and £12,696. Smyth himself stated in May 1697 that he owed the Company £10,335. Figures sent to Hugh Fraser in London in December 1699 put the balance at £10,821, while Walter Herries thought that Smyth had embezzled £8,500. The report by Dunlop and Blackwood in 1698 put the total at £8,285, although it might be expected that an official investigation would tend to minimise the size of the loss to avoid further embarrassment.[42] Late 17th century accountancy was not an exact science. In conclusion it can be said with certainty that at least £8,300, or about £830,000 today, was lost, and perhaps more. The main point is that a very significant sum, equivalent to about 10 per cent of the entire capital at the end of 1696, simply disappeared.[43] It was no wonder that the directors tried to keep this quiet. According to their critic, Walter Herries, they 'bit their Lips, but endeavour'd to keep it hush for some time, that the World might not perceive how they were bubbl'd'.[44]

Men such as Smyth are often spewed out during the bust phase of the business cycle. They get away with juggling liabilities in an environment of rising asset prices and economic confidence. When the cycle turns and prices fall, credit is much more difficult to secure and they are unable to pay their debts. The hole in Smyth's finances was

---

[40]   RBS, D/1/2, 16 December 1698.

[41]   Herries, *Defence*, 12.

[42]   NLS, Adv MS 83.3.7, f22, 83.8.7, f150, 153–4, 83.7.9, f85–6, f173–4. This sum included an additional £1,250 of interest payments, 83.7.8, f213, 83.8.4, f217–18, 83.8.7, f148–9, Herries, *Defence*, 11.

[43]   Forrester argues that £3,000 of the loss can be explained by currency movements during the crisis of 1696-7, but a number of directors were merchants experienced in European trade and it seems unlikely that they would not have drawn attention to such an obvious reason. Forrester, *Man who saw the Future*, 171.

[44]   Herries, *Defence*, 11.

large and cash provided by Scottish investors briefly plugged some of the gap. Smyth was a slippery character at ease in a world of multiple identities and his linguistic skills enabled him to change his name and move from bankruptcy to bankruptcy. Not enough questions were asked by Paterson and the directors about the talented Mr Smyth/ Schmitten/Le Serrurier. Such questions never are during periods of excessive optimism.

CHAPTER TEN

Assets

Fifty Thousand Pounds, which you squander'd away on those Six Hulks you built at Amsterdam and Hamburgh, purely to make a Noise there of your Proceedings.

WALTER HERRIES[1]

To what ends is there so great naval preparation design'd to put the Company upon spending so much of their Stock so foolishly ... were it not more prudent and advisable to fraught and hire ships for the first expedition.

ROBERT DOUGLAS[2]

They are about 1200 good men, and 60 pretty officers, and seven Counsellers who have the government, They wer very hearty, and very well provyded with all necessarys, as ever any equipement of this kind that went out of Europe, God prosper them, and find them a happy landing.

LORD BASIL HAMILTON[3]

THE FUNCTION OF A joint-stock company is to raise capital and invest it in assets which provide a financial return for shareholders. In the summer of 1696 the Company of Scotland was awash with cash. The expectations of investors had been heightened by the ebullient capital raising and there was pressure on the directors to spend the money they controlled. Over the following years the majority of the cash was allocated to purchase ships, cargoes and provisions for the colonial expedition to Darien.

Ships

Ships were naturally a key asset of an overseas trading company.[4] In

---

[1]   Herries, *Defence*, epistle dedicatory.

[2]   NLS, Adv MS 83.7.4, f25.

[3]   NAS, GD 406/1/9062.

[4]   Davies, *Royal African Company*, 185–208.

the 16th century and down to the mid-17th century Scots had a considerable reputation as shipbuilders, but the industry declined in the second half of the 17th century, and by the 1690s only a small proportion of vessels sailed by Scottish merchants were built at home.[5] As a result the Company could not turn to domestic shipbuilders to construct the large ships required for long-distance voyages to Asia, Africa and the Caribbean. In late 1695, when the directors in England investigated fitting out ships for the East Indies, there were no plans to build any new vessels, and it seems they hoped to freight shipping assets from London merchant syndicates. But in January 1696 the EIC petitioned the Commons about ships refitting in the Thames for the Scottish Company and the House of Lords threatened legislation prohibiting English shipbuilders from building ships for the Company or overseeing construction work in Scotland.[6]

Denied access to the English shipping industry, the Company was forced to look to the major European shipping centres of Amsterdam and Hamburg. On 23 June 1696 the Glasgow merchant James Gibson and Edinburgh merchant Alexander Stevenson were appointed to travel to the Continent and purchase, or build, five or six ships of about 600 tons 'fit for voyages to the East-Indies'. Walter Herries provided mocking descriptions of the two men sent on this mission, highlighting their staunch Presbyterian affiliations. Stevenson, who had been kirk treasurer of Edinburgh, was a 'zealous and Long-grace Sayer' and Captain James Gibson a 'Malignant of Glasco'.[7] They were also to investigate the acquisition of three or four lesser ships of 200 to 400 tons.[8] The directors had decided to buy or construct a substantial fleet of up to ten vessels.

In Amsterdam Gibson purchased the *St Francis*, a three year old ship with 44 guns, which was renamed the *Union* (and later the *Unicorn*), and arranged for the construction of a vessel with a 135 foot keel, which was to become the Company's most expensive asset, the *Rising Sun*.[9] In Hamburg Stevenson organised the construction of four new vessels. In late September Rycaut noted that 'the building of ships goes briskly forward and their Commissary, or overseer of their

---

5   Smout, *Scottish Trade*, 47.

6   BL, B/41, 84, JHL, XV, 618.

7   Herries, *Defence*, 9.

8   RBS, D/2, f3.

9   NLS, MS 1914, f43.

workmen, seems to be an active and a cunning person'. Stevenson, however, proved a difficult character, quarrelling with the master-builder and the Company's factors, the Stratfords, who were shocked by the 'indecency' of his language.[10] Nevertheless, the directors who were in Hamburg attempting to raise capital were impressed by the construction activity. Erskine and Paterson wrote confidently that the ships were 'to be the best that ever was built here and perhaps the Cheapest that has been built in Europe'.[11]

On 10 November Stevenson informed the directors that he expected two of the ships to be launched within a month if the weather held.[12] But the winter of 1696/7 was severe and by January there were significant delays in construction. In February he did not think that two ships would be finished before August.[13] As a result the directors instructed the builders to concentrate their efforts on the two closest to completion so they could be finished as soon as possible, and at last in early March two vessels were launched and named the *Caledonia* and the *Instauration*.[14] The *Caledonia* was a large ship of 600 tons burden with 56 great guns, and the *Instauration* 350 tons.[15] The two remaining vessels lay unfinished on the stocks, but were named the *Lyon* and the *Thistle*.

The capital spent on shipping assets represented the largest single component of Company expenditure. Despite assurances from the Stratfords and the directors on the Continent that the ships were good value, very large sums were lavished on these vessels. The costs of constructing and fitting out the three large ships that sailed on the first expedition, the *St Andrew*, the *Caledonia* and the *Unicorn*, were £11,574, £10,715 and £8,687 respectively. The flagship on the second expedition, the 450 ton *Rising Sun*, cost the vast sum of £14,946.[16] This was a massive amount to spend on a merchantman. The English 800 ton *Charles the Second*, which cost £15,680 in 1683, was prob-

---

[10]   *Ibid.*, 89.

[11]   *Ibid.*, f58–9.

[12]   *Ibid.*, 62.

[13]   *Ibid.*, f42, f44–5.

[14]   *Ibid*, f57–8, *Darien Shipping Papers*, 17.

[15]   *Ibid.*, 131, E.J. Graham, *A Maritime History of Scotland, 1650–1790* (East Linton, 2002), 86.

[16]   NLS, Adv MS 83.3.7, E. J. Graham, 'In Defence of the Scottish Maritime Interest, 1681–1713,' *SHR*, 71, (1992), 102.

ably the largest merchant ship built in England in the whole 17th century.[17] The sums spent were substantial when compared with other contemporary joint-stock companies. The EIC bought shares in ships that were owned by other merchants. For example, in the years 1695 and 1696 a stake in the *Northam* was purchased for £2,000, 50 per cent of the *Stepney Friget* for £1,200, and 50 per cent of the *East India Merchant* for £828.[18] The Royal African Company, in contrast, owned only a few of its ships and hired the rest.[19] When it did buy vessels it spent considerably smaller amounts than the Company of Scotland: £450 for a 90 ton ship in 1699 and £500, £487 and £475 for three ships of 100 tons in 1700. Company of Scotland expenditure on shipping assets was therefore far above that of their principal competitors.

This profligacy may reflect the inadequacies of Scottish naval power in the late 17th century, as the Scottish Navy composed only three ships in 1696 and the directors believed that the expedition required a heavily armed fleet to protect their settlement from Spanish attacks.[20] But there was possibly another reason. In the summer of 1696 the Company was flush with capital. When capital is very plentiful it is often poorly allocated. It was suggested by contemporaries that the directors hoped to pay for the ships with cash raised abroad and that building expensive vessels was aimed at impressing potential investors.[21] In other words, in order to persuade investors that the shares were a worthwhile investment, an expensive fleet was constructed, but in order to pay for the impressive fleet, foreign investors were required. This was a very high risk circular strategy and may explain the intense anger of the directors when the international roadshow failed to deliver a penny. The capital raised in Scotland would now be soaked up paying for assets in Amsterdam and Hamburg.

In September 1696 the London Scottish merchant Robert Douglas

---

[17]   R. Davis, *The Rise of the English Shipping Industry in the Seventeenth and Eighteenth Centuries*, (London, 1962), 87.

[18]   BL, B/41, 74, 78, 103.

[19]   Davies, *Royal African Company*, 194–7. They were hired at rates between £5 10s and £6 per ton for a return voyage in peacetime and £12 to £13 10s during periods of war.

[20]   Graham, 'Scottish Maritime Interest,' 100, 103.

[21]   *Darien Shipping Papers*, 18–19.

provided some sober advice: 'To what ends is there so great naval preparation design'd to put the Company upon spending so much of their Stock so foolishly ... were it not more prudent and advisable to fraught and hire ships for the first expedition'.[22] A fleet could indeed have been sent to Darien at a much lower cost. This was evident from sums spent on shipping assets later in the Company's history. The total cost of four large ships ordered in 1696 (*Caledonia*, *Rising Sun*, *St Andrew* and *Unicorn*) was £47,435, while four ships purchased in later years (*Olive Branch*, *Dispatch*, *Speedy Return* and *Hope*) totalled only £6,624, or 14 per cent of the 1696 amount (see Appendix 9).

Cargoes

The cargoes carried by the fleet were the second major expenditure. The goods taken on the expedition would hopefully kick-start the economy of the colony and provide a profit for the Company. They were also assets which could, if necessary, be liquidated to purchase further provisions. Walter Herrries' mocking inventory has echoed through the historiography of Darien:

> Scotch Cloath 8000 peices white, ditto Brown 4 or 5000. ditto dyed and strypt 2000 Sterling Searges 8000 Ells, Mens and Womens Shoes 5 or 6000 pair, Slippers about 1500 pair, Mens Course Stockins 4000 pair, Womens ditto 2000 pair, Scotch Hats a great quantity, English Bibles 1500, Perewigs 4000. some Long, some short, Campaigns, Spanish Bobs and Natural ones; and truly they were all Natural, for being made of Highlanders Hair, which is Blanch'd, with the Rain and Sun, when they came to be open'd in the West-Indies, they lookt like so many of Samsons Fireships that he sent amongst the Philistines, and could be of no use to the Collony, if it were not to mix with their Lyme when they Plaster'd the Walls of their Houses. This was all the Merchandable Cargoe, save about 500l. worth of Hamburgh Linnen and Holland, and to the same value of little Trincums bought in Holland for a Guinea or Indian Trade, and about 2 or 3 Hoggsheads of Beezwax.[23]

[22]   NLS, Adv MS 83.7.4, f25.

[23]   Herries, *Defence*, 22.

Herries described this as a 'ridiculous cargo' and the image of vessels carrying useless wigs and bibles has proved a powerful one, influencing historians down to the present day.[24]

Analysis of the cargo inventories of the first expedition, however, shows that the *Caledonia* carried only ninety-six periwigs, making up 1 per cent of the value of the cargo. Religious literature (bibles, new testaments, confessions of faith and catechisms) only represented 0.4 per cent of the value.[25] On the *Unicorn* there were also 96 periwigs or 0.8 per cent of the cargo and religious literature composed only 0.3 per cent.[26] The *St Andrew* carried only 27 periwigs, or 0.4 per cent of the cargo, and bibles worth 0.4 per cent.[27] In total the fleet carried only 219 periwigs, rather than the 4,000 noted by Herries.[28] Bibles and wigs were therefore an insignificant part of the cargoes and irrelevant in financial terms. They were of course manna for a propagandist like Herries.

Textiles were the most common item carried to Darien, reflecting the nature of the Scottish manufacturing economy at the time. Linen production had grown considerably in the course of the 17th century, driven by the English market, and it was now one of Scotland's principal exports.[29] About 25 per cent of the goods carried on the *St Andrew* by value (£1,338) were different types of textile including calico, 'harn wraper,' blue linen, brown linen, Montrose linen, diaper, fine linen, muslin, serge and Yorkshire cloth. The first expedition carried 41,079 ells of green linen, 11,375 ells of fine linen, 2,241 ells of harn, 1,569 ells of 'masquerade and druggett,' and 439 ells of hodden gray.[30] Herries underestimated the quantity of textiles taken by the ships.

---

[24] *Ibid.*, 150. See for example N. Davidson, *Discovering the Scottish Revolution 1692–1746* (London, 2003), 99, and *Scotland: A History*, ed. J. Wormald (Oxford, 2005), 167.

[25] £57 of periwigs and £20 of religious literature out of a total cargo of £5,678, NLS, Adv MS 83.5.9, 19–33, Adv MS 83.6.6, f172.

[26] £54 of periwigs and £20 of religious literature out of a total cargo of £7,117, NLS, Adv MS 83.5.8, f54, f56, 83.5.9, 34–53.

[27] £19 of periwigs and £21 of religious literature out of a total cargo of £5,424, NLS, Adv MS 83.5.8, f127, f129, Adv MS 83.5.9, 1–18.

[28] Prebble correctly states that Herries grossly exaggerated the number of wigs. Prebble, *Darien*, 97.

[29] Smout, *Scottish Trade*, 233–4.

[30] RBS, Cargo Book, D/5, f18, 29, 31. An ell was equivalent to 3 1/12 feet.

The other trading goods carried in the holds were combs, hats, shoes, and slippers. The *St Andrew*, for example, carried £360 of shoes and pumps for men and women, £81 of combs, £80 of hats, and £25 of tobacco pipes.[31] The directors expected that these items, including the wigs and bibles, would be sold in the colonial markets of America, or perhaps in the Spanish empire as contraband.

The rest of the cargo included multifarious utensils required for the construction and protection of the colony such as axes, nails, locks, knives, tools, saws, shot, and guns. Such items made up about 57 per cent of the value of the cargo on the *St Andrew*. There were £903 of guns and pistols, £520 of powder, and £498 of iron work (hoops, ladles, axes, knives, and chain hammers).[32]

The first expedition carried in total £18,921 of goods to Darien.[33] This was a very considerable quantity of assets but a substantial proportion of the items were for construction and defence of the colony and only about £8,000 available for immediate sale.[34] About 8 per cent of the £100,000 provided by the first call on the shareholders was spent on assets that might actually produce a financial return.

Provisions

There was also substantial expenditure on provisioning the expedition, organised by the committee 'for equipping ships', which met for the first time on 30 November 1697.[35] Securing items such as beef, pork, oats, bear (barley), butter, cheese, raisons, suet, live pigs and poultry, fresh water, and wheat for flour and 'bisket', was far from easy, as the Scottish agricultural economy was in severe difficulties and prices of commodities at very high levels. Indeed provisioning occurred at the worst possible time as prices in 1698 were at their highest in decades. For example the price of oats rose from £4 6s 8d Scots in 1694 to £10 Scots in 1698 (+230 per cent), before dropping to £8 Scots in 1699. Edinburgh wheat prices rose from £7 Scots in 1692 to peak at £17

---

[31]   NLS, Adv MS 83.5.8, f126-134.

[32]   *Ibid.*, f125, f130, 83.5.9, 18. Items for colonial construction made up 57 per cent of the cargo of the *Unicorn* and 59 per cent of the *Caledonia*.

[33]   The *Unicorn* (£7,117), the *Caledonia* (£5,678), the *St Andrew* (£5,424), the *Endeavour* (£403) and the *Dolphin* (£299), NLS, Adv MS 83.3.7, f11.

[34]   NLS, Adv MS 83.5.9.

[35]   NLS, Adv MS 83.7.2, f19, f36.

Scots in 1698 (+245 per cent), before falling to £14 Scots in 1699, while Edinburgh peas and beans rose from £4 Scots in 1692 to £13 Scots in 1698 (+325 per cent).[36] In total, £6,547 was spent on provisioning the first expedition; about £5 10s per man.[37] This included £1,953 of wheat, £1,773 of ships biscuit, £684 of stock-fish, £593 of bear, £529 of salted beef, £420 of pork, £309 of butter, and smaller amounts of currants, raisons, hops, salt, and cheese. The agricultural price environment meant that the Company was able to purchase about half the amount of provisions that the same quantity of money would have provided a few years before.

There does appear to have been reasonably careful supervision of the provisioning process. On 14 April the 'committee in constant waiting' reported it had examined the condition of the beef, pork and other provisions and found them in 'extraordinary good case and well cur'd'.[38] On 21 June the directors ordered all the ships' commanders to produce inventories of provisions, stores and goods, and before they set sail the pursers provided accounts of provisions to be laid before the directors.[39] On 4 July a problem with brackish water on the *St Andrew* was identified and fresh water ordered to be taken on board.[40] After the fleet sailed, director Robert Blackwood reported that he had been on board the ships with the clerks and accountants and that invoices had been produced for all ships except the *Unicorn* as accountant John Dickson had left the receipts at Leith.[41]

Many tradesmen and merchants benefited from contracts to secure goods and provisions for the Company and a number of these merchants were directors. Mr Robert Blackwood purchased £162 of goods, Robert Watson £1,061, William Arbuckle £2,200, William Wooddrop £2,213 and George Clark £2,629.[42] The director who

---

[36]   Gibson and Smout, *Prices, Food and Wages*, 86, 103, 110.

[37]   Assuming that 1,200 men travelled on the first expedition. Detailed invoices have not survived but the amount spent on provisions can be calculated from the ledger of the Committee of Improvements. There are inventories for the second expedition and the relief ships, NLS, Darien Papers, Adv MS 83.4.5.

[38]   RBS, D/3, 112.

[39]   RBS, D/1/1, 483, 501–2.

[40]   *Ibid.*, 540.

[41]   RBS, D/1/2, 20 July 1698.

[42]   RBS, D/1/1, 438, NLS, Adv MS 83.3.6, f5, f14, f35, f63.

spent the largest amount was James Balfour, who purchased goods worth £8,412. It is unclear how much profit was made on these transactions, although it may have been in a range between 10 per cent and 20 per cent.[43] If Balfour made a 20 per cent margin he would have made a profit of £1,402, more than compensating him for his cash investment of £850 in the Company.[44] The perception that Balfour had feathered his own nest may have been behind a threat by the Edinburgh mob to pull down his house in October 1699.[45]

The Dutch factors jointly managed £32,929 of Company expenditure, and Isaac Cossart and Alexander Henderson £8,805 and £3,061 individually.[46] In total £44,795 was spent by these men, representing about 29 per cent of the entire capital.[47] This of course wasn't money going into their pockets as they earned 0.5 per cent on bill transactions and 2 per cent on items relating to the construction and fitting out of the ships.[48] They also supplied goods themselves and presumably made a profit on these; Henry Wylenbrock provided 788 guilders of gunpowder, and Alexander Henderson 89 guilders of brandy, for the *Rising Sun*.[49] In Hamburg the Stratfords oversaw expenditure of £9,239.[50] A large proportion of the Company's capital, about 35 per cent in total, was therefore spent on the Continent, and many Dutch and German merchants and craftsmen were prime beneficiaries of the cash provided by Scottish investors, although some Scottish merchants who were members of the Scottish community in Amsterdam also benefited.[51]

---

[43] *Ibid.*, 509. The directors ordered the committee in constant waiting to make sure that all the prices of goods in Company invoices for the expedition were advanced by 20 per cent 'in consideration of Extraordinary expenses, and as being the practice of all merchants.'

[44] Balfour subscribed £2,000 and the cash calls amounted to £850.

[45] NAS, GD 158/965, 147. Marchmont mistakenly described Balfour as a Jacobite.

[46] NLS, Adv MS 83.3.6, f13, f17.

[47] During its existence the Company raised £153,448 5s 4 2/3d from a subscribed capital of £400,000.

[48] NLS, Adv MS 83.7.9, f1–2, f5–6.

[49] *Ibid.*, f17–18.

[50] NLS, Adv MS 83.3.6, f20.

[51] D. Watt, 'The Dutch and the Company of Scotland trading to Africa and the Indies,' *Dutch Crossing*, 29, (2005), 130.

Human Capital

The directors finally decided to proceed with Paterson's plan for a colony at Darien in October 1697 and thereafter all energy was directed to preparing the fleet and arranging the employment of human capital for manning the ships and establishing the colony. On 26 November the council general resolved that the first expedition was to include three large ships, two tenders and 900 sea and land men.[52] They had originally considered sending six large ships on the first colonial expedition, but lack of capital forced them to send only three.[53] There was not yet enough cash to complete the construction of the *Rising Sun*, *Lyon* and *Thistle*.

By November the *Caledonia* and the *Instauration* had arrived in the Firth of Forth.[54] They were joined by the *Union* and two tenders, the *Dolphin* and the *Endeavour*. The *Dolphin* was a snow of two masts with ten guns which had originally been a French prize called the *Royal Louis* and was bought in Amsterdam by James Gibson. The *Endeavour* was a pink purchased in Newcastle by Dr Munro.[55] In a patriotic gesture on St Andrew's Day (30 November) the *Instauration* was renamed the *St Andrew*.[56]

The directors resolved that the government of the colony was to be vested in the authority of a council of seven persons of equal power, rather than in one individual as governor, and this was approved by the council general.[57] The seven men appointed were Major James Cunningham of Eickett, 'a Pillar of the Kirk'; James Montgomery, grandson of the Earl of Eglinton, who had been an ensign in the Scots Guards; the lawyer Daniel MacKay; Captain Robert Pennecuik, who had served in the English Navy; Captain William Veitch, a Flanders veteran; the Scots Hamburg merchant Robert Jolly, described by Herries as a 'jolly Scotch over-grown Hamburger'; and Robert Pincarton, 'a good down right, rough spun Tar', who had served as boatswain with Sir William Phips on the salvage mission that returned

---

[52] RBS, D/3, 58.

[53] NLS, MS 1914, 60–1, f54–5.

[54] RBS, D/1/1, 357–8.

[55] Prebble, *Darien*, 96, Insh, *Company of Scotland*, 104. The costs of the *Dolphin* and *Endeavour* were £921 and £592 respectively.

[56] RBS, D/1/1, 365.

[57] RBS, D/1/1, 374, D/3, 63.

with a vast quantity of treasure from a Spanish wreck north of Hispaniola in 1687.[58] Herries claimed that Cunningham, Veitch and Pennecuik obtained their positions because of their Presbyterian credentials, and mockingly described them all as 'the seven wise men, who were to divide Mexico and Peru amongst them'.[59]

Under the councillors in the government of the colony was a military establishment of 12 captains as overseers, 24 lieutenants as assistants and 22 ensigns as under-assistants.[60] As an 'encouragement' the directors decided to provide these men with free shares in the Company's stock; each councillor received £400, each overseer £150, each assistant £100, and each deputy assistant £50.[61]

The souls of the colonists were not forgotten. Three ministers were to be sent with the fleet, each receiving an inducement of £10 for 'buying books or other ways as they shall think fitt' and a salary of £120 per annum payable by the colony.[62] Surprisingly there was reluctance among ministers to join the venture, perhaps reflecting the experience of exile of many Presbyterians in the 1680s and the short supply of ministers in the 1690s. It was hoped that the services of Alexander Shields, author of the 742 page Presbyterian classic *Hind Let Loose*, would be secured, and director Hugh Cunningham and Captain William Veitch were sent to St Andrews to persuade him.[63] Shields declined the Company's offer. The two other candidates, Mr Adam Scott and Mr Thomas James, also proved difficult to convince. Lord Ruthven and Scott of Thirlestane visited Adam Scott and persuaded him that his skills were needed, and the presbytery of Edinburgh dispatched a contingent of worthies to convince James, with further pressure being applied by director Hugh Cunningham in early July. Under this barrage he finally relented and declared that he

---

58 *Ibid.*, 97, 114. Prebble provides more detailed descriptions of these men, Prebble, *Darien*, 109–112, Herries, *Defence*, 34–6. The Spanish plate ship *Concepción* was shipwrecked off the north coast of Hispaniola in 1641, P. Earle, *The Wreck of the Almirata: Sir William Phips and the search for the Hispaniola Treasure* (London, 1979).

59 Herries, *Defence*, 36.

60 Prebble, *Darien*, 100, NLS, Adv MS 83.2.2 lists 22 ensigns rather than 24.

61 RBS, D/1/1, 465.

62 *Ibid.*, 424–5.

63 *A Hind let Loose, or an Historical Representation of the Testimonies, of the Church of Scotland* (1687).

was willing to accompany the fleet 'providing that Mr Paterson do go, as believing him to be a propagator of virtue and discourager of vice'. A further inducement of £100 of free shares was provided to both ministers, but only these two were recruited for the first expedition.[64]

In April the directors were offered advice from a man who had actually been to Darien. The ship's surgeon Lionel Wafer had accompanied Dampier across the isthmus in 1680 and had injured his leg in the jungle in an explosion of gunpowder. He was forced to remain with the Tule Indians, the indigenous people of the isthmus; his time spent among them provided detailed information which formed the basis of *A New Description of the Isthmus of Darien*, published in 1699.[65] According to Herries, Wafer offered to provide the Company with details about Darien for the large sum of £750, to be paid over two years, with an upfront fee of £50, and to delay publication of his book for 20 guineas more.[66] He travelled to Scotland secretly under the name of Brown but was stopped by the secret committee of the Company at Haddington and taken to Fletcher of Saltoun's house so that he would not be seen in Edinburgh by Paterson or Lodge, who 'at this time were kept in the Dark as to the Companies Resolutions'. There he was interviewed over two or three days and 'unbossom'd himself freely' about Darien, offering to lead the Scots to a treasure of Nicaragua wood, and informing them that 300 men might cut down enough timber in six months to cover the whole cost of the expedition. But once the directors had word of the location of the valuable timber they had no further need for him. He was given 20 guineas for his trouble and escorted from Edinburgh by Walter Herries himself, who was told his 'Mournful story' on the road.[67] At this time Wafer was something of a celebrity because of the publication of Dampier's book in 1697. George Home noted in his diary on 2 July that there was word from London that Wafer was missing and that it was rumoured he had come to Scotland and engaged himself with the Company. There were also stories that Dampier was setting out for the Caribbean to prevent the Scots taking possession of the isthmus.[68]

---

64   RBS, D/1/1, 460–1, 464, 514, 518, 522, 527, 537, 558. The worthies were Mr George Hamilton, Mr David Blair and 'lay elder' Captain Coutts.
65   D. and M. Preston, *Pirate of Exquisite Mind*, 86–7.
66   Herries, *Defence*, 39.
67   Ibid., 40–3.
68   NAS, GD 1/891/2, 2 July 1698.

The official Company response is found in the minute book of the directors. On 19 April a letter from Baillie of Jerviswood was read to the court, containing proposals made by Wafer to serve the Company. The directors resolved unanimously not to employ him.[69] Wafer's association with the Company remains mysterious, especially as the principal source for the arrival of Mr Brown is Walter Herries, and the veracity of his account cannot be substantiated by other pieces of evidence. Wafer may have simply come north, presented his case, and been rejected. The Company was unlikely to pay such a large amount of cash to one man given it was having problems financing the expedition to the isthmus; there were also his problematic buccaneering associations.

The Scots were in contact with another group of pirates according to Mr Orth, Sir Paul Rycaut's secretary, who informed the English government that a majority of Henry Avery's crew were employed on Company ships that sailed from Hamburg to Scotland in September 1697. Avery had seized the *Gang-i-Sawai* with 600 pilgrims from Mecca and unleashed an orgy of butchery, rape and torture which reputedly earned half a million pounds in gold, silver and diamonds.[70] He disbanded his crew at New Providence in the Bahamas and disappeared into legend. The Scots were now, apparently, trying to tap into the extensive seafaring knowledge of those who had sailed with him. Another letter from Orth informed the English government that Avery's pilot was to be employed by the Company and was in Edinburgh.[71] It seems unlikely there was any truth in these stories. Avery's crew were probably too rich to necessitate employment with the Company.[72] The association with piracy, however, was a way of tarnishing the reputation of the Scots and making it easier for the English government to justify action against them.

The Company continued to make other appointments. Alexander Hamilton became chief accountant and keeper of the merchandise of the colony and Mr Benjamin Spence, a Jew recruited in Amsterdam, was engaged as secretary of Spanish and Portuguese. He could speak, read, and write three or four other languages.[73] Archibald MacKinlay,

---

[69]   RBS, D/1/1, 447.

[70]   E.J. Graham, *Seawolves: Pirates and the Scots* (Edinburgh, 2005), 133–6.

[71]   *Darien Shipping Papers*, 39, 40–1.

[72]   Graham, *Seawolves*, 121.

[73]   RBS, D/1/1, 461–2, 558, Gallup-Diaz, *Door of the Seas*, 128.

John Clark and John Scott became pursers of the three main ships; Archibald Stewart and Andrew Livingston surgeons of the tenders after being examined in anatomy, surgery and medicine; Hugh Ross one of the chief clerks of the colony, following a testimonial from director Hugh Dalrymple, now President of the Court of Session. Ross had served his father, the famous jurist Lord Stair, for several years.[74]

By 3 June the fleet was ready in the 'River' of Leith and financial incentives were provided to boost confidence ahead of the long voyage. To aid recruitment, the seamen received one month's wages in advance, two months' more before departure, and one month in six was to be paid to their attorneys during their absence. This suggests that skilled seamen were in short supply, although there were plenty of others who wanted to sail as planters or gentleman volunteers. Cash advances were also made to each overseer (£12), assistant (£8), and deputy assistant (£6), which came to the large sum of £480, and on 4 July £8,200 of free shares were transferred to the councillors and military establishment. Two days later the directors specified the hierarchy of command for the voyage. Captain Robert Pennecuik, commander of the *St Andrew*, was to be commodore of the fleet, followed by Captain Robert Pincarton of the *Union* and Captain Robert Drummond of the *Caledonia*.[75] The two tenders, the *Dolphin* and the *Endeavour*, were captained by Thomas Fullarton and John Malloch, who had both served in the English Navy.[76] On 30 June, between 11 and 12 in the morning, the fleet was inspected by the directors.[77]

Last-minute preparations continued. Roderick MacKenzie received a warrant from the Lord Lyon's office for a coat of arms, which was illuminated by the herald painter and engraved on a great seal and signet for use by the colony.[78] On Captain Pincarton's request the *Union* was renamed the *Unicorn*. The Kirk was asked to intervene on the Company's behalf: 'to appoint prayers in such manner as they shall think fitt for a fair wind and success to the said intended expedition (as being a National concern)'.[79]

Further appointments were made in the last days before departure. Andrew Scott, brother of director Sir Patrick Scott of Ancrum, was

74 RBS, D/1/1, 482, 494, 496.

75 *Ibid*, 478, 480, 483, 488, 535, 544–5.

76 Prebble, *Darien*, 115.

77 RBS, D/1/1, 498, 516–17.

78 *Ibid*., 469.

79 *Ibid*., 522.

recommended to the Council of the colony. Mr John MacKay, an 'absolute master of the several species of mathematicks', was willing to go as a volunteer and was allowed to choose the ship he wanted to sail on. William Simpson was appointed printer of the colony and was ordered on board the *Unicorn* to examine the Company's printing press. A quarter of his monthly wage of 40s was to be paid to his wife in Scotland. Other recruits included Laurence Crawford and William Young, who both had considerable experience of colonial life in America, and two men named John Balfour: Mr John Balfour, volunteer; and John Balfour, merchant and volunteer.[80]

'Fundamental Constitutions' providing rules for organising the colony were drawn up by the council general. The thirteen articles specified that the colony was to be governed by a 'Parliament or Council-General', persons of any nation were to have liberty to settle there and a register was to be kept of incomers. The Company reserved 5 per cent of all lands and grounds possessed by the colony, 5 per cent of all gold-dust, gold, silver or other metals or minerals, pearls, wrecks, ambergris, precious wood, jewels, gems or stones of value. From 1 January 1702, European, Asian and African goods imported into the colony would be charged a duty of 2 per cent if in Scottish ships or ships belonging to the colony, and 3 per cent if in the ships of other nations. Goods imported from American plantations by any nation would pay only 1 per cent to encourage this trade. The tariffs on exports were to be 2 per cent in Scottish ships and 4 per cent in foreign ones.[81] All public inns and drinking houses were to remain at the disposal of the colonial government.

The Company and the colony were divided into distinct legal entities. The colony would ultimately be charged by the Company for the expense of buying and fitting out the fleet, and so the cost of the colonial expedition became a £70,000 debt on the colony, to be paid back in annual instalments of £7,000 from 1 June 1698. The directors expected their settlement would quickly provide a very significant financial return. This was extremely optimistic as the £8,000 of assets would realistically only make a profit of £1,600 if a margin of 20 per cent could be achieved. There were also optimistic plans to raise more capital at the isthmus. Those who settled there were to be allowed to subscribe for shares in the Company before 1 June 1701, up to a total of £50,000, with the first quarter payable in money or goods.[82]

80 Ibid., 527, 529, 552, 558.

81 RBS, D/2, f15–18.

82 *Ibid.*, f18–21.

On 13 July a cash sum of £320 was provided as a 'stock purse' for the fleet; a liquid reserve in case of emergency. Each large ship was given £100 and the tenders £10 each. The small size of these payments reflected the Company's lack of capital. There was also a credit of £100 to buy fresh provisions in Orkney if they landed there.[83]

None of the ships or cargoes sent to Darien was insured. An insurance market did not exist in Scotland in the late 17th century, although there were developed markets in London and Amsterdam, and most overseas trading ventures by this time were insured. Indeed the Dutch factors, on orders from the directors, had insured some of the Company's goods when they were transported from Amsterdam to Hamburg in April 1697.[84] Because the destination of the expedition was supposedly secret and the establishment of a new colony a very high risk venture, insurance would have been extremely difficult to obtain anyway. Insurers in England and Holland might have found themselves under political pressure not to insure assets belonging to the Company. But this was beside the point, for there was simply not enough capital to cover the costs of insurance. If the ships or goods were damaged or destroyed there would be no compensation, although the Company might claim that under a provision in their act of parliament there was redress from the King.

The vast majority of those who sailed on the first expedition were Scots, although there were some men from other nations, including a few Englishmen. Many Dutch sailors had been employed to sail the ships back to the Firth of Forth in late 1697, but in December the Glasgow merchant William Wooddrop reported that all the Dutchmen had been paid off at Leith 'except one who was aboard and willing to go the voyage'.[85] Later, under Spanish interrogation, interpreter Benjamin Spence stated there had been six Italians and three Frenchmen on his ship, presumably international seamen.[86]

---

[83]   RBS, D/1/1, 559.

[84]   NLS, MS 1914, f81. The goods included sails, anchors and iron hoops for the ships in Hamburg. Two thirds of their value was insured for 3 per cent. In February 1697 the directors considered whether they should insure goods being sent on two ships from Bordeaux, but decided against because of the 'extravagant ensurance now demanded upon goods from France.' Unfortunately one of the ships was taken by a Spaniard of 24 guns and condemned as a prize. RBS, D/1/1, 193, 231.

[85]   NLS, Adv MS, 83.7.2, f2.

[86]   Gallup-Diaz, Door of the Seas, 128.

The fleet finally sailed from Leith on 14 July 1698. Even Herries rested his satiric pen, for a moment, to describe 'the glorious show our Ships made from the Castle-hill of Edinburgh'.[87] Sir John Dalrymple, a historian of the Company writing in the 18th century, described the scene:

> The whole city of Edinburgh poured down upon Leith, to see the colony depart, amidst the tears, and prayers, and praises of relations and friends, and of their countrymen. Many seamen and soldiers, whose services had been refused, because more had offered themselves than were needed, were found hid in the ships, and, when ordered ashore, clung to the ropes and timbers, imploring to go, without reward, with their companions.[88]

Unfortunately little contemporary evidence survives about the celebrations accompanying the glorious beginning of Scotland's imperial future. The ships carried more than the target of 900 colonists outlined by the council general the previous November. Having witnessed the scene, Lord Basil Hamilton expressed the hopes of the nation:

> They are about 1200 good men, and 60 pretty officers, and seven Counsellers who have the government, They wer very hearty, and very well provyded with all necessarys, as ever any equipement of this kind that went out of Europe, God prosper them, and find them a happy landing.'[89]

---

[87] Herries, *Defence*, 45.
[88] Dalrymple, *Memoirs*, ii, 96–7. Prebble seems to have based his grandiloquent descriptions on this source. Prebble, *Darien*, 117.
[89] NAS, GD 406/1/9062.

CHAPTER ELEVEN

Cash is King

Money may be called the Blood which circulates thro' all the Veins of the Body, and convoys Life and Vigor to every part.
JAMES DONALDSON[1]

Money has not only the character of mere money or a mere thing, but also beyond this, a certain seminal character of something profitable, which we commonly call capital.
SAN BERNARDINO OF SIENA (1380–1444)[2]

IT IS A CLICHÉ OF modern finance that 'cash is king'; that the management of cash is vital to success or failure in any business venture. This is true today and it was true in the late 17th century. 'We are blunt marchants unless we be in cash' commented a Scottish merchant in 1686.[3] The cash books of the Company of Scotland survive in the National Library of Scotland and are an untapped source for examining the management of capital by the Company.[4] All payments of cash to the Company and by the Company are itemised and allow a 'net cash position' to be calculated, an objective liquidity ratio or indicator of the Company's financial health throughout its history. High net cash is positive and low net cash negative. The change in net cash between 1696 and 1705 is shown in Figure 3.

---

[1]   James Donaldson, *The Undoubted Art of Thriving* (Edinburgh, 1700), 6.
[2]   Translated from the Latin and quoted in M.N. Rothbard, *Economic Thought before Adam Smith: An Austrian Perspective on the History of Economic Thought*, 2 vols (Aldershot, 1995), i, 85.
[3]   Smout, *Scottish Trade*, 116.
[4]   NLS, Darien Papers, Cash Book 1696–1700, Adv MS 83.5.2, Cash Book 1700–7, Adv MS 83.5.3. Rough drafts were kept by the accountants, see Adv MS 83.4.8–9, 83.5.1.

Figure 3

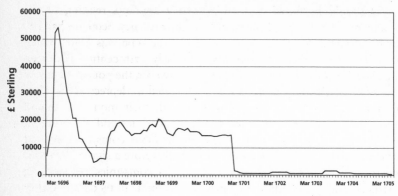

Source: NLS Adv MS 83.5.2–3.

This one chart provides a dramatic picture of the Company of Scotland's financial history. Indeed the line on the graph charts the rises and falls, the shifts between optimism and pessimism, characterising that history. No great experience of financial analysis is required to understand that the trend was very negative and the Company was not financially healthy.

Within this grim picture a number of distinct periods are discernible. There was a steep rise in cash during the first call on capital, or capital raising, to peak at just over £56,000 in July 1696. This was the zenith of the Company's fortunes in financial terms. There was then an equally precipitous decline in cash, which we might describe as a period of 'cash burn,' through the second half of 1696 and the first half of 1697, to bottom at only £4,084 in August 1697. The steepness of the fall indicates that management of cash was out of control; the Company was spending its resources at an unsustainable pace, and came very close to running out of money and destroying its credit. If this had happened the international financial community would have lost trust in the Company and the ships being built in Amsterdam and Hamburg would not have been completed. No shipping assets would have been available for a Darien expedition. From the second half of 1697 there was a moderate recovery, followed by a period of steady cash, averaging about £16,000, until a collapse between late June and

early July 1701. From this point the Company was basically moribund in financial terms and was accumulating significant liabilities
which reached over £14,000 by 1707.[5]

It should be noted that all monetary amounts relating to the
Company were in pounds sterling, a foreign currency. Scotland had her
own currency, the pound Scots, which at the time was worth much
less; the official exchange rate since the early 17th century had been
12 pound Scots to each English pound. However, the pound Scots was
regarded as a 'soft' currency which had tended to depreciate in value.
Canny Scottish merchants did not hold all their money in pound
Scots, but maintained an array of other currencies and also bullion,
which was a more reliable store of value as many coins were clipped
or debased. Capitalisation in sterling was therefore a sign of financial
security for investors. For the same reason companies in emerging
markets today raise capital and produce accounts in US dollars rather
than local currencies. The Company was faced with a further practi-
cal consideration. There was no natural buyer of large amounts of
Scottish coin. If capital had been raised in pounds Scots there would
have been significant problems changing it into other currencies to
buy ships, provisions and cargoes.

The first capital raising had been a startling success, with £400,000
pledged by August 1696. However, it must be emphasised that subscription was not the same as cash payment and many historians have
failed to grasp this point. Subscription involved signing the subscription book and was a promise, legally enforceable, to pay the various
calls for cash made by the Company. The payment of cash was a
separate event in the vast majority of cases. For example, in March
1696 £216,865 was subscribed but only £7,000 paid in cash. The first
call on shareholders was for a quarter of the amount they had subscribed – £100,000 out of £400,000 – so that a shareholder who had
subscribed £100 had to pay £25 to the Company. Payments were
accepted in coin, bullion (lumps of silver or gold), and Bank of
Scotland notes. Monthly cash payments by investors are shown in
Figure 4.

5   NLS, Adv MS 83.8.6, f205.

Figure 4

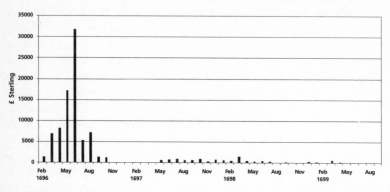

Monthly Payments from First Capital Raising 1696–1699

Source: NLS Adv MS 83.5.2.

Payments by shareholders were initially made at a healthy rate. Cash flowed into the Company over the spring and summer of 1696, peaking in June when £31,938 was paid in this one month. However, in the autumn the pace decreased and from December 1696 until May 1697 practically no cash was received. There was a slight pick up in May 1697 and then a long tail of late payments through to August 1699, three and a half years after the first payments were made. The directors found that extracting all the cash promised by subscribers was extremely difficult. Large shareholders who were reluctant to part with their money included the Campbell chief, Archibald, Earl of Argyll, who did not provide his cash until December 1698, five months after the first expedition had sailed, and another Campbell, John, Lord Glenorchy, who did not pay until March 1699; his payment coincided with news that the first expedition had successfully landed at Darien.[6] Walter Herries thought that £10,000 of the first call was not paid, but analysis of the cash books shows that late payment was initially much more significant; nearer £20,000 had not been paid by the end of 1696, representing 20 per cent of called-up capital. There was reluctance amongst a significant group of shareholders to hand over their cash.[7]

---

[6]   NLS, Adv MS 83.5.2 , 106, 124.

[7]   Prebble and Insh are misleading on this, suggesting that the first call was raised with little trouble. Prebble, *Darien*, 60, Insh, *Company of Scotland*, 67.

Herries commented that 'some great Men could not be forc'd to pay ... thinking their Countenance to the thing to be enough for their share; others were Sick and a great many Stark Dead of the Project, but most of them not able to raise their Quota'.[8] It was suggested at the time that some members of the government deliberately withheld their cash to undermine the Company.[9] But a close examination of late-payers shows that they included directors such as Lord Belhaven, Hugh Cunningham, and Sir John Swinton of that Ilk, members of the political opposition.[10] The principal reason appears to have been economic. Unfortunately, the capital raising coincided with catastrophic financial conditions in Scotland and elsewhere in Europe. Even the bluest chip of joint-stocks would have faced severe difficulties persuading investors to hand over cash. Indeed, timing could not have been worse as the Company sought to gather money at the beginning of the bust phase of the economic cycle. Sterling had collapsed in 1695 and the period 1695–7 was one of tight liquidity and monetary crisis, precipitating the English recoinage of 1696, a Scottish devaluation in the same year, very high interest rates, disruption of credit markets, and a general shortage of specie throughout Western Europe. It was the worst possible environment for persuading investors to exchange hard-earned silver or gold coins for the riskier option of shares in an overseas trading company. In Scotland the situation was worsened by an agricultural crisis precipitated by harvest failure in August 1695, which resulted in a steep rise in grain prices, draining liquidity. The harvest in 1696 was also poor and after a respite in 1697, 1698 was disastrous, causing dearth and famine in many areas of the country.[11] These years entered Scottish folk memory as King William's 'seven ill years'.

The success of the capital raising itself acted to tighten liquidity, given its size relative to the Scottish coinage. So much of the nation's coin was being handed over to the Company that the shortage throughout the country was intensified. Money was a very scarce

---

8   Herries, *Defence*, 23.

9   K. van den Steinen, 'In Search of the Antecedents of Women's Political Activism in early 18th Century Scotland: the Daughters of Anne, Duchess of Hamilton' in *Women in Scotland c.1100–c.1750*, (eds.) E. Ewan and M.M. Meikle (East Linton, 1999), 117.

10   NLS, Adv MS 83.5.2, 41–106.

11   Smout, *Scottish Trade*, 246–8.

commodity in Scotland, especially after the summer of 1696, and the
directors faced a battle with their own shareholders to convince them
to pay up. Nevertheless 80 per cent of the first call was paid relatively
quickly; testament to the confidence of the majority of subscribers.

Many attempts were made to persuade late-payers to provide the
cash they had promised and this proved a continuous headache for
the directors.[12] In July 1696 the court warned that any subscriber who
had not paid by 10 August was to have their shareholding pursued
according to the law or disposed of. But this was only the first of a
series of deadlines which proved ineffectual. Finally, in June 1697, the
directors let the law follow its course and the legal process of diligence
was instituted. Those who had not paid were 'put to the horn' and
denounced as rebels, which occasioned a pick up in payments. For
example, George Home of Kimmerghame was finally persuaded to
pay when threatened with such an eventuality in May 1698.[13]

The source of the cash provided by subscribers remains uncertain.
It has been suggested that much of it came from English moneylenders
but there is no evidence for this.[14] In the dire financial conditions of
1695-7 it seems very unlikely that any English investors would have
contemplated moving cash into a very high risk asset like the
Company of Scotland. Subscriptions probably came from a pool of
capital that had been accumulated over the previous decades as the
Scottish economy slowly recovered from the devastation of the Civil
Wars of the mid-17th century.

The cash that was paid to the Company was quickly spent. A significant amount was allocated to a business unrelated to overseas
trading. In the summer of 1696 a banking venture was launched and
between July and October the Company lent £20,025 to its own
shareholders: equivalent to 20 per cent of called-up capital, but an
even higher 24.6 per cent of actual capital at the end of October. It
appears to have been made in cash rather than notes.[15] Paterson, of
course, had some experience of banking; for a short time he was a

---

[12] Cash was still being collected from reluctant shareholders down to
      1706-7.

[13] NAS, GD 1/891/2, 24 May 1698.

[14] Jones, '"The Bold Adventurers,"' 37. The only direct evidence I have
      found is a late payment of £500 in 1699 by Lord Glenorchy in London,
      RBS, D/1/2, 2 January 1699.

[15] Shareholders borrowed up to two thirds of the amount they had handed
      over to the Company at an interest rate of 4 per cent.

director of the Bank of England, but given the deteriorating liquidity environment in Scotland in 1696, such an allocation was unwise, as it locked a significant amount of capital in a peripheral business, and this capital proved very difficult to recover.[16]

The directors soon reached the conclusion that a combination of foreign trading and banking was financially inept and loans were called back in. Repayments began in October 1696, but it proved a slow process. From August 1697 diligence had to be used to force borrowers to repay, in the same way that reluctant subscribers were being persuaded.[17] Fifty per cent of the sums lent out had not been repaid by November 1697, and it was only between December and March 1698 that the bulk of the rest was returned. By July 1699 the Company had recovered £20,147.[18] The banking venture provided a return on capital of 0.6 per cent.[19] Given the lending rate was 4 per cent, about £800 was lost as bad debt. In financial terms this was a miserable return; however, with hindsight, given that the Darien colony was a financial disaster and swallowed up every last mouthful of capital, it proved the best performing part of the Company of Scotland business portfolio, along with the investment in Edinburgh property.

Figure 5

Monthly Debt Repayments by Subscribers 1696–1699

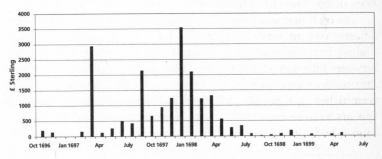

Source: NLS Adv MS 83.5.2.

---

[16] The directors had considered launching a banking business in London in November 1695. *JHC*, xi, 404.

[17] RBS, D/1/1, 294.

[18] NLS, Adv MS 83.5.2.

[19] Return = (£20,147 – £20,025) / £20,025.

The Company faced other financial woes in 1696 when £1,245 was lost in foreign exchange transactions, much of it related to the recoinage of the English currency.[20] When added to the losses from the Smyth affair this represented about 10 per cent of called-up capital. By early 1697 the Company had invested 20 per cent of its capital in a banking business, 20 per cent had not been paid by investors, and 10 per cent had been lost. The directors did not have access to 50 per cent of the capital. The Company's financial management during its early history was clearly disastrous.

Substantial expenditure on shipping, combined with capital allocation to banking, difficulties in raising capital, and losses led to the collapse in net cash. By August 1697 the Company was close to running out of money, with potentially serious repercussions for its credit. For a number of months previously the directors were aware that their cash was disappearing at an unsustainable rate and they began to have second thoughts about overall strategy.

In February 1697 they had informed John Haldane of Gleneagles, who was still on the Continent, that if they could not raise cash in Holland or Hamburg he was to 'take all prudent measures for disposing of the two Ships at Amsterdam', namely the *Rising Sun* and the *Union*.[21] Another letter ordered Lieutenant Colonel John Erskine to sell one of the ships being built at Hamburg; probably the *Instauration* or the *Caledonia*.[22] The directors had decided on a substantial asset liquidation which would have represented a drastic curtailment of Company ambitions. If it had been carried out a significant colonial enterprise like the Darien venture could not have taken place. Instead the Company might have sent its remaining ships to the East Indies.

On 25 February a committee of directors stated that 'without the help of considerable Forreign Subscriptions this Company is not at Present in a condition or able to put Mr Paterson's said design in execution'. Those advocating a policy of retrenchment and the abandonment of a Darien project were led by directors William Hay of Drummelzier, a Borders laird, and Robert Watson, an Edinburgh merchant. Other Darien sceptics outside the court included the merchant Robert Douglas, who was experienced in the East Indies trade and

---

[20]   NLS, Adv MS 83.3.6, f12.

[21]   RBS, D/1/1, 195.

[22]   In March 1698 further attempts were made to sell the *Rising Sun* in Amsterdam and the *Lyon* and *Thistle* in Hamburg, which were both unfinished. Buyers could not be found. In September 1700 there was another effort to sell the *Lyon* and *Thistle*. RBS, D/2, f11–13, f80.

had written a long attack on Paterson's plan in 1696, and the Highlander George MacKenzie, Viscount Tarbat, an experienced politician and shareholder, who believed the Company had insufficient capital for such a venture.[23] Both urged a strategy of sending ships to Asia like the English and Dutch East India Companies.

However, having flirted with a policy of retrenchment, the directors changed their minds, abandoned plans to sell the ships, and reverted to Paterson's Darien venture, despite recognition by many on the court that they did not have sufficient capital for such an expedition. In October 1697 Mr Robert Blackwood drew the attention of his fellow directors to 'how absolutely necessary it is that the court come to immediate Resolutions concerning the place or places to which the Company are to direct their first expedition'.[24] A committee was appointed to consider the matter, made up of Sir Francis Scott of Thirlestane, John Haldane of Gleneagles, John Drummond of Newton, Blackwood himself, and William Wooddrop.

A series of destinations were examined, including the Amazon, the Bay of Mexico, Crab Island, Chile, and Old Providence, but all were perfunctorily rejected as unsuitable. Location for the 'smuggling or sloop trade' with the Spanish Empire was highlighted as crucial and Central America chosen after 'long and serious deliberation', because of its position, climate, fertile soil, and the absence of European settlement. Darien was unsurprisingly identified as the most promising area on account of its pivotal location and potential to become a centre for the slave trade, timber extraction and gold mining. Several objections were considered, including the unhealthy climate, infertility of the land, lack of good harbours, potential for English, French and Spanish opposition, but these were all dismissed. The key issue of the Spanish presence on the isthmus was addressed in detail, but it was argued that the Company's act of parliament gave it the right to settle in places not inhabited or by consent of the local indigenous population. The devastating attacks by the buccaneers highlighted Spanish weakness.[25] Their empire was in decline and incapable of mounting a major offensive to oust a newcomer from Darien.

---

[23]   NLS, Adv MS 83.7.4, f58.

[24]   RBS, D/1/1, 335.

[25]   The discussions of this committee have not survived or were never committed to paper, but the deliberations of another committee for providing sailing orders in 1698 provide an insight into what was decided in 1697, University of London, Goldsmith's Library of Economic Literature, MS 63, item 6.

The reasons for this volte-face are not explicitly provided in any source, but it is possible to make a number of suggestions. Firstly, the Company was not able to sell its ships on the Continent; potential buyers were waiting for lower prices, given the rumours circulating about the Company's finances since the Smyth affair, and the directors were unwilling to sell at large discounts to the sums they had just paid to construct or buy the ships. Secondly, the return of the directors who had been in Holland and Hamburg (Paterson, Gleneagles, and Erskine) may have altered the balance of power on the court, resulting in the ascendancy of a pro-Darien faction. According to their arch-critic Walter Herries, the directors were 'bewitch'd to the Golden Dreams of Paterson the Pedlar, Tub-preacher, and at last Whimsical Projector'.[26] Paterson's return to Scotland may have refocused attention on Darien despite his tarnished reputation. Thirdly, there was public opinion to consider. News of potential asset sales had leaked out and was undermining the confidence of shareholders.[27] Many investors were frustrated by the Company's apparent inactivity, as Paterson and the directors had wetted their appetites in 1695–6 with glowing descriptions of the opportunities for wealth creation. It would be very painful to admit they had failed, and were planning to abandon a major colonial attempt by selling assets only recently bought or built. Finally, cash balances were rising by October 1697 (see Figure 3) and, perhaps crucially, the Company had gained some control of its capital as expenditure slowed, cash was extracted from late-payers, and loans to shareholders were recalled. The directors were clearly divided in 1697 and there was not unanimous support for a colonial attempt in Central America, but for a number of reasons a majority were convinced to support the fateful decision to send the fleet to Darien. Perhaps they decided that not to do so would have provoked too much criticism in the short-term.

---

[26]   Herries, *Defence*, epistle dedicatory.

[27]   NLS, MS 1914, f101–2.

CHAPTER TWELVE

Disaster in Darien

I shall only say of the Country that it is one of the fruitfullest spots of ground on the face of the Earth and best situat for trade.

DANIEL MACKAY[1]

The Affair of Darien; which, I think, had not one Branch belonging to its Contrivance, but what was Big with necessary Abortions.

DANIEL DEFOE[2]

THE FLEET OF FIVE ships sailed from Leith on 14 July 1698. It crossed the Firth of Forth to anchor off Kirkcaldy, where final checks were carried out. William Paterson, accompanied by his wife and clerk, took his place on the *Unicorn* on 16 July and three days later the voyage northwards began with the intention of augmenting provisions at the Orkney Islands.[3] But the ships lost contact in thick fog and slipped between Orkney and Shetland without making land.[4] The *Endeavour* and *Unicorn* soon found each other and headed south, passing St Kilda, west of the Outer Hebrides, on 1 August. After another three weeks at sea they reached the Portuguese colony of Madeira, off the north coast of Africa, where they were joined by the other ships four days later.

At Madeira, Paterson was elected to the Council in place of the absent Captain William Veitch, who had withdrawn from the expedition because of ill health before it had departed. On the island the Scots bought 27 pipes of wine, nearly 3,000 gallons, and a small amount of fresh produce.[5] George Douglas wrote to his brother from

---

[1] NAS, Leven and Melville Muniments, GD 26/13/101.

[2] Defoe, *History of Union*, 34.

[3] *Darien Papers*, 178, NLS, Adv MS 83.7.2, f55, Prebble *Darien*, 118. It was not until 5 July that William Paterson finally decided to sail, NLS, Adv MS 83.7.2, 537–8.

[4] Prebble, *Darien*, 122.

[5] Ibid., 124–6, Insh, *Company of Scotland*, 122. One source states that the cargo on the *Endeavour* was sold to purchase this, although Herries claimed the stock purses were used. Herries, *Defence*, 48.

Funchal, the principal settlement, informing him that after six weeks at sea there had been minimal loss of life 'save a Dutch sailer and a Scots barber'.[6] Further sailing orders were opened, directing the expedition to Crab Island in the Caribbean (now Vieques, between Puerto Rico and the Virgin Islands), and then to the Bay of Darien and Golden Island.[7]

The ships left Madeira on 2 September to cross the Atlantic and experienced 'as pleasant and favourable a passage as could be desired by Sea-fareing men'.[8] Eight days out they slipped over the Tropic of Cancer, where customary celebrations were held:

> The ships performed the usual ceremony of ducking several of the Ships Crew, who had not passed before; they were hoisted to the main yard arm, and let down 3 several times with a soss into the sea out over head and ears, their legs being tyed somewhat closs, which was pretty good sport.[9]

As they sailed south, disease began to take its toll. John Stewart, a gentleman in Captain Dalziel's company, died of fever and was 'heaved over board.' As a result, the decks were washed with vinegar and smoked to prevent the spread of sickness.[10] On 28 September, after almost four weeks at sea, the Caribbean island of 'Deseada', where it was mistakenly believed Columbus had made land after his first voyage across the Atlantic in 1492,[11] was sighted. On the following day the surgeon's mate, Walter Johnston, died from an overdose of laudanum taken to ease his fever.[12] Two days later the ships passed between the islands of Antigua and Montserrat, both English plantations, to reach the Caribbean Sea.[13]

---

[6]   NAS, Douglas of Strathendry, GD 446/39/13.

[7]   Prebble, *Darien*, 131, Insh, *Company of Scotland*, 118.

[8]   *Darien Papers*, 79.

[9]   *Ibid.*, 60.

[10] *Analecta Scotica: Collections illustrative of the Civil, Ecclesiastical, and Literary History of Scotland*, 2 vols (Edinburgh, 1834), i, 356.

[11] *Darien Shipping Papers*, 72. There is uncertainty about the island where Columbus first made landfall. According to a recent biography he could have arrived at almost any of the islands in the Bahamas or Turks and Caicos, F. Fernández-Armesto, *Columbus* (London, 1996), 81.

[12] *Analecta Scotica*, i, 357.

[13] Prebble, *Darien*, 130.

The Council met on board the *St Andrew* on 2 October and decided to send the *Unicorn* and *Dolphin* to the tiny Danish island of St Thomas, where Paterson was to find a pilot to guide the fleet to the Spanish Main, and obtain any information about the 'state of Darien'. The rest of the ships made for Crab Island, where they landed and took possession in name of the Company of Scotland. However, Scottish sovereignty was to be short-lived as a party of Danes arrived on a sloop to stake the Danish claim over the island. Privately they told the Scots they hoped they would settle there to provide a bulwark between themselves and the Spanish in Puerto Rico.[14]

At St Thomas a pilot was found, the ex-buccaneer Robert Allison, who offered to guide the ships to Golden Island, where eighteen years before, under Captain Sharp, he had prepared to march across the isthmus to Santa Maria. He was now a merchant hoping to trade with the new Scottish colony and was accompanied by a Scottish doctor, Mr Crawford, who hailed from Linlithgow.[15] They brought encouraging news from the Danish colony. Twenty-five families had offered to resettle with the Scots if they were provided with transportation.[16]

On 5 October the *Unicorn* and *Dolphin* joined the other ships at Crab Island and two days later the fleet set sail, leaving behind Michael Pearson, an unfortunate individual who had presumably lost his mind, for rather than returning to his ship he ran off into the woods and did not return.[17]

For ten days they sailed south west across the Caribbean until, on 17 October, at about 2am, land was sighted. Dawn confirmed the 'prodigiously high' promontory of rock rising behind the Spanish city of Cartagena (in Colombia).[18] Thereafter progress along the north coast of South America was slow because of 'calms, rains, contrary winds and sickness'.[19] On 22 October Adam Bennet, son of Sir William Bennet of Grubbet, and Adam Cunningham, brother of Sir William

[14] *Ibid.*, 131. Insh, *Company of Scotland*, 124, *Darien Shipping Papers*, 78. Herries commented that no one in the fleet had ever been to the Spanish Main, Herries, *Defence*, 51, *Darien Shipping Papers*, 79.

[15] D. and M. Preston, *Pirate of Exquisite Mind*, 61.

[16] *Analecta Scotica*, i, 358–9.

[17] *Darien Shipping Papers*, 80.

[18] *Analecta Scotica*, i, 359, Insh, *Company of Scotland*, 125, *Darien Shipping Papers*, 80.

[19] *Darien Papers*, 79–80.

Cunningham of Caprington, both died of fever. The following day one of the ministers, Mr Robert James, perished and was given 'four dropping guns fired at his throwing over'.[20] More deaths followed: John Aird, James Graham, Alexander Taylor, Robert Goudie, John Luckieson, and the English volunteer John Malbin.[21] The surgeon Hector MacKenzie referred to 'a general distemper that seized most yea almost all our people', which he blamed on 'unwholesome' water taken on board at Crab Island.[22] Herries noted that the men 'fell down and died like rotten Sheep'.[23]

In the evening of 27 October the ships anchored in a sandy bay about nine miles west of the Gulf of Darien.[24] Their arrival was watched by some of the local people of the isthmus, the Tule, who dispatched a welcoming party in two canoes. The Scots provided food and drink and they spent the night on board the St Andrew, leaving the next morning bearing hats, looking glasses and knives as gifts.[25]

The Tule who inhabited the coastal areas of the isthmus were divided into a series of kin-based tribal communities or clans and had considerable experience of foreign incursions and interaction with the Spanish, English, Dutch, French, and buccaneers. Relations with the Spanish, which dated back to the early 16th century, shifted between tentative alliance and violent struggle.[26] Over the following weeks the Scots established communications with a number of local chiefs, including Captain Andreas, his brother Pedro, and Captain Ambrosio. At the time, the Tule were well known to Europeans from their description in Dampier's travelogue, published in February 1697, which had reached a third edition by May.[27]

---

[20] *Analecta Scotica*, i, 360. James had been minister of the parish of Cleish in the presbytery of Kinross. *Fasti Ecclesiae Scoticanae*, v, 61.

[21] *Analecta Scotica*, i, 360.

[22] *Darien Papers*, 79.

[23] Herries, *Defence*, 51.

[24] *Darien Shipping Papers*, 80. Prebble states this was on 28 October, Prebble, *Darien*, 136. A league was about three miles.

[25] *Darien Shipping Papers*, 80. The San Blas Kuna Indians, the descendants of the early modern indigenous peoples of Panama, use the word 'Tule' to describe themselves. They migrated to the San Blas Islands in the second half of the 19th century. Gallup-Diaz, *Door of the Seas*, xi.

[26] *Ibid.*, 29. The Scots were later given a detailed description of the local political map by a Frenchman who had lived among the Tule for four years. *Darien Shipping Papers*, 83–7.

[27] Gallup-Diaz, *Door of the Seas*, 84.

On 1 November the Scottish fleet anchored within half a mile of Golden Island. It was explored but no convenient harbour found. However, the following day brought an exciting discovery. Captain Pennecuik noted in his journal: 'we went in Boats to sound a bay about 4 Miles to the East of Golden Island and found it a most Excellent Harbour'.[28] This was to be the site of New Caledonia. The bay was almost two miles in length and was formed by a narrow peninsula of high ground joined to the mainland. There was a narrow entrance of about half a mile, with a rock above water, but wide channels on either side. Water depths in the bay were between three and a half and six fathoms.

The Scots were delighted with the site of their colony. Pennecuik wrote: 'This Harbour is capable of containing a 1000 sail of the best Shipps in the World. And without great trouble Wharfs may be run out, to which Shipps of the greatest Burthen may lay their sides and unload'.[29] Another report enthusiastically stated: 'it may be made impregnable, and there is bounds enough within it, if it were all cultivated, to afford 10,000 Hogsheads of Sugar every year'.[30]

On their arrival the colonists were mesmerized by Darien's exotic natural beauty. The contrast with their dank homeland could not have been more complete; the seas, creeks, and jungle offering an explosion of biodiversity. A journal kept on the *Endeavour* captured the breathtaking diversity of animal life:

> Turtle, Manatee, and a vast variety of very good small Fish, from the bigness of a Salmon to that of a Perch. The Land affords Monkeys of different sorts, Wild Deer, Indian Rabbits, Wild Hog, Parrots of many kinds, Parakites, Macaws, Pelicans, and a hundred more Birds we have got no name to. There are moreover Land-Crabs, Souldiers, Land-Turtle, Lizards, Guanhas, back-Lizards and Scorpions: I had almost forgot Patridges, Pheasants, and a kind of Turkey.[31]

There were 'monstrous Plants' with leaves longer than three ells.[32]

---

[28]   *Darien Shipping Papers*, 80–1.

[29]   Ibid., 82.

[30]   Ibid., 74.

[31]   Ibid., 74–5.

[32]   Ibid., 75. Darien still attracts adventurers today and continues to be wild, difficult to control, and the preserve of bandits, guerrillas and drug-traffickers. *The Rough Guide to Central America* (London, 2001), 747.

The great variety of trees and shrubs included 'Cedar trees, Locust and Bullet trees, wild Cotton trees of vast bigness, Cabbage trees, Palmetto trees, Maccaw trees', as well as mangrove and many more the Scots did not have names for. The fruits and produce were similar to other West Indian plantations: Indian corn, plantain, bananas, yams, potatoes, cassava roots, sugar cane, 'cotton-wool' trees, peppers, pineapples, melons, oranges, coconut, and lime. There was also a 'beast called an Ant-Bear' and a 'remarkable creature called by the English a Sloath'.[33]

Early modern Darien equates closely to the modern Panamanian province of the same name and is divided into Atlantic and Pacific areas by the Serranía del Darien.[34] Spanish presence in the region was restricted to settlements at Cartagena, Portobello and Panama and was not large in numerical terms. There were about 500 adult householders in Panama City and only about 50 permanent house-holders in Portobello. The total number of Spanish in the region was about 4,000, but there was a large slave population which fluctuated between three and fourteen thousand in the early modern period.[35]

Disease was a prevalent feature of life at the isthmus and a wide variety of deadly ones ravaged newcomers: small-pox, plague, cholera, dysentery, typhoid, and the mosquito borne yellow fever and malaria. The Scots categorised all these under the general terms of 'fever' or 'flux'. The area was also home to a wide range of plant diseases and insects which hindered agriculture, and rains brought storms and flooding from May to November.[36] The geography was not conducive to colonial development by northern Europeans.

Unaware of these geographical disadvantages, the construction of New Edinburgh began in earnest. Men were first dispatched from the ships to clear ground and make huts for the sick. The Council deter-mined the best location for a defensive settlement to be named Fort St Andrew and resolved to build a battery on the west side of the entrance to the harbour. All hands were employed to clear vegetation.[37]

Excavations by archaeologists have provided a detailed view of

[33]   Rev Mr Francis Borland, *The History of Darien* (Glasgow, 1779), 14–16.

[34]   Gallup-Diaz, *Door of the Seas*, xiii.

[35]   *Ibid.*, xviii.

[36]   Borland, *History of Darien*, 8.

[37]   *Darien Shipping Papers*, 83.

the Scottish fort constructed on the west side of the peninsula. The defences on the landward side included an earthen rampart running from the north to south shore, with cannon positions and four bastions projecting outwards, fronted by a moat. Two batteries defended the seaward side. Some maps of the colony indicate that the settlement of New Edinburgh was 300m further south, but archaeology suggests the wooden huts were built within the defences. There was one stone building (3m in diameter) which was probably a powder store.[38] A ditch eight feet deep and 12 wide was dug across the neck of land that joined the mainland to the peninsula, which was about 180 paces in width. The area beyond the ditch was cleared for a distance of a musket-shot.[39]

In order to cement relations with the Tule, a party of colonists was sent on a short expedition to Captain Ambrosio's village about 16 leagues to the west.[40] They were also instructed to examine the coast for other suitable settlement sites, suggesting that the location of Caledonia Bay was not regarded as perfect.[41] Another party was sent to search for the Nicaragua wood described by Wafer, but returned empty handed.[42] Relations with the Tule were formalised in early December when Captain Andreas was received into the protection of the colony, promising to defend the Scots to the last drop of blood.[43] In February 1699 a more formal treaty of 'Friendship, Union, and Perpetual Confederation' was entered into between the Council and the most powerful of the local Tule chiefs, the 'Excellent Diego Tucupantos and Estrara, Chief and Supreame Leader of the Indians Inhabitants of the lands and possessions in and about the Rivers of Darieno and St Matolome'.[44] The treaty specified that other Tule leaders might be admitted under the terms on application.

The Tule provided the colonists with mouth-watering descriptions of local mineral deposits, which were to excite investors in Scotland when details were sent home. A nearby mountain was the location of

[38] M. Horton, *Caledonia Bay Panama 1979: A preliminary report on the archaeological project of Operation Drake* (London, 1980), 5–10.

[39] Insh, *Company of Scotland*, 135.

[40] *Ibid.*, 130–2.

[41] *Darien Shipping Papers*, 88.

[42] Insh, *Company of Scotland*, 133.

[43] *Ibid.*, 134–5, *Darien Shipping Papers*, 91.

[44] *Darien Papers*, 87–8, Prebble *Darien*, 176.

several gold mines.[45] Captain Pacigo of Carret Bay, one of the chiefs, showed the Council a sample of 'extraordinary fine' gold and told them of several good mines within two miles of the colony.[46] According to one report, 100 ounces of gold was seen on the *Endeavour*, but Herries noted that the amounts offered for sale were usually between half an ounce and an ounce.[47]

The number of dead continued to rise during the early days of colonial life: sailor Hugh Barclay, trumpeter Henry Grapes, volunteers Archibald Wright and James Wemyss, planters James Clerk and John Fletcher, and Paterson's wife Hannah Kemp, who had guns fired at her burial, all succumbed in the first week or so. The dead in the following weeks included Recompence Standburgh, mate on the *St Andrew*; Mr Adam Scott, the other minister; and two boys, William MacLellan and Andrew Brown.[48]

Despite the excitement generated by the establishment of New Caledonia, some were already not convinced about the colony's prospects, or had quickly sickened of the back-breaking toil of clearing virgin jungle in the tropical heat. On 29 November ten planters deserted with firearms taken from the *Unicorn*. The Council did not take kindly to such treachery and, when captured two days later, the runaways were placed in irons and fed on bread and water.[49] The severity of the punishment, however, did not deter others. Seven more ran off on 16 December.[50]

There was soon news that the Spanish were preparing an attack on the settlement from the Englishman Captain Richard Long, who had reached the isthmus on the *Rupert* before the Scots and was keeping a careful watch over their activity, although he told them he was in the area to find wrecks for salvage.[51] Captain Andreas warned that

45   *Darien Shipping Papers*, 85.
46   *Ibid.*, 95.
47   *Ibid.*, 76, Herries, *Defence*, 149.
48   *Exact List of all Men, Women, and Boys that Died, Analecta Scotica*, i, 361–2.
49   *Darien Shipping Papers*, 90.
50   *Ibid.*, 93.
51   Prebble, *Darien*, 147. On 15 November he dined on the *St Andrew* and on 17 November on the *Unicorn*, *Darien Shipping Papers*, 88. Long believed he had staked an effective claim to the Gulf of Urabá for the English crown, Gallup-Diaz, *Door of the Seas*, 111.

his intelligence suggested a major attack was imminent by land and sea. But morale was high and the Scots were in defiant mood. Pennecuik noted in his journal: 'we wish nothing more than that the Spaniard would attack us'. The battery containing sixteen 12 pound guns was finished and the *Endeavour*, which the Council had initially planned to send back to Scotland, was converted into a fireship for the colony's defence.[52]

It was necessary to establish communication with the directors in Edinburgh and on 18 December the Council decided to send chief accountant Alexander Hamilton home on the *Maurepas*, a French ship of forty-two guns commanded by Captain Duvivier Thomas, which had arrived at the colony a week before.[53] Major Cunningham of Eickett also wanted to leave. The Council thought the departure of one of their number would undermine confidence and considered keeping him by force, but ultimately consented.[54] Hamilton and Cunningham were joined by another man unimpressed with what he had found on the isthmus. The surgeon Walter Herries was afflicted by a 'mallady imaginaire', and had sickened of colonial life. His experience left him with a very bitter taste in the mouth.

The *Maurepas* left on Christmas Day but disaster struck when she was hit by mountainous waves on leaving the bay, and in half an hour was 'all in pieces'. Twenty-four of the 54 on board drowned, including a servant of Herries.[55] According to reports, the ship carried 60,000 pieces of eight in gold and silver and 30,000 in goods.[56] Her shipwreck highlighted a fundamental disadvantage of the location of the colony. It was easy for ships to enter the bay, but difficult for large vessels to depart in the dry season, when northerly winds blew them back in.[57]

---

[52] *Darien Shipping Papers*, 93–4.

[53] *Ibid.*, 92. Thomas was commissioned by the French government to hunt French pirates in the Rio Coco region and the San Blas islands on the Atlantic coast, Gallup-Diaz, *Door of the Seas*, 113.

[54] *Darien Papers*, 182.

[55] *Ibid.*, 148.

[56] A piece of eight was the principal coin of the Atlantic world in the 17th and 18th centuries and was worth 4s 6d. 60,000 pieces of gold was worth the considerable sum of £13,500. McCusker, *Money and Exchange*, 7–8.

[57] Borland, *History of Darien*, 10.

Hamilton, Cunningham and Herries sailed instead on a Jamaican sloop.[58] Hamilton carried official journals, letters for the court of directors, and a list of the dead. The reports of colonial life reflected the optimism of the early period of settlement and highlighted the presence of gold on the isthmus. The councillor Daniel MacKay wrote: 'I shall only say of the Country that it is one of the fruitfullest spots of ground on the face of the Earth and best situat for trade'.[59] Paterson's optimism remained unbounded. He informed director Sir Patrick Scott of Ancrum that if provisions arrived soon, Darien 'will in a small time be the most flourishing colony and settlement in the East or West Indies'. As a man at home in the coffee-house culture of the late 17th century he was hungry for news and asked the Company to send small vessels every few weeks with London and Dutch newspapers.[60]

But behind these optimistic proclamations lay a darker reality. Disease and insufficient provisions were beginning to sap the confidence of the settlers. Hunger was already apparent before the departure of Herries, Hamilton and Cunningham. The short allowance of food drove men to sell their shirts to the Tule for plantains, feast on small land crabs until the supply ran out, and then in desperation on the 'inner rind of the bark of the great Tree'. Despite the fertility of the seas, insufficient fish could be caught because each ship carried only one small net.[61]

At the beginning of February the *Dolphin* was sent on a trading mission to Curaçao, the Dutch trading entrepôt off the northern coast of South America, and then to the Windward Islands and St Thomas to buy rum, sugar, and a couple of sloops.[62] But on 26 February the Jamaican Captain Ephraim Pilkington returned to the colony on the *Maidstone* and reported that the Scottish tender had been taken by the Spanish. She was badly holed on a rock near Cartagena and forced to make for the Spanish city, where her crew were imprisoned for piracy and her £1,400 of goods seized.[63] This marked the loss of a substantial proportion (18 per cent) of the trading assets.

[58] *Darien Shipping Papers*, 95–7, Prebble, *Darien*, 155. The sloop had arrived on 20 December.

[59] NAS, GD 26/13/101.

[60] NAS, Scott of Ancrum, GD 259/4/3/18.

[61] Herries, *Defence*, 147.

[62] Prebble, *Darien*, 171, *Darien Papers*, 182.

[63] Prebble, *Darien*, 178.

There was another encounter with the Spanish at this time.[64] On intelligence from Captain Pedro that an attack was imminent, a force of 160 men led by Captain James Montgomery, one of the councillors, and Captain Robert Drummond, commander of the *Caledonia*, was dispatched to intercept them. Two Scots were killed and 12 wounded in a skirmish with a small contingent of 25 Spaniards and 12 Tule, which was the scouting party of a much larger force.[65] George Douglas wrote to his brother about the Scottish victory, celebrating the spoils of war, which were no doubt savoured by the ravenous Scots: 'After they fled we remained possessors of their victual which was for the most part Bread and cheese'.[66]

By early March the colonists were hoping desperately for the arrival of provisions from Scotland as they continued to work on the construction of houses and ramparts.[67] By April there was still no word from home. Another letter from young ensign George Douglas reflected the rising pessimism. He told his brother that half the men were sick. If a second equipage did not arrive soon they would run out of provisions. The fortifications would not be finished for another year. Many were threatening to leave.[68]

Disease and hunger were breeding disagreements among the councillors: 'jarrings, divisions, bitterness and misunderstandings'.[69] A parliament was convened in an attempt to resolve the problems of government. Eight representatives from eight areas of New Edinburgh met on 24 April and drew up rules and ordinances for the 'good order and Government' of the colony.[70] The twenty-fifth article specified that those who deserted would be whipped and serve a week of hard labour for every day of their absence.[71]

On 18 May more dreadful news reached the colony. Under orders from the English government, Sir William Beeston, governor of Jamaica, had published a proclamation on 9 April declaring that the Scottish settlement had broken the peace between William and the

---

[64] *Ibid.*, 172–4.

[65] Gallup-Diaz, *Door of the Seas*, 130.

[66] NAS, GD 446/39/14.

[67] NAS, GD 446/39/15.

[68] NAS, GD 446/39/16.

[69] Borland, *History of Darien*, 20.

[70] *Darien Papers*, 186, Prebble, *Darien*, 194.

[71] *Darien Papers*, 113–118.

Spanish, and prohibiting the supply of provisions to the Scots or the holding of any sort of correspondence with them, under severe penalties. Similar proclamations were issued in Barbados and New York. There were also rumours from Jamaica that the Scottish parliament had abandoned the colony. Depressed by disease, hunger and the absence of further supplies, the morale of the colonists collapsed and sentiment shifted towards complete abandonment. Paterson and Captain Thomas Drummond argued against this, with Paterson suggesting alternative strategies, including taking to the ships and waiting for supplies, or retaining 25 to 30 men on the isthmus with a sloop.[72] But the majority supported leaving immediately. The provisions were divided up and 900 survivors boarded the ships.[73] Borland later reported that he was told by survivors that nearly 300 men were buried on the isthmus.[74] On 16 June Paterson, who had succumbed to fever, was 'brought on board the Unicorne in a great hurry'.[75] The ships sailed three days later but did not clear the harbour until 22 June because of contrary winds.[76] Those who were too weak to travel were left behind. One source puts this number at six and another at between 18 and 20.[77]

Undernourished and succumbing to disease, the colonists died in droves on the voyage north across the Caribbean. By the time they reached Jamaica seven weeks later, 100 of those on board the St Andrew were dead. On the island many seamen deserted and some of the colonists signed themselves up as bonded servants.[78] The Endeavour sank on 1 July after those she carried were transferred to the Caledonia. According to Robert Drummond, 105 corpses were dropped overboard during her six week voyage to New York. Ten days after their arrival, the Unicorn reached Sandy Hook having lost all her topmasts except the main one.[79] The 20 land men who were 'able to move' had been employed continuously on the pumps to keep the ship above water. Paterson estimated that nearly 150 of the 250 on board

[72] Prebble, Darien, 197, Darien Papers, 191–2.

[73] Insh, Company of Scotland, 165.

[74] Borland, History of Darien, 22.

[75] Darien Papers, 193.

[76] Insh, Company of Scotland, 165.

[77] Borland, History of Darien, 25, RBS, D/1/2, 28 November 1699.

[78] Borland, History of Darien, 24, Prebble, Darien, 204–6.

[79] Darien Shipping Papers, 114–15.

perished during the voyage. They included the surgeon Hector MacKenzie, who died on 12 July of a distemper 'contracted by his unwearied paynes and industrie among the people on shore, as well as on board, for many weeks'.[80] The Scots presented an apocalyptic vision on their arrival in New York: 'famine and death was discerned in ther countenances at the first aspect'.[81]

Walter Herries later summed up the Scottish colonial experience at Darien between November 1698 and June 1699: 'we were sent to the back of Gods elbow, where we could see nothing but Death, starving and the Spanish Mines before our Eyes'.[82] His description of the Scottish colony was in stark contrast to the optimistic ones that had reached the directors in March 1699: 'Caledonia, where there's nothing to be had but hard Labour, Sweat, Hungry Bellies and Shallow Graves'.[83]

80 *Darien Papers*, 196–7.
81 *Ibid.*, 143–4.
82 Herries, *Defence*, 49.
83 Herries, *Caledonian Project*, 51.

CHAPTER THIRTEEN

Caledonia Now or Never

The first puff of the Haggis is the worst.

EARL OF MARCHMONT[1]

THE MANIPULATION OF CHILDREN for political ends is not a new phenomenon. On 22 May 1700 George Home noted in his diary:

> Thir were about 300 boys or more met the Duke of Queensberry as he went to Edinburgh with a petition in favours of Calidonia in Latine he desired they might give it to the secretary which they refused so he bid them come up to his coach and he took it in himselfe.[2]

This was a classic piece of political theatre. James Douglas, second Duke of Queensberry, was leader of the Court Party and King's commissioner in parliament. Despite being the most powerful nobleman in Scotland, he was unable to ignore a petition presented by a crowd of children, marking a propaganda coup for the opposition.

The fate of the Darien colony had made the previous seven months a period of tortuous political difficulties for the Scottish government. The first hints of disaster had reached Scottish shores the previous autumn, but most were reluctant to believe the worst. On 17 September 1699 the Earl of Orkney wrote to his brother Hamilton: 'I can think of nothing but poor Darien that the Scots have diserted which I wont give certaine faith till I hear it confirmed'.[3] Two days later the directors were informed of similar rumours by Robert Blackwood, who was in London.[4] Hamilton thought the stories were politically motivated: 'only a trick of some of our Enimies'. and John Murray, Earl of Tullibardine, that they were simply wrong.[5] Nonetheless they spread

---

[1]   NAS, GD 158/965, 139.
[2]   NAS, GD 1/891/3, 22 May 1700.
[3]   NAS, GD 406/1/7707.
[4]   RBS, D/1/2, 19 September 1699.
[5]   NAS, GD 406/1/7860, GD 406/1/4445.

quickly and by 10 October reached Swinton fair in the Borders where George Home heard them: 'this troubled us all yet we hope this is still a contrivance of Secretary Vernons to hinder the sailing of our ships he not knowing but they are already saild.'.[6]

The terrible news was soon confirmed, however, by letters from New York, where the *Caledonia* and *Unicorn* had arrived in early August. It was a devastating blow for the directors, who only a few months before had been basking in imperial bliss. A council general was summoned for 18 October to determine the response.[7] Despite the significant setback the Company remained firmly committed to maintaining a presence on the isthmus and it was decided to provide a credit of £2,000 in New York for refitting the *Caledonia*, with five months' provisions for those willing to return to the colony. Captain Alexander Campbell of Fonab, who had offered his services to the Company, was given a credit of £1,000 in Jamaica and the Leeward Islands for freighting or buying a sloop to go after the *Rising Sun*, which had recently left from the Clyde. Campbell was a professional soldier from Perthshire who had served in the Low Countries, but had been reduced to half-pay following the Treaty of Ryswick of 1697, which had ended the Nine Years War. Another relief ship was to be bought at Glasgow, fitted out, and dispatched as soon as possible. Tullibardine expressed the dishonour inflicted on the nation: 'the shame it brings to our Country is the worst thing in itt for after we had made such noise abroad and been the envie of Europe we will now become thure scorn'.[8] Prompt and vigorous action was required 'to show the world we have the hearts as well as the estaites of our Predecessors'. He believed an address should be made to the King for summoning parliament to redress the concerns of the nation, but was unsure whether it should come from the shires or the council general.

The finances of the Company also had to be considered. From early 1698, net cash remained around the £16,000 level, suggesting a period of more efficient capital management (see Figure 1). This level was maintained by squeezing further sums from shareholders in a series of five capital raisings with payment dates between 1698 and 1700 (see Figure 6).

---

[6]   NAS, GD 1/891/2, 10 October 1699.

[7]   RBS, D/3, 178.

[8]   NAS, GD 406/1/4444.

Figure 6

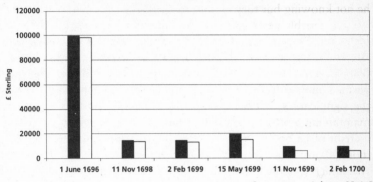

Capital Raisings 1696–1700

Source: NLS, Adv MS 83.1.6.

The small amounts indicate the difficulties experienced raising capital in a tough economic environment. Indeed it could be argued that it was miraculous that the Company was able to extract anything given the scarcity of money in Scotland, and was a reflection of the continuing loyalty and optimism of the shareholders. The dark columns in Figure 6 represent the size of the calls and the white columns the total amount of cash provided. It is obviously more efficient to raise a large sum and the original intention of the directors was to have a second capital raising of £100,000.[9] Instead the series of small ones included two of £15,000, one of £20,000 and two of £10,000. The final two calls were made by the council general on 18 October, when it was known the colony had been abandoned by the first expedition. It was little wonder that the payment ratio, the proportion that was eventually paid, fell from 98.2 per cent for the first call in 1696 to 62.5 per cent for the final one.[10] It was becoming increasingly difficult to raise small amounts of capital.

The Company also sought to raise more cash by borrowing. In the summer of 1698 £4,000 had been lent by a number of directors and councillors (members of the council general) to ensure that the first expedition was entirely provided for. When the council general met on 18 October they borrowed £1,500 from Sir John Shaw of Greenock

---

9   NLS, MS 14493, f130–1.
10 NLS, Adv MS 83.1.6.

to fund a relief ship.[11] These sums were very small compared to the debts of English joint-stock companies at the time. By 1685 the EIC had borrowed £500,000 by issuing bonds and in 1692 the Royal African Company had debts of more than £150,000.[12] The absence of a liquid domestic debt market was another problem faced by the Company.[13] Four directors, Sir Archibald Muir, William Menzies, Robert Blackwood, and Hugh Cunningham, were asked to engage their own private credit at New York, Jamaica, and the Windward Islands.[14] Indeed the financial condition of the Company was so fragile that on a series of occasions between 1697 and 1699 directors provided credit on the Company's behalf, indicating that suppliers viewed the Company as a higher financial risk than individual merchants.[15]

There were other optimistic schemes for recapitalising the Company. In April 1699 the director John Hay, second Marquis of Tweeddale, had recommended another capital raising aimed at those who had not invested in 1696. This would have extended ownership of the enterprise to an even higher proportion of the nation and sucked every last drop of liquidity from the financial system. Perhaps thankfully it was rejected by the directors as unrealistic.[16] In May negotiations took place with potential investors in London, whose interest was stimulated by news that the first expedition had reached the isthmus. A sum of £100,000 was mentioned in letters, but it is unclear whether this represented the size of the investment or the amount to be spent on cargoes by the merchants behind it.[17] Either

---

[11]   NLS, Adv MS 83.3.8, 71–4, RBS, D/1/1, 13 July 1705. The council general authorized the directors to make over outstanding debts, the Company's ships in Hamburg and the house in Milne's Square as security, RBS, D/3, 118.

[12]   K.G. Davies, 'Joint Stock Investment in the Later 17th century,' *EcHR*, second series, 4, (1952), 291, Davies, *Royal African Company*, 78.

[13]   An illiquid debt market had existed in Edinburgh from the late 16th century which allowed merchants and lawyers to lend to the nobility. This market collapsed during the Civil Wars and an overhang of unpaid debt remained a constraint on economic development after 1660. For more details see D. Watt, '"The laberinth of thir difficulties": the Influence of Debt on the Highland Elite, c. 1550–1700', *SHR*, 85, (2006), 28–51.

[14]   RBS, D/1/2, 10 October 1699.

[15]   RBS, D/1/1, 364, and 10 October 1699.

[16]   NLS, Yester Papers, MS 7020, f144.

[17]   NAS, GD 406/1/4382, 406/1/4377.

way negotiations fizzled out. One pamphlet writer suggested that the Scottish parliament might lend the Company money, but it was not clear where parliament would get the money from.[18]

Following confirmation of the abandonment, the political campaign was also extended. Several motions were raised in the council general about the 'evil consequences' of the proclamations issued in the colonies. A vote on whether to address the King was carried, but an appeal to the Kirk for a 'fast and humiliation' was rejected by the church leadership, who remained loyal to William.[19] From this point a significant breach opened up between the Company and the church, or at least between the Company and those who dominated the General Assembly of the church, who viewed their Calvinist king as a safeguard of the Presbyterian settlement. The directors were deeply frustrated by this, well aware of the propaganda value of a preacher in every parish. Lamenting the Kirk's lack of patriotism, Lord Basil Hamilton believed it had 'sadly abandoned the interest of our Countrey'.[20] The pro-court leaning of the church leadership was to prove an important factor, eight years later, in securing the passage of the treaty of Union.

The day after the appeal to the church was denied, the council general drew up an address which was agreed and transmitted to the secretaries of state to be given to the King. It also voted to address the Scottish privy council.[21]

By the late 1690s Scottish politics had become more clearly defined along party lines as an opposition group emerged in the period 1696–8. Some were opposed to the government because they had lost positions in previous regimes; some were angered by the terrible series of harvest failures; others wanted to push for constitutional reforms.[22] The treatment of the Company by the English in Hamburg provided an issue which bound these disparate elements together. From 1698 the opposition began to be called the 'Country Party' to signify its self proclaimed position as upholder of the nation's rights. The news of the abandonment of Darien stimulated unrest and provided further cement for the opposition. Disgruntled placemen, unhappy shareholders, con-

---

18 Donaldson, *Art of Thriving*, 56.

19 NAS, GD 406/1/4368.

20 NAS, GD 406/1/4549.

21 RBS, D/3, 185.

22 Riley argues that those out of office formed the nucleus of an opposition grouping which made its appearance in the parliament of 1696, Riley, *King William*, 118.

stitutional reformers and Jacobites could all rally under the patriotic banner of Caledonia.

As we have seen, the directors became actively engaged in politics from April 1697, following English intervention to crush the Company's attempt to raise capital in Hamburg. The years following witnessed the gradual transformation of the Company from a financial into a political entity, controlled by the Country opposition, who became dominant in both court of directors and council general. In March 1698 James Maule, Earl of Panmure, the advocate Mr David Drummond, and the second Marquis of Tweeddale were elected as directors by a 'great Majority' of the council general, replacing the merchants John Corse, Robert Watson, and John Graham of Dougalston.[23] Tweeddale, who had succeeded his father in 1697, was one of the principal leaders of the Country Party and must have viewed his election as a political benefit: direct access and influence over an organisation that had showed it could raise money effectively and would prove, he no doubt hoped, a useful tool to attack the Court. Tweeddale and his political supporters, who included Scott of Thirlestane, Scott of Ancrum, Hay of Drummelzier, Baillie of Jerviswood, and Haldane of Gleneagles, now represented the most powerful faction on the court of directors. Panmure and Drummond were Jacobites. Their election is perhaps surprising given the Presbyterian character of the shareholders, but reflected an effort to heighten the political temperature and put more pressure on the government.

Panmure had opposed the Revolution, refused to take the oaths of allegiance to William and Mary, and retired to his estates in Angus. He described his motivation for becoming involved with the Company in a short account of his life which he wrote in the third person:

> He joyend in this company, and being chosen one of the Directurs he applyed himself very much to their busseness, in which he had this view, that if it succeeded (which it was thought it would doe if not obstructed by the Prince of Orange) it would have been a great advantage to the kingdom and if obstructed by that Prince it would not miss to create him a great many Enemies, the most part of the Kingdom being sharers in that Company.[24]

23   RBS, D/3, 104, D/1/1, 399.

24   NLS, Saltoun MS 17804, 'Coppy of a short account of the life of James Earle of Panmure done by himself,' 11.

Mr David Drummond was an advocate who acted as the legal agent for his Jacobite kinsman James, fourth Earl of Perth.[25]

The treatment of the Company in Hamburg had dominated proceedings in the Scottish parliament of 1698. An address was made to the King by parliament on behalf of the Company, referring to 'severall obstructions they have met with in the prosecution of their Trade' and stressing the damage done by the memorial to the Senate of Hamburg. The King was entreated to take measures to vindicate the rights and privileges of the Company.[26] A number of directors, who were also members of parliament, emerged as key figures in the Country Party: Tweeddale, Panmure, Scott of Thirlestane, Haldane of Gleneagles, Scott of Ancrum, and Baillie of Jerviswood. This has led one historian to argue that 'from almost the beginning, the organisation of the African Company had looked remarkably like the opposition going into business'.[27] This was not initially the case, for in 1696 the court of directors had included supporters of the government, such as Cockburn of Ormiston, Hugh Dalrymple, Montgomery of Giffen, and Lord Ruthven. But government supporters were not the most active directors and as the Company was politicised from 1697 it was gradually transformed into an organ of the opposition. The group of Country Party directors met regularly, attending meetings together in the office of the Company, and had access to a vigorous propaganda machine under secretary Roderick MacKenzie. There was also a financial incentive to raise the treatment of the Company to the top of the political agenda as they were all major shareholders.

The relationship between Country Party and Company grew stronger still when Arran, who was now Duke of Hamilton, became more active in Scottish politics and Company affairs.[28] Lord Basil Hamilton had complained that his absence in London was undermining the

---

[25] NLS, Letters of James, Duke of Perth, MS 3288. He was the son of minister David Drummond of Moneydie and became an advocate in 1683.

[26] APS, X, 134.

[27] Riley, *King William*, 132. Riley has portrayed the politics of the 1690s as a bitter struggle between noble factions which rendered Williamite Scotland ungovernable. A recent study of parliament and politics has provided a more optimistic picture. Patrick, 'People and Parliament,' argues for 'the continuing development of an inclusive party political system similar to that evident in England,' vii.

[28] His mother had resigned her estates to King William in July 1698 and on the following day Arran was created fourth Duke of Hamilton.

effectiveness of the opposition in Scotland.[29] Such criticism may have hit home for a more vigorous influence in the Company can be detected following the news of the successful landing at Darien in March 1699, and by early May Hamilton was transmitting advice to the court of directors via the Earl of Panmure.[30] Having stood aloof for so long, he was soon in the thick of things. Gleneagles wrote to him in July: 'Your Grace truly merits the title which Colonel Hamilton gives you of being the great Champion of Caledonia', and by September he was back in Scotland.[31] It seems fair to conclude that his involvement was driven primarily by political expediency, unlike that of his younger brother Lord Basil, who worked tirelessly for the Company and cared deeply about its success.[32]

By 1699 the council general had become a forum in which political battles were being fought between the Court and Country. On 18 October debate raged until ten at night over the issue of addressing the King for a parliament. The supporters of the Court, who argued for delaying an address, were Leven, Annandale, Northesk, Ruthven, Cockburn of Ormiston, and Hugh Dalrymple. But they were only six out of a council of 46.[33] A committee was appointed to draw up the address, composed of Tweeddale, Lord Yester, Lord Basil Hamilton, Lord Belhaven, and Gleneagles; key figures in the Country Party, reflecting the strength of the opposition in the council general.[34] Cockburn of Ormiston believed Hamilton was pulling strings off stage: 'all this had been thought of at Hamilton, and agreed to here before the meeting'.[35]

In January 1700 final domination of the Company by the Country Party was evident. The chancellor Patrick Hume Earl of Marchmont met Annandale, Cockburn of Ormiston and Montgomery of Giffen in the Treasury Chamber: 'I found them hesitating whither they should goe to the meeting of the Directors (of which number they are) or not and decided not to'.[36] By this time government influence was negligible in both court of directors and council general and the Company had

[29] NAS, GD 406/1/9062, 406/1/9064.

[30] NAS, GD 406/1/4383.

[31] NAS, GD 406/1/4423, 406/1/7860.

[32] NAS, GD 406/1/6487, 406/1/4549.

[33] RBS, D/3, 178–9.

[34] As a gesture Hugh Dalrymple, a Court supporter, was added to the committee.

[35] *Carstares SP*, 499-504.

[36] NAS, GD 158/965, 227.

become synonymous with the opposition. This was emphasized in March when Court supporters Annandale, Montgomery of Giffen and Sir Archibald Muir were voted off the court of directors.[37]

The devastating blow of the colony's demise precipitated a wave of anger among shareholders, relatives of those who had sailed to the isthmus, and the general population: 'This mischief of our plantation puts people by themselves, ther had need both of worldly wit, and the assistance of god himself to guyd well now!' commented Duncan Forbes of Culloden on 10 October.[38] George Home noted the rising unrest in his diary: 'Thir is a great Stir at Edinburgh about it and they say treason publiquily spoke'.[39] Jacobites were becoming more confident and more vocal in their opposition. The fate of the colony and the ill-treatment of the Company by William was manna for those implacably opposed to the regime. Marchmont wrote of a 'universall dissatisfaction in this nation most part imputing it to the proclamations in the English plantations passing by other obvious causes'.[40] There was fear that the opposition was manipulating the Edinburgh mob for political ends: 'some take advantage and occasion to impose upon the multitude'. It had become common talk that the King had 'nae kindness for Scotland'. Despite the difficult political situation, Marchmont thought there were still grounds for optimism, quoting the Scottish proverb: 'The first puff of the Haggis is the worst'.[41] In other words he believed that after an intense explosion of anger the political temperature would cool. Surprisingly the King's birthday celebration on 7 November was 'as full of rejoyceing here as I have seen it at any time'.[42] This was perhaps a reflection of the old chancellor's hopes, rather than reality.

---

[37] NAS, GD 158/965, 242.

[38] NAS, GD 158/1063/8.

[39] NAS, GD 1/891/2, 13 October 1699.

[40] NAS, GD 158/1124.

[41] NAS, GD 158/965, 139, 143. This proverb does not appear in collections of Scottish proverbs such as D. Fergusson, *Scottish Proverbs* (Edinburgh, 1641), N. Wood, *Scottish Proverbs* (Edinburgh, 1989), and C.S.K. Walker, *Scottish Proverbs* (Edinburgh, 1996), although a haggis is mentioned in proverbs in A. Ramsay, *The Scottish Proverbs, or, The Wise Sayings of the Old People of Scotland* (Falkirk, 1813): 'The first sup of a fat haggis is the baldest' and A. Henderson, *Scottish Proverbs* (Edinburgh, 1832): 'The first puff o' a fat haggis is aye the bauldest.'

[42] NAS, GD 158/965, 159.

In this intense atmosphere, scapegoats were sought. The Edinburgh mob threatened to pull down the house of director James Balfour, who was accused of delaying a relief ship to Darien for personal profit.[43] Marchmont reflected on this incident: 'I see clearlie Scots natives cannot shake off the Scots nature they are soon raised and incensed before they take leisure to consider well'.[44] On 8 November the directors' journal referred to the 'general Clamour that is made against the Directors for their mis-management, as the ground of the Colony's desertion'. Some were blaming the directors for the disaster and in response they launched a propaganda offensive, appointing a committee to prepare a 'Short and distinct Abstract of the Company's Proceedings, with relation to the Colony, for the Directors vindication'. The propaganda battle between the directors and those who blamed them for the colony's demise marks an important bifurcation in the historiography of the Company. The pamphlet war was voluminous and two parallel views emerged; one in which a well managed Company was undermined by English opposition and another in which the directors squandered the Company's capital.[45] We have seen that the directors had indeed been inept managers of the capital, but over the following years they proved to be relentless and vigorous in the sphere of politics. Despite the accusations of mismanagement against them, support for the Company itself remained intense. Marchmont commented on 25 November: 'from the first, till now, and still on so, there is such an earnestness and disposition towards the matter, without any sparing, either of their persons or purses, that every observer must think it wonderful'.[46]

Politics was tending towards extremes. On the night of 19 December a paper was attached to the Cross at Edinburgh: 'Murther Marchmont Murther Annandale Traitors to thir country King James is our righteous King'.[47] The chancellor Marchmont and the unpopular Court politician William Johnstone, Earl of Annandale, were being accused of deliberately acting with the English government to undermine the Company. This had not been the case, but truth was another casualty of the charged atmosphere.

---

[43] NAS, GD 158/965, 147.

[44] NAS, GD 258/965, 147.

[45] The pamphlet literature on Darien is voluminous. For a selection see the pamphlet section of the bibliography.

[46] *Carstares SP*, 512.

[47] NAS, GD 1/891/2, 20 December 1699.

In an attempt to placate shareholder anger, the council general ordered an investigation into the provisions sent with the first expedition, an issue that had become central to the case against the directors.[48] Tullibardine reported that the popular view from Perthshire was that the desertion was the result of 'bad provisions and cheatry of the persons imployed in packing up the Provisions'.[49] There was now an opportunity to question some of those who had abandoned the colony. The *Caledonia* had reached the Sound of Islay on 19 November and two days later weighed anchor at Greenock.[50]

Captain Robert Drummond's letter from onboard the *Caledonia* was read to the directors on 28 November.[51] It described the desperate situation in Darien before the abandonment; many seized with a 'general Sickness of Fever, Ague and Flux' which killed about 200 at the isthmus. The colonists had experimented in planting yams, Indian corn, and Jamaican peas, which were ready in five weeks, but most of their energies were devoted to the construction and fortification of the settlement. Despite the high death toll a startling optimism remained: 'the Climate was undoubtedly as wholesome as any in America, and the water singularly Good ... the Indians were very angry at them for coming away'. Drummond believed the colony had been abandoned because the proclamations had ended the possibility of securing provisions. He did, however, criticise the poor communication network provided by the Company. They had received no word from the directors all the time they were there, and thought the severity of the proclamations meant that no relief would reach them as the Company was 'wholly crush'd at home'.[52] Between 18 and 20 men had stayed at Darien by their own choice.[53] A sloop had been bought and provisioned in New York and sent back to the colony with Captain Thomas Drummond, Lieutenant Turnbull, and 32 men.

William Paterson, the man behind the golden dream of Darien, was also back in Scotland. On 8 December he gave the directors an

---

[48] RBS, D/3, 193.

[49] NAS, GD 406/1/4442.

[50] Prebble, *Darien*, 268.

[51] RBS, D/1/2, 28 November 1699.

[52] On 29 December and 16 January Captain Drummond was examined in person by the court of directors. RBS, D/1/2, 29 December 1699 and 16 January 1700.

[53] RBS, D/1/2, 28 November 1699.

oral account of events, promising to put a fuller description in writing by the next court.[54] Paterson's report of 19 December is of crucial importance for understanding what went wrong on the first expedition; he was, after all, a merchant with much experience of the Caribbean, one of the councillors, following his election at Madeira, and the man primarily responsible for extolling the virtues of the isthmus. Given the disastrous events in Darien one might have expected some contrition, but Paterson did not blame himself. What he wrote, however, contained a number of bombshells about the conduct of others. There was firstly the issue of the provisions:

> Two or three dayes after we sailled, the Councell was called on board the St Andrew, where they found the provisions and necessarys for the voyage fall exceedingly short of what was given out or expected; whereupon the people were reduced to a much shorter allowance.[55]

This was a truly startling state of affairs given the amount of time and effort expended on preparations for the expedition and the seemingly careful supervision of the provisioning process.

Paterson also informed the directors that at the beginning of October 1698 the *Unicorn* and *Dolphin* had anchored off the tiny Danish island colony of St Thomas, the fleet having separated to find a pilot to guide it to Darien.[56] At St Thomas they met an English sloop captained by Richard Moon, who was recognised by Paterson from his days in the Caribbean. Moon was on a voyage from New York to Curaçao and was persuaded to take his 80 ton ship to meet the rest of the fleet at Crab Island, offering the Scots an opportunity to supplement their meagre rations before they reached the isthmus, as Moon's ship was carrying provisions. Unbelievably no business was done. According to Paterson: 'When he came he found our goods so deare and ill sorted for his purpose, that, upon the conditions he proposed, he would not parte with any of his provisions'.[57] Paterson warned the Council that a failure to transact at reasonable prices would have a serious impact on the future of the colony if word spread that Scottish goods were too

---

[54]   *Ibid.*, 8 December 1699.

[55]   *Darien Papers*, 179.

[56]   Prebble, *Darien*, 131.

[57]   *Darien Papers*, 179.

expensive. But the councillors would not budge from prices listed in the Company invoices and were unwilling to sell their cargo at a lower rate. The colonists were later informed by a Jamaican merchant who came to trade with them at the isthmus that their goods were overvalued by more than 40 per cent. Lack of knowledge about market conditions in the Caribbean was another weakness of the expedition.

A deluge of further criticisms flowed from Paterson's pen: the Council was split by factional disputes and lacked decisive leadership; much time was wasted clearing undergrowth and building huts on another site before the location of Fort St Andrew was finally agreed; there was a lack of sloops suitable for the Caribbean seas; there was poor management of the cargo, which was in 'disorder and confusion',and the remaining provisions were spoiled.[58]

Of course, Darien itself, a disease-ridden jungle with a poor harbour abandoned by the Spanish nearly two centuries before, could not be blamed.[59] Instead Paterson told the directors of the arrival of a French sloop under Captain Tristian, who had been shipwrecked on the isthmus and forced to live with the Tule. The Frenchman admired Darien for 'healthfullness, fruitfulness, and riches, above all other in the Indies', and said he would settle there with at least five hundred French settlers from Hispaniola.[60] Unsurprisingly this party never materialised. Paterson could not face the painful truth that the place he had been praising for most of his life was a chimera. What could not be denied was that he had suffered great personal hardship: his wife had died of fever on 14 November 1698, only 12 days after the Scots had made land, and in early June 1699 he himself had fallen ill. Somehow he survived the voyage to New York: 'when I arrived, I was brought soe low by my distempers and troubles of mynd, that for some time my life was not expected'.[61]

Lieutenant Abraham Loudon, another colonist who was questioned by the directors, also remained loyal to the Central American colony. The abandonment was 'not through any dislike they had to the place, for that it was undoubtedly one of the wholesomest places in the West Indies'. According to Loudon there were no mosquitoes or vermin in

---

[58]   *Ibid.,* 181–2.

[59]   According to Woodward, Darien was finally abandoned in 1524. Woodward, *Central America,* 28.

[60]   *Darien Papers,* 190–1.

[61]   *Ibid.,* 197.

Darien.[62] Those who had experienced the vile conditions on the isthmus were either mesmerized by a fantasy of wealth or, more likely, providing the directors with the story they wanted to hear. The spell of delusion was hard to break and the court was unwilling to admit that its choice of destination had been calamitous. A rare sceptical voice came from inside the Hamilton family. George, Earl of Orkney, wrote to his elder brother Hamilton on 21 December: 'I declare I am sory you have soe good an opinion of the place because I believe it will ingage you all in more expence which will never come to a good account tho I wish with all my hart I be a false prophet'.[63]

Alongside the investigations by the directors, the Country Party launched a vigorous political response. The rising wave of discontent drove momentum for a statement of significance that encapsulated the nation's anger and crystallised as a National Address. In late November discussions took place between Tweeddale, Panmure, Lord Basil Hamilton and others about the exact wording, and by 29 November a draft was produced and sent to Hamilton for his opinion.[64] The government was caught off guard by this political escalation. On 6 December Hamilton led Marchmont into a room in the Treasury full of nobles and lairds and was presented with a large parchment by Lord Basil. The old chancellor thought there were about forty signatures on the address at this point, including Hamilton, Tweeddale, Panmure, Tullibardine, Yester and Belhaven, and the Lords of Session Anstruther, Arniston and Whitelaw.[65] Thereafter copies were sent round the country. In late December Tullibardine was securing signatures in Perthshire and in early January Tweeddale noted that the address had been signed by more than sixty in Teviotdale.[66] On 18 January Roderick MacKenzie was jubilant about its success:

> The National Address goes on wonderfully in the North, there is not scarce a man of Note or consideration in all the Shires of Inverness, Nairn, Murray or Bamf but what have sign'd it, and likewise all the Magistrates of Burghs, Town-Councils and Incorporations in those shires.[67]

---

[62] RBS, D/1/2, 16 December 1699.

[63] NAS, GD 406/1/7795.

[64] NAS, GD 406/1/6949.

[65] NAS, GD 158/965, 178–81.

[66] NAS, GD 406/1/4441, 406/1/4546/1.

[67] NAS, GD 406/1/4569.

Families were divided on the issue. Secretary of State Seafield had not invested in the Company, but signatories in the north included his father, brother, and brother-in-law.[68] The government tried to persuade as many as possible not to sign, but it was an uphill battle. Marchmont noted that 'the promoters of it are so industrious in gathering hands through the Cuntrie that it is a great worke for those who oppose it to meet them in every place that they are'. When the address was presented to the Faculty of Advocates it was put to a vote and carried in favour of signing, despite there being only a minority of about 16 present, less than a third of the faculty. The government was clearly outflanked and unsuccessfully tried to influence institutions such as the Merchant Company, although there was some success in localities dominated by Court politicians.[69] Archibald, Earl of Argyll, vigorously opposed it and made sure no one signed in Argyllshire.[70] Macaulay suggests the National Address may have been signed by 30,000 individuals, but this is an exaggeration as the campaign was focused principally on men of 'note and consideration'.[71] Unfortunately copies have not survived. The address was a well organised political device but did not galvanise the nation like the National Covenant of 1638. There was one crucial missing ingredient: the Kirk did not support it.

In late December there was a shimmer of good news from the Caribbean. Tweeddale noted rumours from London that the colony had been repossessed.[72] However, this was followed by a further blow. On 4 January 1700 the emotionally sensitive Lord Basil wrote to his elder brother Hamilton from London:

> It is not to be expressed the melancholy condition I'm in, I'm touched to the very soull and ashamed to be seen, we shall appear so despicable to the world, it seems God Almighty sees it not time yett to deliver us from our misery, but to tryst us with affliction on the back of Affliction.[73]

---

[68]   NAS, GD 406/1/4555.

[69]   NAS, GD 158/965, 186, 216.

[70]   NAS, GD 24/5/67.

[71]   Macaulay, *History of England*, viii, 236.

[72]   NAS, GD 406/1/4362.

[73]   NAS, GD 406/1/4549.

The relief ships *Olive Branch* and *Hopeful Binning* had sailed from Leith Road on 12 May 1699 with provisions and 300 colonists. When they reached Darien in August they found the colony abandoned by the first expedition. One of the ministers on the second expedition, Francis Borland, described what happened to the *Olive Branch*:

> Within a few days after their arrival, Divine Providence frowned upon them, by a sad disaster. Captain Jamieson's ship being loaded with provisions and Brandy; while some were drawing Brandy in the Hold of the ship, having a lighted candle with them, accidently the fire of the candle catched hold of the Brandy, which forthwith flamed so terribly, that it set the ship on fire, and in a little time destroyed both ship and provisions. The wreck of this ship is yet to be seen in Caledonia harbour.[74]

For Borland this was 'another awful rebuke upon this design and Company.' Tweeddale described its effect as 'lyke a thunderclap unto us'.[75] Most of the new colonists left on the *Hopeful Binning*, but after arriving in Jamaica were struck with a 'great mortality' and the majority died.[76]

The directors' reputation was also being blackened in London. Four Scots officers from the colony, MacLean, Forbes, Stewart, and Streton, arrived at the beginning of January, having sailed to Jamaica on the *St Andrew* and then taken another ship to Bristol. Lord Basil attempted to persuade them to say nothing disrespectful of the Company.[77] But his efforts to hush them up failed as Walter Herries, who had left his eldest son from his first marriage at the isthmus, made contact with them and encouraged them to speak their minds.[78] Lord Basil informed Hamilton that MacLean 'has made a great noise every where to the prejudice of the interest and blameing the management at home for the ruine of all and excusing the proclamations'.[79] Despite the attack on the directors there was again no criticism of Darien itself. MacLean and Forbes gave 'wonderfull accounts of the place and that who ever

---

[74]   Borland, *History of Darien*, 25.

[75]   NAS, GD 406/1/4556.

[76]   Insh, *Company of Scotland*, 193, Borland, *History of Darien*, 26.

[77]   Prebble, *Darien*, 276–8.

[78]   Herries, *Defence*, 158, Gallup-Diaz, *Door of the Seas*, 108.

[79]   NAS, GD 406/1/6986.

has it must be masters of the trade of America'. Lord Basil thought that if the Company could recover the settlement 'it might be called our Dear Calledonia'.[80] In this atmosphere of rumour and counter rumour his emotions were swinging in a manic manner, like the Company's fortunes. By March Scottish confidence returned as stories spread of the arrival of the *Rising Sun* at the isthmus.[81] Marchmont commented: 'I find people much elevated upon a persuasion they have of the Scotes their being repossessed of Darien'.[82]

Nevertheless, the government remained under severe pressure. In January 1700 a gesture was made to deflate the intense atmosphere. Marchmont was advised by Cockburn of Ormiston and the Lord Advocate that 'a little book in octavo of 168 pages having a Dedication to the Court of Directors' should be burned by the common hangman. This was Walter Herries' *A Defence of the Scots Abdicating Darien*, which was full of 'irritating and bitter expressions towards Scotland and several statesmen'. It was also a stringent attack on the management of the directors.[83]

Anti-English sentiment was intensified by debates in the English Houses of Parliament in January and February on the issue of Darien, and a Union proposal by William. The English Tories killed off the attempt to reconstitute the relationship between the two kingdoms with bitter attacks on the Scots. Sir Edward Seymour, an old Tory member of the Commons, famously stated that Scotland 'was a beggar, and whoever married a beggar could only expect a louse for a portion'.[84] The English parliament complained about another pamphlet, *An Enquiry into the Causes of the Miscarriage of the Scots Colony at Darien*, which was condemned as a 'false, scandalous, and traitorous libel' and ordered to be burnt.[85] George Home thought the nations might be 'dasht against one another like two pitchers'. There was fear in government circles of a coup and Marchmont was keeping a careful eye on the loyalty of army officers.[86]

The opposition was uncertain about who should present the

[80]   NAS, GD 406/1/4549.

[81]   *Seafield Correspondence from 1685 to 1708*, (SHS, 1912), 278–9.

[82]   NAS, GD 158/965, 245.

[83]   *Ibid.*, 207.

[84]   *Ibid.*, 230–1. Quoted in Ferguson, *Scotland's Relations*, 201.

[85]   Insh, *Company of Scotland*, 213–17.

[86]   NAS, GD 1/891/3, 23 January 1700, GD 158/965, 213.

National Address at the English court, as a previous address from the Company was ignored when taken south by Lord Basil. In November the council general had resolved that he should be sent to England with an address about the prisoners from the *Dolphin* being held at Cartagena. He was initially reluctant to go, having been nominated in absentia by Gleneagles, and seconded by his three brothers-in-law. When he arrived in London the King refused to see him on the pretext that he had not paid a visit to court before.[87] The Earl of Orkney, his own brother, concurred with William's decision: 'its doun right ill manners to send in a man who never has kissed the kings hands'.[88] Marchmont commented that access to the King was refused because Lord Basil had not attended court on a previous visit to London and had 'never since given any publict evidence of his Loyaltie'.[89]

This setback produced debate about who should bear the National Address and the delay gave rise to hopes in government circles that it was not to be delivered. But unexpectedly at just after six in the morning on 5 March Tweeddale and Gleneagles arrived at Marchmont's house to inform him that they and Sir John Home of Blackadder were leaving immediately.[90] On 25 March they were allowed to kiss the King's hand and the address was presented and read by Sir John. William replied dismissively that he had already appointed a Scottish parliament to meet on 14 May: 'you could not expect that I could call it sooner; had you considered this you might have spared the labour of comeing hither to present the address'.[91] However, the opposition had garnered support from across the nation and articulated discontent over the treatment of the Company. The directors were pleased with the reception at court and their mood was improved by reports that the colony had been repossessed.[92]

In the meantime another desperate event afflicted the citizens of the Scottish capital. On 3 February a fire broke out in the centre of Edinburgh. George Home noted in his diary:

The wind being very high the fire soon broke in upon the Land

---

[87] *Carstares SP*, 514, RBS, D/3, 196, 199, NAS, GD 406/1/4547/1.

[88] NAS, GD 406/1/9071.

[89] NAS, GD 158/965, 213.

[90] NAS, GD 158/965, 241.

[91] Insh, *Company of Scotland*, 208.

[92] NAS, GD 158/965, 260.

wher I was lodged and ther being few or no hands at the
beginning It gaind such strength that it burnt doun the Meal
Market all the back Land wher I lodged which was 13 stories
high beside the cellars and Garrets the highest fabrick of lodgings
I beleive ever was known It advanced toward the Parliament
Closse and burnt out to the street and if it had not pleased God
the wind fell about 5 a clock and turned north west the whole
toun might have been burnt as was the finest part of it.[93]

At 2am on the following morning he ventured onto the High Street to get
a closer look: 'the most terrible sight I ever see the sparks were flying
just like a shower of thick snow.' Fortunately the wind fell and horse
dung applied to Parliament House seems to have been an effective fire
retardant. A 'Great Fire of Edinburgh' was avoided and by 5 February
it was extinguished except in some coal cellars. Between three and 400
families lost their homes and there was devastation between the
Cowgate and the High Street, with the lodgings of the King's
Commissioner, President of Parliament, President of the Session, most
of the Lords of Session, lawyers and clerks, and the office of the Bank
of Scotland, destroyed. Luckily there were no casualties, but the fire
had a serious financial impact on the political and legal establishment.

The nation had experienced a calamitous series of events culminat-
ing in ordeal by fire. 'The Lord is angry with us' commented Duncan
Forbes of Culloden.[94] The privy council declared a national fast on 28
March: a day to contemplate God and ponder the reasons for His wrath.
The directors had appealed for such an event the previous October to
garner support for the Company, but the church had opposed their
request. Now the fast was sanctioned by government. The General
Assembly described the litany of disasters that had befallen the nation,
the 'many dreadfull tokens of the Lords anger':

The continued pinching dearth, notwithstanding of a favourable
Harvest, and relief therby in some measure wherby the number
of the poor and their necessities have been and are greatly
increased The great and unusuall sickness and mortality which
hath gone over all the land and doth yet in pairt continue. The
Rebukes from God on the nation in disappointing severall

---

[93]   NAS, GD 1/891/3, 3 February 1700.

[94]   *Culloden Papers* (London, 1815), 27.

undertakings to advance the Trade and wealth thereof and particularly in the severall Cross providences that the African and Indian Companys Colony in America hath mett with notwithstanding of the many fervent prayers made in their behalf and by a Stupendious Burning within these few days of so considerable a pairt of Edinburgh.[95]

Scotland was a blighted nation. For the Kirk there was little doubt about the reasons: 'the sad effects and bitter fruits of our heinous sins against God'.

The elderly chancellor Marchmont continued to look for a moderate course through the political quagmire; a 'midle way', as he put it. It was hoped that William would come to Scotland to sort out the political crisis, daunt the opposition with the charisma of kingship and the distribution of royal patronage.[96] In January there were rumours that the King was to be in Edinburgh in May and Holyrood House prepared for him.[97]

Tweeddale and his party were welcomed home from London as heroes. As they travelled through southern Scotland there were official greetings, speeches of welcome, and toasts.[98] Some of the directors, Lord Basil, Gleneagles, Mr Robert Blackwood, and Mr David Drummond, travelled to Blackadder in the Borders to join the rapturous return to Edinburgh. George Home noted in his dairy: 'They were met with the mob at Jocks lodge with huzzas and so convoyed to the Marquis's lodging ther was a bonfire made near his lodging and drinking of wine'. Walter Herries' book was again cast into the flames.[99] A letter to the Duke of Queensberry spoke of a 'great parade' which welcomed Tweeddale home and a great number of 'idle' people running around the streets calling 'Caledonia Caledonia'.[100] Many had papers on their hats with 'Calidonia now or never'.[101] The atmosphere was fever pitched.

---

[95]   NAS, PC 1/52, 73–4.

[96]   NAS, GD 158/965, 254.

[97]   NAS, GD 1/891/3, 16 January 1700.

[98]   NAS, GD 1/891/3, 24 and 30 April 1700.

[99]   NAS, GD 1/891/3, 30 April 1700. We are fortunate that some copies of this important historical source have survived.

[100] NRAS, Duke of Buccleuch, Drumlanrig Castle, Letters to the Duke of Queensberry, 1275, volume 116, 30 April 1700.

[101] NAS, GD 1/891/3, 22 May 1700.

It was little wonder that supporters of the government were extremely worried. One commentator feared a repeat of the Covenanting radicalism of the 1640s, which had started a rebellion against the rule of Charles 1 and precipitated the Civil Wars in Scotland, England and Ireland: 'the ferment still continues, and new addresses are daily coming in from all parts of the country ... God help us, we are ripening for destruction. It looks very like Forty-one'.[102]

On 21 May 1700 parliament convened, but William was not in attendance.

---

[102] *Carstares SP*, 527–8. A reference to the Covenanting radicalism of the early 1640s.

CHAPTER FOURTEEN

Second Chance

From such an observable succession of counteracting provi-
dences in this design, who cannot but remark, and see a holy
and sovereign God, signally appearing and fighting against this
undertaking. As if men should say, This design shall succeed,
and God say, It shall not prosper.

FRANCIS BORLAND[1]

ON 11 APRIL 1699 news had reached the directors that the *Dispatch*, a
relief ship bound for Darien, had been beaten back by contrary winds
and driven onto the small island of Texa off Islay. Her crew and cargo
were saved, but the ship would be unable to sail to the isthmus.[2] This
was principally a blow to confidence, as she carried only a small
quantity of provisions. Communication with the colony, however,
would be delayed.[3] In May another two relief ships, the *Olive Branch*
and the *Hopeful Binning,* sailed from the Forth with 300 colonists
and provisions.[4] Thereafter preparations continued for a second
major expedition.

The *Rising Sun* had been launched in Amsterdam two years before,
in May 1697.[5] The directors hoped she would accompany the *Union*
back to Scotland in August, but because of problems securing funds to
cover her construction she remained in the Dutch city over the winter
of 1697/8, where she was visited by the Russian Czar Peter I, who was

---

[1]   Borland, *History of Darien*, 27.

[2]   RBS, D/1/2, 11 April 1699.

[3]   *Darien Papers*, 122. The directors stated in a letter to the Council of the
      colony that she had been sent 'more to shew our good will to you than
      for any other relief she can bring you.'

[4]   Borland, *History of Darien*, 25. The *Hopeful Binning* and *Olive Branch*
      carried cargoes valued at £2,441 and £1,258 respectively.

[5]   NLS, Adv MS, 83.6.4, 75.

on a European tour.[6] Back in the Clyde she was joined by another
Company vessel, the *Hope*, and two ships chartered for the voyage,
the *Duke of Hamilton* and the *Hope of Bo'ness*, both of 300 tons.[7]
The cost of shipping assets was therefore much reduced and significantly smaller cargoes were carried than on the first expedition. The
Rising Sun carried goods of £2,907, the *Hope of Bo'ness* £746, the
Duke of Hamilton £639 and the *Hope* only £285, reflecting the constrained capital position of the Company. There was, however, no
shortage of willing recruits, Marchmont noting the 'unaccountable
inclination among people here to goe hither'.[8]

The second expedition attracted some men of higher social standing
than had sailed on the first. Lord Mungo Murray, the fifth son of the first
Marquis of Atholl, was appointed as an overseer.[9] The Hamiltons hoped
that they might be represented on the expedition and tried to persuade
Lord Archibald, a younger brother of the Duke of Hamilton, to provide
'great Creditt and reputation to the affair'.[10] But he could not be convinced to sail to the isthmus.[11] Lord Basil Hamilton noted that although
two hundred gentlemen were with the fleet 'some persons of more notte
and quality is what we want extreamlie'.[12]

Financial embarrassment at home drove some to seek a new life in
the colony. The goldsmith Andrew Law had been deacon of the
Incorporation of Goldsmiths of Edinburgh and a shareholder in the

6   *Ibid.*, f102–3. James Gibson wrote on 28 November 1697, 'The Ship
     Rising Sun hath been in equal readiness this month by past only waiting
     your orders and our factors licence for sailing which is absolutely refused
     by them, for want of effects ... it is a shame and disgrace attour the loss,
     that the ship Rising Sun should be hauld of from the stream, to winter
     heir.' NLS, Dunlop Papers, MS 9251, f152. Prebble wrongly suggested that
     the *Rising Sun* did not return because she was unfinished, Prebble,
     Darien, 96. For Prebble's grandiloquent description of her see Prebble,
     Darien, 224, Herries, *A Defence*, 26–7.

7   The *Hope* was purchased for the more reasonable price of £1,711, NLS,
     Adv MS 83.3.7, f14, Prebble, *Darien*, 224.

8   NLS, Adv MS 83.3.7, f14, f17, NAS, GD 158/965, 101.

9   RBS, D/1/2, 28 April 1699, 15 May 1699. Lord Mungo's mother was
     Amelia Anne Sophia Stanley, fourth daughter of James, seventh Earl of
     Derby. He was born on 29 Febraury 1668, *Scots Peerage*, i, 476.

10   NAS, GD 406/1/6484.

11   NAS, GD 406/1/6981.

12   NAS, GD 406/1/6946.

Company, before insolvency drove him to volunteer.[13] The Writer to the Signet John Elliot was a subscriber who had failed to pay his cash but was willing to serve the Company in Darien.[14] There were specialists who offered their skills to the Company. A distiller, George Winram, was appointed 'to carry along with him stills and other necessaries for the distilling and fermenting of several sorts of Liquors'; James Hunter was a smith, refiner and coiner, and was accompanied by his wife and two children; Robert Keill, a goldsmith and refiner; and John Jaffrey was made bombardier of the colony.[15] Four new councillors were appointed: Captain William Vietch, Captain James Gibson, Edinburgh merchant James Byres, and Major John Lindsay. One hundred women also travelled to the isthmus. Most are only known by the names of their husbands.[16]

Major John Lindsay and Dr John Munro of Coul were appointed trustees for managing the interests of the Company in the colony, each on the substantial salary of £250. Munro had been responsible for purchasing drugs and medicines and procuring a variety of other goods including the tender *Endeavour* in Newcastle.[17] He was also involved in efforts to recover cash from James Smyth in London in early 1698.[18] James Gibson, who had overseen her construction in Amsterdam, was appointed commander of the *Rising Sun* and commodore of the fleet.[19] The *Hope* was captained by James Miller, and the two chartered ships, the *Duke of Hamilton* and the *Hope of Bo'ness*, by Walter Duncan and Richard Dalling. On 14 July command of the expedition was placed in the hands of a council of Gibson, Munro, Lindsay, Byres, and Veitch.[20] Dr Munro stated that he would only accept his position if promoted to director of the Company. His request was rejected by the court and he did not sail with the fleet.[21]

[13] NAS, GD, 1/482/1, f225, RBS, D/1/2, 30 June 1699.
[14] *Ibid.*, 11 July 1699.
[15] RBS, D/1/2, 5 May 1699, 15 May 1699, 6 June 1699, 13 June 1699, 18 July 1699.
[16] Prebble, *Darien*, 227.
[17] RBS, D/1/2, 10 July 1699, Prebble, *Darien*, 80, 96, 105.
[18] RBS, D/1/1, 399.
[19] Prebble wrongly states that he was a director of the Company, Prebble, *Darien*, 224.
[20] RBS, D/1/2, 14 July 1699.
[21] He did, however, achieve his ambition of becoming a director in 1701.

On her voyage to Scotland from Amsterdam the *Rising Sun* was manned by an international crew, but the majority of foreign sailors were discharged before the second expedition left. However, a small group of ten sailors not born in Scotland sailed on the second expedition: two Dutchmen, Lourance Mikleson and Jacob Jacobson; four Italians, John Baptista, Nicolo Grilo, Symon Amodesto and Lourance Amagie; three Englishmen, John Codd, William Pirrie and Richard Philips; and the Irishman William Houston.[22]

Four ministers, Francis Borland, Alexander Dalgleish, Alexander Shields and Archibald Stobo, accompanied the ships. The directors had attempted to persuade Shields to sail with the first expedition but he had declined. Now he had changed his mind, perhaps influenced by the popular frenzy for Darien. Borland, who was born in East Kilbride in 1666 and ordained in 1692, had spent time in New England and the Dutch colony of Surinam in South America. Stobo had only graduated from Edinburgh University in 1697, and very little is known about Dalgleish.[23] Another candidate, the newly qualified and recently married Mr James Stewart, confessed to 'fornication' with an English woman before the ships sailed. His honesty resulted in his deposition from the ministry and the loss of his position on the ill-fated voyage.[24]

On 21 July the directors moved temporarily to Glasgow to oversee preparations as further recruits continued to come forward.[25] Mr Robert Johnson, a schoolmaster who had lived for several years in the West Indies, was recommended by the Duke of Hamilton. He had prepared a scheme for teaching English quickly to the Tule and was accompanied by his wife and daughter.[26] A laird of some standing in

---

[22] NLS, Adv MS, 83.8.4, f234–5. Gallup-Diaz refers to these individuals as 'non-Scottish mercenaries,' but it seems more likely they were international seamen. Gallup-Diaz, *Door of the Seas*, 128.

[23] RBS, D/1/2, 14 April 1699, *Fasti Ecclesiae Scoticanae*, iii, 254, vii, 665.

[24] NAS, Hay of Park, GD 72/645.

[25] RBS, D/1/2, 21 July 1699. Tweeddale, Annandale, Montgomery of Giffen, Mr David Drummond, Shaw of Greenock, Haldane of Gleneagles, Dougalston, Montgomery, Wooddrop, and Arbuckle attended the court held at the 'Company's Arms' in Glasgow at 2pm on 3 August. The following day they were joined by Lord Ruthven, Cockburn of Ormiston, Scott of Thirlestane, Baillie of Jerviswood, Campbell of Monzie, and Drummond of Newton. *Ibid.*, 25 July 1699, 3–4 August 1699.

[26] *Ibid.*, 14 August 1699.

Presbyterian circles and a major shareholder, John Dunlop of that Ilk, was recommended to the Council of the colony as a 'worthy Gentleman'.[27]

Before the ships departed, the optimistic mood was slightly deflated by rumours that the colony had been abandoned. But, as we have seen, this was dismissed as an attempt by English ministers to undermine the venture.[28] The directors wrote to the Council in Darien explaining the difficulties they had faced obtaining provisions, which were scarce and expensive. They reminded them that the colony was to provide cash to cover the Company's expense of establishing and supporting the settlement.[29] They also asked the Council to formally purchase land on the north of the isthmus from the Tule, as well as on some convenient place on the south side 'for certain reasons, of which you shall be acquainted with in due time'.[30] Amazingly the directors believed they could control both sides of the isthmus.

On 18 August the second fleet of four ships sailed from the Clyde.[31] The directors had responded to criticisms that the journey round the north of Scotland by the first expedition had increased the length and danger of the voyage.[32] The very small stock purses again highlighted the capital constraint under which the Company was operating. Captain Gibson was given £60 for the *Rising Sun* and Captain Miller only £10 for the *Hope*. In addition a credit of £200 was provided for buying fresh provisions in Ireland if they landed there. Mr Jaffrey was ordered to prepare some 'small Fireworks' for the evening of 17 August to celebrate their departure.[33] Unfortunately the ships, carrying in total about 1,300 people, were forced to anchor in Rothesay Bay off Bute and wait for a favourable wind, which took over a month to come.[34] The fleet finally sailed out of Scottish waters on 23 September.

---

[27] *Ibid.*, 5 August 1699.

[28] Insh, *Company of Scotland*, 183–4.

[29] *Darien Papers*, 133–4.

[30] *Ibid.*, 138.

[31] Prebble, *Darien*, 230.

[32] Insh, *Company of Scotland*, 171.

[33] RBS, D/1/2, 17 August and 21 August 1699.

[34] The second expedition carried about 1,300 people in total: 1,200 men and about 100 women and children. Borland, *History of Darien*, 28, Prebble, *Darien*, 230.

Avoiding the route round the north of Scotland, they reached the isthmus in two months, half the time of the first expedition, although the mortality rate was significantly higher, with about 160 dying at sea. The minister Francis Borland, who sailed on the *Hope* and later wrote a detailed account of his experiences, recalled that: 'the Lord's hand was heavy upon us, pursuing us with sore sickness and mortality, which cut off many of us'.[35] The dead included Dunlop of that Ilk, the children Jean Jeffray and Helen Hunter, and the minister Alexander Dalgleish, who died between Montserrat and Darien, leaving a pregnant wife.[36] On 9 November the fleet had dropped anchor at Montserrat but was refused fresh provisions because of the English proclamations. They were told that New Caledonia had been abandoned six months before, but again refused to believe such incredible rumours.[37]

When the ships reached Darien on St Andrew's Day (30 November) they were faced with the bleak reality of a deserted colony. Instead of being greeted by their fellow countrymen they found nothing but a 'waste, howling wilderness'. The huts were burned, the fort ruined, and the ground in front of it overgrown with shrubs and weeds. Borland's mind sought parallels in the Old Testament and he likened their coming to the arrival of David with his small army at Ziklag, described in the Book of Samuel.[38]

A general meeting was held on the *Rising Sun* to discuss the grave situation, and a detailed examination of provisions ordered, which found there was only enough for six months.[39] Byres argued that all the ships should sail immediately for Jamaica, leaving two or three companies of soldiers to maintain a presence on the isthmus. But it was decided instead that everyone should remain at Darien until the fort was rebuilt. Then 500 would hold the colony and the rest sail for Jamaica to preserve provisions.

The Church of Scotland had outlined how the ministers should

---

[35]   Borland, *History of Darien*, 41. The councillor James Byres published a list of those who died on each ship: 66 perished on the *Duke of Hamilton*, 56 on the *Rising Sun*, 39 on the *Hope of Bo'ness* and three on the *Hope*, totalling 164. James Byres, *A Letter to a Friend at Edinburgh from Rotterdam; Giving account of the Scots affairs in Darien* (1702), 152–7.

[36]   Borland, *History of Darien*, 29, Prebble, *Darien*, 235.

[37]   Insh, *Company of Scotland*, 184–5.

[38]   Borland, *History of Darien*, 29.

[39]   Prebble, *Darien*, 238.

care for the souls of the Scottish colonists and propagate the 'glorious light of the Gospel among the Pagan Natives'. In order to achieve this they were to constitute themselves as a presbytery, elect a moderator and a clerk, appoint ruling elders and deacons, and establish kirk sessions and parishes. A few days after their arrival the ministers held a meeting on the *Hope of Bo'ness*, at which they proceeded to attack the morality of their fellow colonists, referring to the 'many grievous and heinous sins and abominations that have abounded and still continue among us' and lamenting the 'Atheistical swearing and cursing, brutish drunkenness, detestable lying and prevaricating, obscene and filthy talking'. As a means of reformation a day of 'thanksgiving, humiliation and prayer' was held on 3 January. In a letter to the Moderator of the General Assembly composed in the 'Woods of Caledonia' they lamented their 'sad and very afflicted state', complaining that nearly a third of the colonists were 'wild Highlanders that cannot speak nor understand Scotch'.[40] Their attempts to convert the Tule had proved fruitless because of the language barrier and a lack of interpreters. The locals were, however, easily taught to curse and swear in Scots or English. The ministers informed their Scottish brethren back home that the establishment of a presbytery had been delayed until the colony was on a surer footing. None of them were willing to settle in such a den of iniquity.[41]

Unsurprisingly, the short rations introduced to preserve provisions soon provoked disquiet among the settlers. Ten planters, including a number of the foreign seamen, stole an eight-oared boat from the *Rising Sun* and made off for the Spanish settlement of Portobello.[42] In an atmosphere of paranoia the planter Alexander Campbell was court-martialled and executed in December for an alleged conspiracy to seize some of the ships and escape the colony.[43] The Council arrested others including Captain Thomas Drummond, a Flanders veteran and participant in the massacre of the MacDonalds of Glencoe, and Alexander Hamilton, the chief accountant who had brought the glorious

---

[40]   Borland, *History of Darien*, 34–7, 39-40, 42, 48, 53. This appears to
       have been an hysterical exaggeration as the list of dead provided by
       Byres suggests that about 10 per cent were Highlanders, Byres, *Letter to
       a Friend*, 152–9.

[41]   Borland, *History of Darien*, 51, 54–5.

[42]   Gallup-Diaz, *Door of the Seas*, 128.

[43]   Prebble, *Darien*, 241–4, Borland, *History of Darien*, 32.

news back to Scotland earlier in the year. Those not stirred to rebel were laid low by sickness and lethargy.[44] Borland graphically described the grim effect of disease: 'Darien, Thou, Land, devourest men, and eatest up thy inhabitants.'.[45]

Meanwhile the Spanish were planning to destroy the colony. The arrival of a minor European power at the isthmus was a threat to Spain's reputation and prestige. After all, if the Scots could take on the might of imperial Spain and establish a permanent position at Darien, surely anyone could. To allow their invasion was a sign of perhaps fatal weakness. There was also a religious dimension. The Spanish, not realising the difficulties under which the Scottish ministers laboured, feared the spread of Protestantism.[46] It was an economic, strategic and religious imperative that the Darien settlement be crushed.

The Spanish intelligence network in the Caribbean had provided early information about the arrival of the first expedition. Initially this provoked a diplomatic response, with Carlos II's representative in London, the Marqués de Canales, protesting formally to William's government. Military preparations were soon under way in New Spain, where Conde de Canillas, President of Panama, and General Don Andrés de Pez planned an overland attack on the Scots from the south with between 1,200 and 1,500 men. But heavy winter rain hampered the expedition and after the inconclusive skirmish in February 1699, when the Scots repulsed a forward party, the attempt was abandoned.[47]

In June military and naval reinforcements composing two warships, a lighter vessel, and five infantry companies reached Panama from Spain, and a further two ships with about 300 men were dispatched in October. It was also decided that a much larger force should be recruited in Spain and diplomacy was successful in persuading Pope Innocent XII to provide a grant of one million escudos on clerical wealth in the Spanish Indies to help finance the expedition. However, departure was postponed until March 1700 because of organisational difficulties.[48]

Alexander Campbell of Fonab had arrived at New Caledonia on

44   Prebble, *Darien*, 102–3, 243–6.

45   Borland, *History of Darien*, 19.

46   C. Storrs, 'Disaster at Darien (1698–1700)? The Persistence of Spanish Imperial Power on the Eve of the Demise of the Spanish Habsburgs,' *European History Quarterly*, 29, (1999), 8–9.

47   *Ibid.*, 11–12, Prebble, *Darien*, 167–9.

48   Storrs, 'Disaster at Darien,' 12–15, 19, 21–3.

11 February 1700, having taken four months to reach the isthmus via London and Barbados, where he had purchased a sloop and bought provisions.[49] On arrival he ordered the release of those imprisoned by the Council, and within a day recommended seizing the initiative by an attack on the Spanish. On 13 February he left Fort St Andrew with two hundred men and a party of Tule and marched to a small village on the banks of the River Acla, where they spent the night. In the morning they were joined by more Tule troops under Captain Pedro and, on climbing a nearby cordillera, spotted Spanish forces fortifying themselves at the frontier post of Toubacanti, a few miles away on the crest of a hill.[50] The following morning (15 February) a patrol was dispatched to gain intelligence, and acting on their information Campbell of Fonab launched a surprise attack on the stockade, despite being unaware of the size of the Spanish force, which in fact numbered only about 200 men under Miguel Cordones.[51] This bold strategy was vindicated when the Spanish fled, although seven Scots died and about fourteen were wounded, including Campbell himself and Lieutenant Turnbull.[52] There was no exact record of Tule and Spanish losses, although rumour and press reports in Scotland were to paint a picture of massive Spanish slaughter. Borland put the Spanish casualties at only eight or nine dead and three prisoners. On the return of the victorious colonists to New Edinburgh on 18 February there were joyous celebrations, or according to Borland, 'excessive drunkenness, profane swearing, ranting, boasting and singing'. The ecstatic mood did not last, for in late February eleven Spanish vessels came into view.[53]

Following the interrogation of two Scottish deserters, Canillas had ordered an immediate attack on the settlement by land and sea under Don Juan de Pimienta, the new Governor of Cartagena.[54] At Golden Island Pimienta was joined by Admiral Don Francisco Salmon and on 1 March 200 men were landed east of the settlement near Carret Bay to establish a beach-head and probe the Scottish defensive positions.[55] Two days later 300 more Spanish troops came ashore and further

[49]   Prebble, *Darien*, 256, Insh, *Company of Scotland*, 188.
[50]   In the Spanish sources 'Tubuganti,' Gallup-Diaz, *Door of the Seas*, 121.
[51]   *Ibid.*, 137.
[52]   See Prebble, *Darien*, 256–61 for a detailed description of Toubacanti.
[53]   Borland, *History of Darien*, 58–9.
[54]   Prebble, *Darien*, 254–5, Storrs, 'Disaster at Darien,' 25–6.
[55]   Insh, *Company of Scotland*, 193–4, Prebble, *Darien*, 287.

troops and ammunition followed.[56] The Scots fortified the colony but were weakened by further small-scale attacks and on 18 March a large Spanish contingent pushed them back behind the ditch, cutting off the fort's water supply. The colonists were forced to dig for water inside the fort, which was 'brackish and unwholesome'. By this time most of the officers were dead and many colonists were dying each day.[57] Without water and under distressing conditions the Council sought terms with the Spanish. A conference was held between Pimienta and Veitch and articles of capitulation signed on 31 March 1700. The Scots were allowed to evacuate the colony with military honours, arms and ammunition, and take what was left of their goods and provisions.[58] The Tule were not forgotten; the seventh article specified that they should not be molested by the Spanish following the withdrawal.[59] The Scots were given two weeks to make preparations and embark. By the evening of 11 April they were aboard their ships.

Mortality rates at the isthmus were far worse than on the first expedition. Byres, who left the colony on 6 February to attempt to obtain provisions in Jamaica, noted that by the time he departed 46 had died at Fort St Andrew, a death rate of 0.7 per day.[60] According to Borland, 300 were buried during the four months and 12 days at Caledonia, an average of 2.3 deaths each day.[61] In the period following Byres' departure the death rate had risen to an average of almost four per day. In total about 460 (35 per cent) of the 1,300 who left the Clyde in August were dead.

The agony of the Scots was symbolised by the dreadful demise of the unfortunate Edinburgh lawyer Daniel MacKay, who had been a councillor on the first expedition and had originally left the colony in April 1699. He attempted to return on the second expedition but just missed the fleet before it sailed and was forced to board the *Speedy Return,* another relief ship dispatched to the isthmus. Between Jamaica and Darien, leaning over the stern while fishing for sharks, he fell into the sea and was torn to pieces by the creatures he was trying to catch.[62]

---

[56]   *Ibid.,* 289.

[57]   Borland, *History of Darien,* 10, 62.

[58]   Insh, *Company of Scotland,* 194–7.

[59]   Borland, *History of Darien,* 67.

[60]   Byres, *Letter to a Friend,* 152–7.

[61]   Borland, *History of Darien,* 73.

[62]   *Ibid.,* 73.

Five ships and two sloops left the colony. If the days in Darien were agony, the voyage to Jamaica was a journey into hell: 'the Poor sick men were sadly crowded together, especially aboard the Rising-Sun like so many Hogs in a sty, or sheep in a fold'. Sometimes eight or nine were buried in a morning on the *Rising Sun* and within a month more than 250 had perished on the ships. Again many survivors decided to remain on Jamaica as indentured labourers rather than risk the journey home. Nearly 100 more died during the three month stay on the island, including minister Alexander Shields, who by this time was 'heart weary and broken with this company of men'. He was buried in a cemetery near Kingston by some kind English residents of Port Royal; a Scotswoman Isobel Murray paying for his funeral expenses. Two young students of divinity, Mr Greg and Mr Potter, also died in Jamaica.[63]

Only the *Speedy Return*, the relief ship that had arrived after the surrender to the Spanish, and Campbell of Fonab's sloop safely returned to Scotland.[64] An old sloop the Scots had obtained was shipwrecked on an island west of Jamaica.[65] The *Hope of Bo'ness* was leaking badly and after the colonists were transferred to the *Rising Sun* she was forced to make for Cartagena to avoid sinking. There she was sold to the Spanish for a small price.[66]

In June another very large Spanish force of ten ships carrying 4,800 men, led by Don Pedro Fernández de Navarrete, finally left Cadiz.[67] This substantial mobilisation indicated that Spain was still a significant power despite her relative decline. The Spanish were, of course, unaware of the difficulties under which the Scots had suffered at Darien and the lack of cash in the Company of Scotland coffers at home. They did not know that the colony would have collapsed anyway. Had the Scots somehow held onto their position at the isthmus for a few more months, they would have faced another intensive Spanish attack. The directors had completely misjudged the ability of Spain to mount a major offensive against them.

On 21 July the *Rising Sun* sailed from Jamaica. In the Gulf of Florida she was hit by a violent storm which smashed her masts and

---

[63] *Ibid.*, 75, 77–9.
[64] Insh, *Company of Scotland*, 197.
[65] Borland, *History of Darien*, 76.
[66] Prebble, *Darien*, 301, Insh, *Company of Scotland*, 197.
[67] Storrs, 'Disaster at Darien,' 24.

turned her into a 'wreck upon the sea'. With difficulty she struggled
to the coast of Carolina where on 24 August she anchored, about nine
miles from the harbour of Charles Town. On the night of 3 September
a devastating hurricane hit the coast and she was sunk. One hundred
and twelve on board perished, including Captain James Gibson and
Alexander Hamilton.[68] It had been an exhilarating but tragically short
journey for the young accountant. The sinking of the Company's most
expensive asset with such terrible loss of life was devastating. Borland
lamented that:

> This last blow, was one of the sorest and most tremenduous of all
> the sad stroaks, which have befallen this design and company
> concerned therein hitherto. *Quis talia fando temperet a*
> *lachrymis?* [69]

There were 15 lucky survivors, including James Byres and the minister
Archibald Stobo and his wife, who were on shore when the hurricane
hit. The *Duke of Hamilton* went down in the same storm in the harbour of Charles Town, but fortunately those on board were saved.
The *Hope* was cast onto rocks on the west coast of Cuba, although
most colonists reached dry land and some eventually returned to
Jamaica. Captain Veitch had died at sea before the shipwreck.[70]

Of fourteen Company ships that sailed from Scotland, 11 (80 per
cent) never returned.[71] The wreck and capture rates of VOC ships in the
period 1675–99 were very low in comparison: for outward voyages
from the Dutch Republic, two per cent were wrecked and one per cent
captured, and on homeward journeys from the East Indies, 3.6 per
cent wrecked and 0.3 per cent captured.[72] This brutal differential
illustrates the massive advantage of a company with a hundred years'

---

[68]   Borland, *History of Darien*, 79-82. The Latin quotation is from Virgil's
       Aeneid (2.8): 'Who in speaking of such matters could refrain from tears?'
       Stobo became minister at Charles Town in Carolina. NAS, GD 1/564/12,
       21 December 1700.

[69]   Borland, *History of Darien*, 81.

[70]   *Ibid.*, 84.

[71]   The 14 ships were the *St Andrew, Caledonia, Unicorn, Dolphin,*
       Endeavour, Dispatch, Olive Branch, Hopeful Binning, Rising Sun, Duke
       of Hamilton, Hope of Bo'ness, Hope, Speedy Return, and *Content.*

[72]   Bruijn, Gaastra and Schöffer, *Dutch-Asiatic Shipping,* 75, 91.

experience of overseas trade backed up with capital provided by the Dutch economic miracle and an extensive communication network.

The Scottish expeditions to Darien in 1698 and 1699 resulted in massive loss of life. Borland put the total deaths on land and sea at nearly 2,000 (71 per cent) and there is evidence for the deaths of at least 1,500.[73] Fate had indeed dealt the Scots a severe blow and the minister sought explanation in divine intervention:

> From such an observable succession of counteracting providences in this design, who cannot but remark, and see a holy and sovereign God, signally appearing and fighting against this undertaking. As if men should say, This design shall succeed, and God say, It shall not prosper.[74]

---

[73] Borland, *History of Darien*, 86. The figure of 1,500 assumes 44 died at sea on the first expedition, 200 at the isthmus (Borland puts this at 300), and 265 on the voyages from Darien; 150 of the 300 colonists on the *Olive Branch* and *Hopeful Binning* in Jamaica; 164 at sea on the second expedition to Darien, 300 at the isthmus, and 362 on the ships after the evacuation, including the sinking of the *Rising Sun*. There were no doubt other deaths in Jamaica, New York, and elsewhere and so Borland's total may be close to the actual loss of life. The total number who sailed was about 2,800: 1,200 on the first expedition, 1,300 on the second, and 300 on the *Olive Branch* and *Hopeful Binning*.

[74] *Ibid.*, 27.

CHAPTER FIFTEEN

Frenzy

Our Soveraignty and Freedom is Violated, Our Laws trampled upon, and Our Trade interrupted; how Our Brethren have been Starved and made Slaves, Our Colony deserted, and Our Ships burnt and lost Abroad, whilst Our Petitions have been rejected, Our Company baffled, Our People Famish'd, Our Metropolis burnt, and Flames of Division kindled amongst Us at Home.[1]

ON 14 MAY 1700 Queensberry was welcomed by Tweeddale and other nobles at Musselburgh and on the links was saluted by a battalion of Foot Guards. The *Edinburgh Gazette* reported his reception on entering the Scottish capital:

For above a Mile before he made his Entry, both sides of the Road was Crowded with vast Multitudes of People, who shewed great Satisfaction by Repeating Huzzaa's, and all other Extraordinary Signes of Respect and Esteem; At which time also, some Field Pieces upon the Abbay Hill Discharged above 40 Shot, and both sides of the Street from the Water-Gate to his Graces Lodging, was lined with Foot Guards, all in very good order. The Cavalcade, what Nobility, Gentry, and Magistrates, and Inhabitants of this City, was Generally computed to be above 1200 Horse, and betwixt 30 and 40 Coaches, and a greater confluence of People than hath been seen of a long time on the like occasion.[2]

The report was censored by the government and provided a sanitised version of the duke's arrival which did not reflect the nation's anger.[3]

---

[1]   *The People of Scotland's Groans and Lamentable Complaints, Pour'd out before the High Court of Parliament* (Edinburgh, 1700), 1.

[2]   *Edinburgh Gazette*, no. 128, 13–16 May 1700.

[3]   A.J. Mann, *The Scottish Book Trade 1500–1720: Print Commerce and Print Control in Early Modern Scotland* (East Lothian, 2000), 148.

Parliament opened a week later on 21 May. The King's letter to his Scottish subjects stated he was 'heartily sorry for the misfortunes and losses that the nation has sustained' and recommended they should encourage manufacturers and improve the 'native product' of their land, rather than concentrating on foreign trade. The Company of Scotland was not mentioned. The opposition attempted to have the issue of Darien considered first 'as a National concern,', but to delay proceedings the Court argued that religious issues should take precedence. A representation by the council general was read in the chamber, asking parliament to 'Vindicat, Support and Protect' the Company, provide compensation for its losses, and maintain their 'just right and title' to the settlement of Caledonia. Petitions were received from shires and burghs asserting and vindicating the Company's right to Darien. But on 30 May Queensberry adjourned the session until 20 June and a series of further adjournments followed.[4] The Court hoped that careful use of management over the summer would weaken the opposition, making it easier to secure supply (tax revenue) from a more pliant parliament. The house was not to meet again until October.

As a result the political atmosphere remained highly charged. William's letter and the adjournment intensified his unpopularity and encouraged Jacobites to become more vocal and visible: 'Monday last was a great day amongst the Jacobites here, being the birthday of the pretended Prince of Wales; and it was solemnized by a great many this year, who never did it before'. A Latin poem by Company shareholder and Jacobite Dr Archibald Pitcairne contained 'a great many satirical and obscene reflections upon the King in it'.[5] There was talk that unless William accepted the legality of the colony another address would be signed by 40,000 and a Convention of Estates called in defiance of royal authority.[6]

Meanwhile the directors continued with business and anxiously waited for news from the Caribbean. In early June they rewarded volunteer George Cowan for his loyalty and bravery in Company service. He had sailed to Darien with the first expedition but was incarcerated in

4   APS, X, 190–1, 193–5, W. Douglas Jones, 'The Darien Reaction: National Failure and Popular Politics in Scotland, 1699–1701' (University of Edinburgh MSc, 2001), 38, NAS, GD 158/965, 289.

5   Carstares SP, 527–8. Archibald Pitcairne (1652–1713) was a doctor, dramatist and poet from an Episcopalian family who subscribed £200 in the Company's stock. ODNB, 44, 422–5.

6   Carstares SP, 527.

a series of Spanish jails following the sinking of the *Dolphin*. Now, miraculously, he was willing to return to the isthmus. Andrew Livingston, the *Dolphin's* surgeon, who was also imprisoned at Cartagena and somehow escaped, was rewarded a gift of four gallons of brandy.[7]

The glorious news of the victory at Toubacanti broke a few weeks later. Details of the battle reached Edinburgh on 19 or 20 June and provoked a storm of rejoicing. Initial reports published in the *Edinburgh Gazette* greatly exaggerated the slaughter and suggested the Scots had killed five hundred Spanish soldiers, making it one of the most brilliant military victories in Scottish history.[8]

To celebrate, all 'true Caledonians' were called on to place illuminations in their windows on the High Street of Edinburgh.[9] The presence of candles in the windows of the tall tenements of the city was a common form of celebration, usually sanctioned by the privy council on the King's birthday.[10] On 20 June 1700 it represented a direct challenge to the authority of the government. The events that followed were a violent climax to a long period of intense political agitation; a patriotic celebration of military success and a declaration of support for the rights of the colony. They quickly deteriorated into a violent attack on those who were perceived to be enemies of the Company.

That evening the windows of the Royal Mile sparkled with defiant support for the Company of Scotland and the Darien colony; banners with 'Caledonia in great characters' and bonfires accompanying the illuminations.[11] By nine o'clock the festive mood had turned sour and, the town guard proving ineffectual, a mob of a few hundred was in

---

[7]   RBS, D/1/2, 4 June and 13 June 1700.

[8]   Jones, 'Darien Reaction,' 29. The *Gazette* had previously reported other grossly inaccurate accounts of Scottish military success. In June and July 1699 there were stories that the Scots had led an army of 6,000 Tule and taken 700 Spanish prisoners and on 5 October the paper reported a significant engagement in which 3,000 Spanish soldiers were overrun and a 'great number' killed.

[9]   *Carstares SP*, 539.

[10] A proclamation by the burgh council in October 1695, for example, commanded the inhabitants of the city and suburbs 'to put illuminations of candles in their windows to the high street on 4 November, the King's birthday.' Fines were imposed on those not doing so or not wearing their best clothes. *Records of the Burgh of Edinburgh*, 183, 240.

[11] NAS, GD 158/965, 271–2.

control of the High Street.[12] The *Edinburgh Gazette* reported that a
large number of boys started throwing stones at windows that were
not lit. They were soon joined by footmen, other 'Inferior Persons,' and
some 'in the fashion of Gentlemen.'[13] Another report noted that some
nobles were seen in the crowd, including Lord Drummond and the
Earl Marischal, well known for their Jacobite sympathies.[14] The houses
of government figures and those associated with the Court Party were
targeted, including the Earl of Melville, Seafield, Lord Carmichael, the
Lord Provost, and other magistrates.[15] Seafield himself was not in town,
but all the windows of his house were smashed while his terrified wife
sought refuge in a back room. The rioters then broke into his cellars
and consumed his wine.[16] After the windows of director, but Court
supporter, Adam Cockburn of Ormiston were broken, some of the
Company's servants arrived with violins and danced in the rooms immediately above his lodgings, to his great annoyance.[17] A minister who had
not prayed for Caledonia, David Blair, had his windows smashed. It was
estimated that £5,000 of glass was destroyed that night.[18]

The mob ordered the city bells to be rung and burst into song with
'Willful Willy, wilt thou be willful still,' mocking the authority of the
King.[19] Some proceeded to the Lord Advocate's house on the High
Street to obtain a warrant for the release of prisoners from the Tolbooth
and Sir James Stewart was threatened until he complied. The rioters were
intent on freeing two prisoners, James Watson and Hugh Paterson.
Watson had printed two Country Party pamphlets written by surgeon-
apothecary Paterson.[20] Both were imprisoned by the privy council
because the pamphlets were viewed as being critical of the government.[21]

[12]   Jones, 'Darien Reaction,' 31.

[13]   *Edinburgh Gazette*, no. 139, 20–24 June 1700.

[14]   NAS, GD 1/891/3, 24 June 1700.

[15]   NAS, GD 158/965, 271–2.

[16]   NAS, GD 1/891/3, 24 June 1700.

[17]   RBS, D/1/2, 25 June 1700.

[18]   *Carstares SP*, 539–40.

[19]   Ibid., 546.

[20]   *People of Scotland's Groans* and *A Short Speech prepared by a worthy
       member to be Spoken in Parliament* (Edinburgh, 1700).

[21]   Insh, *Company of Scotland*, 217–18. A week before their arrest the privy
       council had extended its control over press and pamphlet freedom by the
       creation of a committee 'anent printers and booksellers.' Mann, *Scottish
       Book Trade*, 176.

The door of the city jail was brought down and in the melee a number of other prisoners escaped, including two Frasers being held for accessory to the rape of Lady Lovat. Two men accused of buggery remained incarcerated.[22] By three o'clock the next morning the disorder was over.[23] One report noted that some of the town guard were killed and several seriously wounded, while another said that only one was killed.[24]

Riots of this kind were a common expression of popular politics in the early modern period. There had been a riot in the city in 1682, an anti-Catholic one in 1686, and several at the time of the Glorious Revolution.[25] Rioting was encouraged and manipulated for political ends and the degree of organisation on the night of 20 June 1700 suggests the Toubacanti riot, as it became known, was a premeditated tactic of the Country Party, taking advantage of the groundswell of popular indignation about the treatment of the Company. One report named Tweeddale as the instigator.[26] Melville noted that the opposition in 1700 had overwhelming popular support: 'There is no more speaking to people now, than to a man in a fever'.[27]

Within a week a dozen suspects were arrested and four men, Charles Weir, a trainee cook, Robert Henryson, a servant of James Watson, and the servants Alexander Acheson and John Easton, stood trial on 29 July charged with unlawful convocation, armed assault on the King's officers, and fire-raising.[28] The lenient punishments did not please the government. Argyll referred to them as 'smaller than my tyrant governour has, while at school, inflicted on me for going to play without leave'.[29] The cook was to be scourged and banished from the realm and the other three pilloried and banished.[30] There were further problems carrying out the punishments as the four men were

---

[22]   Jones, 'Darien Reaction,' 31.

[23]   NAS, GD 1/891/3, 24 June 1700.

[24]   Jones, 'Darien Reaction,' 33, NAS, GD 158/965, 271–2.

[25]   *RPC*, third series, vii, 403. A few hundred apprentices were involved. T. Harris, 'Reluctant Revolutionaries? The Scots and the Revolution of 1688-9' in *Politics and the Political Imagination in Later Stuart Britain*, ed. H. Nenner (Rochester, 1998), 101, 106.

[26]   NAS, GD 1/891/3, 24 June 1700.

[27]   *Carstares SP*, 544.

[28]   Jones, 'Darien Reaction,' 34–5.

[29]   *Carstares SP*, 599.

[30]   Insh, *Company of Scotland*, 224, Jones, 'Darien Reaction,' 35.

cheered and kissed by adoring crowds and showered with flowers to
the accompaniment of flutes.[31] The hangman was understandably
intimidated and did not apply the lash with any vigour. The Edinburgh
council then sent for the Haddington hangman to enforce the punishment, but he failed to appear after gauging the atmosphere on the
High Street.[32]

The euphoria, however, did not last. A week later news of the final
capitulation reached Scotland and crushed all optimism. For some,
like Tullibardine, national loss was mixed with personal grief, as he
heard of the death of his brother Lord Mungo Murray at the isthmus.[33]
Despite this setback the political campaign continued. A second National
Address, seeking the recall of parliament to assert the Company's rights,
was being organised before the riot and gained momentum following the
news of the abandonment.[34] The Country Party also launched a campaign calling for a boycott of the purchase of foreign woollen goods
and French wine and brandy.[35]

The only hero to emerge from the Darien disaster, Alexander
Campbell of Fonab, was back in Edinburgh by the middle of July.[36] In
August the directors decided to provide him with a 'distinguishing
mark of their favour till such time as the Company's affairs may admit
of gratifying his services'. In other words they had insufficient funds
for a substantial reward and instead he was to be given a medal, cast
from some of the gold that returned on the *African Merchant*, a ship
sailing under Company commission.[37] The medal was designed and

---

[31]   *Carstares SP*, 615, 618.

[32]   Insh, *Company of Scotland*, 224–5. A proclamation had been issued the
       day before for the arrest of Captain Gavin Hamilton, Captain Kenneth
       Urquhart, and Captain Kenneth MacKenzie, who were identified as the
       main instigators of the riot. Urquhart was arrested but released without
       trial in December. Jones, 'Darien Reaction,' 36.

[33]   NAS, GD 406/1/4687.

[34]   *Carstares SP*, 526, Jones, 'Darien Reaction,' 38. The second National
       Address was delivered in November but as its principal aim had been to
       precipitate the calling of parliament its impact was muted.

[35]   *Ibid.*, 39. NAS, GD 158/965, 277. The second National Address has been
       described as a 'comprehensive manifesto' which combined 'the main
       opposition policies of Caledonia and supply, with the universal appeal of
       religion, and the historical precedent of the Claim of Right,' Patrick,
       'People and Parliament,' 267.

[36]   NAS, GD 1/891/3, 15 July 1700.

[37]   RBS, D/1/2, 20 August 1700.

engraved by Leman de Hooges from a sketch of the engagement drawn by Fonab himself.[38] On one side are the arms of the Company of Scotland; on the other a classical warrior in the foreground leads the attack on Toubacanti. It was 'struck' in Holland but not presented to the Scottish hero until 15 January 1705, almost five years after his famous victory.[39]

The opposition was weakened by the news of the capitulation and began to divide into moderate and extreme factions. The moderates were willing to accept the reality that the dream of a Scottish empire in Central America was over. Queensberry believed that influential director Sir Francis Scott of Thirlestane 'might now be taken off' with the offer of a job, the position of Master of Works. William Paterson had been recruited by the Court and was attempting to persuade Country parliamentarians not to raise the issue of Darien in the present session. Queensberry hoped to secure him £100 for his support of the government. Perhaps surprisingly given the magnitude of the disaster at the isthmus, Paterson continued to be viewed as something of a financial guru, the Lord Advocate referring to his 'prodigious genius' and 'vast extended thought'. Queensberry concluded in a letter to Carstares: 'In short, if money could be had, I would not doubt of success in the King's business here'.[40]

Parliament was finally reconvened on 29 October. Government tactics were to make positive statements to the house, provide legislation to attract some of the opposition, and use bribery and management to persuade others.[41] On this occasion the King referred directly to the Company in his letter, informing parliament that he had, at last, considered the address of 1698, and was 'heartily sorrie for the Companies Loss'. He was willing to assent to 'repairing the losses and supporting and promoting the interest' of the Company, but could not assert their right to Darien: 'our yielding in that matter had infallibly disturbed the general peace of Christendom'.[42]

This somewhat conciliatory response did nothing to placate the anger of most of the Country Party and the atmosphere in parliament remained hostile. The nine hour session on Thursday 31 October was

---

38 Insh, *Company of Scotland*, illustrations facing pages 185 and 193.
39 RBS, D/1/3, 15 January 1705.
40 *Carstares SP*, 584–5, 621–3, 630–2, 646.
41 Riley, *King William*, 149–151.
42 *APS*, X, 201.

described by Marchmont as the 'most clamourous contentious and hot' he had experienced in a parliamentary career dating back to 1665.[43] The mood in the chamber and nation was highlighted when two pamphlets by Walter Herries and a 'scurrilous Lampoon' in rhyme, *Caledonia or the Pedlar turn'd Merchant*, were condemned to be burned at the Cross of Edinburgh by the common hangman. A reward of £6,000 Scots was offered for apprehending Herries. Extracts from the pamphlets were read in parliament and found to be 'blasphemous scandalous and calumnious libells reflecting upon every thing that is sacred and upon the honour of this Nation'.[44]

Caledonia was a scurrilous piece of anti-Scottish doggerel. In its 127 verses the history of the Company of Scotland and the role of Paterson were mocked to brutal effect. A poor example of the poetic art it may have been, but as a piece of raucous Scot-baiting it hit the mark:

> A Sorry Poor Nation, which lies as full North,
> As a great many Lands which are wiser,
> Was resolv'd to set up for a People of Worth,
> That the Loons who laugh'd at Her might prize her.[45]

The Scots were not in the mood for humour. In late November news of the fate of the *Rising Sun* intensified the gloom. 'I am sure there neaver were so many unlucky accidents befell any people as has befallen that Company' reflected the Earl of Selkirk.[46]

Parliament continued its violent course into 1701. Marchmont again lamented that the sessions were the 'hottest mast contentious and disorderlie' he had ever seen.[47] Petitions were still arriving from Company supporters in the shires and burghs and on 10 January par-

---

[43] NAS, GD 158/965, 298A. The focus of the storm was a contested by-election between Lord Basil Hamilton (Country Party) and William Stewart, son of the late Earl of Galloway (Court Party), over who should be parliamentary commissioner of the shire of Wigtown. The election had taken place on 8 October in the Wigtown Tolbooth but the result was disputed. Patrick, 'People and Parliament,' 270–7.

[44] *Caledonia; or, the Pedlar turn'd Merchant. A Tragi-Comedy, As it was Acted by His Majesty's Subjects of Scotland in the King of Spain's Province of Darien* (London, 1700), NAS, GD 158/965, 299–301, APS, X, 211–12.

[45] *Caledonia; or, the Pedlar turn'd Merchant*, 1.

[46] NAS, GD 406/1/8581.

[47] NAS, GD 158/965, 314.

liament approved a series of resolutions attacking English opposition to the Company. The memorial to the Senate of Hamburg was again singled out as 'the occasion of great losses and disappointments' and the proclamations in the English plantations declared to be 'injurious and prejudicial' to the rights and liberties of the Company and 'a great occasion of the loss and ruine of the said colony'. But another resolution, that those advising the King on these occasions were traitors, did not receive wide enough support in the chamber and was withdrawn.[48]

If popular frenzy reached its apotheosis on the streets of Edinburgh on 20 June 1700, the political battle between Court and Country parties finally came to a head in parliament on 14 January 1701. The Country Party wanted an act asserting the Company's right to Caledonia, while the Court Party pressed for a less contentious address to the King.[49] Despite the venomous atmosphere the vote was carried in favour of the Court by 108 to 84. The passage of reformist and popular mercantilist legislation, including acts preventing wrongful imprisonment, banning the import and wearing of foreign woollen manufactures and silk, the export of wool, and the import of French wine and brandy, may have helped to obtain some votes. Other pressures and monetary inducements were also applied.[50] A financial package to recapitalise the Company from the rents of bishoprics and the post office, with tonnage and poundage for twenty-one years, was also rejected by parliament. The Court was willing, however, to support an act extending Company privileges by another nine years following their expiry, and this was passed on 31 January. On the same day the government finally secured much needed supply.[51] Despite the anger and fury of the session the Court had survived. Parliament was adjourned on 1 February.

In March an engraving appeared representing the nation as a young woman, Scotia, and listing the 84 loyal supporters of the colony of Caledonia who had voted against the Court in parliament.[52] In the bottom right hand corner of the engraving, under the shade of a giant thistle, a group of men were banished by an angel into the flames of hell. From the devil's mouth came a quotation from Virgil:

---

[48]   *APS*, X, 242–3.

[49]   Patrick, 'People and Parliament,' 286.

[50]   Riley, *King William*, 150–1, *APS*, X, 272–82.

[51]   *Ibid.*, 257, 282.

[52]   NAS, JC 26/81/31.

'*vendidit hic auro patriam*' (this man sold his country for gold) – a reference to the use of bribery to secure parliamentary votes. From the
angel's mouth: '*Procul o procul este prophani*' (Go far, far away, you
uninitiated).[53] It was understood by contemporaries that the men
depicted in the engraving were members of the government; according
to Marchmont it gave 'great offence and is looked upon as ane alarm
for moveing sedition and disturbance and as a treasonable practice.'.[54]
He had particular reason to be annoyed. The old man with a walking
stick and devil perched on his shoulders represented the elderly chancellor himself.

An attempt was made to suppress the circulation of all copies and
three men, Charles Achmuty, John Thomson, and Roderick
MacKenzie, were quickly arrested on suspicion of being involved in
the engraving's creation. They were all closely associated with the
Company of Scotland. Thomson had been a clerk since September 1696,
Achmuty was originally the Company housekeeper, and MacKenzie
was the indefatigable secretary.[55] The engraving highlights the very
close relationship that had developed between the Company and the
political opposition. Administrative personnel of the Company were
producing anti-government propaganda. Copies were also retrieved
from Country Party leaders Hamilton, Tweeddale, and Lord Whitelaw.
They were all burned by the hangman, except one which was kept for
the King and three or four for the trial.[56] It was thought that some had
been sent to England to be reprinted.

MacKenzie was released on lack of evidence. Thomson and Achmuty
were tried for treason, leasing making, and sedition, but the jury
returned a verdict of 'not proven' on 23 May, despite the defendants
having provided confessions to the privy council.[57] Their accounts
informed the government that the engraving of Scotia was designed
and drawn on paper by Thomson in the Company of Scotland office.
He had shown it to several friends including Achmuty, Matthew

---

[53] *The Darien Adventure* (Edinburgh, 1998), 23–4. Both quotations are from
     Virgil's *Aeneid* (6.621 and 6.259). I would like to thank Allan Hood for
     identifying and translating them for me.

[54] NAS, GD 158/965, 348.

[55] RBS, D/1/1, 144–5.

[56] NAS, GD 158/965, 348–9, 352, 355.

[57] NAS, JC 26/81/31. The statutory crime of leasing making was not clearly
     distinguished from treason but involved bringing dishonour on the King
     and was punishable by death until 1703.

Finlayson, and others, and taken it to Robert Wood, an engraver in
Niddry's Wynd, who engraved the plate at a cost of £6 10s, Achmuty
providing £3 10s. This was a very large amount for a housekeeper to
spend on a piece of propaganda and the money is likely to have come
from another Country Party source.[58] Roderick MacKenzie provided the
list of 84 loyal supporters.[59]

As a burning political issue, however, Darien had run its course.
By late 1701 the political fire, if not extinguished, was considerably
subdued in ferocity and the Court was able to re-establish some control
over Scottish politics. This was principally due to external events. In
March uncertainty on the international scene was undermining share
and bond prices in London, and by the summer Seafield thought war
was inevitable.[60] In September Louis xiv recognised James viii as the
rightful King of Scotland, England and Ireland, reneging on the Treaty
of Ryswick.[61] Marchmont believed that Louis' action was a vital factor
in undermining support for Scottish Jacobitism.[62] There was a shift in
moderate Presbyterian opinion back behind William. He may have
showed little support for the Company of Scotland, but the prospect of
a Jacobite restoration was even more unpalatable for most Presbyterians.
The government grabbed the political initiative for the first time in many
years and organised a counter-addressing campaign in late 1701 to bol-
ster loyalty to William.[63] Now the King received supportive addresses
rather than ones complaining about his treatment of the Company. The
falling political temperature was evident on the King's birthday in
November, when illuminations appointed by the privy council were
'very full and without any disorder'.[64] In December 1701 a Country
Party strategy document made no mention of Darien and the last months
of William's reign were surprisingly quiet on the political front.[65]

---

[58] Achmuty's salary in 1696 was £12 10s.

[59] NAS, JC 26/81/31.

[60] NAS, GD 406/1/6506, Carstares SP, 705–6.

[61] Ferguson, Scotland's Relations, 199.

[62] NAS, GD 158/966, 44.

[63] Ibid.. 44–57. According to Bowie, 'Counter-addressing was rare in early
modern Scottish politics, as the Court did not often seek populist support
for its policies,' K. Bowie, 'Public Opinion, Popular Politics and the Union
of 1707,' SHR, 82, (2003), 249.

[64] NAS, GD 158/966, 42.

[65] NAS, GD 406/1/4919.

CHAPTER SIXTEEN

Other Ventures

I think the Salt and Fishery to be the best and the greatest things that ever was proposed to the Company of Scotland at so little Hazard and Charge.

WILLIAM PATERSON[1]

I dont understand the Africain Company for I thought they were to trade into the Indies and not sett up to ruin manufacteries.

LORD JOHN HAMILTON[2]

Some who, I am perswaded, wish'd very well to the Company, did propose, with great earnestness, That they should bend their Thoughts chiefly to the East-India-Trade.

RODERICK MACKENZIE[3]

I do readily allow, the first Scheme of Trade to the East-Indies had a Probability of Success in it, a Thing I can not grant to the Affair of Darien.

DANIEL DEFOE[4]

FOR GOOD REASON THE Company of Scotland has become known as the Darien Company. The attempt to establish a colony on the isthmus of Central America was central to the Company's history and ate up the vast majority of its capital. There were, however, other business ventures pursued by the directors. We have already noted the unsuccessful banking enterprise of 1696, but this was only one arm of a diversification strategy.

In May 1696 the directors provided a broad remit to the committee of improvements to investigate other profitable opportunities. The committee resolved that a herring and white fishing venture 'may be of great advantage to the Nation' and trade to Archangel in northern

---

[1] NLS, MS 1914, f104.

[2] NAS, GD 406/1/6868.

[3] MacKenzie, *Full and Exact Account*, 34.

[4] Defoe, *History of Union*, 35.

Russia and Greenland might be profitable. It was proposed that lists of cargoes for Archangel and the Gold and Negro Coasts of Africa, with 'Patterns of the several goods and their prices', be obtained from director James Smyth in London.[5] But these initial soundings were soon overshadowed by another enterprise.

Salt

Salt was a valuable commodity in the early modern world and the Scottish salt industry reasonably buoyant in the later 17th century, as war in Europe after 1689 cut off supplies of French and Spanish salt and boosted domestic producers.[6] On 5 June 1696 the directors approved a motion 'concerning the Improvement of Salt' and on 3 August considered several ideas about an 'intended Salt-works and Fishery'. The seriousness of their intent was reflected in the allocation of £10,000 to the enterprise, which represented 10 per cent of the first call on shareholders. An industry 'expert,', the London merchant Robert Cragg, was invited to Edinburgh in November to investigate possible locations for the venture. William Dunlop and the Glasgow directors were empowered to purchase a plot of land on the Clyde and by March 1697 a site had been chosen in the Bay of Ardmore.[7]

The Company also sought to secure a monopoly over their new method of production. On 12 September a draft act of parliament for making improvements in salt and encouraging fisheries was considered by the directors.[8] But opposition emerged from a number of major noble houses, including Hamilton, Mar, Winton, Wemyss, and St Clair, who were dominant in the salt industry. These salt-masters commissioned a pamphlet that warned the act in favour of the Company would 'undoubtedly destroy the Manufactory of making Salt in this Kingdom'.[9] As with much else in the early history of the Company,

---

[5]   NLS, Adv MS 83.7.1, 1–2.

[6]   C.A. Whatley, *The Scottish Salt Industry 1570–1850* (Aberdeen, 1987), 43.

[7]   RBS, D/1/1, 67, 109, 112, 131, 162, 182, 216.

[8]   *Ibid.*, 133.

[9]   *Reasons Offered to his Grace His Majesties High Commissioner and the Honourable Estates of Parliament by the Dutchess of Hamilton, the Earl of Arran, the Earl of Marr, the Earl of Wintoun, the Countess of Weymss, Lord St Clair, the Lairds of Bougie, Bonhard and Grange, and other Salt-Masters and Heretors of Salt-Works, Against The Overtures proposed by the Affrican Company, anent the making of salt of a new Fashion* (Edinburgh, 1696).

William Paterson was deeply involved in promoting the venture. He wrote to the Earl of Arran, who was displeased about the act, stressing the venture would not damage the business of existing salt makers.[10] Lord John Hamilton, Arran's brother, lamented: 'I dont understand the Africain Company for I thought they were to trade into the Indies and not sett up to ruin manufacteries'.[11] The issue highlights the disengagement of the Hamilton interest from the management of the Company during its early history, despite the significant shareholding of the family, and shows that the directors were willing to take on vested interests. In a pamphlet justifying their position they emphasised their democratic mandate stemming from the very large number of people who were directly or indirectly concerned in the Company, which they claimed was not less than 200,000.[12] When the act was brought before parliament on 16 September it was remitted to the committee of trade, but then passed following some concessions to the salt-masters on 12 October.[13] The Company had strong backing in parliament and there was little opposition in the chamber.[14]

The eternal optimist William Paterson remained very confident about the prospects of the business. On his return from the Continent in July 1697, reeling from the Smyth scandal, he praised the venture in typically fulsome terms: 'I think the Salt and Fishery to be the best and the greatest things that ever was proposed to the Company of Scotland at so little Hazard and Charge'.[15] Paterson believed the risk reward profile was very attractive. Despite considerable effort in securing legislation, however, the enterprise proved a short-lived distraction as the directors' attention soon shifted to the high risk colonial enterprise. The business languished and never produced one grain of salt despite considerable time and effort being expended on it. Only £142 of the

---

[10] NAS, GD 406/1/4139.

[11] NAS, GD 406/1/6868.

[12] *Reasons For passing into an Act, an Overture in Parliament, for making Salt of a new Fashion* (Edinburgh, 1696).

[13] *APS*, X, 13, 47, 80. Whatley, *Scottish Salt Industry*, 86.

[14] NAS, GD 406/1/7531. In June 1690 the representation of lairds in parliament was increased by about 50 per cent. They were therefore a parliamentary force to be reckoned with and also held a very significant proportion of the shares in the Company. Patrick, 'People and Parliament,' 74.

[15] NLS, MS 1914, f104. Paterson was invited to inspect salt works in the south of England with Craggs on his return from the Continent.

allocation of £10,000 was ultimately spent, amounting to just 0.1 per cent of the Company's capital.[16]

East Indies

Some of the subscribers did not share Paterson's enthusiasm for a Darien venture. Roderick MacKenzie noted that: 'some who, I am perswaded, wish'd very well to the Company, did propose, with great earnestness, That they should bend their Thoughts chiefly to the East-India-Trade'.[17] Indeed the activity of the Company in London in 1695 suggests that trade to the East Indies was then at the heart of their strategy, and when the directors sought to raise capital in Holland and Hamburg potential subscribers were led to believe that they would be investing in an East Indian company.

Robert Douglas, a London Scot and director of the Company in England, wrote a vigorous rebuttal of Paterson's Darien scheme in September 1696, arguing instead for an East Indian approach. Paterson's views about Darien, as we have seen, were already well known in merchant circles. Douglas warned the directors not to be 'Led blind-fold by Another at his pleasure without ever requiring him to give ane accompt of his design'. Paterson's belief that ships could reach the East Indies more quickly via the isthmus was challenged by Douglas, who argued that although this may have been the case for voyages to and from Japan and China, it was not for journeys to India, the west coast of Sumatra, the Persian Gulf, and the Red Sea. Instead Douglas highlighted the potential profitability of an East Indian trade. The Scots would avoid the huge cost of buying luxury eastern goods from the Dutch and English, which had been estimated to cost the nation about £60,000 per annum, and he claimed the Company had sufficient capital to establish settlements in both East and West Indies.[18]

Daniel Defoe believed an East Indian trade might have been more successful:

I do readily allow, the first Scheme of Trade to the East-Indies

---

[16]   NLS, Adv MS 83.3.6, f12.

[17]   MacKenzie, *Full and Exact Account*, 34.

[18]   NLS, Adv MS 83.7.4, f23–8. The time taken depends upon type of ship, area of sail, season of the year, and the wind. I would like to thank Prof Charles Withers of the Institute of Geography at Edinburgh University for this information.

had a Probability of Success in it, a Thing I can not grant to the Affair of Darien; which, I think, had not one Branch belonging to its Contrivance, but what was Big with necessary Abortions.[19]

As we have already seen, the Company factors in Hamburg, the Stratfords, also advised the directors to pursue a smaller scale East Indian venture, citing the relatively successful example of the Danish East India Company.[20]

Commissions

The Company was initially envisaged as a global trading vehicle. But because most of the capital was spent on the Darien colony there was little left to fund ventures to other locations. As a result the directors issued commissions to syndicates of merchants, allowing them to trade under the provisions of the act and return goods tax free to Scotland. In return the Company received a promise of 5 per cent of the profits.[21] The first proposal of this kind was made by George MacKenzie, Viscount Tarbat, and a group of Edinburgh merchants in June 1698, just before the first expedition sailed for the isthmus. They wanted to raise capital to buy a small ship and cargo for a voyage to the East Indies, but there is no evidence to indicate whether this venture ever materialised.[22]

On 25 August 1698 the Rotterdam merchant Gilbert Stewart applied for a similar commission to trade to Africa and by September 1699 the *African Merchant* was fitted out for a voyage to the Gold Coast.[23] The ship returned safely to Scotland in July 1700 with gold, ivory, rice, and the remains of the cargo that was unsold. The directors bought the gold from Stewart and obtained a warrant from the privy council to coin it in imitation of the gold guineas produced in England from African metal.[24] These pistoles and half-pistoles were to be the

---

[19] Defoe, *History of Union*, 34.

[20] NLS, MS 1914, f75.

[21] *Darien Shipping Papers*, 253-4.

[22] RBS, D/1/1, 517, D/1/2, 11 August 1698. The merchants were Robert Watson, Mr John Duncan, John Marjoribanks, James Marjoribanks and John Geills.

[23] RBS, D/1/2, 12 September 1699.

[24] Some of the gold brought back from Africa on the *Golden Lion* in the 1630s was coined by the Scottish Mint, Law, 'First Scottish Guinea Company,' 185-202.

last gold coins struck by the Scottish Mint. However, as the vessel was trading under commission, only 5 per cent of the profits went to the Company. The venture returned £46,668 Scots, or £3,889 sterling, and the directors therefore expected to recoup £194 sterling.[25] But Gilbert Stewart insisted on an abatement, claiming that the voyage was not as profitable as he had hoped, and offering the court only £100.The directors eventually accepted a compromise figure of £150, which was paid in two instalments: £100 in December 1701 and £50 two years later in December 1703.[26]

Another opportunity that might have developed into a trading relationship of some consequence emerged when negotiations began with Armenian merchants of Amsterdam. The Armenians formed one of the great trading networks in the early modern world, operating in Europe, Russia, the Mediterranean, Asia Minor, Persia, India, Indonesia, the Philippines, and even Tibet. Their success was based on knowledge of supply sources, market conditions and languages, family networks, mobility, and access to capital.[27] In February 1699 Martin Gregory wrote from Amsterdam to James Gibson, the commander of the *Rising Sun*, enquiring about using Company ships to transport cargoes custom free to India.[28] The directors considered the matter, concluded that the proposal was reasonable, and requested that Gregory and other Armenians come to Scotland for negotiations.[29] However, the Armenian connection was soon overshadowed by news of the successful landing of the first expedition at Darien. Scotland was now an imperial power in her own right and the attention of directors was, understandably, focused on securing relief ships to provide the new colony with provisions.

In a letter of 26 June Gregory told Gibson he had heard the *Rising Sun* was to be sent to the West Indies: 'I hope you will persuade the

---

[25]   Insh, *Company of Scotland*, 249, 252.

[26]   RBS, D/1/3, 25 November 1701, NLS, Adv MS 83.5.2, f45, f51.

[27]   M. Aghassian and K. Kévonian, 'Armenian Trade in the Indian Ocean in the 17th and 18th Centuries' in *Asian Merchants and Businessmen in the Indian Ocean and the China Sea*, (eds.) D. Lombard and J. Aubin (Oxford, 2000), 154–177. At times Armenians freighted ships from joint-stock companies of other nations. For example, in 1702 Armenian merchants chartered a ship from the EIC for a voyage from Calcutta to the Persian Gulf. P.D. Curtin, *Cross-cultural trade in world history* (Cambridge, 1984), 197.

[28]   *Darien Shipping Papers*, 221–2.

[29]   RBS, D/1/2, 23 Feb 1699.

honourable Lords to send nott that ship thence, butt to make an agreement with us'. He offered a return of 12 per cent to the Company and the prospect of a steady stream of business of two or three hundred thousand guilders each year (£19,000 to £28,000).[30] The Armenians were clearly serious about the joint venture, for in July Jonas Gregory, the brother of Mr Martin Gregory, and Mr Gregory di Estephan arrived in Edinburgh for discussions. But the directors came to the surprising decision that their proposal was not of sufficient size to warrant further attention.[31] A Scottish-Armenian trade network was to remain one of the great 'what ifs' of Scottish economic history.

Another commissioned vessel was the 250 ton *Speedwell*, owned by a syndicate headed by Mr Robert Blackwood junior, which left for the Portuguese settlement of Macao, at the mouth of the Canton River in China, with a cargo of £11,000.[32] Optimistically the directors authorised chief supercargo Robert Innes to raise up to £15,000 of capital for the Company at Batavia in Java, if the ship found it convenient to stop there, and also to look for suitable locations for Company settlements.[33] This probably reflected the presence of a small Scottish community in the Dutch colony, as a number of Scots were employed in the Far East by the VOC.[34] The *Speedwell* left Scotland in late 1700 or early 1701 and reached Batavia the following July. But ten leagues from Macao she was almost sunk by a typhoon, and two further attempts to reach the Portuguese colony failed. As a result she was forced to turn tail, anchoring in the River of Johore where a new mast was fitted, and reaching the Dutch trading centre of Malacca (in present day Malaysia) in January 1702. There she was careened, but was accidentally run onto rocks and sank, although her cargo was saved and taken to the Dutch settlement.[35]

One venture utilised Company owned vessels. The *Speedy Return*

---

[30] *Darien Shipping Papers*, 225. Based on an exchange rate of 10.61 guilders per £1 sterling. McCusker, *Money and Exchange*, 58.

[31] RBS, D/1/2, 18 July 1699.

[32] Insh, *Company of Scotland*, 268, *Darien Shipping Papers*, 231–3. He was the son of promoter Mr Robert Blackwood.

[33] *Ibid.*, 234–7.

[34] S. Murdoch, 'The Good, the Bad and the Anonymous: A Preliminary Survey of Scots in the Dutch East Indies 1612–1707,' *Northern Scotland*, 22, (2002), 63–76.

[35] Insh, *Company of Scotland* , 271–4, *Darien Shipping Papers*, 238–42.

had reached the isthmus two days after the capitulation to the Spanish and returned to the Clyde with the sloop *Content*.[36] In March 1701 a proposal was made by Captain Robert Drummond and Captain Stewart to take the two ships with Company goods and provisions on a trading venture to Africa. The directors sold a store of brandy to finance the fitting out of the two vessels. They rounded the Cape of Good Hope and headed for the pirate island of St Mary's, off the north east coast of Madagascar, where they sold some of their cargo, picked up slaves and made for Isle Bourbon (present day Réunion), over 300 miles to the east.[37] Madagascar was then the epicentre of pirate activity in the Indian Ocean and an emporium where goods might be sold at very high prices.[38] The two Scottish ships returned to Madagascar but were taken themselves by pirates under Captain John Bowen.[39] Captain Drummond, with a few others, was left stranded on Madagascar, and the rest of the crew forced into Bowen's service. The *Content* was soon leaking badly and was burned off the island, and the *Speedy Return* was later burned at Rajapore in India.[40]

None of these ventures had a particularly positive impact on the Company's cash position and between late June and early July 1701 cash balances fell from £14,680 to £1,407 (see Figure 1). This final collapse was not due to any spending spree by the directors but was an accounting issue caused by recognition that Company notes had no market value. The Company had issued notes in 1696 as part of its abortive banking business and by 1701 a substantial part of the cash reserve was made up of the Company's own notes. These were

---

[36]   The *Speedy Return* was called the *Margaret* before being purchased by the Company and cost £1,426 including her cargo. NLS, Adv MS 83.3.7, f18. The sloop *Content* was also a Company owned vessel costing £905 including cargo, Insh, *Company of Scotland*, 254.

[37]   RBS, D/1/3, 1 March 1701, Graham, *Seawolves*, 148.

[38]   A. Bialuschewski, 'Between Newfoundland and the Malacca Strait: A Survey of the Golden Age of Piracy, 1695–1725,' *Mariner's Mirror*, 90 (2004). Madagascar was viewed as a treasure island in the early 18th century and a number of Madagascar schemes promoted with little success, A. Bialuschewski, 'Greed, Fraud, and Popular Culture: John Breholt's Madagascar Schemes of the Early 18th Century,' paper given at the Interdisciplinary Colloquium on the Financial Revolution in the British Isles, 1688–1756, held at the University of Regina, 20–22 June 2004, Insh, *Company of Scotland*, 258–9.

[39]   Graham, *Seawolves*, 148.

[40]   Insh, *Company of Scotland*, 262, Graham, *Seawolves*, 150–1.

worth something in 1696, when backed up with coin and bullion supplied by the subscribers, but as the financial position deteriorated their value fell, and by 1701 they were worthless. If the net cash position is adjusted to take account of this by removing the value of notes, the financial position of the Company appears even worse (see lower line in Figure 7).

Figure 7

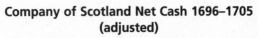

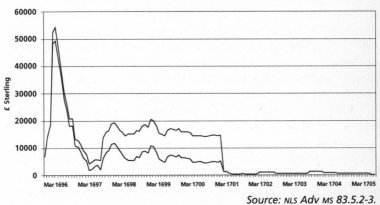

Source: NLS Adv MS 83.5.2-3.

Figure 7 demonstrates quite clearly that the Company was under-capitalised for most of its history, operating with cash balances of about 1.5 per cent of subscribed capital, despite being briefly in a very strong financial position in the summer of 1696.[41] An overseas trading company could not be run on such meagre financial resources. From 1701 the Company was bankrupt in all but name, could not fund its liabilities, and staggered on in a moribund state.

As a result many of the directors, perhaps understandably, lost their appetite for managing a joint-stock company. There were problems securing quorums and the court was forced to meet less often.[42] Roderick

---

[41] Long distance foreign trade required substantial liquid assets. The EIC had more than £500,000 in cash in 1710. Chaudhuri, *Trading World*, 443.

[42] The court met on average 22 times a year between 1702 and 1706, having averaged 75.5 times between 1696 and 1701, and peaking at 120 meetings, or ten per month, in 1699, RBS, D/1/1-3.

MacKenzie, who was at the centre of Company administration for its entire history, stated that the strategy during these frustrating years following the second abandonment was 'to keep up the Face and Constitution of a Company, till better times, by granting Permissions to such as had a mind to Trade'.[43] The Company was unable to raise more capital, although it continued to try to secure cash owed by reluctant shareholders and sold assets such as the *Lyon*, which still lay in Hamburg.[44] A number of other syndicates, including London Scots, Edinburgh merchants, and the Earl of Morton, showed interest in obtaining commissions, but it is unclear how many of these ventures materialised, and none provided a financial return to the Company.[45] The situation might have been different if capital had been available to make significant investments in a larger number of ventures to Africa and the East, as the example of the *African Merchant* had shown.

The Annandale/Worcester

In October 1703 articles of agreement were signed with Captain John Ap-Rice of the 220 ton *Annandale*, a ship with 20 guns and a crew of 50, for a trading venture to the East Indies under commission, with the Company entitled to 5 per cent of the ship and cargo.[46] However on 31 January 1704 the *Annandale* was seized in the Downs at the instance of the EIC, and with her cargo was condemned as lawful prize.[47] This blatant aggression intensified Scottish resentment towards England.

---

[43]   MacKenzie, *Full and Exact Account,* 18.

[44]   NLS, Adv MS 83.5.3. The *Lyon* was sold to a syndicate headed by Edinburgh merchant Alexander Stevenson, who had arranged for her construction in Hamburg in 1696.

[45]   RBS, D/1/2, 5 March 1700, 5 July 1700, D/1/3, 14 November 1701, 16 April 1702, 22 October, 17, 18 and 24 December 1702, 13 July 1703, 20 November 1703, 24 November 1704, 15 August 1706, 4 October 1706, 27 January 1707. The Earl of Morton planned a voyage to the East Indies in the 100 ton *Morton* in 1703 and a group of Edinburgh merchants planned a similar voyage in the *Neptune Galley* in 1707.

[46]   Insh, *Company of Scotland,* 279, *Darien Shipping Papers,* 252–5. Graham states that the Company bought a majority share in her and 75 per cent of the cargo, but little capital was available by this point and there is no evidence of such a transaction in the Company cash books, Graham, *Seawolves,* 156. The ship was transferred in trust to the Company, but could be redeemed at any time, *Darien Shipping Papers,* 254.

[47]   *Ibid.,* 282, Graham, *Seawolves,* 161.

Six months later, in July, an opportunity for revenge presented itself when the *Worcester*, operating under a licence from the EIC, sheltered in the Firth of Forth to repair a leak on her return from the East Indies.[48] The directors authorised Roderick MacKenzie to seize her as a reprisal for the *Annandale* and because she had imported and sold East Indian goods in Scotland, contrary to the rights of the Company.[49]

For a brief period the office of the Company of Scotland buzzed with activity and the court met more frequently. The directors initially resolved that the English crew were to be treated civilly, but in the frenetic political atmosphere of late 1704 events gained a momentum of their own.[50] On 14 December the court was informed about allegations against Captain Thomas Green and on the following day he and his crew were arrested on charges of piracy against the *Speedy Return*.[51] On 16 March 1705 Captain Green, first mate John Madder, and gunner James Simpson, with 12 other members of the crew, were convicted and sentenced to death by the High Court of Admiralty.[52] The news was jubilantly received on the streets of Edinburgh. Green expected to receive a reprieve from the Queen, but the unfortunate trio were executed on Leith Sands on 11 April. They were innocent men who had nothing to do with the demise of the *Speedy Return* and their judicial murder reflected the deteriorating political relationship between Scotland and England. For many their execution was revenge for English opposition and indifference to the Company and colony, and all the Scots who had died. The Scottish government did not intervene to save their lives, influenced by the popular cry for blood.[53]

---

[48] She was a 180 ton ship with 16 guns and a crew of 32.

[49] RBS, D/1/3, 11 August 1704, 12 August 1704. For detailed descriptions of the incident see Insh, *Company of Scotland*, 288–312, Prebble, *Darien*, 1–9, Graham, *Seawolves*, 153–90.

[50] RBS, D/1/3, 15 August 1704.

[51] *Ibid.*, 14 December 1704, Insh, *Company of Scotland*, 296.

[52] *Ibid.*, 300. Seven out of the 15 jurors were shareholders in the Company: Captain John Mathie of Prestonpans (£200), the Edinburgh merchants Robert Forrest (£100), Robert Innes (£100), Robert Walwood (£500), George Clark (£1,000), William Neilson (£100), and the chancellor of the jury Sir James Fleming of Rathobyres (£500). The rest may well have been related to shareholders or those who had sailed to the isthmus. For a list of all the jurors and more details of the trial see Sir R. Carnac Temple, *New Light on the Mysterious Tragedy of the 'Worcester' 1704–1705* (London, 1930), 227–8.

[53] Insh, *Company of Scotland*, 304.

The Company hoped to make some money from the sale of the *Worcester* and her cargo, but faced considerable expenses of £516 7s associated with the legal process of reprisal and the cost of providing for Green's crew during their incarceration.[54] Some of this was recovered in early 1706, but the *Worcester* incident further weakened the Company's finances, although it appears that certain individuals, including Roderick MacKenzie, profited personally.[55]

The other ventures of the Company of Scotland returned very little in financial terms. The salt business produced nothing and the overseas ventures under commission, and in Company owned ships, were also unsuccessful, with the exception of the small amount earned from the *African Merchant*. The banking business did make a return, but locked up cash in non-liquid assets. If the directors had pursued an East Indian strategy, as advocated by Douglas and others, there may have been more success. It is possible that a few ships sent to the Indies each year might have provided a financial return and allowed the accumulation of capital and management experience. There were, however, no free lunches in the tough economic world of the 1690s and such a strategy would still have faced bitter opposition from the joint-stock companies of other nations. Securing insurance in London and Amsterdam might also have proved problematic. The difficulties associated with establishing a foreign trading company from scratch without naval protection were very great indeed, and such an effort was beyond the abilities and experience of the directors of the Company of Scotland.

---

[54]   RBS, D/1/3, 18 April 1705.

[55]   £123 was paid to the Company in January 1706. NLS, Adv MS 83.5.3. MacKenzie bought £10,000 Scots of goods from the *Worcester* but the Company received nothing. It may have been a 'gift' for arrears of salary. Carnac Temple, *New Light*, 348.

CHAPTER SEVENTEEN

Bail-out

And now we are come to the great Article of the Equivalent,
which has of it self made more Noise in the World, than all the
other Articles.

DANIEL DEFOE[1]

Amongst all the Articles of the Treaty of Union, there has been
none more talked of, and less understood, than the Fifteenth, con-
cerning the Rise, Nature, and Management of the Equivalents.[2]

It is Not Arithmetick only that can make a man understand
the Equivalent.

DAVID NAIRNE[3]

The Equivalent (alias Price of Scotland) came to Edinburgh on
the Fifth of August, the Day the Earl of Gourie designed to
perpetrate his horrid Conspiracy against King James VI.

GEORGE LOCKHART OF CARNWATH[4]

BEING A SHAREHOLDER IN the Company of Scotland proved a financially
fruitless and emotional journey. The Company was strapped for cash for
most of its history and finally ran out in the summer of 1701. Most
of the assets were literally sunk and after 1700 there was no market
in the shares.[5] The investors faced the grim reality that all their money
was lost.

---

[1] Defoe, *History of Union*, 'An Abstract of the Proceedings,' 147.

[2] *An Essay upon The XV Article of the Treaty of Union, Wherein the*
Difficulties That arise upon The Equivalents Are fully Cleared and
Explained (1706), 3.

[3] NAS, Mar and Kellie Muniments, GD 124/15/449/48.

[4] George Lockhart of Carnwath, *Memoirs concerning the Affairs of Scotland,*
from Queen Anne's Accession to the Throne, to the Commencement of
the Union of the Two Kingdoms of Scotland and England, In May 1707
(London, 1714), 340.

[5] NLS, Adv MS 83.2.2, 85–86. There was only one share transaction recorded
in the Transfer Book for the whole of 1701, one in 1702, and none from
1703 to 1705.

However, after a long series of catastrophes their luck was about to change. As part of negotiations over an Incorporating Union between Scottish and English commissioners in 1706, a very large lump sum of money emerged called the Equivalent, which was to be paid to certain Scots on achievement of Union. Most of it was earmarked for the shareholders of the Company of Scotland and was an unusual departure in corporate history; a shareholder bail-out with cash provided by a foreign government. Not only were the investors to receive all the cash they had paid to the Company but also, amazingly, interest payments of 5 per cent per annum, as if their money had been invested in some bank deposit or gilt-edged government bond, rather than a company that had lost every penny of its capital. This was an extraordinarily handsome return for the shareholders – a bail-out of 142 pence in the pound – and was a truly incredible result for the directors, who had squandered the capital of the Company and now, as major shareholders, were to be generously rewarded for their mismanagement.[6]

There was, of course, more at stake than this. The Union of 1707 was not made to compensate the directors and shareholders of the Company of Scotland. It occurred because the English government and Houses of Parliament believed it was in the English national interest.[7] Another war with France was at a crucial phase. There were concerns about the drift of politics in Scotland where parliament was flexing its independence and threatening the future of the Regal Union. The English government feared that the Scots might revert to a French alliance and provide another front on their northern border. A Union which removed Scotland's parliament and locked her into a Protestant succession made strategic sense and was worth paying for. Union was thus a 'political job' in the English national interest.[8] To

---

6   The shareholders advanced £153,448 to the Company and the total reimbursement from the Equivalent including interest was calculated to be £217,833 (£219,094 reduced by £1,261 which had not been repaid by those who had borrowed from the Company in 1696). £217,833 divided by £153,448 equals 1.42, NLS, Adv MS 83.1.6.

7   Riley has argued that union was principally the result of short-term political machinations of the Whig Junto. P.W.J. Riley, 'The union of 1707 as an episode in English politics,' *EHR*, 84, (1969), 498–527.

8   Ferguson famously described union as 'probably the greatest 'political job' of the 18th century',' W. Ferguson, 'The Making of the Treaty of Union of 1707,' *SHR*, 43, (1964), 110.

make it possible, however, the Scottish political nation had to be per-suaded that it was also in their interest.

A number of sweeteners were therefore offered to the Scots to secure the passage of the Union treaty through the Scottish parliament. Political management was intensified; promises of pensions and jobs were made and peerages created to secure votes.[9] There was also resort to more blatant bribery. In 1706 the English government provided a secret payment of £20,000 (£2.8m today) which was distributed by the Earl of Glasgow. Although ostensibly for arrears of salary, the majority went to Queensberry (£12,325) and the rest to figures such as Ormiston, Cromarty, Tweeddale, the Argyll interest and other sup-porters of the Court.[10]

Free trade with England and the growing colonial and plantation markets was also offered as a long-term economic inducement. Scottish merchants would be free to expand their activity in tobacco and sugar begun clandestinely in America and the Caribbean. The Scots were also to keep their private law, heritable jurisdictions, the rights of their ancient burghs and a separate act would safeguard the Presbyterian structure of the Church of Scotland. The Scottish currency was to dis-appear, but it was not viewed as an important component of national identity, and there was no campaign to save it.[11] One inducement, however, dwarfed the others. The Scots were to receive a payment of £398,085 10s (£55.5m today); equal to the nominal capital of the Company of Scotland, 2.6 times the actual cash raised by the Company, and perhaps 50 per cent of the Scottish coinage. The payment of such a large sum would re-liquefy the Scottish monetary system.

The Equivalent was a complex financial mechanism that dealt with a number of important issues at the heart of the Union treaty; in particular tax, debt and the Company of Scotland. The English writer Daniel Defoe, who was in Edinburgh as a spy and propagandist for

9   Ferguson, *Scotland's Relations*, 220–1.
10   P.W.J. Riley, *The Union of England and Scotland: A study in Anglo-Scottish politics of the eighteenth century* (Manchester 1978), 256–9, 336–8, Ferguson, *Scotland's Relations*, 247–8.
11   The 16th article of the treaty specified that after union 'the Coin shall be of the same standard and value throughout the United Kingdom, as now in England.' By the early 19th century Scottish bank notes were consid-ered an aspect of national identity, when Sir Walter Scott, in the guise of Malachi Malagrowther, launched a campaign to preserve the Scottish one pound note.

the English government during the Union debates in the Scottish parliament, believed the Equivalent was central to achieving Union:

> Without this it had been impossible to bring this Union to a Conclusion; Nor was the way ever seen clear towards a Union till the project of an Equivalent was thought of.[12]

The term 'equivalent' was first applied to transactions by French and Danish Kings but came to prominence in England during the reign of James VII in the late 1680s. James was attempting to enhance the rights of his fellow Catholics, constrained by the test acts of 1673 and 1678, by which only those taking the Anglican sacrament and an oath against the doctrine of transubstantiation could hold public office and sit in parliament. It was suggested that the sacramental tests might be exchanged for an 'equivalent' security for Protestants. The pamphlets of William Penn, the King's Quaker ally, assumed that any loss of Protestant security by repeal of the test acts would be counterbalanced by an 'equivalent' law guaranteeing liberty of conscience. The notion was mocked in *The Anatomy of an Equivalent*, published anonymously by George Savile Marquis of Halifax in 1688:[13]

> The World hath of late years never been without some extraordinary Word to furnish the Coffee-Houses and fill the Pamphlets... Thus, after *Whig*, *Tory*, and *Trimmer* have had their time, now they are dead and forgotten, being supplanted by the word *Equivalent*, which reigneth in their stead.[14]

The term 'equivalent' was therefore on the lips of the chattering classes of London during the Revolutionary crisis of 1688–9. When it was resurrected in the early 18th century, within the context of Anglo-Scottish relations, it was not a neutral term, but one that reminded Scots and English of the dangers of a Catholic revival and the necessity of safeguarding Protestantism. The 'Equivalent' of the fifteenth article of the Treaty of Union of 1707 was a lump sum dressed in political clothing. It was not just cash, but moral money for Protestants.

---

[12] Defoe, *History of Union*, 95.

[13] *The Works of George Savile Marquis of Halifax*, ed. Mark N. Brown, 3 vols (Oxford, 1989), i, 265–91.

[14] *Ibid.*, 265.

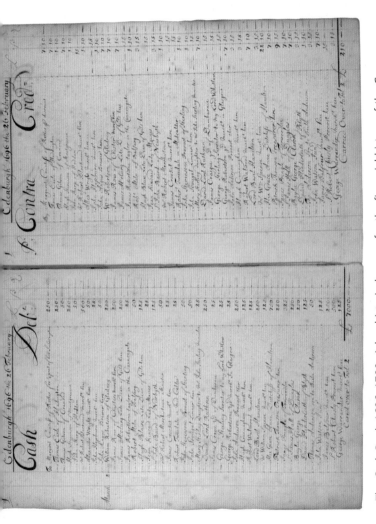

The Cash Book 1696–1700. A key historical source for the financial history of the Company.

Reproduced by permission of the Trustees of The National Library of Scotland

John Blackadder was in Flanders in 1696 and was the only Scottish shareholder based overseas. (Artist: Unknown)

Scottish National Portrait Gallery

See the Following MAPP of this NECK and Harbour, with a Plenary Explication thereof.

a shows the Isle of Pines
b Golden Island.
c where the Spanish Fleet did ride
d Brandies Bay.
e Acla the Greater.
h CALEDONIA Harbour and Road.
i The Look out.
k Mountains and Woods.
l Rocks.
m The Plantan Tree.
n The Narrow Neck.
o The Orange Grove
p Indian Habitations.
r Litle Islands and Rocks.
s Indian dwellings.
t Acla the Lesser.
v Mountains and Woods.
w The watering place.
u The Maccaw-Tree, full of prickles
x The Orange-Tree.
y The Fort.
z The Cockernut-Tree.
l The wild Cabage-Tree.
C Caret-Bay river and Indians dwelling Westward
R About this Bay, the Spaniards landed men against us.

N North.
S South.
E East.
W West.

The crude map of the colony from the account of Francis Borland, one of the ministers on the second expedition.

The last gold coins struck by the Scottish Mint. The gold was from a trading venture to Africa by the *African Merchant*.

John Hamilton, Lord Belhaven: director of the Company and Country Party
supporter who vigorously opposed Union.
(Artist: Sir John Baptiste de Medina)

Scottish National Portrait Gallery

Hugh Dalrymple: director of the Company and President of the Court of Session from 1698 who supported the Court Party.
(Artist: attributed to Sir John Baptiste de Medina)

Scottish National Portrait Gallery

John Hay, second Marquis of Tweeddale: director of the Company and Country Party leader who broke to form the *Squadrone Volante*.
(Artist: attributed to Jacob Ferdinand Voet)

Scottish National Portrait Gallery

Adam Cockburn of Ormiston: director of the Company and Lord Justice
Clerk who supported the Court Party.
(Artist: attributed to William Aikman)

Scottish National Portrait Gallery

Patrick Hume, Earl of Marchmont, was a shareholder, Court supporter and
King William's loyal Chancellor. (Artist: William Aikman)

In a private Scottish collection © The Trustees of the National Museums of Scotland

George MacKenzie, Earl of Cromarty, was a Court politician,
shareholder in the Company and sceptic about Darien.
(Artist: after Sir John Baptiste de Medina).

Scottish National Portrait Gallery

The death of King William in March 1702 had ushered in a period of deepening crisis between the two kingdoms. The constitutional relationship, as it had existed since 1603, was under severe strain, intensified by changes in the constitution following the Glorious Revolution, including the abolition of the committee of the articles and more regular parliaments, which gave rise to a more vigorous and independent Scottish parliament.[15] There was also simmering resentment over the treatment of the Company by the English government, which had highlighted the inadequacies of Regal Union, and a backdrop of general discontent caused by continuing economic stagnation.

Two other issues were of vital importance in the Anglo-Scottish crisis: the succession and war. King William was childless and on 30 July 1700 the Duke of Gloucester, the last surviving child of his heir Anne, died at the age of eleven. By the Act of Settlement of 1701 the English parliament excluded Catholics from the throne and chose the elderly Sophia dowager Electress of Hanover and her heirs as successors to Anne. There was no discussion with the Scots on this important issue, although Scotland was included in limitations imposed on the Hanoverian successor: no person holding the crown was to leave England, Ireland or Scotland without the consent of parliament.[16] Such arrogance intensified Scottish resentment towards their southern neighbours.

The other factor was the War of the Spanish Succession; another bloody struggle between France and Britain over control of the Spanish empire fought from 1702 to 1714. In Scotland war was declared on 30 May by proclamation of the privy council and not by parliament. The Scottish parliament did not meet until 9 June, even though an act of 1696 had specified it should gather within 20 days of the King's death. The legality of the session was challenged by the Country Party and in protest Hamilton led 74 members out of the chamber. This proved a tactical blunder allowing Queensberry to obtain supply and pass an act permitting the crown to nominate commissioners to treat for Union.[17]

An incorporating Union was achieved by Cromwell through military

---

[15] Ferguson, *Scotland's Relations*, 183. A.J. Mann, 'Inglorious Revolution: Administrative Muddle and Constitutional Change in the Scottish parliament of William and Mary,' *Parliamentary History*, 22, (2003), 121–44.

[16] Ferguson, *Scotland's Relations*, 197–8.

[17] *Ibid.*, 201.

force in the 1650s and a number of 17th century monarchs had proposed closer union.[18] In February 1700 William backed the policy in an address to the House of Lords and again in his last message to the Commons in 1702, as a solution to the problems he faced governing Scotland. From her succession Queen Anne was also firmly committed to such a policy.[19] During negotiations between Scottish and English commissioners at the Council Chamber in the Cock Pit in London between October 1702 and February 1703, the term 'equivalent' re-emerged into the political landscape. The Scots first raised the payment of an 'equivalent' as compensation for equality of taxation proposed by the English as part of Union.[20] At this time English taxes were much higher and so Scottish taxes were expected to rise towards English levels following a treaty. But by 18 January the 'equivalent' had developed into a compensation payment for higher tax and as an investment fund to encourage fishing and manufactures in Scotland, which was to be paid from Scottish revenue at £10,000 per annum.[21]

The negotiations of 1702/3 reached agreement on a number of points: free trade between the two kingdoms and the English plantations, a commitment to the same level of taxes on imports and exports and the abolition of the Navigation Acts. An area of difficulty remained the large debts England had accumulated since the Revolution and whether Scotland should have any obligation to pay a proportion of them after Union. By 28 January 1703 there was agreement that neither kingdom should be burdened with debts contracted before Union, that no duties or taxes levied in Scotland should be applied to paying English debts, and that there should be time allowed for the Scots to reap the benefit of free trade before equal taxation was introduced. Negotiations continued but reached deadlock over the issue of the Company of Scotland. On 25 January the Scottish commissioners, referring to the 'great losses' from the Darien colony, argued that the catastrophe had discouraged investment in the economy, and as a result, a sum should be paid for encouraging fishing, linen and other

---

[18] There were attempts in 1604, 1668, 1670, and 1689. *Ibid.*, 102–3, 153–4, 156, 171–2, 201–2.

[19] *Ibid.*, 179.

[20] As a large free trade zone was being created it was reasonably argued that there should be a move towards the same level of taxation so that Scotland would not have an unfair advantage.

[21] *APS*, xi, Appendix, 156.

manufactures and that the privileges of the Company should continue after Union. The English replied in true mercantilist spirit that having two such companies in one kingdom would undermine trade. On 1 February the Scots claimed inaccurately that £200,000 had been invested in the Company and that the privileges should be bought out by the English government.[22]

The negotiations did not proceed any further. In early 1703 the English were not fully committed and on a number of occasions an insufficient number of English commissioners attended to achieve quorums. Negotiations were adjourned until October but the commission did not meet again.

Despite this failure, however, the attempt of 1702/3 was very important for the later negotiations in 1706, for agreement was reached in a number of areas and the issues to be resolved were highlighted. A number of these 'loose strings' came together three years later in a different and much larger 'equivalent': trade, tax, debt and the Company of Scotland. The Equivalent that emerged in 1706/7 was not, as some have taken it to be, a literal compensation for higher taxes that would be used to pay English national debts, but rather a negotiated financial settlement which pulled together a number of key aspects of the treaty into a monetary amount that would be paid to the Scots immediately after Union, to encourage the passage of the treaty through the Scottish parliament.

In 1704 a new ministry led by Tweeddale attempted to resolve the Anglo-Scottish political crisis by carrying the Hanoverian succession without Union and obtaining supply in return for an act enabling the Scottish parliament to approve nominations to officers of state.[23] The creation of the Tweeddale ministry marked a significant fracture in the Country Party; the breakaway of its more moderate elements. Tweeddale and his supporters became known as the New Party and later the *Squadrone Volante*.[24] They also dominated the court of directors of the Company of Scotland, and so from this point the Company can no longer be viewed as an instrument of the opposition. The directors, as the most significant shareholders, had lost large amounts

---

22   *Ibid.*, 155, 159, 161.

23   Ferguson, *Scotland's Relations*, 216–17.

24   *Ibid.*, 229. Meaning 'Flying Squadron,' the term had originally been applied to the Cavaliers, another political grouping which included Jacobites and Episcopalians.

of money. The fruits of government office might provide some compensation. Tweeddale became chancellor, Lord Belhaven a treasury
commissioner, Baillie of Jerviswood treasurer-depute, Sir Francis Scott
master of works and Robert Blackwood was knighted.[25] But
Tweeddale could never count on more than thirty votes in parliament
and was unable to secure a majority. The Old Party, those who had
held office in previous administrations, refused to support his ministry
and the rest of the Country Party feared that accepting the limited
reform on offer would end momentum for further constitutional change.
He was forced to pass the controversial Act of Security to obtain six
months supply which poured more flames on Anglo-Scottish relations.
According to Defoe the act was 'magnified in England, to such a
Hight, that it was look'd upon as in effect a Declaration of War'.[26] The
act declared that parliament was to meet 20 days after the Queen's
death and, if there were no heirs of her body, it was to nominate a successor, providing they were of the royal line of Scotland and
Protestants. The candidate was not to be the same as the successor to
the crown of England unless particular conditions acceptable to the
Scottish parliament were met.[27] The act deliberately left the succession
open and sustained the crisis in Anglo-Scottish relations. The English
parliament retaliated with the Alien Act of February 1705 which
specified that unless a Union treaty was in train or the Hanoverian
succession accepted by 25 December, all Scots, except those already
domiciled in England or her possessions, would be treated as aliens
and trade with England in cattle, linen and coal would cease. The
judicial murder of Captain Green and two of his crew for piracy on

---

[25]   A list of the New Party of 1704 can be found in Riley, *Union*, 110, foot-
       note 152. The first reference to Sir Robert Blackwood in the directors'
       journal is 28 August 1704. RBS, Court of Directors, D/1/3, 28 August
       1704. In March 1699 Mr Robert Blackwoood was voted off the court and
       replaced by Baillie Robert Blackwood. It was this Baillie Robert
       Blackwood who was knighted. The exact relationship between these two
       men is not clear. His fellow director, Edinburgh merchant James
       MacLurg, was knighted by April 1701, but was excluded from the court
       on 7 March 1704. RBS, D/1/3, 1 April 1701, D/1/3, 7 March 1704.

[26]   Defoe, *History of Union*, 50.

[27]   The conditions were that in the present session of parliament the govern-
       ment should be settled to secure the honour and independence of the king-
       dom, the freedom and power of parliament and the religion, liberty and
       trade of the nation from English or any foreign influence. APS, xi, 69.

11 April was another consequence of the escalating crisis between the two kingdoms.[28]

The threat of economic sanctions had the desired effect. In 1705 an administration led by John Campbell, the 24 year old second Duke of Argyll, broke the parliamentary deadlock. He made use of his military skills to control parliament and was aided by some typically ambivalent behaviour from Hamilton, who called for a vote allowing the queen to nominate Union commissioners, having assured his supporters that they were no longer required in the chamber.[29]

On 16 April the commissioners met again in the Council Chamber of the Cockpit at Whitehall and 25 articles were quickly thrashed out by 22 July. The strongly pro-Union bias of the Scottish commissioners ensured a successful outcome, as did the informal negotiations that had been ongoing for a year or more with the Whig Junto on what demands the English parliament would accept.[30] The first four articles encapsulated the essential aspects of the treaty: the two kingdoms were to be united into one by the name of Great Britain, the Hanoverian succession accepted; the kingdom represented by one parliament and a large free trade zone created comprising the United Kingdom, its dominions and plantations.[31] The rest of the articles fleshed out the detail and provided assurances and inducements to the Scots. Provisions were made to exempt particular commodities such as coal, salt and malt from duties for various periods after Union to alleviate the pain of higher taxation.[32]

The fifteenth article provided for the payment of the Equivalent:

> Whereas by the Terms of this Treaty the Subjects of Scotland for preserving an Equality of Trade throughout the United Kingdom, will be lyable to severall Customs and Excises now payable in England, which will be applicable towards payment of the Debts of England, contracted before the Union; It is agreed, That Scotland shall have an Equivalent for what the

---

[28] Ferguson, *Scotland's Relations*, 198, 208–10, 217, 223–5.

[29] *Ibid.*, 231.

[30] R.A. Sundstrom, *Sidney Godolphin: Servant of the State* (London, 1992), 191.

[31] *APS*, xi, 406–13.

[32] C.A. Whatley, 'Salt, Coal and the Union of 1707: A revision article,' *SHR*, 66, (1987), 26–45.

Subjects thereof shall be so charged towards payment of the said Debts of England.[33]

The money was to be paid shortly after Union and Queen Anne was to appoint commissioners accountable to the new parliament of Great Britain for its distribution. The Scots had accepted a number of points proposed by the English in 1702/3: equality of taxation and an obligation to pay a proportion of English pre-Union debts. In return they were to receive significant compensation: a large lump sum paid immediately by the English government, rather than from Scottish revenues over a number of years.

The Equivalent perplexed many at the time, as is indicated by the large number of contemporary pamphlets that tried to explain it, and has confused many students of Scottish history since, concerned as it was with the dry and thorny issues of debt, taxation and a shareholder bailout.[34] It brought all these issues together and has been well described as an 'ingenious device'.[35] Its confusing and paradoxical nature was one of its principal strengths, making it difficult to successfully attack. The opposition in the Scottish parliament created much noise about the fifteenth article, but were unsure whether to attack it in principal or in detail, and their assaults were ultimately ineffectual.

In 1702/3 a much smaller amount of £10,000 per annum had been suggested by the Scots. The sum payable under the fifteenth article was a vastly greater £398,085 10s. In the period from 1702/3 to 1706/7 the 'equivalent' was transmogrified from a small yearly payment to a one-off bonanza just short of £400,000. This sharp appreciation was

---

[33] APS, xi, 409–10. There was also provision for a further sum, the so-called 'rising equivalent' that would be due to the Scots for the rise in Scottish revenues applied to the payment of English debts following union. P.W.J. Riley, *The English Ministers and Scotland 1707–1727* (London, 1964), 205. The Scots would be entitled to £792 from every £1,000 rise in customs revenue and £625 from every £1,000 rise in the excise.

[34] Pamphlets about the Equivalent included *An Essay upon The XV Article of the Treaty of Union, Wherein the Difficulties That arise upon The Equivalents Are fully Cleared and Explained* (1706) and *Trialogus. The Seventh Conversation on 15th Article of the Treaty* (1706). In December 1706 the Earl of Cromarty sent several copies of a pamphlet he had written called *The Equivalent Explain'd* to the directors of the Company. It caused great offence as it contained 'several false and Scandalous Reflections on the Managers and servants of this Company.' RBS, D/1/3, 27 and 28 December 1706.

[35] M. Lynch, *Scotland: A New History* (London, 1991), 310.

not due to the statesmanlike benevolence of English politicians, although this view was accepted by some later historians, and can be traced back to a pamphlet of the arch-unionist Cromarty: 'It is a Mistake to think, That in this, England is buying or bargaining with us for our Union; no, It is but a Just Reciprocal Administration'.[36] It rather reflected the heightened desire of the English government to achieve Union. Marlborough had won famous victories at Blenheim in August 1704 and at Ramillies in May 1706. The English government did not want an unstable Scotland just as the tide was turning their way. It was better to pay up a reasonable amount to secure a more pliant northern neighbour.

The size of the Equivalent was thus a political decision. Nevertheless it was deemed necessary to justify it as reasonable and financial mathematics were utilised to assure politicians and the 'public' that the sum was equitable. The proportion of Scottish revenues that would be used to pay English debts was calculated and applied to estimates of the Scottish customs and excise in the future.[37] Some of the English duties appropriated to pay debts were due to expire in 1710, but the majority were for 98 and 99 years, and so a discounted cash flow calculation, of the kind well known to present day financial analysts, was employed; a stream of future cash flows discounted to produce a present value.[38] The cash flows were estimates of Scottish government revenue from customs and excise and proved optimistic.[39] The discount rate was set at 6.6 per cent, or in the parlance of the early 18th century, 15 years and three months purchase. Any analyst who has worked in the financial markets will know that a calculation of this nature can be manipulated by flexing the discount rate or the size of future cash flows, to produce an answer that is close to the one that 'feels' right. In 1705 William Paterson calculated equivalents ranging from £600,000 to £1m.[40] The

---

[36] George Mackenzie, Earl of Cromarty, *The Equivalent Explain'd* (1706).

[37] Riley, *English Ministers*, 204–6.

[38] See Riley, *Union*, 185 and Riley, *English Ministers*, chapter 14. APS, xi, Appendix, 199, indicates that £329,156 or 82 per cent of the calculation was based on a discounted cash flow.

[39] Riley, *English Ministers*, 206. In 1706 the excise was farmed at £33,500 a year and the committee of commissioners assumed it would produce this. The customs was farmed at £28,500 for the period of the war yet the committee estimated it would produce £30,000.

[40] *Writings of William Paterson*, 216–225.

wide range from £10,000 to £1m indicates that the Equivalent was a negotiated settlement.

There was therefore no 'correct' figure for the Equivalent. Sir David Nairne the Scottish secretary-depute noted that 'it is Not Arithmetick only that can make a man understand the Equivalent'.[41] What was important in 1706 was that the size of the payment was acceptable to the Scottish and English parliaments. If it was not, the treaty was a dead duck. If the payment was too large it would precipitate a backlash in the English parliament. That there was minimal opposition there, suggests that English parliamentarians considered it to be reasonable. If the sum was too low the treaty would be rejected by the Scottish parliament. That it passed by a reasonable margin of votes suggests that most Scottish parliamentarians thought the price was high enough, when considered alongside other inducements. Both sides would no doubt have preferred better terms; the Scots more, the English less, but what emerged was a bargain between two political nations and resulted in a 'price' acceptable to the majority of Scottish and English parliamentarians.

Experts were employed to legitimise the calculations. David Gregory professor of astronomy at Oxford University, Sir David Nairne, and, perhaps remarkably, given his responsibility for the loss of so much Scottish cash, William Paterson, were appointed to examine the Scottish revenues.[42] A Scottish parliamentary committee was also nominated in October 1706 to scrutinise the Equivalent which included a number of directors of the Company of Scotland: Tweeddale, Baillie of Jervis-wood, Haldane of Gleneagles, Lieutenant Colonel Erskine and Hugh Montgomery. They stood, of course, to benefit handsomely from it and were unlikely to put up much opposition.[43] A report provided by two professors of mathematics, Dr James Gregory of Edinburgh and Dr Thomas Bowar of Aberdeen University, concluded in December that the calculation was 'exact and well founded'.[44]

On 6 November 1706 a council general of the Company attended by 46 directors and councillors discussed the fifteenth article. Debates raged about whether the Company should continue to exist once compensation was paid.[45] Some argued that the majority of shareholders just wanted their money back, others that there should be compensation

[41] NAS, GD 124/15/449/48.

[42] Riley, *English Ministers*, 205.

[43] *APS*, xi, 308–9, NAS, GD 158/938/1.

[44] *APS*, xi, 350.

[45] MacKenzie, *Full and Exact Account*, 10.

without dissolution. On 27 November a representation to parliament
was approved and published which provided the Company's view of the
Equivalent: the sum proposed was inadequate, interest should be calculated at 6 per cent and not 5 per cent, the part for shareholders and
creditors of the Company should be paid directly to the council general for distribution, and the Company should continue to exist upon
the same footing as the EIC.[46] None of these points were ultimately
accepted and they were not pushed with any degree of vigour. There
was talk of a parliamentary enquiry into the mismanagement of the
Company which may have discouraged most of the directors from
being too vocal in opposition. As a bargaining chip they peddled the
story that a group of London merchants had declared they would
offer a million pounds to have unquestionable right to the Company's
privileges.[47]

The identity of those who were to benefit from the Equivalent was
vital and influenced support for the treaty in the Scottish parliament. The
order of payment was a matter of some debate and was not finalised
until 25 March 1707 by the 'Act concerning the Publick Debts'.[48] This
provided a detailed breakdown of the beneficiaries: firstly those who lost
out from the recoinage; secondly, and most significantly, £232,884 5s
2/3d for the shareholders and creditors of the Company; thirdly a sub-
sidy of £2,000 per annum for seven years to the wool industry, fourthly
an unspecified amount to the commissioners who had negotiated
Union, and finally the military and civil lists (the public debts of
Scotland).[49] What was important, however, for securing the passage of
the treaty, was expectation rather than actual payment.

The largest group of beneficiaries were the shareholders and creditors of the Company of Scotland who were to receive 58.5 per cent.

---

[46]   *To His Grace, Her Majesty's High Commissioner, and the Right Honourable
       Estates of Parliament. The Humble Representation of the Council-General of
       the Company of Scotland Trading to Africa and the Indies* (Edinburgh,
       1706).

[47]   MacKenzie, *Full and Exact Account*, 6–8, 37.

[48]   The fifteenth article itself provided less detail about the order of payment:
       firstly losses from the recoinage, secondly the capital fund of the
       Company of Scotland with interest at the rate of 5 per cent, and finally
       the public debts of Scotland divided into civil and military parts. APS, xi,
       410, NAS, Cromarty Muniments, GD 305/1/159/118.

[49]   APS, xi, 490. The act also provided a detailed breakdown of the order of
       payment within the civil and military lists. The sum due to the commis-
       sioners who negotiated union was later calculated to be £30,500.

As we have seen, there were a large number of shareholders, perhaps three thousand or more, and the majority were Presbyterian supporters of the Revolution of 1688–9. There were some Jacobites and Episcopalians but they were only a small minority. The Equivalent principally rewarded the Presbyterian interest and therefore sustained divisions within the Scottish body politic.

The sums received by shareholders were substantial. Investors who subscribed the minimum £100, and had paid all the calls for cash, received £60 8s (£8,416 today). Subscribers of £500 received £302 (£42,079) and subscribers of £1,000 received £604 (£84,158). These were very substantial tax-free lump sums. The creditors ranged from Roderick MacKenzie, the Company secretary, who received £600 (£83,601) to John Spence, boatswain's boy on the *Rising Sun*. Spence was dead by 1707 and the sum of £3 6s (£460) went to David Hutchison, writer in Edinburgh, who had right by assignation from the boy's cousin and executor Marion Spence in Prestonpans.[50]

A market in Company shares returned during the negotiations and some shareholders decided not to wait for payment from the Equivalent but to sell immediately. Others had lost their subscriptions because of the legal process of debt recovery. In total about a quarter of the shares of the Company changed hands in 1706/7.[51] Sellers included important political figures such as Fletcher of Saltoun, as well as directors Sir Francis Scott of Thirlestane and Lieutenant Colonel John Erskine. Speculators emerged to take advantage of the opportunity. Captain Francis Charteris of her Majesty's Guards bought stock with a face value of £4,900. This investment was perhaps the beginning of his personal fortune, for he went on to accumulate vast riches and become a notorious gambler and rake.[52] An Edinburgh writer John Gordon was the most active investor in the shares, buying stock of £33,555. If this was bought at discounts of up to 90 per cent of par, as described by Defoe, he would have realised spectacular profits of over 600 per cent.[53] It remains unclear where Gordon obtained so much money; the

---

[50]   NLS, Adv MS 83.2.4, 121, 186.

[51]   NLS, Adv MS 83.2.4.

[52]   By the time of his death in 1732 he had amassed £100,000 and an annual income from property of £7,000 per annum. This was more than the cash raised by the Company of Scotland. *ODNB*. 11, 209–11.

[53]   A purchase at a 90 per cent discount to par on stock that was fully paid up would have realised a profit of 604 per cent (i.e. buying at £10 and selling

job of Edinburgh writer in the early 18th century was not that lucrative, and he may have been acting as a front for others who were convinced Union would be achieved and the Equivalent paid.[54]

The other principal beneficiaries were to be those owed money by the Scottish government, but there was some uncertainty about exactly who these individuals were and the size of the amounts they were due. The lists that were drawn up emphasise the importance of the Equivalent as a mechanism of reward.[55] The military list included 935 individuals, and an unspecified number of invalids, and totalled £95,041.[56] The majority of the military elite and officer class expected to receive substantial compensation from the Equivalent. The amounts involved were very significant indeed; for example the Viscount of Teviot was due £2,296 (£319,911 today), Lord Strathnaver £1,700 (£236,868) and Ludovick Grant of that Ilk £1,090 (£151,874). There were also smaller amounts owed to army surgeons, majors, lieutenants, quartermasters, adjutants, cornets and ensigns. That the individuals had a legal right to these sums as arrears of salary, as pointed out by some historians, is beside the point.[57] The Scottish government had very little chance of repaying their debts unless there was a miraculous improvement in the economic condition of the nation and the state's ability to raise tax. Such payments would alleviate the financial position of the Scottish military elite, and were again principally a reward for the Presbyterian

at £60 8s) when redeemed through the Equivalent. Defoe describes transactions occurring at discounts of 90 per cent and a document of 31 January 1707 stated that 'since there hath bin, and doubtless still will be, considerable parts of the said Capital Stock, Sold, and disposed of by Poor and necessitous Persons, for less than half, or possibly than a fourth part of what the principal and Interest may amount to.' NAS, GD 305/1/160/80.

54 By February 1707 there was so much activity in the Company's stock that the accountants were being distracted from their work and the directors ordered that no further transfers be admitted from 13 February until further notice. However, buying and selling continued in a 'grey market.' On 8 March, for example, the Hammermen of Glasgow decided to sell their £100 holding for a minimum of £42 and they secured a price of £45 in the market. If they had waited until the Equivalent arrived in August they would have received £60 8s or 34 per cent more. RBS, D/1/3, 13 February 1707, Shaw, Political History, 8–9.

55 RBS, CEQ/15/1.

56 Ibid., 1–22.

57 J. MacKinnon, The Union of England and Scotland: A Study of International History (London, 1896), 236.

mainstream who dominated the military establishment. Crucially it made the likelihood of a coup by the army against Union unimaginable, as Union itself provided the only realistic prospect of payment of arrears.

The civil list comprised 435 individuals and an unspecified number of invalids who were owed £79,790.[58] The debts were for fees, salaries and pensions during the reigns of William and Anne and included £600 (£83,601 today) owed to Sir John Maxwell of Pollock as Justice Clerk, £1,200(£167,201) to Sir James Stewart as Lord Advocate and £1,050 (£146,301) to Sir Hugh Dalrymple as President of the Session. There were other large sums due to a number of nobles including Queensberry, Tweeddale, Cromarty, Melville, Forfar and Atholl, and debts to a wide range of minor officials such as £205 (£28,564) to the botanist Mr James Sutherland, £40 (£5,573) to keeper of the library at Holyroodhouse Mr David Simpson, and £80 (£11,147) and £105 (£14,630) respectively to the historiographers Daniel Campbell and David Crawford. Others who expected to benefit included previous moderators of the General Assembly, professors of St Andrews University and clerks of the Session. There were also over 200 charity payments due to widows and the poor, including £10 (£1,393) to Helen Brown, £15 (£2,090) to Anne Watt and £20 (£2,787) to Jean Mason. The public debts of Scotland were therefore calculated to be £174,831 in total, with sums owed to 1,370 individuals and an unspecified number of invalids.[59]

A substantial number of Scots expected to benefit financially from the Equivalent, perhaps 3,000 Company of Scotland shareholders and a further 1,500 or so from the military and civil lists, making a total of about 4,500 individuals. This was much larger than the small political elite of about 200 that sat in parliament.[60] The Equivalent provided a mechanism for extending the direct short-term financial benefits of Union to a relatively large number of individuals.

Those who expected to receive payments did not all vote in favour of Union. The Glasgow merchant and ex-director Hugh Montgomery voted in favour of article 15 but against ratification of the treaty.[61] A variety of factors influenced each individual: pressure from kinsmen,

[58]   RBS, CEQ/15/1, 23–32.

[59]   In 1710 another 112 payments of £10,992 were found. RBS, CEQ/15/2.

[60]   P.H. Scott refers to 'the narrow circle of Parliamentarians who might be tempted by the Equivalent.' P.H. Scott, *Andrew Fletcher and the Treaty of Union* (Edinburgh, 1992), 178.

[61]   APS, xi, 375, 405. He was voted off the court of directors in March 1701.

ideological commitment or patriotism as well as financial incentives. The number and size of these payments, however, must have made it very difficult for those who were not particularly committed one way or the other, to vote against Union. The majority of shareholders voted in favour of the treaty.[62] The early modern world was laced with uncertainty and the economic fabric of the nation had been torn apart by the dearth and famine of the 1690s. Scarcity of money remained a constant concern. For many it would have been financial madness to reject so much largesse. After all, how long would Union last? Cromwell's attempt had crumbled in 1660. A motion in the House of Lords to dissolve the Union in 1713 failed by only four votes, and the Union was abolished by Bonnie Prince Charlie during the Jacobite Rebellion of 1745/6.[63] It is only with hindsight that the Incorporating Union of 1707 appears a solid and lasting political arrangement. There must have been pressure on members of parliament from kinsmen and friends who had invested in the Company, or were owed sums from the military and civil lists. The vast majority of directors, who were the largest shareholders, unsurprisingly supported the treaty.

When combined with an act securing the Presbyterian establishment in Scotland, which silenced much of the church's opposition, the adroit use of political management and bribery, and the carrot of free trade, the passage of the treaty was assured. Some were going to be very handsomely rewarded, especially if they were owed sums as shareholders of the Company and from the civil and military lists. For example Tweeddale received £590 as a shareholder and was owed £828 from the civil list.[64] He expected to be paid the large sum of £1,418 (£197,576 today). Other directors who had not sold their shares also received very generous amounts.[65]

---

[62] Shaw has shown that 69 per cent of shareholders who voted for the first article voted yes and 75 per cent of those who had sold their shares voted no. Shaw, *Political History*, 3–5.

[63] Lynch, *Scotland*, 322–3, B. Lenman, *The Jacobite Risings in Britain 1689–1746* (London, 1984), 253.

[64] NLS, Adv MS 83.2.4, 9, RBS, CEQ/15/1, 25.

[65] John Haldane of Gleneagles £604 (£84,158), William Arbuckle £604 (£84,158), Sir Patrick Scott of Ancrum £604 (£84,158), James Pringle of Torwoodlee £604 (£84,158), Mr Francis Montgomery of Giffen £1,070 (£149,088), and George Baillie of Jerviswood £1,070 (£149,088). The executors of Lord Ruthven, John Drummond of Newton and James Balfour received £604 (£84,158), £755 (£105,197), and £885 (£123,311) respectively. NLS, Adv MS 83.2.4, 7, 15, 26, 27, 38, 42, 44, 65.

As it was anticipated there would be little opposition to the treaty
in the English parliament it made political sense to secure its passage in
Scotland first. The Scottish parliament opened on 3 October 1706 in
a thronged and tense Edinburgh. The tactics of the opposition were to
disrupt and delay proceedings and hope for a popular uprising against
the treaty. Riots rocked Edinburgh and Glasgow in November and
December and anti-Union addresses flooded into parliament.[66] Three
hundred armed Cameronians entered Dumfries and burnt the articles
of Union.[67] However, the opposition was divided and poorly led by
the vacillating and unpredictable Hamilton, who may have been
bribed by the Court. At a crucial point, when there were plans to
withdraw from parliament, he called off on the plea of toothache and
then, when persuaded to return to the chamber, refused to play an
active role. An armed rising by Cameronians and Jacobites proved a
fiasco as the leader, James Cunningham of Eickett, who had sailed on
the first expedition to Darien and left the colony with Walter Herries,
turned out to be in the pay of Queensberry.[68] This attempt emphasised
that the political centre was not willing to engage in violence to support the continued existence of the Scottish parliament.

There was the threat of English military force. During the debates
in parliament three regiments of foot were on the Border and there
were three regiments of horse, one of foot and one of dragoons ready
in the north of Ireland. By 10 December 800 horse were also on the
Border.[69] These numbers, however, were not large enough to mount an
invasion of Scotland, but could be used to quell major civil unrest. English
military intervention was therefore a risk but highly unlikely unless
there was a major Jacobite rising, as large numbers of Scots were serving in Anne's army on the Continent and their continuing loyalty
would have been undermined by an attack on their homeland.

The fifteenth article was intensely debated in the chamber. Sir John
Clerk of Penicuik noted how it 'engrossed everyone's attention, full of
difficult, controversial material which gave the parties ample scope to
belabour each other with calumny and abuse'.[70] Defoe commented

---

66 APS, xi, 300, Ferguson, *Scotland's Relations*, 255, 267–8.
67 APS, xi, 331.
68 Ferguson, *Scotland's Relations*, 264, 267–8.
69 P.H. Scott, *1707: The Union of Scotland and England* (Edinburgh, 1979),
    48.
70 Sir John Clerk of Penicuik, *History of the Union of Scotland and England*,
    ed. D. Duncan (SHS, 1993), 148.

that 'the very Word [Equivalent] became Proverbial and was the Jest of Conversation' and that it met with the 'greatest Opposition, and was Treated with the most Contempt in Scotland of any other part of the Union'.[71] However on 30 December 1706 the amended fifteenth article was carried by 112 votes to 54. Lord Belhaven was the only director to vote against as the Jacobite Panmure did not attend parliament. The treaty itself was ratified on 16 January 1707 by 110 votes to 69.[72]

There was an intellectual battle over Incorporating Union waged in the large number of contemporary pamphlets.[73] Some individuals were long-term vocal supporters of Union such as Cromarty, others vociferous opponents like Fletcher of Saltoun. It remains difficult to gauge how significant this debate was in influencing members of the Scottish parliament. In the end parliament reflected the mood of the Presbyterian mainstream. Most were probably reluctant unionists persuaded by the cash on offer and the act safeguarding the Presbyterian settlement. In December 1705 Baillie of Jerviswood had stated that it 'would not be my choice ... Nevertheless, the Union is certainlie preferable to our present condition, and of two evils the least is to be chosen'.[74] The evidence of riots, anti-Union addresses and opposition in parliament suggests that the majority of the country did not favour the treaty.[75] The unionist Clerk of Penicuik later stated that three quarters of the kingdom were against Union.[76] The rest of the population grumbled but did not take up arms.

The Equivalent was therefore at the heart of the treaty and crucial in securing its passage through parliament. Defoe highlighted the importance of the compensation it provided for shareholders of the Company:

The Surprize of this Offer had Various Effects upon the

---

[71]   Defoe, *History of Union*, 112, 147.

[72]   *APS*, xi, 375–6, 404–6.

[73]   Bowie, 'Public Opinion,' 226-60, Ferguson, *Scotland's Relations*, 238–44, Riley, *Union*, 215–45.

[74]   *Correspondence of George Baillie of Jerviswood 1702–1708* (Bann. Club, 1842), 143–4, 145–6.

[75]   Ferguson, *Scotland's Relations*, 267. Pro-unionist historian James MacKinnon stated that 'The Union, was, in fact, carried by the Parliament, with the assistance of the Church, against the country' J. MacKinnon, *Union of England and Scotland*, 326.

[76]   *Sir John Clerk's Observations on the present circumstances of Scotland, 1730*, ed. T.C. Smout, (SHS, 1965), 192.

People; for this Stock was a dead Weight upon a great many Families, who wanted very much the Return of so much Money: It had not only been long disburs'd, but it was, generally speaking, abandoned to Despair, and the Money given over for lost; Nay, so entirely had People given up all Hopes, That a Man might even, after this Conclusion of the Treaty, have bought the Stock at 10 Pound for an Hundred; And after all this, to find the whole Money should come in again with Interest for the Time, was a Happy Surprize to a great many Families, and took off the Edge of the Opposition, which some People would otherwise have made to the Union in general.[77]

The staunch Jacobite and anti-unionist Lockhart of Carnwath's view was more strident:

The Truth of the Matter lies here, a Sum of Money was necessary to be distributed amongst the Scots; and this Distribution of it amongst the Proprietors of the African Company, was the cleanliest Way of bribing a Nation, to undo themselves; and alas! It had the design'd Effect.[78]

There is truth in both these descriptions. Interestingly, the Equivalent was very close to the £400,000 promised to the Scots for delivering Charles I into the hands of the English parliament in 1647.[79] The sum does indeed seem to have been about the 'price of Scotland'. Lockhart and others who opposed the treaty such as Lord Belhaven, the Earl of Panmure and the Duchess of Hamilton still took the cash when it arrived.[80] Defoe cuttingly reflected: 'Nor among the most Malecontent persons could I ever find any, that when the Money upon the African Stock came to be paid, would think the Species Unhallowed enough to refuse their share of it'.[81]

Historians have underplayed the significance of the Equivalent. For those who viewed Union as a piece of statesmanship the payment of such a large sweetener was problematic and is not discussed in

---

[77] Defoe, *History of Union*, 87.
[78] Lockhart, *Memoirs*, 272.
[79] D. Stevenson, *Revolution and Counter-Revolution in Scotland, 1644–1651* (London, 1977), 73, 80.
[80] NLS, Adv MS 83.2.4, 20, 40, 54, 72.
[81] Defoe, *History of Union*, Appendix part 1, 23.

detail.[82] More recent historians have focused on patronage, influence, bribery and corrupt nobles and, although they have mentioned it, they have not stressed its centrality.[83] Others have highlighted the importance of longer term economic factors or the rational patriotic pro-Union views of some in the Scottish parliament with the aim of 'putting economics back into the Union'.[84] However, the very large payments to many Scots is evidence that Union was not so much about long-term economic benefits as about short-term monetary ones. Bribery and patronage were important but were dwarfed by the Equivalent that should be returned to its central place in what Defoe called the 'Great Transaction'.[85] Union was a short-term financial bargain between two political elites. The Equivalent ensured that a majority in parliament put 'cash in hand' before sovereignty and nationalism. It was pragmatic rather than idealistic politics and the decision has divided Scots ever since.

When the United Kingdom came into existence on 1 May 1707 many did not believe the financial bonanza would be paid. On 31 May, the Edinburgh writer Harry Maule wrote to the Earl of Mar:

> The equivalent is so much despaired of here that among the vulgar the greatest part beleeve it's gone to Spain, and some beleeve that the bridge of Berwick is fallen with the weight of it, and all is lost.[86]

---

[82] For example MacKinnon, *Union of England and Scotland*, 236–7, spends much more time on the £20,000 bribe. An excellent survey of the historiography is provided in C.A. Whatley, *Bought and sold for English Gold?: explaining the Union of 1707* (East Linton, 2001).

[83] Ferguson, *Scotland's Relations*, Riley, *Union*, Scott, *Andrew Fletcher*. Ferguson recognizes its vital importance as 'a liberal coating of sugar for an otherwise bitter pill,' but his analysis of it is very brief, Ferguson, *Scotland's Relations*, 249.

[84] Smout does not discuss the Equivalent in any detail in *Scottish Trade*, C.A. Whatley, 'Scotland, England and 'The Golden Ball': putting economics back into the Union of 1707,' *The Historian*, 51, (1996), 9–13.

[85] Defoe, *History of Union*, dedication.

[86] HMC, *Manuscripts of the Earl of Mar and Kellie*, i, 397. The uncertainty affected trading in the shares of the Company which fell 12 or 15 per cent following the achievement of union. The debt market was more positive about the prospect of payment. Diligence, the legal process of debt recovery, was much diminished on expectations of a flood of liquidity from the Equivalent. HMC, *Mar and Kellie*, i, 399.

However, it was welcomed with military honours at Berwick and finally reached Edinburgh on 5 August in 12 or 13 wagons guarded by 120 Scots dragoons. Despite efforts by the magistrates, who had doubled the city guard, those who delivered it were stoned.[87] Defoe referred to the 'Reproaches and Railings at the poor Innocent People that brought it, nay, at the very Horses that drew the Carriages'.[88] Some were unconvinced that money was being delivered, believing the wagons were full of ammunition and stones. Others were apprehensive that the regalia of Scotland were to be seized and sent south.[89]

Nevertheless the money was delivered: £100,000 in silver coins and £298,085 in exchequer bills; pieces of paper redeemable at the Bank of England for silver.[90] The Scottish government were concerned that the bills would be refused and complaints about the mix of cash and paper provoked the English government to send £50,000 in gold to replace £50,000 of bills.[91] Despite grumbles most was paid in paper; members of the Court Party took all their payments in exchequer bills, others took half in money and half in bills and some were offered bills to jump the queue. No one was refused cash who demanded it.[92]

The issuance of certificates for payment began on 12 August at the office of the Company of Scotland that had been taken over by the commissioners of the Equivalent. The shareholders and creditors of the Company were first to be paid. By 30 August warrants for nearly £60,000 had been issued and over £50,000 paid by the cashiers, of which £36,000 was in exchequer bills.[93] The numbers flocking to Milne's Square to obtain certificates was reminiscent of the early months of 1696 when the Company had offered shares to an expectant nation, but the mood was entirely different. The vast majority of shareholders and creditors were paid by the end of the year, but there

---

[87] A. Lang, *A History of Scotland from the Roman Occupation* (Edinburgh, 1907), iv, 139–40, HMC, Mar and Kellie, i, 411.

[88] Defoe, *History of Union*, Appendix part 1, 22–3.

[89] Lang, *History of Scotland*, 140. Unfortunately he does not give the source of this information.

[90] More than half of the first delivery of money was in sixpences, A.L. Murray, 'Sir Isaac Newton and the Scottish recoinage, 1707–10,' *Proc Soc Antiq Scot*, 127, (1997), 925.

[91] NAS, Montrose Muniments, GD 220/5/128/1.

[92] Defoe, *History of the Union*, Appendix Part 1, 24–5.

[93] NAS, GD 220/5/137.

was not enough to honour the military and civil lists. This under-standably led to ill-feeling even amongst those who had supported Union in parliament and was to become a contentious issue in the period following 1707.[94]

The payment of the majority of the Equivalent in English paper rather than coin or bullion highlights the importance of the financial revolution as a factor in the Union of 1707. England was able to raise paper money at a time of war, when cash was in short supply, and per-haps more remarkably, the Scots were willing to accept pieces of foreign paper, indicating their trust in the credit of the Bank of England and the English state. Union therefore reflected the financial sophistication of both Scots and English. Despite the vast difference in power and finan-cial muscle between the English and Scottish states, a shared commercial culture existed in both kingdoms; a culture that had spawned the Company of Scotland. The Scots were not 'bought and sold for English gold' as Robert Burns lamented, but more prosaically for a combination of gold, silver and exchequer bills.

The fifteenth article also ended the existence of the Company of Scotland. If many lamented the demise of Scotland's parliament, few shed tears about the final extinction of the Company. The fifteenth article ended the dream of an independent Scottish empire funded by a joint-stock:

> Upon payment of which Capital Stock and Interest It is agreed
> The said Company be dissolved and cease And also that from the
> time of passing the Act of Parliament in England for raising
> the said sum of £398,085 10s the said Company shall neither
> Trade nor Grant Licence to Trade Providing that if the said
> Stock and Interest shall not be payed in twelve months after
> the Commencement of the Union That then the said Company
> may from thence forward Trade or give Licence to Trade until
> the said hail Capitall Stock and Interest shall be payed.[95]

The Scots would now develop their empire within a British context. The politicisation of the Company had intensified the political storm

---

94   RBS, REQ/1. In 1714 the small amount of £2,576 was still due, of which
      at least half belonged to seamen who had sailed to Darien in 1698 and
      1699, Riley, *English Ministers*, 214–228.

95   *APS*, xi, 410.

of 1700–1 and highlighted the tensions incipient in the Regal Union. Paradoxically in 1706–7 the disgruntled shareholders provided a mechanism to solve the Anglo-Scottish constitutional crisis in the short-term. The disastrous history of the Company did not lead directly to Union, for Union was dictated by English strategic interests, but the very large number of shareholders made it much more easily achievable.

The directors met for the last time on 18 August 1707. Only one of the nine who attended, Lieutenant Colonel John Erskine, had been present all those years before when the first court assembled in optimistic mood on 12 May 1696.[96] The directors resolved to register accounts relating to the winding-up of the Company with the Court of Session. They also considered a representation by William Paterson. The fifty-seven year old projector was after a share of the Equivalent. He had not invested a penny of his own money in the Company, but hoped that the provisions he had obtained for organising the capital raising in London in 1695, might form the basis of a claim. Paterson was called into the directors' chamber and told the decision of the court. He had no legal right to a share. An address was drawn up recommending him to 'her Majesty's Royal Bounty', but it was noted in the minutes that this 'did not satisfy Mr Paterson.'. The court was adjourned and did not meet again.[97]

---

[96]   The others present were Sir Hugh Cunningham, Dr Dundas, Alexander Wedderburn, John Jamieson of Balmuir, George Warrander, James Fairholm, Robert Inglis, and Alexander Monteith.

[97]   RBS, Court of Directors, D/1/3, 18 August 1707.

Postscript: The Wealth of Nations

BY THE TIME Adam Smith's *An Inquiry into the Nature and Causes of the Wealth of Nations* was published in London in 1776, Scotland and England were poised to make the great leap forward into an industrial future. Scotland, a minor economic power in the late 17th century, was to spearhead this brave new world with her southern neighbour.[1]

In the seven decades since the Union there had been significant economic progress. The tobacco trade and linen industry expanded in the years immediately following 1707, and there were signs of growth in grain exports, banking and shipping. Substantial acceleration, however, began in the 1740s driven by linen and the 'golden age' of tobacco. The fifteen-fold increase in the circulation of banknotes between 1744 and 1772 reflected a decisive shift into a new financial era. Gradual improvement in agriculture became a revolution in the 1760s and 1770s. The picture was not all rosy as some industries, such as fine woollens, paper-making and brewing, struggled to compete with higher quality English imports or suffered in the higher tax environment.[2] But the 18th century was generally characterised by wealth accumulation, confidence and a spirit of improvement, reflected in the cultural attainments of the Scottish Enlightenment.[3]

At the time of Union the Earl of Cromarty had predicted the Scots would become guardians of the 'Golden Fleece' of empire, and indeed, exploitation began in earnest after 1707.[4] In 1722 John Drummond of Quarrel became the first Scottish director of the EIC and during the 18th century Scots were active participants in the opportunities

---

[1]   *Transformation of Scotland*, 34–5, Whatley, *Scottish Society*, 2.

[2]   Graham, 'Scottish Maritime Interest,' 108, Whatley, *Scottish Society*, 53–8, 67, *Transformation of Scotland*, 23–4, 29. It has been estimated that between 1707 and the 1750s there was a fivefold increase in the level of taxation, but only between 15 and 20 per cent left Scotland.

[3]   M. Glendinning, R. MacInnes and A. MacKechnie, *A History of Scottish Architecture* (Edinburgh, 1996), 71–146. For two recent discussions of the Scottish Enlightenment see A. Herman, *The Scottish Enlightenment: The Scots' Invention of the Modern World* (London, 2002) and J. Buchan, *Capital of the Mind: How Edinburgh changed the World* (London, 2003).

[4]   *The Equivalent Explain'd* (Edinburgh, 1706), 7.

offered by the company in the East.[5] In the West Indies, they became the most important group to establish new landed dynasties in Antigua, and by the middle of the century a quarter of landholders in Jamaica were Scots.[6] This was a powerful irony, as the island had refused to provision the Darien colony and a significant number of colonists had remained there as indentured labour after escaping from the isthmus. By 1776 15,000 Highlanders had settled in Georgia and Carolina and 60,000 Lowland emigrants in Boston, Carolina, Chesapeake and New Jersey.[7] The British Empire was to have a distinctly Scottish flavour, and so was the British Army with Scots making up a quarter of regimental officers by the mid-18th century.[8]

The role of Union in this transformation has been a matter of some debate.[9] What is incontrovertible is that it provided Scots with three crucial benefits that were absent in the late 17th century: markets, liquidity and the backing of a vigorous state apparatus. Scottish merchants now had access to the largest free-trade zone in the world. Interest rates remained relatively low, currency risk was substantially reduced, and despite intermittent difficulties caused by bad harvests and Jacobite rebellions, there was not another liquidity crisis on the scale experienced in the late 1690s.[10] The financial revolution, with its key institutions of central bank, national debt and efficient tax-raising bureaucracy allowed England to outpace the much more populous France, and emerge as the dominant world power in the early 18th century.[11] Scotland now had the protection of a substantial 'fiscal-

---

[5]   Between 1775 and 1785, 47 per cent of writers, 49 per cent of cadets, 60 per cent of licensed free merchants, and 52 per cent of assistant surgeons in Bengal were Scots, H.V. Bowen, *Elites, Enterprise and the Making of the British Overseas Empire 1688–1775* (London, 1996), 163–4.

[6]   Scots held 40.4 per cent of the value of all goods recorded between 1771 and 1775. Bowen, *Elites*, 163.

[7]   *Transformation of Scotland*, 31.

[8]   L. Colley, *Britons: Forging the Nation 1707–1837* (London, 2003), 126.

[9]   For a detailed discussion see Whatley, *Scottish Society*, 51–2. Whatley has stated that 'the recent tendency has been to downgrade the significance of 1707.'

[10]   L.M. Cullen, 'The Scottish Exchange on London, 1673–1778,' in *Conflict, Identity and Economic Development: Ireland and Scotland 1600–1939*, (eds.) S.J. Connolly, R.A. Houston and R.J. Morris (Preston, 1995), 29–44.

[11]   J. Brewer, *The Sinews of Power: War, Money and the English State, 1688–1783* (London, 1989), 250.

military' state. Union therefore provided significant economic opportunity at a lower level of risk. Success was not guaranteed but reflected the Scottish response. As we have seen, a vigorous commercial culture existed well before 1707. Indeed its origins can be traced back to the period following the Reformation of 1560.[12] For Scotland the journey from Darien to the Wealth of Nations was not inevitable, but Union provided an environment in which the vibrancy of Scottish entrepreneurial culture could flourish.

Some of the directors at the heart of the management of the Company of Scotland did not live to enjoy the generous bail-out of 1707. Lord Basil Hamilton, inveterate Company supporter, director and patriot, met a tragic end at the age of only 29, when he was drowned while attempting to rescue a servant boy from a river near his house in Galloway in August 1701. Edinburgh merchant James Balfour, who was intimately involved in the establishment of the Company, had died by March 1700 and John Drummond of Newton by 1707.[13]

Others perhaps sought a quiet retirement after the frenetic years at the centre of national events. The elusive Sir Francis Scott of Thirlestane died in 1712 and Tweeddale in 1713. John Haldane of Gleneagles served in the British parliament in 1707, but lost his seat in the following year. Thereafter he was sustained by a clutch of offices and pensions and lived until 1721.[14] Lieutenant Colonel John Erskine became an improving laird and elder of the Kirk and died in 1743.[15] Panmure remained a committed Jacobite, joined the 1715 rebellion and fought in the inconclusive battle of Sheriffmuir. In January 1716 he entertained the Old Pretender at Brechin Castle, but was forced into exile when the rebellion failed, and he died in Paris in 1723. The advocate of Jacobite sympathies Mr David Drummond remained in Edinburgh as treasurer of the Bank of Scotland from 1700 until 1741.[16]

Some of the merchants benefited from their association with the Company. James MacLurg was knighted by April 1701, Robert Blackwood by August 1704 and Hugh Cunningham by November 1706. They prospered, invested in land and became known by their territorial

---

[12] Watt, 'Influence of Debt', 29, 36–7.

[13] NAS, GD 1/891/3, 2 September 1701, RBS, D/1/2, 8 March 1700, NAS, Commissary Court Records, CC 8/8/83.

[14] *House of Commons*, iv, 151–3.

[15] *Journal of the Hon. John Erskine*, xliii.

[16] *Scots Peerage*, vi, 431, ODNB, 37, 431–2, Saville, *Bank of Scotland*, 91.

designations; Sir James MacLurg of Vogrie, Sir Hugh Cunningham of Bonnington and Sir Robert Blackwood of Pitreavie. Blackwood rose to become Lord Provost of Edinburgh in 1711.

The man who had accompanied Gleneagles and Erskine to the Continent in 1696 and severely dented the Company's reputation, the talented James Smyth, re-emerged from historical obscurity in 1713 to lead a colonial revolt against the Danish West India Company on the tiny island of St Thomas, where his father had been a factor of the Elector of Brandenburg, and where the Scots had sought a pilot to guide them to Darien.[17]

Paterson himself lived on until 1719. He was briefly a member of the Union parliament for the burghs of Dumfriesshire, but settled in London where he continued to write on financial matters and press for compensation from the Equivalent. Although his claim seemed dubious to the directors of the Company in 1707, after much persistent lobbying he was eventually successful and awarded the very large sum of £18,241 (£2.25m today) by act of parliament in 1714.[18] This marked another remarkable triumph for the old projector's powers of persuasion. In January 1707 he had written to Queensberry anticipating the benefits of Union and proposing the construction of another canal; not across the isthmus of America, as he had done in a pamphlet of 1701, but rather between the Firths of Forth and Clyde. He recommended that the duke should have a proposed route surveyed to determine the project's practicability and cost.[19] Such careful planning was not part of his Darien scheme, but bringing together the North Sea and the Atlantic Ocean was more in keeping with the realities of Scottish power and finance, and was finally realised in 1790 after 22 years of digging.[20]

The memory of Darien was fresh in the minds of Scots in the early 18th century. One pamphlet of 1706 noted that 'because we have been so oft bitten with Projects....we are now turned Infidels, and believe

17 Forrester, *Man who saw the Future*, 179.
18 Bannister, *William Paterson*, 408, 427. When he died he left an estate of £6,400 (£783,700 today).
19 Paterson, *Proposal to Plant a colony*, 140, NRAS, Duke of Buccleuch, 1275, bundle 1166.
20 Construction began in 1768 but it was not completed until 1790. R.H. Campbell, *Scotland since 1707: The Rise of an Industrial Society* (Edinburgh, 1985), 43-5.

nothing.'[21] Nevertheless, investors have short memories and Scots were active speculators in the bubbles of 1719 (Mississippi) and 1720 (South Sea).[22] Hugh Dalrymple, a director of the Company, noted: 'I who never had much faith in stocks hav bein of late unfortunately drawen in to be prettie deeply concerned in England'.[23] Indeed it was the Scotsman John Law who unleashed the full fury of the new financial world when his policies in France initiated the Mississippi Bubble in 1719, possibly influenced by what had happened in Scotland in 1696.[24]

However, in 1719/20 the domestic capital market did not feature. Scots directed their attention to London where they could now take advantage of a larger pool of wealth and float companies without facing the ire of the English political and commercial establishment. Amazingly, a group of Scots, including two men who had been directors of the Company of Scotland, Hugh Montgomery and Lieutenant Colonel John Erskine, attempted to launch a company for a colonial project described as an 'affair of the Golden Islands'. An expedition was planned for November 1720, but perhaps thankfully the collapse of the bubble put an end to this small-scale re-enactment of the Darien fiasco.[25]

The domestic capital market remained fairly barren for much of the 18th century. A few major joint-stock companies were established, including the Royal Bank of Scotland, British Linen Company and the Forth and Clyde Canal, but nothing to compare with the Company of Scotland in terms of social spread and number of investors. Commercial development was principally funded through small-scale business concerns and partnerships, with financial investment focused on the opportunities offered by the more liquid London market.[26] A revi-

---

[21] *An Essay upon The XV Article of the Treaty of Union, Wherein the Difficulties That arise upon The Equivalents Are fully Cleared and Explained* (1706).

[22] Lewis Grant commented in 1720 that 'our countriemen have a Considerable share in this Loss,' NAS, GD 248/170/3/87.

[23] NAS, GD 110/1264.

[24] For a meticulous and engrossing study of Law's life, monetary theory, and the events of 1719–20 see Murphy, *John Law*.

[25] NAS, Earls of Eglinton, GD 3/5/940/1–2.

[26] R.C. Michie, *Money, Mania and Markets: Investment, Company Formation and the Stock Exchange in Nineteenth-Century Scotland* (Edinburgh, 1981), 6–14.

talised Scottish capital market only re-emerged in the 19th century on
the back of wealth created by industrialisation.[27]

Darien itself continued to haunt the Scottish imagination as totem
of national disaster, reminder of English perfidy or historical curiosity.
In 1736 Highlanders in Georgia named their settlement after the
colony in a gesture of defiance to the Spanish in Florida.[28] The minister and philologist David Malcolm published a book in 1738 which
attempted to show an affinity between the languages of the ancient
Britons and the Tule of the isthmus.[29] Thereafter Darien became a
topic of concern for historians and writers, and has continued to have
a cultural influence to the present day.[30]

The dream of a Scottish presence in Central America never quite died.
In early 1823 a ship containing 200 emigrants left Leith bound for a
new life on the Mosquito Coast, in present day Honduras north of
Darien. The venture was promoted by charismatic soldier Sir Gregor
MacGregor, the self-styled Cazique of Poyais, as a way of restoring
Scottish honour for the events on the isthmus in the 17th century.
MacGregor sold plots of land and attempted to raise £200,000 from the
London capital market, then in the throes of a Latin American debt bub-
ble. The marketing literature painted a picture of colonial sophistication.
The capital town of St Joseph was replete with boulevards, colonnaded
buildings, cathedral and bank. But when the colonists arrived they found
that Poyais existed only in the imagination of MacGregor. They were
the victims of one of the most audacious swindles in history.[31]

---

[27] *Ibid.*, 6, 266. It was not until 1824 that the first stockbrokers appeared in
       Scotland, and 1844 that the first stock exchange was founded.

[28] A.W. Parker, *Scottish Highlanders in Colonial Georgia: The Recruitment,
       Emigration, and settlement at Darien, 1735–1748* (Athens, 1997), 53.

[29] *An Essay on the Antiquities of Great Britain and Ireland...especially an
       Attempt to shew an Affinity betwixt the Languages of the Ancient
       Britains, and the Americans of the Isthmus of Darien* (Edinburgh, 1738).

[30] The Scottish colonial attempt at Darien has formed the basis of a number of
       historical novels: E. Warburton, *Darien; or, The Merchant Prince. A
       Historical Romance*, 3 volumes (London, 1852), F.G. Slaughter, *Darien
       Venture* (London, 1978) [first published in New York in 1955 under the
       name C.V. Terry], D. Galbraith, *The Rising Sun* (London, 2000), and D.
       Nicol, *The Fundamentals of New Caledonia* (Edinburgh, 2003).

[31] D. Sinclair, *Sir Gregor MacGregor and the Land that Never Was: The
       Extraordinary Story of the Most Audacious Fraud in History* (London,
       2003), Michie, *Money, Mania and Markets*, 29. MacGregor's knighthood
       was also fictitious. Sinclair suggests that he may have been related to the
       offspring of one of the Scots at Darien and a Tule woman.

The dream of controlling the isthmus passed on to others. In 1825 a group of wealthy New York businessmen created a canal company, but were unable to raise capital to fund the venture.[32] Finally, the Californian gold rush provided a powerful catalyst as prospectors sought a faster route to the West avoiding the long overland journey across the United States. Between 1850 and 1855 47 and a half miles of railway were laid at a cost of £8m, making it the most expensive track on earth on a pound per mile basis. It allowed the isthmus to be crossed in just over three hours, but an estimated 6,000 workers died during construction.[33]

Following his success in linking the Mediterranean and Red Sea by the Suez Canal, Ferdinand de Lesseps attempted a similar feat across the American isthmus in the 1880s. In three days 100,000 individuals subscribed for shares when his company was floated in France, but insurmountable technical problems, funding difficulties and disease led to its bankruptcy and the abandonment of the project after a decade of work costing 1.4bn francs ($287m). Twenty thousand people are thought to have died in the attempt and the company's demise provoked a political storm, fraud trials and a surge of anti-Semitism.[34] There are strong parallels with the Scottish experience of the 1690s: charismatic leader, financial mania, disaster, political storm, although Scottish prejudice was directed against the English.

A canal was finally constructed by the government of the United States of America. The massive effort began during the presidency of Theodore Roosevelt, the great-great-great-great grandson of Scottish minister Archibald Stobo, who survived the second expedition to Darien and settled in Carolina after the sinking of the *Rising Sun*.[35] Roosevelt was not driven by dreams of wealth, but rather the United States' destiny as world power. Work began in 1904 and the canal opened in 1914; a potent symbol of the rise of the United States, just as Europe entered a period of dark self-destruction. Government financial backing, developments in medical science, improvements in excavation equipment and the choice of a lock system, rather than the sea level canal attempted by de Lesseps, ensured American success. The project was

---

[32] W. LaFeber, *The Panama Canal: The Crisis in Historical Perspective* (New York, 1989), 7.

[33] D. McCullough, *The Path Between the Seas: The Creation of the Panama Canal 1870–1914* (New York, 1977), 33–6.

[34] *Ibid.*, 130–203.

[35] *Fasti Ecclesiae Scoticanae*, vii, 665.

completed below budget at $352m and was six months ahead of schedule, although 5,609 lives were lost during construction.[36] It had taken the vast resources of a rising global superpower to build and control a sea-passage across the isthmus. It was a colossal engineering undertaking, described as the 'largest, most costly single effort ever before mounted anywhere on earth'.[37] In the late 17th century a nation with a navy of three ships had dreamed of doing the same.

[36] McCullough, *Path Between the Seas*, 247–611.
[37] *Ibid.*, 11.

Conclusions

THE DARIEN DISASTER joined the Massacre of Glencoe and the harvest failures to characterise the bitter 'ill years' of King William's rule in Scotland. The pre-Union period has been presented as a time of darkness from which the nation was fortunate to escape in 1707.[1] This study, however, has revealed a more complex reality and highlighted three distinct phases in the Company's history.

The first phase, involving the establishment of the Company and the subscription process, was a major success, reflecting a spirit of secular improvement. The capital raising was a significant event in financial history, anticipating later bubbles, and extending direct and indirect share ownership further than before. This was a remarkable achievement for a relatively poor nation that did not possess the liquid wealth or state power of the Dutch or English. An explanation of why it happened must take account of a number of features of late 17th century Scotland: the presence of a legal framework which facilitated the exchange of cash for shares, a capitalist ethic open to the influence of Dutch and English financial models and perhaps most importantly, confidence. By the 1690s Scotland was a dynamic and relatively sophisticated society, eager for improvement and on the

---

[1] See in particular H. Trevor-Roper, 'The Scottish Enlightenment' in *Studies on Voltaire and the Eighteenth Century*, 58, (1967), 1636: 'at the end of the 17th century Scotland was a by-word for irredeemable poverty, social backwardness, political faction,' and the grim portrayal of Scottish politics in Riley, *King William*. Whatley has also provided a bleak analysis of Scottish society and the economy in the late 17th century. C.A. Whatley, *Scottish Society 1707–1830: Beyond Jacobitism, towards industrialization* (Manchester, 200), 6, 16–47. Herman has described Scotland on the eve of union as a country 'whose southern half was in the grip of a Taleban-like clerical tyranny, and northern half in chaos,' A. Herman, 'Scots genius can lead way to new Europe,' *Scotsman*, 10 January 2006. Others have stressed more positive aspects of the pre–1707 period, see T.M. Devine, 'The Union of 1707 and Scottish Development,' *Scottish Economic and Social History*, 5, (1985), 25–6, Patrick, 'People and Parliament,' 383–4. For a detailed consideration of this issue see D. Stevenson, 'Twilight before night or darkness before dawn? Interpreting 17th-century Scotland' in *Why Scottish History Matters*, ed. R. Mitchison (Edinburgh, 1991).

highroad to Enlightenment, although constrained by a problematic constitutional relationship with England.[2]

The second 'management' phase was truly disastrous. A very large amount of capital was delivered by a very large number of shareholders to an inexperienced court of directors. When capital is raised with little difficulty it is often misallocated, and this was clearly the case with the Company of Scotland. A diversification strategy was ill-considered and excessive sums spent on shipping assets. At all stages there was inappropriate appreciation of risk. A large quantity of the capital was transferred to one man and a significant proportion lost. Opposition from the English, Dutch and Spanish was underestimated and none of the assets were insured. In the knowledge that the Company had squandered its capital and was, as a result, undercapitalised, the directors decided to establish a colony in a location of significant economic and strategic importance to Spain, which had not been surveyed by an advance party, and without a communication and financial network in the Caribbean or America. They briefly flirted with a policy of retrenchment, but ultimately pursued one of extravagant risk. Significant mismanagement of the cargo and provisions on the first expedition followed and the climate and location proved calamitous. Lack of capital made funding relief ships very difficult in the dire financial environment of the late 1690s.

The failure of the colony and the loss of all the capital was principally the result of decisions taken by the directors. Historians have generally pointed to a number of factors to explain the disaster, including English and Spanish opposition, mismanagement and poor conditions on the isthmus.[3] This account places the responsibility firmly on the shoulders of those who ran the Company. There was opposition from the English, Dutch and Spanish, but this should have

---

[2]   Another indication of 'enlightenment' in the financial sphere was the groundbreaking monetary analysis of John Law described by Schumpeter as 'in the front rank of monetary theorists of all times,' J. Schumpeter, *A History of Economic Analysis* (London, 1954), 295. Murphy refers to *Money and Trade* published in 1705 as a 'majestic work towering over the contemporary writings of the early 18th century,' Murphy, *John Law*, 77.

[3]   For a discussion of the historiography see D. Watt, 'The management of capital by the Company of Scotland 1696–1707,' *Journal of Scottish Historical Studies*, 25, (2005), 97–118.

been anticipated, and was not the principal reason why every penny of the shareholders' capital was squandered. The directors lost touch with reality, influenced by the manic overconfidence of the nation.

The Company of Scotland was thus an early example of a corporate cock-up on the grand scale. In his *Proposals for a Council of Trade* William Paterson himself reflected on the importance of management in any major commercial endeavour, and he may well have had the directors of the Company in mind when he wrote: 'The main hazard in an affair of this nature always has been, and ever will be, of a rash, raw, giddy, and headless direction'.[4]

A number of weaknesses in the corporate structure might be highlighted to partly account for this outcome: the court of directors was too large and contained many inexperienced lairds; a rotating president did not provide clear leadership. The directors were also victims of the success of the capital raising. If a much smaller amount had been secured, there would have been less potential for mismanagement, and the political ramifications of failure would have been much reduced.

William Paterson was central to the formation of the Company and its success in raising capital. He described the isthmus with such glowing enthusiasm that a majority of the directors were convinced a Scottish Company could sustain a colony there. The notion that a company from a state with practically no naval power and very limited financial resources could control both sides of the isthmus of America, at a time of intense international trade rivalry, was delusion, and reflected the loss of reality typical of a financial mania. Paterson was at heart a marketing man who brilliantly articulated the new financial age, but his skills did not extend to the pragmatic details of managing a major business venture.

The third phase saw the Company transformed from a financial entity into a political one. A vigorous propaganda campaign was launched by the directors to deflect blame from themselves onto the English government. This began following English opposition to efforts to raise capital in Hamburg and reached a peak during the political storm of 1699–1701, by which time the Country Party and the Company were almost synonymous. The financial revolution in Scotland therefore followed a different path from England, where a symbiotic relationship developed between joint-stock companies and the state; the

---

4   Bannister, *William Paterson*, 247.

Bank of England and EIC providing large amounts of cash to fund King William's war effort.[5] The politicisation of the Company of Scotland and its domination by the Country opposition seriously weakened both the Company, which could not depend on state support, and the Scottish state, which received no financial benefit from the Company's existence. Scotland's 'financial revolution' did not give rise to a powerful 'fiscal-military' state as it did in England. Indeed, it could be argued, it was a contributing factor to the demise of an independent Scottish state in 1707.[6]

The sense of grievance, expressed in pamphlets, addresses and in parliament, called into question the existing constitutional relationship between Scotland and England. But, paradoxically, the large number of disgruntled shareholders provided a mechanism of reward, allowing the English government to purchase incorporating Union relatively easily in 1706/7. The Equivalent was central to the achievement of Union which was a pragmatic transaction reflecting the political realities of the early 18th century, rather than an act of statesmanship or national humiliation. Compensation to investors was generous in financial terms, but hardly equitable, as the directors who were responsible for squandering the capital received the largest payouts.

In the years from 1695 to 1707 the Scots experienced a painful journey from the idealism of independent empire to the realism of incorporating Union.

---

[5]   B.G. Carruthers, *City of Capital: Politics and Markets in the English Financial Revolution* (Princeton, 1996), 18, 138–58. Carruthers highlights that Whigs and Tories fought political battles for control of the English joint-stock companies, but this struggle did not undermine the financial benefits received by the state. Indeed the parties competed to provide the government with larger amounts of cash.

[6]   Brewer, *Sinews of Power*, xvii, 250.

Chronology

1617   Scottish East Indian and Greenland Company established.

1625   Death of James VI. Reign of Charles I begins.

1634   Scots Guinea Company established.

1638   National Covenant.

1642   Civil War.

1649   Charles I executed.

1660   Restoration. Reign of Charles II begins.

1680   Dampier and Wafer cross the isthmus.

1682   Carolina Company founded.

1683   East New Jersey colony established.

1684   Colony of Stuarts Town in South Carolina established.

1685   Death of Charles II. Reign of James VII begins.

1686   September: Scottish colony in South Carolina destroyed.

1688   Glorious Revolution. Reign of William and Mary begins. East New Jersey becomes part of New England.

1689   Jacobite uprising.

1692   Massacre of Glencoe.

1693   Act for Encouraging Foreign Trade.

1695   26 June: Act establishing the Company of Scotland.

17 July: Act establishing the Bank of Scotland.

29 August: First official meeting of English promoters.

6 November: English subscription book opened.

6 December: Last meeting of the directors in England.

12 December: House of Lords address King William about the Scottish Company.

1696   21 January: House of Commons threatens to impeach those promoting the Company.

26 February: Subscription book opened in Edinburgh.

5 March: Glasgow subscription book opened.

12 May: First court of directors elected.

5 June: Directors decide to apply capital to a salt business.

23 June: James Gibson and Alexander Stevenson appointed to buy and build ships on the Continent.

July: Paterson presents his colonial ideas to the court of directors.

1 August: Subscription books closed at £400,000.

9 September: Appointment of entourage for international road-show to the Dutch Republic and Hamburg.

12 October: Legislation passed by Parliament for the Company's salt monopoly.

1697   January: Appointment of Dutch factors.
        25 February: Directors decide against pursuing Paterson's
        Darien scheme.
        March: Details of 'Smyth affair' leak out.
        March: Launch of the *Caledonia* and *Instauration* in Hamburg.
        April: Memorial to the Senate of Hamburg.
        May: *Rising Sun* launched in Amsterdam.
        2 July: Dampier and Wafer questioned by English government
        about the isthmus.
        August: Company cash falls to £4,084.
        20 September: Treaty of Ryswick ends the Nine Years War.
        November: *Caledonia* and the *Instauration* reach the Firth of
        Forth.
        7 October: Mr Robert Blackwood calls for an immediate
        decision on the colonial destination.

1698   14 July: First expedition sails from Road of Leith.
        2 September: The fleet depart from Madeira to cross the Atlantic.
        1 November: Fleet anchors at Golden Island.
        2 November: Site of New Caledonia established.
        25 December: *Maurepas* attempts to leave Caledonia Bay.

1699   February: *Dolphin* forced to make for Cartagena and crew
        imprisoned.
        February: Skirmish with the Spanish.
        February: Company begins negotiations with Armenian merchants.
        25 March: Official confirmation of the successful landing by the
        first expedition.
        9 April: Sir William Beeston publishes proclamation prohibiting
        the provisioning of the colony.
        11 April: News that the *Dispatch* has grounded off Islay.
        12 May: Relief ships *Olive Branch* and *Hopeful Binning* sail
        from Leith Road.
        18 May: News of the proclamations reach the colony.
        16 June: Paterson helped on board the *Unicorn*
        19 June: Darien is abandoned for the first time.
        1 July: The *Endeavour* sinks.
        August: *Olive Branch* and *Hopeful Binning* reach Darien.
        18 August: Second expedition sails from the Clyde.
        23 September: Fleet finally leaves Scottish waters.
        October: Confirmation of the abandonment reaches Scotland.
        19 November: *Caledonia* reaches the Sound of Islay.
        30 November: Second expedition reaches Darien.
        December: National Address promulgated.

1700   Jan-Feb: Debates in English Houses of Parliament about Darien and Union.

3 February: Fire in Edinburgh.

11 February: Alexander Campbell of Fonab reaches Darien.

15 February: Skirmish of Toubacanti.

1 March: Spanish troops land near Carret Bay.

5 March: Tweeddale, Gleneagles and Home of Blackadder take National Address to court in London.

25 March: National Address presented and read to King William.

28 March: National Fast in Scotland.

31 March: Articles of capitulation signed with the Spanish.

21 May: Parliament opens in Edinburgh.

30 May: Parliament adjourned.

20 June: Toubacanti riots in Edinburgh.

July: *African Merchant* returns from voyage to Africa.

3 September: Hurricane sinks the *Rising Sun* and *Duke of Hamilton*.

29 October: Parliament reconvenes.

1701   14 January: Court wins battle in parliament.

June/July: Collapse of Company cash balances.

July: *Speedwell* reaches Batavia.

September: Louis XIV recognises James VIII and reneges on the Treaty of Ryswick.

1702   January: *Speedwell* sinks at Malacca.

8 March: Death of King William.

October: Union negotiations commence.

1703   February: Union negotiations end.

1704   31 January: *Annandale* seized in the Downs.

July: *Worcester* arrives in Firth of Forth.

1705   February: English Alien Act.

16 March: Captain Green and crew convicted and sentenced to death.

11 April: Green, Madder and Simpson executed at Leith.

1706   16 April: Union commissioners meet at Whitehall.

3 October: Scottish parliament opens.

6 November: Council general of the Company discusses Union.

30 December: Fifteenth article passed.

1707   16 January: Treaty of Union ratified by Scottish Parliament.

25 March: Act concerning the Public Debts.

1 May: United Kingdom comes into existence.

5 August: Equivalent arrives in Edinburgh.

18 August: Last meeting of the court of directors.

Principal Characters

ARBUCKLE, William: Glasgow merchant, director.

ANNANDALE, William Johnstone, first Marquis of (1664–1721): Court politician, shareholder.

ARGYLL, Archibald Campbell, first Duke of (d.1703): Court politician, shareholder.

ARGYLL, John Campbell, second Duke of (1680–1743): Court politician, soldier.

BALFOUR, James (d.1700): Edinburgh merchant, promoter, director.

BAILLIE, George of Jerviswood (1664–1738): Borders laird, Presbyterian, Receiver-General, director, Country Party, Treasurer-Depute in New Party administration.

BELHAVEN, John Hamilton, second Lord (1656–1708): promoter, director, Country Party.

BLACKWOOD, Mr Robert: Edinburgh merchant, promoter, director.

BLACKWOOD, Sir Robert: Edinburgh merchant, director.

BORLAND, Francis (c.1666–1722): minister on the second expedition, wrote a detailed description of his experiences.

CAMPBELL, Alexander of Fonab (c.1660–1724): soldier, fought in the Low Countries, sailed to Darien after second fleet, led Scots to victory at Toubacanti.

CHIESLY, Sir Robert: Lord Provost of Edinburgh, promoter, shareholder.

CLARK, George: Edinburgh merchant, director.

CLERK, Sir John of Penicuik (1676–1755): Court supporter, composed *Leo Scotiae Irritatus*, historian of the Union.

COCKBURN, Adam of Ormiston (c.1656–1735): Presbyterian, Lord Justice Clerk, director, Court politician.

CORSE, John: Glasgow merchant, director.

CROMARTY, George MacKenzie, first Earl of (1630–1714): Court politician, Lord Clerk Register, shareholder, member of council general, Darien sceptic.

CUNNINGHAM, Hugh: Edinburgh merchant, director.

CUNNINGHAM, James of Eickett: soldier, councillor on the first expedition, led armed rising against Union but was in the pay of Queensberry.

DALGLEISH, Alexander (d.1699): minister on the second expedition.

DALRYMPLE, Hugh (1652–1737): third son of Viscount Stair, advocate, director, President of the Court of Session from 1698, Court supporter.

DAMPIER, William (1651–1715): buccaneer, travel writer, crossed the isthmus in 1680 and circumnavigated the globe three times.

DEFOE, Daniel (1660?–1731): author, propagandist, English spy in Edinburgh, historian of the Union.

DOUGLAS, Robert: London Scottish merchant, investor and director in London, Darien sceptic.

DRUMMOND, Mr David (1656–1741): advocate of Jacobite sympathies, active director, Treasurer of the Bank of Scotland from 1700.

DRUMMOND, John of Newton (d.1707): Edinburgh merchant, laird, active director.

DRUMMOND, Captain Robert: commander of the *Caledonia* on the first expedition.

DUNLOP, William (1653/4–1700): Presbyterian minister, participant in colonial venture to South Carolina, Principal of Glasgow University, shareholder, member of the council general.

ERSKINE, Lieutenant Colonel John (1662–1743): Presbyterian, son of Lord Cardross, active director, sent on mission to the Dutch Republic and Hamburg, Country Party.

FULLARTON, Thomas: Captain of the *Dolphin* on the first expedition.

GIBSON, James (d.1700): Glasgow merchant, sent to Amsterdam to oversee ship construction, commander of the *Rising Sun* on the second expedition.

HALDANE, John of Gleneagles (1660–1724): Perthshire laird, active director, sent on mission to the Dutch Republic and Hamburg, Country Party, *Squadrone Volante*.

HAMILTON, Alexander (d.1700): chief accountant on the first expedition, brought the news of the successful landing back to Scotland, returned to the isthmus and died when the *Rising Sun* sank.

HAMILTON, Basil, Lord (1671–1701): younger brother of fourth Duke, director, Country Party.

HAMILTON, Anne Duchess of (1632–1716): leading Scottish noblewoman, mother of the fourth Duke and Lord Basil, first to subscribe the subscription book.

HAMILTON, James fourth Duke of (1658–1712): shareholder, leader of the Country Party.

HERRIES, Walter: born in Dumbarton, ship's surgeon recruited by Gleneagles in London, sailed on first expedition, left early and returned to London, wrote vigorous attack on the directors.

HAY, William of Drummelzier (1649–1734): Borders laird, half-brother of first Marquis of Tweeddale, director, Darien sceptic.

HOME, George of Kimmerghame: Borders laird, shareholder, diarist.

HOME, Sir John of Blackadder: Borders laird, director, accompanied the National Address to court.

JAMES, Mr Thomas (d.1698): minister on the first expedition.

JOLLY, Robert: councillor on the first expedition.

LAW, John (1671–1729): monetary theorist who rose to become Controller-General of France and unleashed the Mississippi Bubble in 1719.

LODGE, Daniel: accountant at the Bank of England and disciple of Paterson, organised capital raising in Scotland, director.

LOCKHART, George of Carnwath (1681?–1731): Jacobite laird, shareholder.

MACKAY, Daniel: Edinburgh lawyer, councillor on the first expedition, sailed home to Scotland and then back to Darien again, devoured by sharks.

MACKENZIE, Roderick: secretary, propagandist, Country Party administrator.

MACLURG, James: Edinburgh merchant, active director.

MALLOCH, John: Captain of the *Endeavour* on the first expedition.

MARCHMONT, Patrick Hume, first Earl of (1641–1724): Presbyterian, extraordinary Lord of Session, Chancellor, shareholder, Court politician.

MAXWELL, Sir John of Pollock (1648–1732): Presbyterian, Lord of Treasury, Lord Justice Clerk, director, Court politician.

MONTGOMERY, Francis of Giffen (d.1729): second son of Hugh, seventh Earl of Eglinton, director, Court supporter.

MONTGOMERY, Hugh: Glasgow merchant, director.

MUNRO, Dr John of Coul: Company servant, director.

MUIR, Sir Archibald of Thornton: Lord Provost of Edinburgh, director, Court supporter.

PANMURE, James Maule, fourth Earl of (1658/9–1723): Jacobite, active director, Country politician.

PATERSON, William (1655–1719): merchant, financial revolutionary, promoter of Darien, key director, sailed to Darien, Court supporter after his return.

PENNECUIK, Captain Robert: commander of the *St Andrew* on the first expedition, councillor.

PINCARTON, Captain Robert: commander of the *Unicorn* on the first expedition, councillor.

PRINGLE, James of Torwoodlee: Borders laird, Presbyterian, director.

QUEENSBERRY, James Douglas, second Duke of (1662–1711): Court politician, shareholder.

RUTHVEN, David second Lord, (d.1701): Presbyterian, director, director of the Bank of Scotland.

RYCAUT, Sir Paul (1629–1700): diplomat and author, English Resident in Hamburg and indefatigable opponent of the Company.

SCOTT, Mr Adam (d.1698): minister on the first expedition.

SCOTT, Sir Francis of Thirlestane (1645–1712): Borders laird, most active director, followed Tweeddale in politics, Country Party politician.

SCOTT, Sir Patrick of Ancrum (d.1734): Borders laird, advocate, director, followed Tweeddale in politics.

SEAFIELD, James Ogilvie, first Viscount and Earl of (1663–1730): Court politician, joint Secretary of State, Chancellor.

SHAW, Sir John of Greenock: laird, director.

SHIELDS, Alexander (1661–1700): charismatic minister on the second expedition.

SMYTH, James: London merchant, subscriber in London, director, associate of Paterson, sent to Dutch Republic and Hamburg.

STEVENSON, Alexander: Edinburgh merchant, sent to Hamburg to oversee ship construction.

STEWART, Sir James of Goodtrees (1635–1713): Presbyterian exile, Lord Advocate, framed the Company's act, opposed Union.

STOBO, Archibald (d.1741): minister on the second expedition.

SWINTON, Sir John of that Ilk (d.1724): Borders laird, Presbyterian, director.

TWEEDDALE, John Hay, first Marquis of (1626–1697): politician, shareholder, Lord Chancellor.

TWEEDDALE, John Hay, second Marquis of (1645–1713): director, Country Party leader, *Squadrone Volante*.

VEITCH, William: councillor on first expedition but did not sail because of ill health, sailed on the second expedition.

WAFER, Lionel (d.1705): ship's surgeon and buccaneer, crossed the isthmus with Dampier in 1680, offered his services to the Company.

WATSON, Robert: Edinburgh merchant, director, Darien sceptic.

WILLIAM III and II (1650–1702): Stadholder of the United Provinces, King of Scotland, England and Ireland, unsympathetic to the Company.

WOODDROP, William: Glasgow merchant, director.

Promoters listed in the Act of Parliament of 1695

Nobles
Lord Belhaven

Lairds
Adam Cockburn of Ormiston
Mr Francis Montgomery of Giffen
Sir John Maxwell of Pollock

Sir Robert Chiesly
Sir John Swinton of that Ilk

Edinburgh Merchants
George Clark
Mr Robert Blackwood

James Balfour

Glasgow Merchant
John Corse

London Merchants
William Paterson
James Foulis
David Nairn
Thomas Deans
James Chiesly
John Smith

Thomas Coutts
Hugh Frazer
Joseph Cohaine
Daves Ovedo[1]
Walter Stuart

Source: APS, ix, 378.

[1] The clerk writing the act thought the name Joseph Cohen D'Azevedo represented two individuals. James Smyth's name was also incorrect.

APPENDIX II

Court of directors elected by shareholders on 12 May 1696

Nobles

Lord Belhaven   Lord Ruthven

Lairds

Adam Cockburn of Ormiston   Sir John Maxwell of Pollock
Mr Francis Montgomery of Giffen   Sir John Swinton of that Ilk
William Hay of Drummelzier   John Haldane of Gleneagles
Mr Hugh Dalrymple   Sir Archibald Muir of Thornton
Lieutenant Colonel John Erskine   George Baillie of Jerviswood
Sir John Home of Blackadder   James Pringle of Torwoodlee
Sir Francis Scott of Thirlestane   John Drummond of Newton
Sir Patrick Scott of Ancrum

Edinburgh Merchants

George Clark   James MacLurg
Mr Robert Blackwood   James Balfour

Glasgow Merchants

Hugh Montgomery   John Corse
William Arbuckle   William Wooddrop

Directors added by votes of the above court

William Paterson   James Campbell
James Smyth   Sir John Shaw of Greenock
Daniel Lodge   Robert Watson

Source: Royal Bank of Scotland Archive [RBS], Journal of the Court of Directors, D/1/1, 32-3, 36, 40-1, 48, 113.

APPENDIX III

Director Attendance 1696 to 1701

	1696	1697	1698	1699	1700	1701	Total	%
Number of Courts	56	89	92	120	58	38	453	
Sir Francis Scott of Thirlestane	55	61	82	112	50	30	390	86
John Drummond of Newton	49	43	21	90	41	32	276	61
James MacLurg (Sir from 1 Apr 1701)	52	71	58	59	17	9	266	59
Lieutenant Colonel John Erskine	36	33	52	77	33	21	252	56
Mr David Drummond			71	96	50	24	241	53
Hugh Cunningham (Sir from 7 Nov 1706)		45	76	49	34	21	225	50
John Haldane of Gleneagles	31	21	52	67	23	10	204	45
James Balfour	38	50	67	50			205	45
Second Marquis of Tweeddale			57	74	37	14	182	40
Sir Patrick Scott of Ancrum	40	21	22	40	35	15	173	38
William Hay of Drummelzier	32	44	41	46	3	(off 12 March)	163	36
Lord Ruthven	33	31	39	38	13	4	158	35
Robert Blackwood (Sir from 28 Aug 1704)				70	51	30	151	33
Sir John Shaw of Greenock	14	15	29	48	26	7	139	31
Mr Robert Blackwood	23	43	72	4 (off 7 March)			142	31
Earl of Panmure			57	48	22	9	136	30
George Clark	37	58	31	4 (off 7 March)			130	29

	1696	1697	1698	1699	1700	1701	Total	%
William Wooddrop	39	26	23	23	3	3	117	26
George Baillie of Jerviswood	29	21	2	29	21	10	112	25
Adam Cockburn of Ormiston	22	35	11	36	1		105	23
William Menzies		26	20	39	12	(off 12 March)	97	21
William Arbuckle	37	8	16	16	8	6	91	20
Hugh Montgomery	25	12	14	29	7	(off 12 March)	87	19
Mr Francis Montgomery of Giffen	19	21	12	31	(off 5 March)		83	18
William Paterson	48	16	15	1	3		83	18
Robert Watson	19	57	3				79	17
John Jamieson of Balmuir					42	33	75	17
Sir Archibald Muir of Thornton	46	9	17	39	(off 5 March)		72	16
John Graham of Dougalston		17	28	27			72	16
Dr Dundas					35	31	66	15
Mr Patrick Campbell of Monzie				57			57	13
Sir John Swinton of that Ilk		8 (off 12 / 46 March)					54	12
Daniel Lodge	51	2					53	12
Sir John Home of Blackadder		7 (off 12 / 43 March)					50	11
John Corse	35	13					48	11
Sir John Maxwell of Pollock	34		10	1 (off 7 March)			45	10
Lord Belhaven	29	1	2	5	1		38	8
Mr Hugh Dalrymple	25	3	1	6	1		36	8
Earl of Annandale				32	(off 5 March)		32	7
Dr Munro						27	27	6

	1696	1697	1698	1699	1700	1701	Total	%
James Pringle of Torwoodlee	24	(off 12 March)					24	5
Adam Hepburn of Humby						20	20	4
Lord Basil Hamilton					15	4	19	4
Mr James Campbell	17						17	4
Sir Robert Chiesly						15	15	3
James Smyth							0	

Source: RBS, D/1/1–3.

Shareholder Breakdown

Amount subscribed	Number of shareholders	% of total
£100 or less	648	49.1
£101–£200	283	21.4
£201–£400	123	9.3
£500	115	8.7
£501–£999	24	1.8
£1,000	92	7.0
£1,001–£3,000	35	2.7

Source: Darien Papers, *371–409.*

Institutional Investors

Good Town of Edinburgh £3,000
Convention of Royal Burghs £3,000
Burgh of Glasgow £3,000
Easter Sugary of Glasgow £3,000
Town of Perth £2,000
Merchant Company of Edinburgh £1,200
Faculty of Advocates £1,000
Merchants' House of Glasgow £1,000
Town of Brechin £700[1]
Incorporation of Surgeons of Edinburgh £600
Town of Dumfries £500
Guildry of Aberdeen £500
Town of Selkirk £500
Cowan's Hospital Stirling £500
Incorporation of Marie's Chapel £400
Town of Haddington £400
Trades House of Glasgow £400
Guildry of Linlithgow £300
Incorporation of Skinners of Edinburgh £300
Incorporation of Tailors of the Canongate £300
Guildry of Stirling £200
Hammermen of Edinburgh £200
Incorporation of Baxters of Edinburgh £200
Burgh of Linlithgow £200
Guildry of Dundee £200
Trinity House of Leith £200
Burgh of Stirling £200
Incorporation of Tailors of Glasgow £200
Incorporation of Baxters of Glasgow £200
Incorporation of Maltmen of Glasgow £200
Burgh of Ayr £200
Town of Paisley £200

---

[1]   Two separate subscriptions of £400 and £300.

Burgh of Renfrew £150
Nether Hospital of Stirling £100
Incorporation of Cordiners of Edinburgh £100
Seaman's Box of Dundee £100
Incorporation of Tailors in Easter Portsburgh £100
Incorporation of Baxters of the Canongate £100
Town of Dunbar £100
Incorporation of Hammermen of the Canongate £100
Incorporation of Wrights of the Canongate £100
Incorporation of Cordiners of the Canongate £100
Town of Inverkeithing £100
Burgh of St Andrews £100
Town of Inverness £100
Town of Queensferry £100
Burgh of Cupar £100
Hammermen of Glasgow £100
Wrights of Glasgow £100
Incorporation of Coopers of Glasgow £100
Incorporation of Masons of Glasgow £100
Incorporation of Cordiners of Glasgow £100
Burgh of Irvine £100

£27,150

Source: Darien Papers, *371–409.*

The Largest Shareholders

Shareholders who invested £3,000

James Duke of Queensberry
Anne Duchess of Hamilton
Lord Basil Hamilton
John Lord Belhaven
Mr Robert Blackwood

John Stewart of Grandtully
Good Town of Edinburgh
Convention of Royal Burghs
Burgh of Glasgow
Easter Sugary of Glasgow

Other shareholders who invested above £1,000

Nobles

Margaret Countess of Weymss
Archibald Earl of Argyll
John Lord Glenorchy

William Lord Jedburgh
David Earl of Leven

Lairds

James Pringle of Torwoodlee
Patrick Porteous of Halkshaw
Henry Rollo of Woodside
John Drummond of Newton

Charles Hope of Hopetoun
Sir William Scott younger of Harden
Sir John Swinton of that Ilk
Lieutenant Colonel John Erskine

Merchants

John Duncan
William Arbuckle
James Balfour
Sir Robert Chiesly

John Corse
William Menzies
George Warrander

Others

Merchant Company
    of Edinburgh

Mr William Dunlop
Town of Perth

Source: Darien Papers, *371–409.*

Female Shareholders

Anne Duchess of Hamilton £3,000
Margaret Countess of Weymss £2,000
Susan Countess of Dundonald £1,000
Margaret Countess of Roxburgh £1,000
Lady Margaret Hope of Hopetoun £1,000
Margaret Countess of Rothes £1,000
Margaret Lady dowager of Nairne £500
Katherine Trotter Lady Craigleith £500
Elizabeth Lady Borthwick £400
Marie Douglas Lady Hilton £400
Lady Margaret Napier £400
Lady Campbell £200
Henrietta Dalyell of Glenae £200
Mrs Agnes Dalyell, eldest daughter of late Sir Robert Dalyell of Glenae £200
Mrs Christian Dundas, daughter of William Dundas of Kingscavil advocate £200
Veronica Erskine, daughter of David Lord Cardross £200
Dame Helen Fleming £200
Barbara Fraser, relict of George Stirling surgeon apothecary in Edinburgh £200
Dame Margaret Graham, Lady Kinloch £200
Christian Countess, dowager of Haddington £200
Margaret Hamilton, Lady Bengowar £200
Dame Bethea Harper, Lady Cambusnethan £200
Rachel Johnstoun, relict of Mr Robert Baillie of Jerviswood £200
Mrs Margaret Marjoribanks, daughter of Andrew Marjoribanks £200
Dame Jean Mercer, Lady Aldie £200
Mary Murray, Lady Enterkin elder £200
Patricia Ruthven, grandchild to Earl of Bramford £200
Dame Elizabeth Trotter, Lady Nicolson £200
Margaret Muirhead, daughter of James Muirhead surgeon apothecary in Edinburgh £200
Margaret Adamson, eldest daughter of the late Patrick Adamson merchant in Kelso £100

Jean Arthur, daughter of John Arthur of Newton £100

Katherine Binning, Lady Bavelaw £100

Elizabeth Blackwood, daughter of Robert Blackwood merchant in Edinburgh £100

Bessie Bogle, relict of Robert Bogle elder merchant of Glasgow £100

Marion Borthwick, relict of James Cunningham cooper in Leith £100

Christian Boyd, relict of Peter Gemmell merchant in Glasgow £100

Mrs Elizabeth Brisbane, daughter of deceased John Brisbane of Bishopstown £100

Mrs Margaret Brown, daughter of Laird of Blackburn £100

Agnes Campbell, relict of Andrew Anderson his Majesty's printer £100

Christian Carr, sister of John Carr of Cavers £100

Mrs Janet Carse, sister of Mark Carse of Cockpen £100

Marion Cleghorn, relict of Thomas Robertson late baillie of Edinburgh £100

Katharine Charteris, daughter of Laurance Charteris advocate £100

Mrs Christian Cockburn, daughter of Adam Cockburn of Ormiston Lord Justice Clerk £100

Isobel Cranston, sister of Dr Cranston £100

Ann Cunningham, daughter of late James Cunningham indweller in Alloway £100

Marion Davidson, relict of Mr John Glen minister £100

Susanna Douglas, relict of Ninian Anderson merchant in Glasgow £100

Penelope Erskine, sister of Alexander Erskine of Cambo £100

Cecilia Fotheringham, Lady Kelcy £100

Isobel Foulis, Lady Drylaw £100

Lady Grange £100

Jean Gray, relict of Adam Watson merchant in Edinburgh £100

Christian Grierson daughter of deceased John Grierson £100

Mrs Katherine Hall, daughter of deceased Sir John Hall of Dunglass £100

Mrs Anne Hamilton, daughter of deceased Sir William Hamilton of Preston £100

Mrs Jean Hay, spouse of Captain Lothian £100

Margaret Hepburn, daughter of deceased George Hepburn merchant in Edinburgh £100

Janet Home, Lady Eccles £100

Jean Jamieson, daughter of Edward Jamieson minister £100

[...] Johnstoun, Lady Bogie £100

[...] Johnstoun, Lady Graden £100

Alison Kerr, relict of John Kerr merchant in Kelso £100
Lady Lillias Kerr, sister of Earl of Lothian £100
Jean Kincaid, relict of George Thomson of Maines £100
Mrs Ann Livingston, sister of George Livingston of Saltcoats £100
Jean Lockhart, relict of James Graham vintner in Edinburgh £100
Catherine MacKail, daughter of Helen Watson £100
Mrs Jean Murray, daughter of Woodend £100
Margaret Nicholson, Lady Dalry £100
Dame Isobel Nicholson, Lady Cockpen elder £100
Bessie Peaddie, relict of John Maxwell merchant of Glasgow £100
Marian Preston, daughter of Sir William Preston of Valleyfield £100
Elizabeth Ronald, daughter of John Ronald surgeon in Edinburgh £100
Mary Rymour, relict of David Monteir merchant in Edinburgh £100
Elizabeth Scott, relict of Captain James Wauchope £100
Dame Jean Scott, Lady Harden £100
Jean Scott, Lady Eliston £100
Mary Simpson, relict of Robert Lundie minister of Leuchars £100
Marion Somerville, relict of Andrew Purdie tailor burgess of
    Edinburgh £100
Helen Stewart, relict of Dr Murray £100
Mrs Anne Stewart, daughter of deceased John Stewart of Kettleston
    £100
Marie Stirling, daughter of deceased Mr John Stirling minister at
    Edinburgh and Irvine £100
Elizabeth Stirling, daughter of Barbara Fraser relict of George Stirling
    £100
Elizabeth Syme, relict of Sir Robert Colt advocate £100
Helen Trotter, Lady Crumstone £100
Isobel Tyrie, Lady Glasclune £100
Helen Watson, relict of Gilbert MacKail merchant in Edinburgh £100
Elizabeth White, Lady Southhouse £100
Isobel Yeoman, relict of Robert Robertson merchant in Haddington
    £100
Rachel Yeoman, relict of George Forrester of Knap £100

£21,000

Source: Darien Papers, *371–409.*

APPENDIX VIII

The Establishment in December 1696

Name	Position	Salary
Roderick MacKenzie	secretary	£150
James Dunlop	chief accountant	£120
Gavin Plummer	chief cashier	£120
Robert Douglas	accountant	£80
Andrew Teuchler	accountant	£60
John Dickson	accountant	£50
John Symmer	accountant	£35
Andrew Cockburn	assistant to chief cashier	£60
John Thomson	clerk	£30
James Lindsay	clerk	£30
Patrick Scott	clerk	£30
Matthew Finlayson	clerk	£30
Adam Nisbet	teller	£25
Gilbert Moore	teller	£25
Robert Pringle	teller	£25
William Hopkirk	messenger	£12 10s
Charles Achmuty	housekeeper	£12 10s

Source: NLS, Darien Papers, Adv MS 83.5.2, f42.

APPENDIX IX

Cost of Ships

Rising Sun	£14,946
St Andrew	£11,574
Caledonia	£10,715
Unicorn	£8,687
Thistle	£2,975
Lyon	£2,852
Olive Branch	£2,228
Hope	£1,711
Dolphin	£921
Endeavour	£592
Speedy Return and cargo	£1,426
Dispatch and cargo	£1,260
Content and cargo	£905

Source: NLS, Darien Papers, *Adv* MS *83.3.7, f7, f8, f12, f14, f18, f21.*

APPENDIX X

Cost of Cargoes

Unicorn	£7,117
Caledonia	£5,678
St Andrew	£5,424
Rising Sun	£2,907
Hopeful Binning	£2,441
Olive Branch	£1,258
Margaret of Dundee	£1,204[1]
Hope of Bo'ness	£746
Duke of Hamilton	£639
Susanna of Bristol	£572
Endeavour	£403
Dolphin	£299
Hope	£285

Source: NLS, Darien Papers, *Adv MS 83.3.7, f11, f14, f17, f18, f20, f21.*

---

[1] The *Margaret* and the *Susanna* were relief ships.

Bibliography

Abbreviations:

Bann. Club	Bannatyne Club
EcHR	Economic History Review
EHR	English Historical Review
JEcH	Journal of Economic History
HMC	Historical Manuscripts Commission
Proc Soc Antiq Scot	Proceedings of the Society of Antiquaries of Scotland
SHR	Scottish Historical Review
SHS	Scottish History Society

Primary Sources

Bank of England Archive
Directors Minute Book 27 July to 20 March 1694
Original Subscriptions to Capital 1694
Stock Ledger 1694–6 RDS 3/28

Bank of Scotland Archive
Adventurer's Journal 1/91/1–2
Minutes of the Court of Directors 1/5/3
Original Subscription List Acc 02/8
Letter Book 1696–1711 1/149/1

British Library, India Office Records
Court of Directors Minute Book April 1695 to April 1699 B/41
Home Miscellaneous Series H/2, H/3, H/44

Edinburgh City Archive
George Watson and George Watson's Hospital Acc 289, Acc 789
Darien Company Papers 1696–1709 A0021
Minutes of the Merchant Company Acc 264

Glasgow City Archive
Sederunt Book of Hammermen of Glasgow T–TH 2/1/1
The Masons of Glasgow Minute Book 1681–1772 T–TH 12/1/2
Minute Book of the Incorporation of Maltmen of Glasgow T–TH 6/1/2

National Archives of Scotland
GD 1/564/12 Letterbook of Robert Blackwood
GD 1/634/1–2 Dean of Guild of Linlithgow Council Books

GD 1/482/1 Minute Book of the Incorporation of Goldsmiths of
    Edinburgh 1525–1725
GD 1/891/1–3 Diary of George Home of Kimmerghame
GD 3 Earls of Eglinton
GD 6 Biel Muniments
GD 18 Clerk of Penicuik Muniments
GD 24 Abercairny Muniments
GD 26 Leven and Melville Muniments
GD 45 Dalhousie Muniments
GD 72 Hay of Park
GD 110 Hamilton-Dalrymple of North Berwick Muniments
GD 112 Breadalbane Muniments
GD 124 Mar and Kellie
GD 150 Morton Papers
GD 158 Hume of Marchmont
GD 170 Campbell of Barcaldine
GD 205 Ogilvy of Inverquharity
GD 220 Montrose Muniments
GD 259 Scott of Ancrum
GD 305 Cromartie Muniments
GD 406 Hamilton Muniments
GD 446 Douglas of Strathendry
Justiciary Court Records JC 26/81/31
Commissary Court Records

National Library of Scotland

Darien Papers Adv MS 83.1.1–83.9.3
MS 1496 Delvine Papers
MS 1913 Scots White Paper Manufactory
MS 1914 Darien Company
MS 3288 Letters of James, Duke of Perth
MS 7018-7020 Yester Papers
MS 9251 Dunlop Papers
MS 14493 Yester Papers
MS 17804 Saltoun

National Register of Archives

Duke of Buccleuch 1275
Stirling-Maxwell of Pollock 2312
Earl of Annandale and Hartfell 2170

The Royal Bank of Scotland Archive

Journals of the Court of Directors of the Company of Scotland D/1/1–3

Instruction Book of the Court of Directors D/2
Acts, Orders and Resolutions of the Council General of the Company
    of Scotland D/3
First General Account of the Debts due to the Army and Civil List
    CEQ/15/1
Second General account of Public Debts CEQ/15/2

University of London, Goldsmith's Library of Economic Literature
MS 63, item 6

Reference

G.F. Black, *The Surnames of Scotland* (New York, 1962)
Fasti Ecclesiae Scoticanae, 11 vols (Edinburgh, 1915–2000)
The House of Commons 1690–1715, (eds.) E. Cruikshanks, S. Handley
    and D.W. Hayton, 5 vols (Cambridge, 2002).
The Lord Provosts of Edinburgh 1296 to 1932 (Edinburgh, 1932)
Ordnance Gazetteer of Scotland, 6 vols (London, 1894–5)
Oxford Dictionary of National Biography, (eds.) H.C.G. Matthew and
    B. Harrison, 61 vols (Oxford, 2004)
The Scots Peerage, ed. J.B. Paul, 9 vols (Edinburgh, 1904–14)
The Parliaments of Scotland, Burgh and Shire Commissioners, ed. M.D.
    Young, 2 vols (1992)

Printed Primary

The Account Book of Sir John Foulis of Ravelston 1671–1707 (SHS, 1894)
Acts of the Parliaments of Scotland, (eds.) T. Thomson and C. Innes
    (Edinburgh, 1814–75)
*Analecta Scotica: Collections illustrative of the civil, ecclesiastical, and
    literary history of Scotland*, 2 vols (Edinburgh, 1834–7)
The Annandale Book, ed. Sir W. Fraser (Edinburgh, 1894)
Andrew Fletcher of Saltoun, Selected Political Writings and Speeches,
    ed. D. Daiches (Edinburgh, 1979)
*Calendar of State Papers Colonial Series, East Indies, China and Japan,
    1617–1621* (London, 1870)
Correspondence of George Baillie of Jerviswood 1702–1708 (Bann.
    Club, 1842).
Culloden Papers (London, 1815)
The Darien Papers, ed. J.H. Burton (Bann. Club, 1849)
The Earls of Cromartie, ed. Sir W. Fraser (Edinburgh, 1876)
Early Letters of Robert Wodrow 1698–1709 (SHS, 1937)
Edinburgh Gazette
Extracts from the Records of the Burgh of Edinburgh 1689 to 1701, ed.
    H. Armet (Edinburgh, 1962)

Extracts from the Records of the Convention of the Royal Burghs of Scotland, 1677–1711 (Edinburgh, 1880)

Extracts from the Records of the Burgh of Glasgow 1691–1717 (Scottish Burgh Records Society, 1908)

Extracts from the Records of the Merchant Guild of Stirling A.D. 1592–1846, (eds.) W.B. Cook and D.B. Morris (Stirling, 1916)

Extracts from the Records of the Royal Burgh of Lanark (Glasgow, 1893)

Extraordinary Popular Delusions and the Madness of Crowds and Confusion de Confusiones, ed. M.S. Fridson (New York, 1996)

HMC, *Manuscripts of the House of Lords, 1695–7*, ii, (London, 1903)

HMC, *Manuscripts of the Duke of Portland*, iv, (London, 1897)

The Household Book of Lady Grisell Baillie 1692–1733 (SHS, 1911)

Jounral of the Hon. John Erskine of Carnock 1683–87 (SHS, 1893)

Journals of the House of Commons

Journals of the House of Lords

Letters of George Lockhart of Carnwath 1698–1732, ed. D. Szechi (SHS, 1989)

Letters Illustrative of the Reign of William III from 1696 to 1708, ed. G.P.R. James, 3 vols (London, 1841)

Memoirs of the Maxwells of Pollock, ed. Sir W. Fraser (Edinburgh, 1863)

Memoirs of the Secret Services of John Macky (London, 1733)

Miscellany of the Scottish History Society, ii, (1904)

More Culloden Papers, ed. D. Warrand (Inverness, 1923)

The Minute Book of the Faculty of Advocates, 1661–1712, ed. J.M. Pinkerton (Stair Society, 1976)

Narrative of Mr James Nimmo 1654–1709 (SHS, 1889)

Register of the Privy Council of Scotland, (eds.) J.H. Burton, P. Hume Brown, D. Masson and H. Paton (Edinburgh, 1877–1970)

Royal Letters, Charters, and Tracts, relating to the Colonization of New Scotland, and the Institution of the Order of Knight Baronets of Nova Scotia 1621–1638 (Bann. Club, 1867)

Papers Relating to the Ships and Voyages of the Company of Scotland trading to Africa and the Indies 1696–1707, ed. G.P. Insh (SHS, 1924)

The Records of a Scottish Cloth Manufactory at New Mills, Haddingtonshire 1681–1703 (SHS, 1905)

Scotland and the Americas, c.1650–c.1939: A Documentary Source Book (SHS, 2002)

Seafield Correspondence from 1685 to 1708 (SHS, 1908)

Selections from the Family Papers preserved at Caldwell (Maitland Club, 1854)

State-Papers and Letters addressed to William Carstares, ed J. McCormick (Edinburgh, 1774)

Various Pieces of Fugitive Scottish Poetry; principally of the seventeenth century (Edinburgh, 1825)

Various Pieces of Fugitive Scottish Poetry; principally of the seventeenth century, second series (Edinburgh, 1853)

View of the Merchants House of Glasgow; containing Historical Notices of its Origin, Constitution and Property and of the Charitable Foundations which it administers (Glasgow, 1866)

The Writings of William Paterson, Founder of the Bank of England, ed. S. Bannister, 3 vols (New York, 1968)

The Works of George Savile Marquis of Halifax, ed. M.N. Brown, 3 vols (Oxford, 1989)

Rev Mr Francis Borland, *The History of Darien* (Glasgow, 1779)

James Byres, *A Letter to a Friend at Edinburgh from Rotterdam; Giving account of the Scots affairs in Darien* (1702)

George Lockhart of Carnwath, *Memoirs concerning the Affairs of Scotland, from Queen Anne's Accession to the Throne, to the Commencement of the Union of the Two Kingdoms of Scotland and England, In May 1707*, (London, 1714)

Sir John Clerk's Observations on the present circumstances of Scotland, 1730, ed. T.C. Smout, (SHS, 1965)

Sir John Clerk of Penicuik, *History of the Union of Scotland and England*, ed. D. Duncan (SHS, 1993)

Sir John Dalrymple, *Memoirs of Great Britain and Ireland from the Battle of La Hogue till the capture of the French and Spanish Fleets at Vigo*, 2 vols (Edinburgh, 1788)

William Dampier, *A New Voyage round the World* (London, 1698)

Daniel Defoe, *An Essay upon Projects* (London, 1697)

Daniel Defoe, *History of the Union of Great Britain* (Edinburgh, 1709)

William Forbes, *A Methodical Treatise, concerning Bills of Exchange* (Edinburgh, 1703)

Alexander Hamilton, *A Scottish Sea Captain in Southeast Asia 1689–1723*, ed. M. Smithies (Chiang Mai, 1997)

Sir David Hume of Crossrigg, *A Diary of the Proceedings in the Parliament and Privy Council of Scotland May 21 1700–March 7 1707* (Bann. Club, 1828)

John Law, *Essay on a Land Bank*, ed. A.E. Murphy (Dublin, 1994)

Adam Smith, *The Wealth of Nations*, ed. A. Skinner (London, 1999)

Pamphlets

An Answer To Some Queries, &c Relative to the Union: In a Conference Betwixt a Coffee-Master, and a Countrey-Farmer (1706)

By the King, A Proclamation For Apprehending and Securing the Person of Roderick MacKenzie (London, 1695/6)

The Case of Mr William Paterson In Relation to His Claim on the Equivalent; As the same is stated in A Petition given in by Himself and

A Report made by Mr Roderick MacKenzie; To the Honourable Court of Exchequer in North-Britain (Edinburgh, 1708)

Certain Propositions Relating to the Scots Plantation of Caledonia, and the National Address for supporting therof, briefly offered to Publick View, for removing Mistakes and Prejudices (Glasgow, 1700)

The Circumstances of Scotland Consider'd, with respect to the present Scarcity of Money: together with some Proposals for suppling the Defect thereof, and rectifying the Balance of Trade (Edinburgh, 1705)

Constitutions of the Company of Scotland Trading to Africa and the Indies (Edinburgh, 1696)

The Company of Scotland, Trading to Africa and the Indies, do hereby give Notice (n.d.)

A Defence of the Scots Settlement At Darien with An Answer to the Spanish Memorial against it. And Arguments to prove that it is the Interest of England to join with the Scots to protect it. To which is added, A Description of the Country, and a particular Account of the Scots Colony (Edinburgh, 1699)

The Defence of the Scots Settlement at Darien, Answer'd, Paragraph by Paragraph. By Philo-Britain (London, 1699)

Description of the Province and Bay of Darian...Being vastly rich with Gold and Silver, and various Commodities. By I. B. a Well-wisher to the Company who lived there Seventeen Years (Edinburgh, 1699)

A Discourse concerning the Fishery within the British Seas (Edinburgh, 1695)

Edinburgh, the 17th day of April, 1696, At a General Meeting of the Company of Scotland Trading to Africa and the Indies (Edinburgh, 1696)

Edinburgh the 12th day of May 1696. At A General meeting of the Company of Scotland Trading to Africa and the Indies (Edinburgh, 1696)

At Edinburgh, The 9th day of July, 1696. The Court of Directors of the Company of Scotland Trading to Africa and the Indies (Edinburgh, 1696)

At Edinburgh, The 9th day of July, 1696. Whereas the Books of Subscription to the Company of Scotland (Edinburgh, 1696)

At Edinburgh The 30th day of December 1696 (Edinburgh, 1696)

The Equivalent Explain'd (Edinburgh, 1706)

An Essay At Removing National Prejudices Against A Union with Scotland To be continued Part 1 (Edinburgh, 1706)

An Essay for Promoting of Trade, and Increasing the Coin of the Nation (n.d.)

An Essay upon The XV Article of the Treaty of Union, Wherein the Difficulties That arise upon The Equivalents Are fully Cleared and Explained (1706)

An Exact LIST *of all Men, Women, and Boys that Died on Board the Indian and African Company's Fleet, during their Voyage from Scotland to America, and since their Landing in Caledonia* (Edinburgh, 1699)

A Full and Exact Collection of All the Considerable Addresses, Memorials, Petitions, Answers, Proclamations, Declarations, Letters and other Publick Papers, Relating to the Company of Scotland Trading to Africa and the Indies, since the passing of the Act of Parliament, by which the said Company was established in June 1695, till November 1700 (1700)

A Further Explication of the Proposal relating to the Coyne (n.d.)

An Historical Account of the Establishment, Progress and State of the Bank of Scotland; And of several Attempts that have been made against it, and the several Interruptions and Inconveniencies which the Company has encountered (1728)

The History of Caledonia: or, The Scots Colony in Darien in the West Indies. With an Account of the Manners of the Inhabitants, and Rules of the Countrey. By a Gentleman lately Arriv'd (London, 1699)

A Just and Modest Vindication of the Scots Design, For the having Established a Colony at Darien (1699)

A Letter concerning Trade, From several Scots-Gentlemen that are Merchants in England, To their Country-men that are Merchants in Scotland (1706)

A Letter containing Remarks on the Historical Account of the Old Bank; by a Gentleman concerned in neither Bank (Edinburgh, 1728)

A Letter from a Gentleman in the Country to His Friend at Edinburgh: Wherein it is clearly proved, That the Scottish African, and Indian Company, is Exactly Calculated for the Interest of Scotland (Edinburgh, 1696)

A Letter from Mr Hodges at London to A Member of the Parliament of Scotland (Edinburgh 1703)

A Letter to a Member of Parliament concerning Manufacture and Trade (1704)

A Letter to a Member of Parliament concerning the Bank of Scotland and the Lowering of Interest of Money (Edinburgh, 1696)

A Letter to a Member of Parliament, from a wel-wisher of his Country, in relation to Coin (n.d.)

A Letter to a Member of Parliament, Occasioned, By the growing Poverty of the Nation, from the Want and Decay of Trade, and wrong Management thereof. With Some Overtures, for encreasing and promoting the One, and Rectifying the other (Edinburgh, 1700)

Memorial and Intimation from the Governour and Company of the Bank of Scotland, concerning the present State thereof (1704)

Money Encreas'd. And Credit Rais'd; A Proposal (Edinburgh, 1705)

A New Darien Artiface Laid Open (London, 1701)

The Occasion of Scotland's Decay in Trade, with a proper Expedient for Recovery thereof, and The Increase of our Wealth (1705)

The People of Scotland's Groans and Lamentable Complaints, Pour'd out before the High Court of Parliament (Edinburgh, 1700)

A Premonitor Warning or Advice, by a true Lover of his Country Unto All whose Hands This may come (1702)

A Present Remedie for the want of Money (n.d.)

A Proposal anent Usury and procuring of Money (1705)

Proposals For A Fond to Cary on a Plantation (1695)

A Proposition for Remeding the Debasement of Coyne in Scotland (n.d.)

Reasons For passing into an Act, an Overture in Parliament, for making Salt of a new Fashion (Edinburgh, 1696)

Reasons Offered to his Grace His Majesties High Commissioner and the Honourable Estates of Parliament by the Dutchess of Hamilton, the Earl of Arran, the Earl of Marr, the Earl of Wintoun, the Countess of Weymss, Lord St Clair, the Lairds of Bougie, Bonhard and Grange, and other Salt-Masters and Heretors of Salt-Works, Against The Overtures proposed by the Affrican Company, anent the making of salt of a new Fashion. (Edinburgh, 1696)

Scotland's Present Duty: or a Call to The Nobility, Gentry, Ministry, and Commonality of this Land, to be duely affected with, and vigorously to act for, our Common Concern in Caledonia, as a Means to Enlarge Christ's Kingdom, to Benefit our Selves, and do Good, to all Protestant Churches (1700)

Scotland's Right to Caledonia (Formerly called DARIEN) (1700)

A Serious Advice to the African and Indian Company (n.d.)

A Short account from, and Description of the Isthmus of Darien, where the Scots Collony are settled (Edinburgh, 1699)

A Short and Impartial View of the Manner and Occasion of the Scots Colony's Coming away from Darien. In a Letter to a Person of Quality (1699)

A Short Speech prepared by a worthy member to be Spoken in Parliament (Edinburgh, 1700)

The Sighs and Groans, of a Sinking Kingdom, in a Humble Address to the Parliament of Scotland (1700)

Some Considerations concerning the Prejudice which the Scotch Act Establishing a Company to Trade to the East and West-Indies, (with large Priviledges and on easie Terms) may bring to the English Sugar Plantations, and the Manufactory of Refining Sugar in England (London, 1695)

Some Seasonable and Modest Thoughts Partly occasioned by, and partly concerning the Scots East-India Company Humbly offered to R. H. Esq. a Member of the present Parliament. By an unfeigned and hearty Lover of England (Edinburgh, 1699)

*Some Thoughts concerning the Affairs of this Session of Parliament,
1700* (1700).

*To His Grace, Her Majesty's High Commissioner, and the Right
Honourable Estates of Parliament. The Humble Representation of
the Council-General of the Company of Scotland Trading to Africa
and the Indies* (Edinburgh, 1706)

Trialogus. The Seventh Conversation on 15th Article of the Treaty (1706)

James Armour, *Proposals for making the Bank of Scotland more Useful
and Profitable; And for raising the Value of the Land-Interest of
North-Britain* (Edinburgh, 1722)

Lord Belhaven, *The Countrey-Man's Rudiments; or, An Advice to the
Farmers in East-Lothian how to Labour and Improve their Ground*
(Edinburgh, 1699)

Lord Belhaven, *A Speech in Parliament on the 10th day of January 1701,
by the Lord Belhaven on the Affair of the Indian and African
Company, and its Colony of Caledonia* (Edinburgh, 1701)

Lord Belhaven, *A Speech in Parliament Upon the Act for Security of the
Kingdom, in case of the Queens Death* (Edinburgh, 1703)

Lord Belhaven, *The Lord Belhavens Speech in Parliament, The 17th of
July 1705* (Edinburgh, 1705)

Lord Belhaven, *The Lord Beilhaven's Speech in Parliament The Second
day of November 1706* (Edinburgh, 1706)

Daniel Defoe, *An Enquiry into the Disposal of the Equivalent* (1706)

James Donaldson, *The Undoubted Art of Thriving* (Edinburgh, 1700)

Walter Herries, *A Defence of the Scots Abdicating Darien: Including an
Answer to the Defence of the Scots Settlement there* (1700)

Walter Herries, *An Enquiry into the Caledonian Project, with a Defence
of England's Procedure (in point of Equity) in Relation thereunto.
In a Friendly Letter from London, to a Member of the Scots African
and Indian Company in Edinburgh, to guard against Passion*
(London, 1701)

James Hodges, *Considerations and Proposals, for Supplying the present
Scarcity of Money, and advancing Trade* (Edinburgh, 1705)

John Holland, *A Short Discourse on the Present Temper of the Nation*
(Edinburgh, 1696)

John Holland, *Some Letters relating to the Bank of Scotland written by
the late John Holland, Esq; published with Explanatory Remarks In a
Letter to the Proprietors by Richard Holland M.D.* (Edinburgh, 1723)

John Law, *Money and Trade Considered, with a Proposal for Supplying
the Nation with Money* (Edinburgh, 1705)

Roderick MacKenzie, *A Letter from a Member of the Parliament of
Scotland to his Friend at London concerning their late Act for
establishing a Company of that Kingdom trading to Africa and the
Indies* (London, 1695)

Roderick MacKenzie, *A Full and Exact Account of the Proceedings of the Court of Directors and Council-General of the Company of Scotland Trading to Africa and the Indies, with relation to the Treaty of Union, now under parliament's Consideration* (1706)

William Paterson, *A Proposal to Plant a colony in Darien; to protect the Indians against Spain; and to open the trade of South America to all nations* (London, 1701)

George Ridpath, *Scotland's Grievances Relating to Darien* (1700)

J[ames] S[myth], *Some Account of the Transactions of Mr William Paterson, In Relation to the Bank of England, and the Orphans Fund. In a Letter to a Friend* (London, 1695)

John Spreul, *An Accompt Current betwixt Scotland and England* (Edinburgh, 1705)

Poems

Caledonia; or, the Pedlar turn'd Merchant. A Tragi-Comedy, As it was Acted by His Majesty's Subjects of Scotland in the King of Spain's Province of Darien (London, 1700)

The Golden Island or the Darian Song In Commendation of All Concerned in that Noble Enterprize Of the Valiant Scots. By a Lady of Honour (Edinburgh, 1699)

A Pil, for Pork-Eaters: or, a Scots Lancet for an English Swelling (Edinburgh, 1705)

Secondary Sources

M. Aghassian and K. Kévonian, 'Armenian Trade in the Indian Ocean in the Seventeenth and Eighteenth Centuries' in *Asian Merchants and Businessmen in the Indian Ocean and the China Sea*, (eds.) D. Lombard and J. Aubin (Oxford, 2000)

A. Anderson, *An Historical and Chronological Deduction of the Origin of Commerce*, 2 vols (London, 1764)

D. Armitage, 'The Scottish Vision for Empire: Intellectual Origins of the Darien Venture' in *A Union for Empire: Political Thought and the British Union of 1707*, ed. J. Robertson (Cambridge 1995)

H. Arnot, *The History of Edinburgh from the Earliest Accounts to the Present Time* (Edinburgh, 1788)

M. Balen, *A Very English Deceit: The South Sea Bubble and the World's First Great Financial Scandal* (London, 2003)

S. Bannister, *William Paterson, The Merchant Statesman and Founder of the Bank of England: his Life and Trials* (Edinburgh, 1858)

D.D. Black, *The History of Brechin* (Brechin, 1839)

H.V. Bowen, *Elites, Enterprise and the Making of the British Overseas Empire 1688–1775* (London, 1996)

J. Brewer, *The Sinews of Power: War, Money and the English State, 1688–1783* (London, 1989)

K.M. Brown, 'From Scottish Lords to British Officers: State Building, Elite Integration and the Army in the Seventeenth Century' in *Scotland and War AD79–1918*, ed. N. MacDougall (Edinburgh, 1991)

J.R. Bruijn, F.S. Gaastra and I. Schöffer, *Dutch-Asiatic Shipping in the 17th and 18th Centuries* (The Hague, 1987)

J. Buchan, *Capital of the Mind: How Edinburgh changed the World* (London, 2003)

Bishop Burnet, *History of his Own Time*, 4 vols (London, 1818)

R.H. Campbell, *Scotland since 1707: The Rise of an Industrial Society* (Edinburgh, 1985)

B.G. Carruthers, *City of Capital: Politics and Markets in the English Financial Revolution* (Princeton, 1996)

D. Catterall, *Community without Borders: Scots Migrants and the changing face of power in the Dutch Republic, c.1600–1700* (Leiden, 2002)

K.N. Chaudhuri, *The Trading World of Asia and the English East India Company 1660–1760* (Cambridge, 1978)

J. Childs, *The Nine Years' War and the British Army 1688–1697: The operations in the Low Countries* (Manchester, 1991)

L. Colley, *Britons: Forging the Nation 1707–1837* (London, 2003)

Companies and Trade, (eds.) L. Blussé and F. Gaastra (The Hague, 1981)

L.M. Cullen, 'The Scottish Exchange on London, 1673–1778' in *Conflict, Identity and Economic Development: Ireland and Scotland 1600–1939*, (eds.) S. J. Connolly, R. A. Houston and R. J. Morris (Preston, 1995)

F. Cundall, *The Darien Venture* (New York, 1926)

A. Cunningham, *The History of Great Britain: from the Revolution in 1688, to the Accession of George the First*, 2 vols (London, 1787)

P. D. Curtin, *Cross-cultural trade in world history* (Cambridge, 1984)

The Darien Adventure (Edinburgh, 1998)

N. Davidson, *Discovering the Scottish Revolution 1692–1746* (London, 2003)

K.G. Davies, *The Royal African Company* (London, 1957)

R. Davis, *The Rise of the English Shipping Industry in the Seventeenth and Eighteenth Centuries* (1972)

J. Day, *Money and Finance in the Age of Merchant Capitalism* (Oxford, 1999)

G.S. de Krey, *A Fractured Society, The Politics of London in the First Age of Party 1688–1715* (Oxford, 1985)

T.M. Devine, 'The Colonial Trades and Industrial Investment in Scotland, c. 1700–1815, in *The Organization of Interoceanic Trade in European Expansion, 1450–1800*, (eds.) P. Emmer and F. Gaastra (Aldershot, 1996)

T.M. Devine, 'The Scottish Merchant Community, 1680-1740,' in *The Origins and Nature of the Scottish Enlightenment*, (eds.) R.H. Campbell and A. S. Skinner (Edinburgh, 1982)

T.M. Devine, *Scotland's Empire 1600-1815* (London, 2003)

H.T. Dickinson, *Liberty and Property: Political Ideology in Eighteenth-Century Britain* (London, 1977)

P.G.M. Dickson, *The Sun Insurance Office 1710-1960* (London, 1960)

P.G.M. Dickson, *The Financial Revolution in England: A Study in the development of Public Credit 1688-1756* (Aldershot, 1993)

H.M. Dingwall, *Late Seventeenth-century Edinburgh: A demographic study* (Aldershot, 1994)

D. Dobson, *Scottish Emigration to Colonial America, 1607-1785* (Athens, 1994)

P. Earle, *The Wreck of the Almirata: Sir William Phips and the search for the Hispaniola Treasure* (London, 1979)

J.A. Fairley, *Agnes Campbell, Lady Roseburn* (Aberdeen, 1925)

R. Feenstra, 'Scottish-Dutch legal Relations in the Seventeenth and Eighteenth Centuries' in *Scotland and Europe 1200-1850*, ed. T.C. Smout (Edinburgh, 1986)

W. Ferguson, *Scotland's Relations with England: A Survey to 1707* (Edinburgh, 1977)

D. Fergusson, *Scottish Proverbs* (Edinburgh, 1641)

J.R. Fisher, *The Economic Aspects of Spanish Imperialism in America, 1492-1810* (Liverpool, 1997)

M. Flinn (ed.), *Scottish population history from the 17th century to the 1930s* (Cambridge, 1977)

A. Forrester, *The Man Who Saw the Future* (London, 2004)

M. Fry, *The Scottish Empire* (Edinburgh, 2001)

D. Galbraith, *The Rising Sun* (London, 2000)

J.K. Galbraith, *The Great Crash 1929* (London, 1975)

I.J. Gallup-Diaz, *The Door of the Seas and Key to the Universe: Indian Politics and Imperial Rivalry in the Darién, 1640-1750* (New York, 2005)

G. Gardner, *The Scottish Exile Community in the Netherlands, 1660-1690: 'Shaken together in the bag of affliction'* (East Linton, 2004)

P. Gauci, *The Politics of Trade, The Overseas Merchant in State and Society 1660-1720* (Oxford, 2002)

A.J.S. Gibson and T. C. Smout, *Prices, Food and Wages in Scotland 1550-1780* (Cambridge, 1995)

K. Glamann, *Dutch-Asiatic Trade 1620-1740* (The Hague, 1981)

M. Glendinning, R. MacInnes and A. MacKechnie, *A History of Scottish Architecture* (Edinburgh, 1996)

J. Goodare, *State and Society in Early Modern Scotland* (Oxford, 1999)

J. Goodare, 'The Estates in the Scottish Parliament, 1286-1707' in *The Scots and Parliament*, ed. C. Jones (Edinburgh, 1996)

E.J. Graham, *A Maritime History of Scotland, 1650–1790* (East Linton, 2002)

E.J. Graham, *Seawolves: Pirates and the Scots* (Edinburgh, 2005)

General Sir J. Aylmer L. Haldane, *The Haldanes of Gleneagles* (London, 1929)

T. Harris, 'Reluctant Revolutionaries? The Scots and the Revolution of 1688–9' in *Politics and the Political Imagination in Later Stuart Britain*, ed. H. Nenner (Rochester, 1998)

F.R. Hart, *The Disaster of Darien: The Story of the Scots Settlement and the Causes of its Failure 1699–1701* (London, 1930)

D. Hayton, 'Traces of Party Politics in Early Eighteenth-Century Scottish Elections' in *The Scots and Parliament*, ed. C. Jones (Edinburgh, 1996)

E. Healey, *Coutts and Co. 1692–1992: The Portrait of a Private Bank* (London, 1992)

A. Henderson, *Scottish Proverbs* (Edinburgh, 1832)

A. Herman, *The Scottish Enlightenment: The Scots' Invention of the Modern World* (London, 2002)

P. Hopkins, 'Sham Plots and Real Plots in the 1690s' in *Ideological Conspiracy: Aspects of Jacobitism, 1689–1759*, ed. E. Cruickshanks (Edinburgh, 1982)

J. Hoppit, *A Land of Liberty? England 1689–1727* (Oxford, 2000)

M. Horton, *Caledonia Bay Panama 1979: A preliminary report on the archaeological project of Operation Drake* (London, 1980)

G.P. Insh, *The Company of Scotland Trading to Africa and the Indies* (London, 1932)

G.P. Insh, *Scottish Colonial Schemes 1620–1686* (Glasgow, 1922)

G.P. Insh, *Historian's Odyssey: The Romance of the quest for the Records of the Darien Company* (Edinburgh, 1938)

J.I. Israel, 'The Amsterdam Stock Exchange and the English Revolution of 1688,' in J.I. Israel, *Conflicts of Empires: Spain, the Low Countries and the Struggle for World Supremacy 1585–1713* (London, 1997)

J.I. Israel, *European Jewry in the Age of Mercantilism 1550–1750* (London, 1998)

D.W. Jones, 'London merchants and the crisis of the 1690s' in *Crisis and order in English towns 1500–1700*, (eds.) P. Clark and P. Slack (London, 1972)

H. Kamen, *Spain in the Later Seventeenth Century, 1665–1700* (London, 1980)

H. Kamen, *Spain's Road to Empire: The Making of a World Power, 1692–1763* (London, 2002)

C.P. Kindleberger, *Manias, Panics, and Crashes: A History of Financial Crises* (New York, 2000)

W. LaFeber, *The Panama Canal: The Crisis in Historical Perspective* (New York, 1989)

A. Lang, *A History of Scotland from the Roman Occupation* (Edinburgh, 1907)

M. Lee, Jr., *The 'Inevitable' Union and other essays on Early Modern Scotland* (East Linton, 2003)

B. Lenman, *The Jacobite Risings in Britain 1689–1746* (London, 1984)

M-H Li, *The Great Recoinage of 1696 to 1699* (London, 1963)

London 1500–1700: The Making of the Metropolis, (eds.) A. L. Beier and R. Finlay (Harlow, 1986)

M. Lynch, *Scotland: A New History* (London, 1991)

T.B. Macaulay, *The History of England from the accession of James the Second*, 8 vols (London, 1849–61)

D. McCullough, *The Path Between the Seas: The Creation of the Panama Canal 1870–1914* (New York, 1977)

J.J. McCusker, *Money and Exchange in Europe and America, 1600–1775: A Handbook* (Williamsburg, 1978)

J. MacKinnon, *The Union of England and Scotland: A Study of International History* (London, 1896)

D. MacPherson, *Annals of Commerce, Manufactures, Fisheries, and Navigation* (London, 1805)

David Malcolm, *An Essay on the Antiquities of Great Britain and Ireland...especially an Attempt to shew an Affinity betwixt the Languages of the ancient Britains, and the Americans of the Isthmus of Darien* (Edinburgh, 1738)

A.J. Mann, *The Scottish Book Trade 1500–1720: Print Commerce and Print Control in Early Modern Scotland* (East Linton, 2000)

G. Marshall, *Presbyteries and Profits: Calvinism and the Development of Capitalism in Scotland, 1560–1707* (Edinburgh, 1992)

N. Mayhew, *Sterling: the Rise and Fall of a Currency* (London, 1999)

R.C. Michie, *Money, Mania and Markets: Investment, Company Formation and the Stock Exchange in Nineteenth-Century Scotland* (Edinburgh, 1981)

N. Munro, *The History of the Royal Bank of Scotland 1727–1927* (Edinburgh, 1928)

A.E. Murphy, *John Law: Economic Theorist and Policy-Maker* (Oxford, 1997)

L. Neal, *The Rise of Financial Capitalism: International Capital Markets in the Age of Reason* (Cambridge, 1990)

D. Nicol, *The Fundamentals of New Caledonia* (Edinburgh, 2003)

A.W. Parker, *Scottish Highlanders in Colonial Georgia: The Recruitment, Emigration, and settlement at Darien, 1735–1748* (Athens, 1997)

H. Roseveare, *The Financial Revolution 1660–1760* (Harlow, 1991)

J. Prebble, *Darien: The Scottish Dream of Empire* (Edinburgh, 2000)

D. and M. Preston, *A Pirate of Exquisite Mind: The Life of William Dampier* (London, 2004)

Jacob M. Price, *Tobacco in Atlantic Trade: The Chesapeake, London and Glasgow 1675–1775* (Aldershot, 1995)

A. Ramsay, *The Scottish Proverbs, or, The Wise Sayings of the Old People of Scotland* (Falkirk, 1813)

P.W.J. Riley, *The English Ministers and Scotland 1707–1727* (London, 1964)

P.W.J. Riley, *King William and the Scottish Politicians* (Edinburgh, 1979)

P.W.J. Riley, 'The structure of Scottish politics and the Union of 1707' in *The Union of 1707: Its Impact on Scotland*, ed. T.I. Rae (Glasgow, 1974)

P.W.J. Riley, *The Union of England and Scotland: A study in Anglo-Scottish politics of the eighteenth century* (Manchester 1978)

M. Roberts, *The Swedish Imperial Experience 1560–1718* (Cambridge, 1979)

M.N. Rothbard, *Economic Thought before Adam Smith: An Austrian Perspective on the History of Economic Thought*, 2 vols (Aldershot, 1995)

The Rough Guide to Central America (London, 2001)

R. Saville, 'Scottish Modernisation Prior to the Industrial Revolution, 1688–1763' in *Eighteenth Century Scotland: New Perspectives*, (eds.) T. M. Devine and J. R. Young (East Linton, 1999)

R. Saville, *Bank of Scotland: A History 1695–1995* (Edinburgh, 1996)

J. Schumpeter, *A History of Economic Analysis* (London, 1954)

Scotland: A History, ed. J. Wormald (Oxford, 2005)

P.H. Scott, *1707: The Union of Scotland and England* (Edinburgh, 1979)

P.H. Scott, *Andrew Fletcher and the Treaty of Union* (Edinburgh, 1992)

Sir Walter Scott, *The Tales of a Grandfather* (London, 1933)

W.R. Scott, *The Constitution and Finance of English, Scottish and Irish Joint-Stock Companies to 1720*, 3 vols (Cambridge, 1910–12)

J.S. Shaw, *The Political History of Eighteenth-Century Scotland* (Basingstoke, 1999)

E. Simon, *Hamburg: A Gateway for the World, 1189–1989* (London, 1989)

D. Sinclair, *Sir Gregor MacGregor and the Land that Never Was: The Extraordinary Story of the Most Audacious Fraud in History* (London, 2003)

F.G. Slaughter, *Darien Venture* (London, 1978) [first published in New York in 1955 under the name C.V. Terry]

T.C. Smout, *Scottish Trade on the Eve of Union 1660–1707* (Edinburgh, 1963)

T.C. Smout, 'Scottish-Dutch Contact 1600–1800' in *Dutch Art and Scotland: A Reflection of Taste* (Edinburgh, 1992)

R. Sobel, *The Great Bull Market: Wall Street in the 1920s* (New York, 1968)

K. van den Steinen, 'In Search of the Antecedents of Women's Political Activism in early Eighteenth-Century Scotland: the Daughters of Anne, Duchess of Hamilton' in *Women in Scotland c.1100–c.1750*, (eds.) E. Ewan and M.M. Meikle (East Linton, 1999)

D. Stevenson, *Revolution and Counter-Revolution in Scotland, 1644–1651* (London, 1977)

D. Stevenson, 'Twilight before night or darkness before dawn? Interpreting seventeenth-century Scotland' in *Why Scottish History Matters*, ed. R. Mitchison (Edinburgh, 1991)

R.A. Sundstrom, *Sidney Godolphin: Servant of the State* (London, 1992)

D. Szechi, *The Jacobites: Britain and Europe 1688–1788* (Manchester 1994)

D. Szechi, *George Lockhart of Carnwath 1689–1727: A Study in Jacobitism* (East Linton, 2002)

J. Taylor, *A Cup of Kindness: The History of the Royal Scottish Corporation, a London Charity, 1603–2003* (East Linton, 2003)

Sir R. Carnac Temple, *New Light on the Mysterious Tragedy of the 'Worcester' 1704–1705* (London, 1930)

J.D. Tracy, *A Financial Revolution in the Habsburg Netherlands: Renten and Renteniers in the County of Holland, 1515–1565* (London, 1985)

The Transformation of Scotland: The Economy Since 1700, (eds.) T. M. Devine, C. H. Lee and G. C. Peden (Edinburgh, 2005)

R.E. Tyson, 'Famine in Aberdeenshire, 1695–1699: Anatomy of a Crisis' in *From Lairds to Louns: Country and Burgh Life in Aberdeen*, ed. D. Stevenson (Aberdeen, 1986)

J. de Vries and Ad van der Woude, *The First Modern Economy: Success, Failure and Perseverance of the Dutch Economy, 1500–1815* (Cambridge, 1997)

K. Walker, *Scottish Proverbs* (Edinburgh, 1996)

A Union For Empire: Political Thought and the British Union of 1707, ed. J. Robertson (Cambridge, 1995)

E. Warburton, *Darien; or, The Merchant Prince. A Historical Romance*, 3 vols (London, 1852)

C.A. Whatley, *The Scottish Salt Industry 1570–1850: an economic and social history* (Aberdeen 1987)

C.A. Whatley, *Scottish Society 1707–1830: Beyond Jacobitism, towards industrialization* (Manchester, 2000)

C.A. Whatley, *Bought and sold for English Gold?: explaining the Union of 1707* (East Linton, 2001)

C.W.J. Withers, *Geography, Science and National Identity, Scotland since 1520* (Cambridge, 2001)

N. Wood, *Scottish Proverbs* (Edinburgh, 1989)

R.L. Woodward, Jr., *Central America: A Nation Divided* (Oxford, 1999)

N. Zahedieh, 'Economy' in *The British Atlantic World, 1500–1800*, (eds.) D. Armitage and M.J. Braddick (Basingstoke, 2002)

Articles

D. Armitage, 'The Projecting Age': William Paterson and the Bank of England',' *History Today*, 44 (5), (1994), 5–10

D. Armitage, 'Making the Empire British: Scotland in the Atlantic World 1542–1717,' *Past and Present*, 155, (1997), 34–63

A. Bialuschewski, 'Between Newfoundland and the Malacca Strait: A Survey of the Golden Age of Piracy, 1695–1725,' *Mariner's Mirror*, 90, (2004)

A. Bialuschewski, 'Greed, Fraud, and Popular Culture: John Breholt's Madagascar Schemes of the Early Eighteenth Century,' paper given at the Interdisciplinary Colloquium on the Financial Revolution in the British Isles, 1688–1756, held at the University of Regina, 20–22 June 2004

K. Bowie, 'Public Opinion, Popular Politics and the Union of 1707,' *SHR*, 82, (2003), 226–60

A.M. Carlos and S. Nicholas, 'Giants of an Earlier Capitalism: The Chartered Trading Companies as Modern Multinationals,' *Business History Review*, 62, (1988), 398–419

A.M. Carlos and J. L. Van Stone, 'Stock Transfer Patterns in the Hudson's Bay Company: A Study of the English Capital Market in Operation, 1670–1730, *Business History*, 38, (1996), 15–39

A.M. Carlos and S. Nicholas, 'Agency Problems in Early Chartered Companies: The Case of the Hudson's Bay Company,' *JEcH*, 50, (1990), 853–75

K.G. Davies, 'Joint-Stock Investment in the Later Seventeenth century,' *EcHR*, second series, 4, (1952), 283–301

T.M. Devine, 'The Union of 1707 and Scottish Development,' *Scottish Economic and Social History*, 5, (1985), 23–40

J.A. Downie, 'The Commission of Public Accounts and the formation of the Country Party,' *EHR*, 91, (1976), 33–51

W. Ferguson, 'The Making of the Treaty of Union of 1707,' *SHR*, 43, (1964), 89–110

W. Ferguson, 'Imperial crowns: a neglected facet of the background to the Treaty of Union of 1707,' *SHR*, 53, (1974), 22–44

C.P. Finlayson, 'Edinburgh University and the Darien Scheme,' *SHR*, 34, (1955), 97–102

L.G. Fryer, 'Robert Barclay of Ury and East New Jersey,' *Northern Scotland*, 15, (1995), 1–17

L.G. Fryer, 'Documents relating to the formation of the Carolina Company in Scotland, 1682,' *South Carolina Historical Magazine*, 99, (1998), 110–133

E.J. Graham, 'In Defence of the Scottish Maritime Interest, 1681–1713,' *SHR*, 71, (1992), 88–109

J. Halliday, 'The Club and the Revolution in Scotland 1689–90,' *SHR*, 45, (1966), 143–159

E.J. Hamilton, 'American Treasure and the Rise of Capitalism (1500–1700), *Economica*, 9, (1929), 338–357

E.J. Hamilton, 'John Law of Lauriston: Banker, Gamester, Merchant, Chief?,' *American Economic Review*, 57, (1967), 273–82

D.R. Hidalgo, 'To Get Rich for Our Homeland: The Company of Scotland and the Colonization of the Isthmus of Darien,' *Colonial Latin American Historical Review*, 10, (2001), 311–50

J. Hoppit, 'Financial Crises in Eighteenth-century England,' *EcHR*, second series, 39, (1986)

H. Horwitz, 'The East India Trade, the Politicians, and the Constitution: 1689–1702,' *Journal of British Studies*, 17, (1978), 1–18

G.P. Insh, 'The Carolina Merchant: Advice of Arrival,' *SHR*, 25, (1928), 98–108

G.P. Insh, 'The Founders of the Company of Scotland,' *SHR*, 25, (1928), 241–54

W. Douglas Jones, '"The Bold Adventurers": A Quantitative Analysis of the Darien Subscription List (1996), *Scottish Economic and Social History*, 21, (2001), 22–42

A.J. Mann, 'Inglorious Revolution: Administrative Muddle and Constitutional Change in the Scottish Parliament of William and Mary,' *Parliamentary History*, 22, (2003), 121–144

R. Law, 'The First Scottish Guinea Company, 1634–9', *SHR*, 76, (1997), 185–202

C. MacLeod, 'The 1690s Patents Boom: Invention or Stock-Jobbing,' *EcHR*, second series, 39, (1986), 549–571

B. McPhail, 'Through a Glass, Darkly: Scots and Indians Converge at Darien,' *Eighteenth-Century Life*, 18, (1994), 129–47

S. Murdoch, 'The Good, the Bad and the Anonymous: A Preliminary Survey of Scots in the Dutch East Indies 1612–1707,' *Northern Scotland*, 22, (2002), 63–76

A.L. Murray, 'The Scottish treasury 1667-1708,' *SHR*, 45, (1966), 89-104

A.L. Murray, 'Sir Isaac Newton and the Scottish recoinage, 1707-10', *Proc Soc Antiq Scot*, 127, (1997), 921–44

L. Neal, 'How it all began: the monetary and financial architecture of Europe during the first global capital markets, 1648–1815,' *Financial History Review*, 7, (2000), 117–140

L. Neal, 'The Money Pitt: Lord Londonderry and the South Sea Bubble; or, How to Manage Risk in an Emerging Market,' *Enterprise and Society*, 1, (2000), 117–40.

S. Pincus, '"Coffee Politicians Does Create": Coffeehouses and

Restoration Political Culture,' *Journal of Modern History*, 67, (1995), 807–34

M.G.H. Pittock, 'John Law's Theory of Money and its roots in Scottish culture,' *Proc Soc Antiq Scot*, 133 (2003), 391–403

S. Quinn, 'Gold, silver, and the Glorious Revolution: arbitrage between bills of exchange and bullion,' *EcHR*, second series, 49, (1996), 473–490

S. Quinn, 'The Glorious Revolution's Effect on English Private Finance: A Microhistory, 1680-1705,' *JEcH*, 61, (2001), 593–615

P.W.J. Riley, 'The Formation of the Scottish Ministry of 1703,' *SHR*, 44, (1965), 112–34

P.W.J. Riley, 'The union of 1707 as an episode in English politics,' *EHR*, 84, (1969), 498–527

C. Roberts, 'The Constitutional Significance of the Financial Settlement of 1690,' *Historical Journal*, 20, (1977), 59–76

D. Rubini, 'Politics and the Battle for the Banks, 1688-1697,' *EHR*, 85, (1970), 693–714

E.S. Schubert, 'Innovations, Debts, and Bubbles: International Integration of Financial Markets in Western Europe, 1688–1720, *JEcH*, 48, (1988), 299–306

T.C. Smout, 'The Glasgow merchant community in the seventeenth century,' *SHR*, 47, (1968), 53–71

D. Stevenson, 'The financing of the cause of the Covenants, 1638–51,' *SHR*, 51, (1972), 89–123

C. Storrs, 'Disaster at Darien (1698–1700)? The Persistence of Spanish Imperial Power on the Eve of the Demise of the Spanish Habsburgs,' *European History Quarterly*, 29, (1999), 5–38

H. Trevor-Roper, 'The Scottish Enlightenment,' *Studies on Voltaire and the Eighteenth Century*, 58, (1967)

D. Watt, 'The Dutch and the Company of Scotland trading to Africa and the Indies,' *Dutch Crossing*, 29, (2005), 125–143

D. Watt, '"Laberinth of thir difficulties": the Influence of Debt on the Highland Elite, c. 1550-1700,' *SHR*, 85, (2006), 28–51

D. Watt, 'The management of capital by the Company of Scotland 1696–1707,' *Journal of Scottish Historical Studies*, 25, (2005), 97–118

J. Wells and D. Wills, 'Revolution, Restoration, and Debt Repudiation: The Jacobite Threat to England's Institutions and Economic Growth,' *JEcH*, 60, (2000), 418–41

C.A. Whatley, 'Salt, Coal and the Union of 1707: A revision article,' *SHR*, 66, (1987), 26–45

C.A. Whatley, 'Economic Causes and Consequences of the Union of 1707: A Survey,' *SHR*, 68, (1989), 150–181

C.A. Whatley, 'Scotland, England and 'The Golden Ball': putting economics back into the Union of 1707,' *The Historian*, 51, (1996), 9–13

I.D. Whyte, 'The growth of periodic market centres in Scotland
    1600–1707,' *Scottish Geographical Magazine*, 95, (1979), 13–26

N. Zahedieh, 'Trade, Plunder, and Economic Development in Early
    English Jamaica, 1655–89,' *EcHR*, second series, 39, (1986),
    205–222

N. Zahedieh, 'Credit, Risk and Reputation in Late Seventeenth-Century
    Colonial Trade,' *Research in Maritime History*, 15, (1998), 53–74

Theses

W. Douglas Jones, 'The Darien Reaction: National Failure and Popular
    Politics in Scotland, 1699–1701' (University of Edinburgh MSC, 2001)

D.J. Patrick, 'People and Parliament in Scotland 1689–1702' (University
    of St Andrews PhD, 2002)

Website

Lawrence H. Officer, 'Comparing the Purchasing Power of Money in
    Great Britain from 1264 to 2005,' Economic History Services, URL:
    http://www.eh.net/hmit/ppowerbp/

Index

Some other books published by **LUATH** PRESS

Caledonia's Last Stand: in search of the Lost Scots of Darien
Nat Edwards
ISBN 1 905222 84 X PBK £12.99

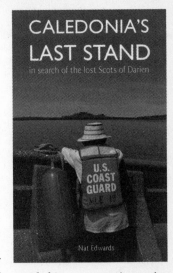

On 2 November 1698 a fleet landed on the isthmus of Darien to create a colony and launch a new Scottish trading empire. Eighteen months later, the colony had seen the loss of ten ships, over £150,000 and the lives of 2,000 souls.

More than 300 years later, an expedition to Darien uncovers a tantalising legacy. Nat Edwards takes us back to Panama on an exciting and often dangerous quest to discover the real story behind the disastrous attempt at building a Scottish Empire. Interweaving the contemporary accounts of buccaneers, Spanish generals and the settlers with his own experiences in Darien, Nat Edwards provides a narrative that is thoughtful, sinister and hilariously funny by turns.

The Fundamentals of New Caledonia

David Nicol

ISBN 0 946487 93 6   HBK   £16.99

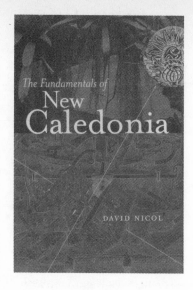

This is the tale of ane lyar and and mis-representer of persones – a time traveller carrying little more that a few half-remembered science fiction yarns for guidance.

Press-ganged by the late 17th century Company of Scotland, he embarks on the ill-destined venture that set out to create a New Caledonia and came to be known as the Darien disaster.

Their tropical colony was projected to build a trading emporium at the heart of Europe's colonial expansion. But in a short time the ambition of Scotland's merchant class was ruined.

In this feverishly written journal, the would-be settlers must adapt to a new world that crumbles about them even as it is being invented.

Apprenticed to a ship surgeon, the narrator faces an eternal conundrum of time travel. Is it reasonable, or fair, to try and alter the course of history?

Only by confronting the powerful can he begin to understand this world. Only by applying his singular insight can he begin to diagnose the settler's plight. And only by embarking on his own personal odyssey can be find remedy.

The Company of Scotland was established by an act of parliament. It planned a colony that would announce itself in a founding declaration, and govern itself by a set of rules and ordinances.

These were the founding principles of a new society. Together with basic ideas and practices in economics, politics, religion, medicine, navigation and law, these principles were tested to destruction.

They are presented here as The Fundamentals of New Caledonia – an historical fiction of a new world.

Women of the Highlands

Katharine Stewart

ISBN 1 905222 74 2 HBK £14.99

The Highlands of Scotland are an evocative and mysterious land, cut off from the rest of Scotland by mountains and developing as a separate country for hundreds of years. Epitomising the 'sublime' in philosophical thought of the 18th century, the Highlands have been a source of inspiration for poets and writers of all descriptions.

Katharine Stewart takes us to the heart of the Highlands with this history of the women who shaped this land. From the women of the shielings to the Duchess of Gordon, from bards to conservationists, authors to folk-singers, *Women of the Highlands* examines how the culture of the Highlands was created and passed down through the centuries, and what is being done to preserve it today.

Katharine Stewart's latest book has the authority of being part of the living tradition it describes.

MARGARET ELPHINSTONE

Selim Aga: A Slave's Odyssey

James McCarthy

ISBN 1 905222 17 3 HBK 16.99

Selim Aga was just eight years old when he was abducted from the remote Nuba Mountains of Sudan by Arab slavers and auctioned 2,000 miles away in the Cairo slave market.

Selim was bought and sold at least eight times before being released from slavery by Robert Thurburn, the British Consul at Alexandria, who took him to his family home in Aberdeenshire in 1836. Little is known of his time in Scotland but what is certain is that Selim grasped every experience and opportunity to learn, and later became an author, lecturer and explorer, as Sir Richard Burton's manservant in West Africa.

James McCarthy's biography is a fascinating piece of detective work that sets Selim's life in the context of European imperialism and the international trade in human cargo. A rare and highly significant document, Selim's own remarkable narrative of his early life is also presented here in its entirety.

Grounded in the horrors of actual fact... thoroughly researched... but this is not [James McCarthy's] only service to history. As well as telling Selim's life, he reprints also two autobiographical essays by Selim: a narrative of his early enslavement and a memoir of his 1863 trip with Burton.

THE FINANCIAL TIMES

Fascinating both for its historical background and as a record of one individual's courage, versatility, strength and, against all the odds, survival.

JAMES ROBERTSON

Reportage Scotland:
Scottish history in the voices
of those who were there

Louise Yeoman
ISBN 1 84282 051 6   PBK   £6.99

Events – both major and minor – as seen and recorded by Scots throughout history.

Which king was murdered in a sewer?

Who was the half-roasted abbot?

Which cardinal was salted and put in a barrel?

The answers can all be found in the eclectic mix covering nearly 2,000 years of Scottish history. Historian Louise Yeoman's rummage through the manuscript, book and newspapers archives of the National Library of Scotland has yielded an astonishing range of material, from a letter to the King of Picts to Mary Queen of Scots' own account of the murder of David Riccio; from the execution of William Wallace to accounts of anti-poll tax actions and the opening of the new Scottish Parliament. The book takes pieces from the original French, Latin, Gaelic and Scots and makes them accessible to the general reader, often for the first time.

The result is compelling reading for anyone interested in the history that has made Scotland what it is today.

Marvellously illuminating and wonderfully readable.

SCOTLAND ON SUNDAY

A monumental achievement in drawing together such a rich historical harvest.

THE HERALD

The Quest for the Celtic Key

Karen Ralls-MacLeod and Ian Robertson
ISBN 1 84282 031 1   PBK   £7.99

Full of mystery, magic and intrigue, Scotland's past is still burning with unanswered questions. Many of these have been asked before, some have never before been broached – but all are addressed with the inquisitiveness of true detectives in *The Quest for the Celtic Key*.

Was Winston Churchill really a practising member of a Druid order?

What are the similarities between Merlin and Christ?

Did Arthur, king of the Britons, conquer Scotland and was he buried in Govan?

What is hidden in the vaults at Rosslyn Chapel?

Encompassing well-known events and personae, whilst also tackling the more obscure elements in Scottish history – the significance of the number 19, the power of the colour green and the spiritual meaning of locations across Scotland – *The Quest for the Celtic Key* illustrates how the seemingly disparate 'mysteries of history' are connected.

An enthralling and informative journey through time which deserves a place on every Scottish bookshelf.

SCOTS MAGAZINE

A well laid-out, concise and fascinating book which offers the uninitiated in Scottish history a fresh and clearly laid path to the past.

WEST LOTHIAN COURIER

100 Favourite Scottish Poems

Edited by Stewart Conn
ISBN 1 905222 61 0   PBK   £7.99
ISBN 1 905222 62 9   HBK   £14.99
[Large Print]

Scotland has a long history of producing outstanding poetry. From the humblest but-and-ben to the grandest castle, the nation has a great tradition of celebration and commemoration through poetry. *100 Favourite Scottish Poems* – incorporating the top 20 best-loved poems as selected by a BBC Radio Scotland listener poll – ranges from ballads to Burns, from 'Proud Maisie' to 'The Queen of Sheba', and from 'Cuddle Doon' to 'The Jeelie Piece Song'.

Edited by Stewart Conn, poet and inaugural recipient of the Institute of Contemporary Scotland's Iain Crichton Smith Award for services to literature (2006).

Published in association with the Scottish Poetry Library, a unique national resource and advocate for the enriching art of poetry. Through its collections, publications, education and outreach work, the SPL aims to make the pleasures of poetry available as widely as possible.

Both wit and wisdom, and that fusion of the two which can touch the heart as well as the mind, distinguishes the work selected by Stewart Conn [in] this lovely little book.
THE SCOTSMAN

A highly varied collection and one that should fulfill Conn's hopes of whetting the reader's appetite... this is both a taster and a volume of substance.
THE HERALD

The Love Songs of John Knox

Alistair Findlay
ISBN 1 905222 30 0 PBK £7.99

This collection consists of poems and musings on contemporary Scottish culture, literature and identity, thematically linked by the iconic – and controversial – figure of John Knox. Knox's voice has echoed down the centuries, lampooned by Burns, mimicked by Carlyle, given homage by MacDiarmid, secularised in the radical polemics of Jon Maclean and Willie Gallacher, and continues today with Alistair Findlay. In amusing reveries and letters to historical figures, Knox takes on a new role and highlights not only the clash of past ideas with those of the present, but also the similarities between them. Written in a blend of Scots and traditional English, Findlay's Knox addresses issues ranging from prostitution and revolution to Celtic FC and war in Iraq.

... there is an interplay between the historic Knox and 21st century Scotland which provides constant surprise, interspersed with laughter, together with stimulus for reflection on the changed place of faith, Christian faith in particular, in this post-modern era.

JOHN MILLER, Former Moderator of The General Assembly of the Church of Scotland.

I don't think any Scottish poet has produced, or is likely to produce, a bath of poems as witty and sharp as this, in and for a long time.

DENNIS O'DONNELL

Luath Press Limited

committed to publishing well written books worth reading

LUATH PRESS takes its name from Robert Burns, whose little collie Luath (*Gael.*, swift or nimble) tripped up Jean Armour at a wedding and gave him the chance to speak to the woman who was to be his wife and the abiding love of his life. Burns called one of 'The Twa Dogs' Luath after Cuchullin's hunting dog in *Ossian's Fingal*. Luath Press was established in 1981 in the heart of Burns country, and is now based a few steps up the road from Burns' first lodgings on Edinburgh's Royal Mile.

Luath offers you distinctive writing with a hint of unexpected pleasures.

Most bookshops in the UK, the US, Canada, Australia, New Zealand and parts of Europe either carry our books in stock or can order them for you. To order direct from us, please send a £sterling cheque, postal order, international money order or your credit card details (number, address of cardholder and expiry date) to us at the address below. Please add post and packing as follows: UK – £1.00 per delivery address; overseas surface mail – £2.50 per delivery address; overseas airmail – £3.50 for the first book to each delivery address, plus £1.00 for each additional book by airmail to the same address. If your order is a gift, we will happily enclose your card or message at no extra charge.

Luath Press Limited
543/2 Castlehill
The Royal Mile
Edinburgh EH1 2ND
Scotland

Telephone: 0131 225 4326 (24 hours)
Fax: 0131 225 4324
email: sales@luath.co.uk
Website: www.luath.co.uk